FIVE THOUSAND AMERICAN FAMILIES —

PATTERNS OF ECONOMIC PROGRESS

VOLUME X

Analyses of the First Thirteen Years of the Panel Study of Income Dynamics

Edited by Greg J. Duncan and James N. Morgan

With Contributions by James N. Morgan, Richard D. Coe, Daniel H. Hill, Linda Datcher, Greg J. Duncan, Jeffrey Liker, Mary Corcoran, Michael Ponza, Martha S. Hill

1983

SURVEY RESEARCH CENTER
INSTITUTE FOR SOCIAL RESEARCH
THE UNIVERSITY OF MICHIGAN

ISR Code # 4590

FIVE THOUSAND AMERICAN FAMILIES--
PATTERNS OF ECONOMIC PROGRESS, VOLUME X

Library of Congress Catalog Card No. 74-62002
ISBN 0-87944-286-7 (clothbound)

Published 1983 by:
Institute for Social Research,
The University of Michigan, Ann Arbor, Michigan

6 5 4 3 2 1
Printed in the United States of America

CONTENTS

INTRODUCTION

This volume contains analysis of the first 13 years of the
Panel Study of Income Dynamics. Some of the chapters focus on
information gathered from new questions asked in the 13th wave of
interviewing. These include James Morgan's chapter on patterns
of help given or received by Panel households, Morgan's analysis
of questions on the impact of inflation, Richard Coe's analysis
of questions asking elderly respondents why they did not
participate in the Supplemental Security Income program, and
Daniel Hill's chapter on the burdens of recent energy price
increases.

Techniques of panel data analysis have become increasingly
sophisticated in the past decade. Linda Datcher applies a new
model of the dynamics of earnings developed by John Hause to
Panel Study men of both races and examines the implications of
the model for "better" estimates of the extent of persistent
earnings affluence and poverty for black and white workers. Greg
Duncan and Jeffrey Liker estimate a structural equations model of
the relationship between a sense of personal efficacy and
economic success in an attempt to disentangle the reciprocal
relationship between the two. Mary Corcoran, Duncan, and Michael
Ponza use the Panel data on women workers to estimate the effects
on their wages of dropping out of the labor force, of working
part time and full time, and of working in predominately male and
female jobs. Martha Hill uses the full power of the Panel to
show how patterns of family composition affect the economic
status of children.

We acknowledge with gratitude a grant from the
Alfred P. Sloan Foundation, which supported most of the research
that produced these chapters, and we also thank the following
colleagues for reading parts of the manuscript and giving us the
benefit of their helpful suggestions and criticisms:

Frank Andrews, University of Michigan
Carolyn Shaw Bell, Wellesley College
Carolyn Edwards, U.S. Department of Agriculture
Jennifer Gerner, Cornell University
Sandra Hofferth, The Urban Institute
George Johnson, University of Michigan
Nicholas Kiefer, Cornell University
N. Anders Klevmarken, Goteborg University
Jacob Mincer, Columbia University
Solomon W. Polachek, University of North Carolina
Willard Rodgers, University of Michigan
Frank P. Stafford, University of Michigan

Chapter 1

THE REDISTRIBUTION OF INCOME BY FAMILIES AND INSTITUTIONS AND EMERGENCY HELP PATTERNS

James N. Morgan

INTRODUCTION

There are many ways in which a society provides for its dependent members, ranging from the nuclear family of husband and wife taking care of their children to national tax and income maintenance systems. The term "transfer" is used in economics to cover some transfers but not others. It includes some contributory transfers such as pensions, Social Security, unemployment compensation, and workers compensation, which are more in the nature of insurance than altruism. Since reciprocal arrangements such as insurance face a market test and are already well documented, we focus here on the other forms of help given and received. Some of these may also involve reciprocity, at least over a period of time, as when children later take care of parents who took care of them, though as we shall see, that particular form of reciprocity seems to be rare. Nor does it involve a legal commitment by the children.

We know a great deal about the impact of the public transfer mechanisms, about the noncontributory transfers such as Aid to Families with Dependent Children (AFDC), Supplementary Security Income (SSI), and welfare, and about the impact of the taxes that support them. We also know something about institutional philanthropy, and contributions of time and money to churches and charities (Morgan, Dye, and Hybels, 1979). A major finding of our study of philanthropy was that giving time and giving money went together, rather than being substitutes for one another. Patterns of help among older people and their children were reported for a three-nation study in 1962 and for a 1975 reassessment in the United States (Shanas, 1967, 1978).

In examining the status of children, Hofferth (1982) examines jointly the family composition and whether or not the family is currently giving or receiving help to or from

1

relatives. She treats the child-year as the unit of analysis, and is concerned with increasing length of time children spend in families other than two-natural-parent families. Interfamilial help patterns appear to substitute in small part for the direct financial contributions of absent parents to their children, particularly in one-parent families and among blacks. Work is also underway at Wellesley by Laura Lein and others on family and community help patterns.

There is also a substantial new set of writings on the aggregate dynamics of intergenerational transfers concerned with the effects of differing sizes of age cohorts and differing needs for investments in human capital in developed countries on fertility and on intergenerational transfers (Becker, 1981; Caldwell, 1980; Willis, 1981). There is also research literature on voluntarism (Menchik and Weisbrod, 1981). A recent analysis of data from the Survey of Income and Education shows that, in black and Hispanic households, nonnuclear family members contribute significantly to family income (Angel and Tienda, 1982).

Estimating transfers within families involves comparing the contribution of each person with an estimate of that person's consumption or share in the family income. We have published two previous studies of these intrafamily transfers, showing their patterns and estimating their aggregate magnitudes. These turned out to dwarf all other transfers, both those that show up in the national accounts, and the organizational philanthropy, which does not (Baerwaldt and Morgan, 1973; Morgan, 1978). Both estimates included as part of the contribution of individuals in the family the value of their housework and child care time, and as part of the family income some nonmoney items such as imputed rent. It is clear that the family is by far the most important welfare or redistributional mechanism even in an advanced industrial country like the United States with extensive public and private income maintenance programs.

This analysis will focus on the process by which the well being of individuals is changed from what it would be if they had to depend on their own productive efforts (or their past savings or insurance), to what it actually is after the various intrafamily interfamily, and government noncontributory transfer systems have come into play. More important, since previous

analysis of interfamily transfers have shown them to be
relatively unimportant, we provide some qualitative evidence on
emergency interfamily help patterns, in both time and money,
based on a new set of questions in the 1980 wave of interviews.

THEORETICAL MODEL

Giving or receiving help can be thought of as a hierarchical
or sequential set of arrangements, starting with the most
primitive and universal support system—the nuclear family.
People probably have more control over who lives with whom than
they do over their own earnings. There is abundant evidence from
people's attitudes and their behavior that they prefer to live in
nuclear families without extra relatives or adult children;
hence, the transfers that take place from doubling up are clearly
not costless. Even the timing of when children leave home can be
affected by economic needs, and tends to be delayed in bad times.
(It is also later for boys than girls, presumably because they
mature and marry later.)

Given a set of families, one can think of decisions about
asking for or giving help to family members living elsewhere—the
extended family of anthropology. Previous data have shown
relatively little regular money given or received in this way,
and we shall not repeat those findings here. Indeed, it was this
infrequency of help by nuclear families to the extended family,
either by doubling up or by regular money transfers, that led to
the new sequence of questions in 1980 on emergency help given or
received, in time or money, actual or potential. All of these
family help patterns might be thought of as alternatives rather
than sequences. One can help relatives by housing them, sending
them regular remittances, or providing money (gifts or loans) or
time in emergencies.

Finally, one can think of help from institutions or
government programs as the last stage fall-back source, although
it might be argued that their very availability has reduced the
extent of interfamily help and even intrafamily transfers by
encouraging undoubling and divorce. We omit the insurance-type
contributory transfer mechanisms, though their existence, of
course, can affect the need for other transfers.

To recapitulate, one can think of an individual deciding
with whom to live and share, then deciding about helping

relatives by housing them or sending money, or about getting help by doubling up with relatives or getting money from them. Then public systems of taxation and welfare come into play to redistribute income further. Finally, giving or getting emergency help takes place. These findings can be interpreted using utility maximization theories, but studies would still have to be done to permit full modeling, asking directly about expectations of reciprocity or other evidences of implied contracts.

We shall not attempt to model these transfers either as a conditional set or as a complex set of joint decisions, but will look at whether any of the forms of giving help relate to variables that proxy for the capacity to give, the likely need to give, or the desire to do so, and whether any of the forms of getting help relate to variables indicating the need for help or whether help is likely to be available.

Our focus is not on estimating overall inequality of income before and after the redistribution produced by transfers, so we shall not be concerned with the discussion of new measures of inequality that improve on the Gini coefficient (by being decomposable into inequality within subgroups of society and inequality between groups).

We turn first to intrafamily transfers, including those between a nuclear family and the other people they live with.

INTRAFAMILY TRANSFERS

Estimating intrafamily transfers requires dealing with the first two of the three problems that beset attempts to measure well-being in general. Comprehensive measures of well-being (1) include nonmoney components, (2) allow for the differential needs of individuals of different age and sex, and (3) take account of the economies of scale from living together. We do not need to estimate economies of scale (the marginal cost of an added person) in deciding the allocation of consumption among members of a given family. First, to develop a better measure of family income, we add to total family money income the following:

> imputed rent on the net equity of homeowners
>
> value of free rent given to those who neither
> own nor rent
>
> value of food stamp subsidies

value of time spent on housework and child care

value of heating subsidy (1979 only)

These noncash incomes must be attributed to individuals if we are to assess individual contributions. Because the primary adults are generally the legal owners of houses, we divide imputed or free rent evenly between husband and wife if there is a wife; otherwise it is attributed to the family head. The food stamp and heating subsidies are allocated to all family members in proportion to their estimated share in family consumption. Time reported as spent by head or wife or others on housework was valued at an arbitrary $6 an hour in 1979 ($5 in 1975).

Similar attributions are necessary for asset income and transfer incomes other than food stamp subsidies. Asset income of head and wife is divided equally, as is any contributory transfer income. Noncontributory transfer incomes are allocated among all family members in the same way as food stamp subsidies, since all persons presumably help the family qualify for these transfers. For those other than head or wife, contribution is the total taxable plus transfer income plus the value of housework time plus share of head-wife noncontributory transfers (see Appendix C). This process effectively neutralizes noncontributory transfer incomes by allocating them in the same way we allocate estimated consumption of each family member. Deciding who "owns" the family wealth is a cultural matter currently in transition, but the trend seems to be toward the notion that husband and wife contribute equally (though in different ways) to the family accumulation and hence each owns half of it. For example, the new Estate Tax Law no longer requires proof of money contribution by each spouse to purchase assets in that spouse's name.

The allocation of consumption requires that we develop some kind of equivalent adult scale but does not require estimating the marginal rather than average cost of each individual, so we can avoid concerns over economies of scale.

Individuals are assumed to benefit from or consume the total full expanded family income, even though some income is saved or used to pay taxes, since they benefit from the savings or government services too. Starting with the food needs estimates

---

'For a recent re-estimate of that and references, see Lazear and Michael (1980).

that are the basis of the official federal poverty standards, we notice that taking an adult male as the base or numeraire, only the children under fourteen are substantially different. On the basis of those estimates, we assume the consumption of a child aged six through thirteen to be 6/7 of the standard, that of a child three through five years old to be 4/7, and that of a child under three to be 2/7. Adding the digits or fractions for all family members gives a base number of equivalent adults, and each individual is assumed to consume a fraction of that. A single child of four with two parents would be assumed to consume (4/7)/(2+4/7) of the family income (22 percent), while each parent consumes 1/(2+4/7), 39 percent, exhausting the income.

Since one might want to disagree on the treatment of transfers and the valuation of housework time, or try alternatives, we provide separate estimates. Note that all the estimates of average net contribution of benefits understate the aggregate transfers. To estimate them we must add up the individual net transfers, ignoring sign, and then divide by two since each dollar of transfer appears once positively for the contributor and once negatively for some recipients. The average per person, intrafamily transfer can then be multiplied by outside estimates of the total number of individuals in the population to provide an aggregate comparable to the national accounts estimates of government-institutional transfers.[2]

The detailed estimates by age and sex, and separately by relationship to head of the family, for 1975 and for 1979 are given in Appendix C, with contributions to the family estimated separately for labor income, income from capital and/or contributory transfers, noncontributory transfer income, and housework. Since families are at different income levels, distributions of dollars have a scale problem, which suggests that we look at the net contribution of each individual as a fraction of the total family income. These relative contributions or subsidies would seem a better measure of the importance of sharing in the family.

---

[2]There will be noncomparabilities because our sample excludes the noncontinental and institutional populations, and we exclude families that have changed heads or wives during the year 1980. We also include nonsample family members in order to have complete families.

Figure 1.1 uses these average net contribution estimates to show how the young and the old men are largely net beneficiaries from living in families, and the middle-aged are net contributors. The male-female differences around age 50 arise from the higher earnings of men, even though the total hours of work, paid and unpaid, done by women often exceed the hours put in by men. And the continuing major contribution of housework by older women plus our attribution to them of half the couple's capital and contributory transfer income, accounts for their greater contribution than men after age 65. Figure 1.2 shows a similar pattern for 1975, using a smaller population that includes only those in the households both in 1976 and in 1980.

A simpler way of looking at contributions of men and women at different ages is to see how many hours a year they spend either working for money or commuting to work or doing housework and child care. It is clear from Figure 1.3 that women are fully employed earlier in life than are many men and that they reduce their work hours far less rapidly after age 60 than do men. The old motto that men work from sun to sun but women's work is never done seems to apply to the life span as well as the day.

The aggregate importance of intrafamily transfers can be estimated by taking half of the average absolute net contribution per person (to avoid double counting), and multiplying by the number of persons in the population. Previous estimates indicated an aggregate of $313 to $398 billion, or 32 to 41 percent of the Gross National Product for 1970 (Baerwaldt and Morgan, 1973), and $528 to $552 billion, or 31 to 32 percent of the Gross National Product for 1976 (Morgan, 1978). Our income measure includes imputations not in the Gross National Product, and of course, transfers are a redistribution, not a component, of the product. The 1970 estimates used cost of hiring help as the lower bound value for housework, and opportunity wage estimate for the upper bound. The 1976 estimates used $5 per hour and the "opportunity cost" market wage. How we value housework time will clearly matter in estimating intrafamily transfers and the relative contributions of women and men. Our use here of $6 in 1979 is a compromise between a lower estimated cost of purchasing the services and a higher estimated opportunity cost of the wife's or husband's time.

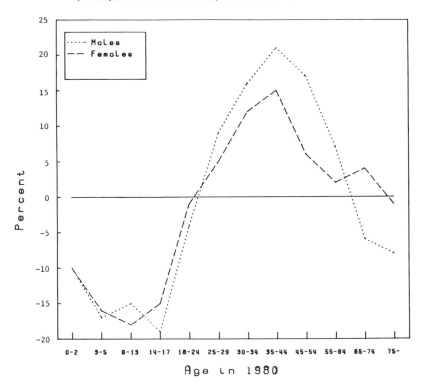

Figure 1.1

1979 AVERAGE NET CONTRIBUTION AS PERCENT OF FAMILY
INCOME BY AGE IN 1980, FOR MALES AND FEMALES

(For 18,920 individuals in sample households in 1980)

Figure 1.2

AVERAGE RELATIVE NET CONTRIBUTION AS RATIO TO FAMILY INCOME IN 1975 AND 1979,
BY AGE IN 1980, FOR 15,152 INDIVIDUALS IN SAMPLE HOUSEHOLDS IN 1976 AND IN 1980

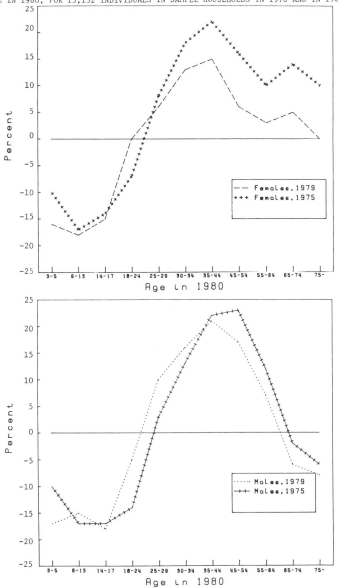

Figure 1.3

PAID WORK, COMMUTING, AND HOUSEWORK HOURS PER YEAR, BY AGE AND GENDER

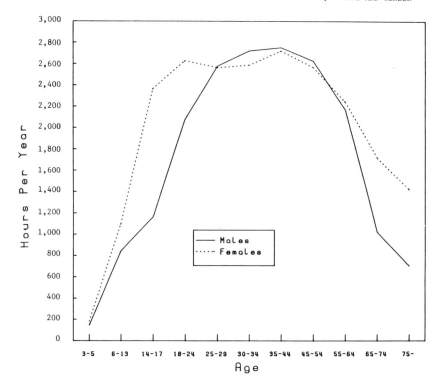

Our new estimates are for 1975 and 1979, using $5 and $6 per hour to value housework. They produce estimates of aggregate intra-family transfers of $548 billion, or 36 percent of the Gross National Product for 1975, and $709 billion, or 30 percent of the Gross National Product for 1975.

We also did a family-level estimate of intrafamily transfers, lumping all individuals other than the husband or wife (or single head) into one entity. This reduced the estimate to $615 billion in 1979, or 26 percent of the Gross National Product, but that is an underestimate because there are some "other" family members with positive net contributions cancelling out the negative net contributions of other extra family members.

It seems clear, then, that these intrafamily transfers, which, unlike most of the public transfer programs are not estimated in the national accounts, are a substantial amount, much larger than public transfers, even if one includes health and education as well as income maintenance programs.

INTRAHOUSEHOLD, INTERFAMILY TRANSFERS

The second level of our hierarchy has been buried in these estimates because it includes individuals living doubled up with relatives who are neither husband, wife, nor their children. There are not many such persons, as our country has gone through extensive undoubling, particularly since the end of World War II, accentuated by improved Social Security benefits, which allowed older people to maintain separate dwellings. Census data show great reductions in the proportions of the aged who live as guests with children, relatives, or others, offset, however, by an increase in the proportion of younger people living as guests, mostly with their parents. The net contribution to or subsidy from the family living together is estimated separately for those who are neither husband, wife, single head, nor children.

Another way to look at doubling up is to consider a nuclear family deciding whether to send money to needy relatives or to invite them to share the house (and presumably the food). Or a needy nuclear family can consider a choice between asking relatives for money or moving in with them. In fact, few make use of any of these options. Less than 10 percent of families house others, and it is most commonly large nuclear families of seven or more who also house other relatives. Sending money is also rare, with about 10 percent sending $500 or more per year to relatives, including children away at college, parents, and presumably ex-spouses and children. It is mostly nuclear families in which the taxable income of the head and wife is $25,000 a year or more that report such regular payments to others. It is clear that giving money tends to replace providing housing as income levels of the donors rise.

There is a lack of symmetry in our analysis possibilities if we try to look at those who receive free housing or remittances, because we have no information about the donors, and because only separate families appear in our analysis as receiving free housing (they neither own nor rent), not those doubled up--except for a few children who left home for a few years, then returned, and are treated as separate families. On the other hand, those who neither own nor rent include some who receive a transfer from some other source than a relative, or who really receive no transfer at all but do some work for their housing (custodians, etc.). However, there remains a general picture of relatively little interfamily help through sending money or providing housing on a regular basis. International or intertemporal comparisons would be revealing but are beyond the scope of this report.

INTERFAMILY AND OTHER TRANSFERS

After this cursory look at transfers that take place within the family and between nuclear and extended families by giving or receiving money or housing, we turn to the main analysis, which takes families as they are and asks what affects the extent to which they give help to, or receive it from, relatives or friends outside their immediate family. That help is in five forms:

Interfamily

Emergency time (in the last five years)

Emergency money loans or gifts (several hundred dollars or more in the last five years)

Regular money ($500 or more per year)

(Regular time was not asked.)

Family-Institution/Government

Regular noncontributory money transfers received (or taxes paid, of $500 or more per year)

Ambiguous

Housing (We count those who neither own nor rent
as receiving it,and those who house others as
giving it.)

(Remember, we exclude contributory [Insurance or
annuity type]) transfers and the related taxes or
premiums or contributions.)

We do not have dollar measures of all these items, but even
for emergency help we have more than a simple yes-no dichotomy.
So we can study both those who receive or give in each, or in one
or more of these categories, or we can build indexes of giving or
receiving activity that take account of more than a simple
dichotomy (gave, did not). For emergency money given or
received, for example, we know whether it was a loan or gift, and
if a loan, whether interest was to be paid.

Figure 1.4 shows the effect of the dominant variable--age--
on whether or not the family gave or received emergency help in
the form of money. But it also shows that the supplemental
question of whether it was a gift or a loan makes quite a
difference--most of the reported money given was reported as a
loan at all ages, but the fraction of recipients thinking of
their emergency money from friends or relatives as a gift rises
from one-third among the youngest to more than nine-tenths among
the oldest respondent families. Figure 5 shows a similar picture
for giving and receiving time to help in an emergency. The young
and old are more likely to receive, and the middle aged are more
likely to be doing the giving.

There are, of course, perceptual and response biases in such
questions. It is not inevitable that the same proportion report
giving and receiving in a nationally representative sample, since
one family could help more than another family. But the overall
proportions probably indicate some tendency to remember giving
more than receiving:

15 percent reported getting help in the form of
time; 28 percent reported giving it

22 percent reported getting help in money; 29
percent reported giving it

The time question was necessarily fuzzy, referring to "a lot of
time," while the money question used the phrase "several hundred
dollars or more." The five-year period reduces errors of timing
(including something earlier than the period asked about), and
gives more people something to report. It probably also would

Figure 1.4

EMERGENCY MONEY HELP GIVEN OR RECEIVED IN THE LAST FIVE YEARS

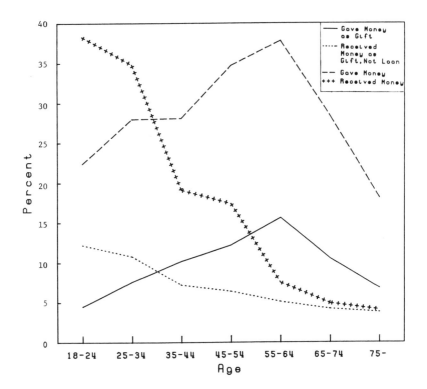

Figure 1.5

TIME GIVEN OR RECEIVED IN AN EMERGENCY IN THE LAST FIVE YEARS

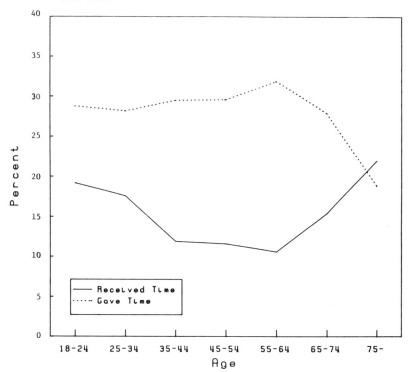

have led to undercounting of the number of instances of help, but
we were not attempting such quantification anyway.

While our explanatory analysis will necessarily keep giving
and receiving money and time separate, it is useful to notice
that the age patterns tend to be similar for both varieties of
help--it is mostly the middle aged who give it and mostly the
young and the very old who get it. Figures 1.6, 1.7, and 1.8
build indexes in three ways (see Appendix A for details). The
details about giving emergency help and providing regular support
of others (or housing them) are used in Figure 1.6 to build an
index of giving aid, and details about receiving emergency money
or time or regular help from relatives or living rent-free are
used to build an index of receiving help. Figure 8 shows even
more strongly that the middle aged do most of the giving, but the
receiving appears to be mostly by the young.

A second procedure is to treat various kinds of giving or
receiving as alternatives and ask what proportion in each age
group gave or received at least one kind of help. (We include
five types. See Appendix A.) Figure 1.7 shows the same humped
giving pattern, but a little upturn in the getting pattern--a
somewhat larger proportion of the very old had at least one kind
of help.

A third set of indexes includes transfers to and from the
government in addition to those to and from family and friends.
(We do not consider contributory transfers such as Social
Security, Workers compensation, and unemployment compensation as
help received for purposes of this analysis, even though they are
commonly lumped in the category of "transfers.") The indexes
simply count the number of types of help given or received.
Figure 1.8 shows a similar pattern, with only a slight upturn in
help received after age 65.

For those interested in the proportions who reported each
kind of help given or received or available, Appendix B gives the
overall distributions of answers to each of the questions.

SOURCES OF FAMILY HELP

Separate from the issue of the extent and variety of help is
its source. Figures 1.9 through 1.12 illustrate a consistent
pattern of younger people expecting and getting help from their
parents, and of older people expecting it from their children.

Figure 1.6
ALTRUISM GIVEN INDEX AND ALTRUISM RECEIVED
(Index by age)

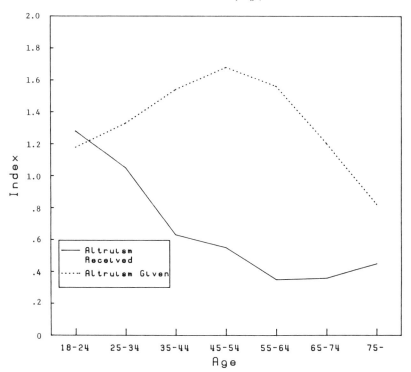

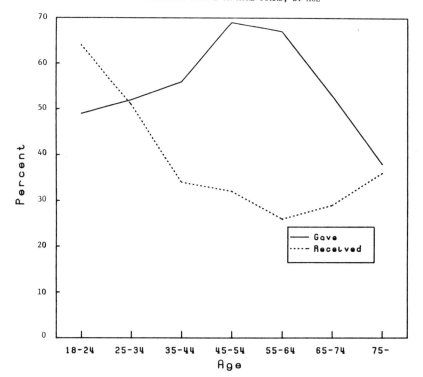

Figure 1.7

GIVING OR GETTING IN ONE OR MORE FORMS, BY AGE

Figure 1.8

NUMBER OF DIFFERENT WAYS OF
GIVING OR GETTING HELP, BY AGE
(Including help to and from government)

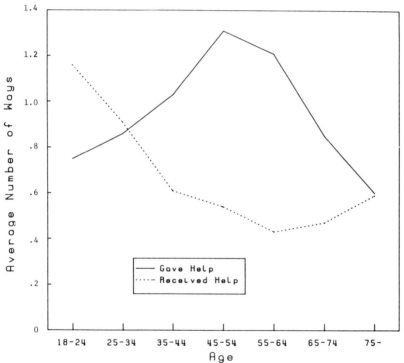

But the last figure, the only one reporting actual help,
indicates that far more actual giving is from older people to
their children than from children to their parents.[3]

Table 1.1 shows the overall proportions mentioning parents,
children, siblings, or in-laws as potential sources of help or
actual recipients of emergency money given. Parents are clearly
more often seen as a source, and children, confirming that, are
far more likely to be the ones receiving the money.

Table 1.1

AVAILABLE SOURCES OF HELP AND ACTUAL RECIPIENTS, BY RELATIONSHIP

| | Help Available | | | Help Given |
| | Time | | | |
Source	Living Nearby	Living Not Nearby	Money	Money
Parents	18.3	11.3	25.6	2.6
Children	15.0	11.1	10.6	9.9
Siblings	13.4	16.7	11.8	5.3
Anyone at all	63.3	55.7	60.0	22.4

Clearly, more people see help available than report actually
giving or receiving it. And the discrepancy is largest for help
from young people to parents. A comparison of Figure 1.11 and
Figure 1.12, the first reporting sources of available emergency
money, and the second, the destinations of actual emergency
money, indicates that actual help is even more dominated by
transfers from parents to children than perceived availability.
A fifth of older people see their children as a potential source
of financial help, but a trivial few young people report giving
or lending anything to their parents. The young people also are
somewhat more likely to see their parents as a source of help
than actually to receive help from them, but the difference is

---

[3]One difficulty is in deciding what people mean when they
report "in-laws"; whether this means son- or daughter-in-law or
mother- or father-in-law. If we assume that most younger people
are referring to mothers- or fathers-in-law, and most older
people to sons- or daughters-in-law, the allocation would simply
reinforce the picture of parents and children.

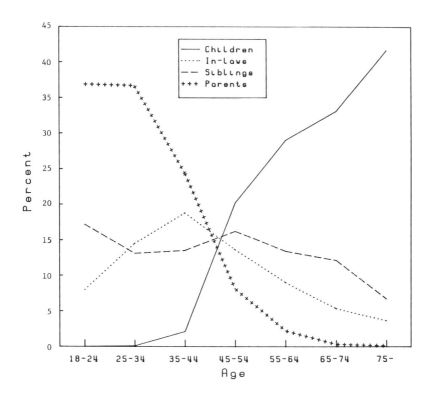

Figure 1.9
SOURCES OF AVAILABLE EMERGENCY TIME-HELP

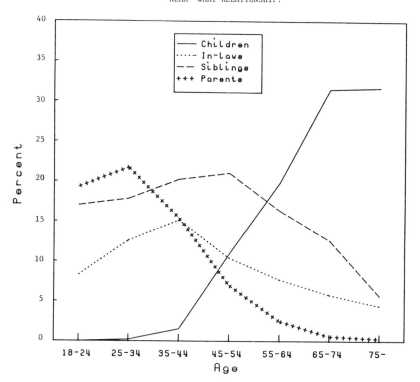

Figure 1.10
TIME HELP AVAILABLE FROM THOSE NOT LIVING
NEAR--WHAT RELATIONSHIP?

Figure 1.11

SOURCES OF AVAILABLE EMERGENCY MONEY

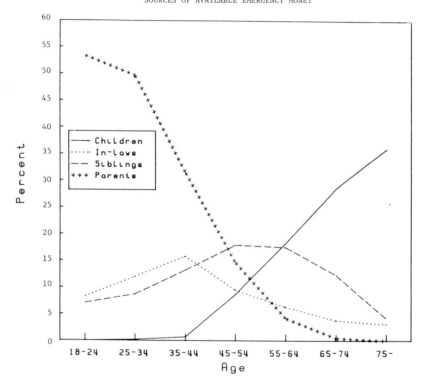

Figure 1.12

RELATIONSHIP OF PERSON TO WHOM MONEY HELP WAS GIVEN, BY AGE OF GIVER

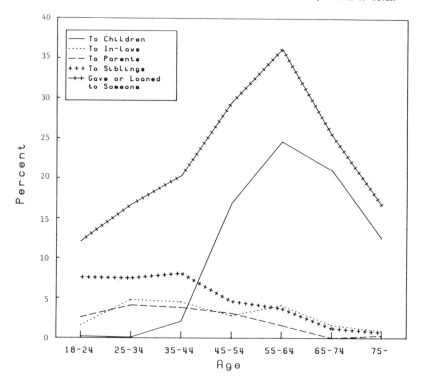

smaller--there are a substantial number of older people, even
past retirement, giving loans or gifts to their children.

ALTERNATIVES TO FAMILY AND GOVERNMENT HELP

People also have savings and insurance to protect them, and
such protection tends to be more nearly universal and greater in
magnitude as people age. Figure 1.13 shows that as people get
older the average number of own sources of help increases while
the adequacy of help available in money and time from relatives
decreases.'

Of course, older people are more likely to need help. The
proportion reporting a disability that limited them "a lot" rose
steadily to 21, 31, and 47 percent of the last three age groups
(55 to 64, 65 to 74, and 75 or older). We reported earlier that
such self-reports are apparently not just rationalization of a
retirement decision, since prior reports of disabilities were in
fact associated with early retirement (Morgan, 1980). It is
possible that better health or the increasing adequacy and
coverage of Social Security plus other pensions has decreased the
need of older people for help, but there are no comparable data
from other times or places to test this possibility.

WHAT ELSE AFFECTS PATTERNS OF HELP?

We have seen dramatic age differences in the giving or
receiving of emergency help and in the relationship of the donors
and recipients. Age serves as a proxy representing a number of
things, of course. Only the middle aged have both children and
parents to help or ask for help. The middle aged also have more
money than the young and more energy than the old, even if they
also have more responsibilities and more demands on their time.

We have other indicators both of the capacity to give help
and of the likelihood of being called on to give it. A third

'Own sources add a digit for: any liquid savings, two
months' income saved up, a year's income saved up, medical
insurance, and available free medical care. Emergency help from
relatives adds points for reporting time help nearby, from a
relative, the other person wouldn't mind, and respondent would
not feel a need to repay, someone else also available, someone
not nearby available, and that person a relative (seven possible
points). To that we add points for emergency money help:
available, from a relative, person wouldn't mind helping with
money, it would be a gift (which implies the last point too), and
respondent would not expect to pay interest.

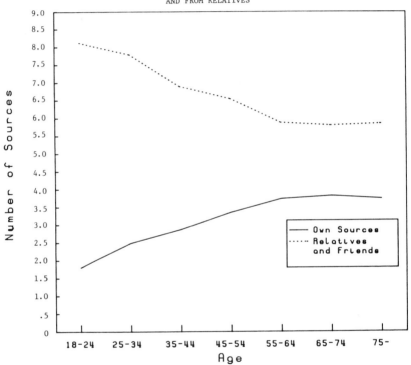

Figure 1.13

AVERAGE NUMBER OF SOURCES OF HELP FROM OWN SAVINGS-INSURANCE
AND FROM RELATIVES

aspect, altruism, or the desire to help, is more difficult. (We found no relationships with religious preference, church attendance, "connectedness," or living in the South for families with the same head since 1972, when we last measured these variables.)

Actually, the expected effect of our measured variables may well be different for giving as against getting help, and for giving money as against time, in rather obvious ways. Items indicating a capacity to give tend to reflect less likely need to get help, while those indicating a higher probability of being called for help also indicated a higher probability of having some to call on for help.

Concept:	Indicated by:
	Married or single female or single male
	Income
	Family size
Capacity to give (or less need to get)	Children under six
	Work hours of head and wife, relative to full time
	Recent change in head or wife
	Number of siblings of head
Probability of being called on to give (or more sources from which to get)	Number of children head ever had minus number at home
	Age
	Race (black)

A number of other possible variables were investigated and discarded as substitutes for the ones we used or as apparently having no effect: religious denomination, education, house equity, savings, growing up on a farm, reporting poor parents,

veteran, years in the same residence, trend or stability of
income, and five-year unemployment total. On the other hand, the
patterns of age and family size and income effects were
sufficiently nonlinear so that sets of dummy variables reflecting
each appeared preferable to parabolic representation. Indeed,
the changes in pattern upon adjustment by regression are
themselves interesting.

We report first the gross and net explanatory power of the
ten predictors for each of the four simple dichotomies: gave
time, gave money, got time, got money, and the overall
explanatory power of the regressions[5] (Table 1.2). For the more
important effects, we give details:

When the hours spent by husband and wife on paid work
commuting and housework were nearly 2,000 hours a year each, or
were more than 3,000, the family was _more_ likely to report giving
time to help others, even taking account of the family size,
income, age of head, etc. And having a child under six at home
made no difference at all. It seems likely that giving help is
more a function of outside demands that we cannot model or
measure than any capacity or willingness to help that we might
try to measure. The mere number of head's siblings or of
children no longer at home did not appear to matter.

Giving money help in emergencies was, as expected, more
frequent at higher incomes and smaller family sizes (greater
capacity), and the age pattern becomes far less pronounced when
adjusted for differences in income, family size, and the other
variables. Figures 1.14, 1.15, and 1.16 illustrate the dramatic
improvement in the estimated effects of family size (in
discouraging) and income (in encouraging) giving money help

---

[5]There are limits below 1.0 on the capacity to account for a
dichotomous dependent variable, some heteroscedasticity problems
when the overall proportion is close to zero or one, and problems
with the assumption of an additive model, which can become
apparent with predictions of probabilities less than zero or
greater than one. However, none of these problems is serious
with large samples. Our average proportions vary from 15 to 29
percent, so the heteroscedasticity adds a minor bit of
underestimation of the error to that already present because of
the sample clustering. Early investigations revealed no
substantial interaction effects. We can clearly explain giving
or getting money better than time. Giving time was more common
among the middle aged and also among Hispanics (and to a lesser
extent, blacks), and given more by single women or married
couples rather than single men.

Table 1.2

FACTORS RELATED TO ACTUAL EMERGENCY HELP IN THE LAST FIVE YEARS (1975-1979)
(For all 6,533 families)

	Number of Categories	Gave				Got			
		Time		Money		Time		Money	
		Gross Eta²	Net Beta²	Gross Eta²	Net Beta²	Gross Eta²	Net Beta²	Gross Eta²	Net Beta²
Capacity									
Income	10*	.002	.002	.045**	.070**	.018**	.002	.006**	.002
Family size	6	.001	.001	.005	.030**	.012**	.001	.004	.001
Married--single man, single woman	3	.002	.002	.006	.001	.029**	.019**	.007	.001
Age	7	.005**	.004	.015**	.005**	.010**	.001	.101**	.106**
Paid work hours/ full time	6	.004	.004	.007**	.001	.008**	.004	.020**	.002
Demands or Needs									
Number of siblings	4	.001	.001	.002	.001	.001	.001	.017**	.004
Number of children not living at home	4	.000	.000	.002	.004**	.003	.002	.014**	.000
Child < six	2	.000	.000	.005**	.000	.006**	.009**	.009**	.000
Recently changed head or wife	3	.001	.001	.000	.000	.006**	.003	.016**	.002
Race	3	.002	.002	.004	.000	.004	.001	.006**	.009**
R² adj.			.01		.07		.05		.12
Mean Proportion		.28		.29		.15		.20	

**Significant at .01 level. These tests are approximate since we are using categorical predictors.

Note: Eta² is a measure of explanatory power identical with the multiple correlation one would get using only the categories of that predictor as dummy variables in a regression. Beta² uses the adjusted coefficients for the subclasses to produce a measure analogous to the partial r-squared. See Andrews et al.

outside the immediate family and the weakening of the apparent age effect. Having children away from home also stimulates providing money help, presumably to them, with the most frequent reports coming from those with only one or two children.

Percent Giving Money Help

Children Away from Home	Unadjusted	Adjusted
None	28	27
One or two	33	33
Three to five	28	31
Six or more	25	31

A number of the apparent effects of income, age, and family size on getting emergency help (time) disappear in the multivariate analysis, presumably because they were spurious representations of the three remaining significant variables: presence of a child under six, unmarried heads, particularly female, and low hours of work-commuting-housework. The proportions were:

Percent Getting Time Help

	Unadjusted	Adjusted
Marital Status		
Married	10	11
Single man	17	16
Single woman	24	23
Preschool Child Present?		
Child under six	21	23
No such child	14	14
(Work + Commuting) ÷ Full Time		
Less than .49	21	19
.50 - .79	20	19
.80 - .99	14	15
1.00 - 1.19	14	14
1.20 - 1.49	13	14
1.50 or more	13	13

(Full time = 2,000 hours for single head; 4,000 hours for married couples.

Finally, getting money help remains dominated by age--it is the young who get help, other adjustments if anything increasing the age discrimination. Apparent effects of having more siblings or fewer children outside the household largely disappear in the

Figure 1.14

GAVE EMERGENCY MONEY, BY FAMILY SIZE
(Unadjusted and adjusted by regression for age, income, etc.)

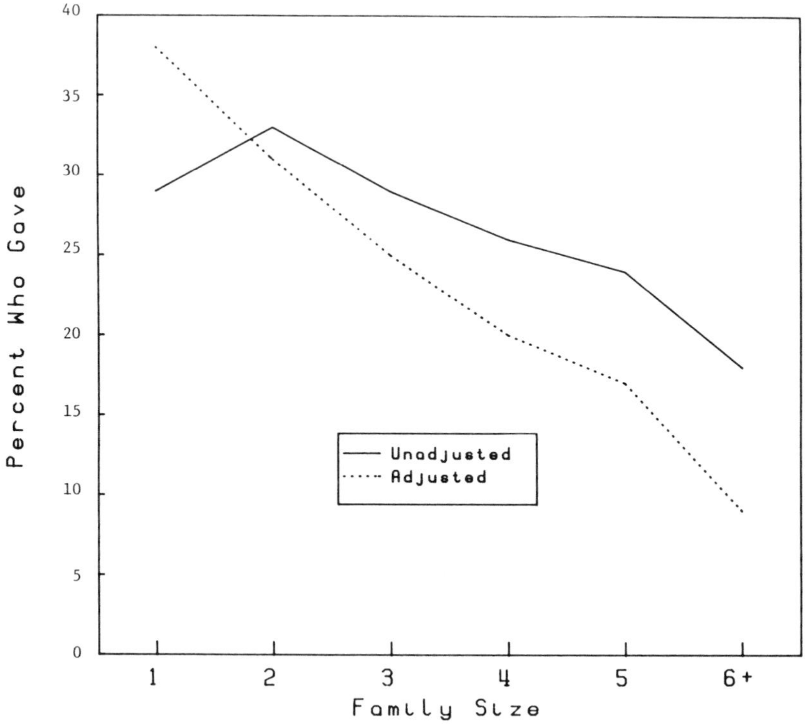

Percent Who Gave

Family Size

— Unadjusted
···· Adjusted

Figure 1.15

GAVE EMERGENCY MONEY, BY INCOME DECILE

(Unadjusted and adjusted by regression for age, family size, etc.)

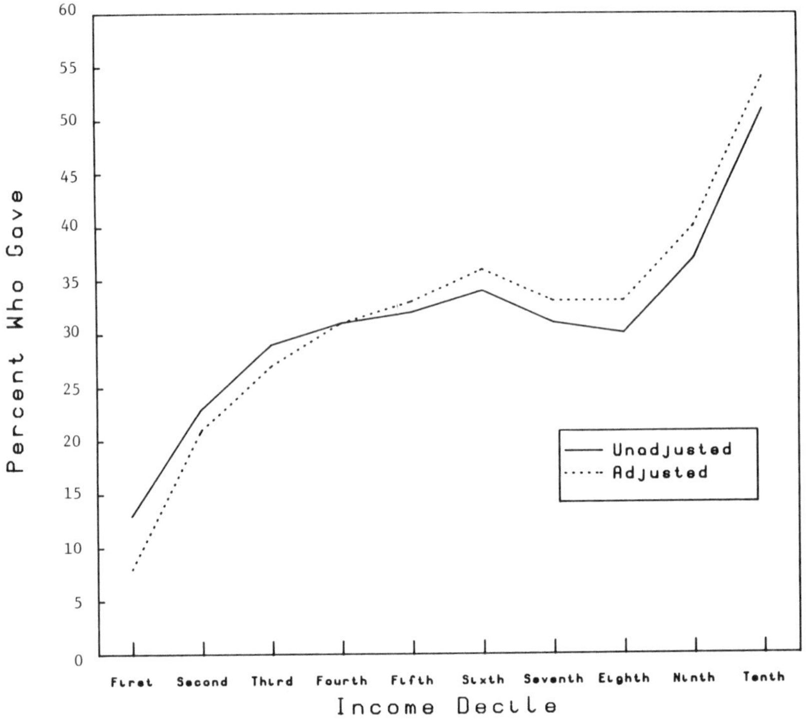

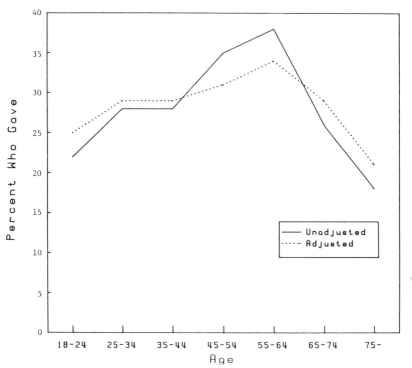

Figure 1.16

GAVE EMERGENCY MONEY, BY AGE

(Unadjusted and adjusted by regression for income, family size, etc.)

multivariate context. Having more siblings is associated with
less likelihood of receiving money, even after the adjustments,
though borderline in significance. Only race remains significant
in addition to age:

Percent Who Got Money Help

Race	Unadjusted	Adjusted
Black	12	10
Hispanic	18	17
Other	22	22

Interfamily aid takes more forms than the emergency money
and time. Regular support given and received amounting to $500 a
year or more, and providing housing for relatives or receiving
free housing, can be combined with emergency time and money help
to create two new variables: whether or not aid was given and
whether it was received in one or more of the four forms (see
Appendix A). Since a larger proportion receives one or more of
four than any of them separately, the statistics are safer, and
there is more variance to account for.

Table 1.3 shows the importance of our standard ten
predictors. For getting help, many of the other variables
besides age and sex-marital status drop substantially in
importance in the multivariate context, most of them below
significance. It is the young and single living alone,
particularly single women, who are most likely to get and to give
some form of family help (Table 1.4). There remains some
tendency for them to get more help if they have fewer siblings
and are not fully employed. Figure 1.17 shows the age pattern,
adjustments for sex-marital status indicating that the upturn in
help at the older ages is attributed more to single status than
to age itself. Those with a child under six or a recent change
in family composition are more likely to report getting some kind
of help. Those with one or two siblings get more help than those
with none or three or more, and there is a systematic but
nonsignificant pattern of more help, the more children one has
living elsewhere.

The patterns for giving help are, of course, different,
particularly with age. Figure 1.18 shows a more pronounced
humping of help giving just before retirement, and less decline
after that when the regression adjusts for marital status, family

Figure 1.17
GOT HELP IN ONE OR MORE OF FOUR WAYS

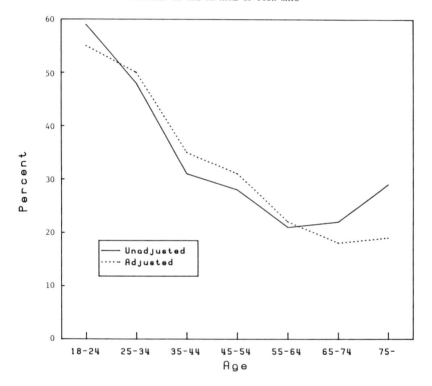

Table 1.3

FACTORS ASSOCIATED WITH GIVING OR GETTING REGULAR OR EMERGENCY HELP IN ONE OR MORE OF FOUR WAYS

(Using categorical predictors)

	Number of Categories	Gave Help		Got Help	
		Gross (Eta²)	Net (Beta Squared)	Gross (Eta²)	Net (Beta Squared)
Age	7	.021**	--	.071	--
Income	10	.023**	.038**	.017	.006
Family size	6	.003	.007**	.022	.002
Married, single man, single woman	3	.004	.028**	.045	.053**
Race	3	.002	.003	.000	.002
Number of siblings of head	4	.001	.000	.008	.006**
Number of children living elsewhere	4	.003	.003	.002	.003
Paid work hours/full time	6	.009**	.002	.001	.003
Child under six	2	.003	.002	.006	.007**
Change in family head or wife	3	.008**	.004	.016	.007**
R² adj.		.062	.057	.119	.081

**Significant at .01 level.

Table 1.4

GAVE OR GOT ONE OR MORE OF FOUR TYPES OF HELP, BY MARITAL STATUS AND SEX OF HEAD
(Unadjusted and adjusted by regression)

| | Gave | | | Got | | | Number of Cases |
	Unadjusted	Adjusted Including Age	Adjusted Excluding Age	Unadjusted	Adjusted Including Age	Adjusted Excluding Age	
Married couples	.52	.45	.46	.26	.28	.26	3,836
Single men	.61	.69	.67	.46	.41	.47	825
Single women	.52	.60	.60	.47	.47	.48	1,872

size, etc. Indeed, after adjustments a tendency also appears for larger families to be more likely to give help.

Figure 1.19 gives the pattern of the most important factor in giving help, the family income of the givers. Note, however, that the effect is somewhat more pronounced without adjusting for age. Indeed, there is a problem of interpretation in using age along with various other demographic variables with which it is highly correlated. One could argue that it is the other factors--family size, marital status, children living away from home--that lead to giving or receiving help, and that most of the apparent effect of age is spurious--working through these other variables. For that reason we provide regressions with and without age, since the increment in explanatory power from adding age to the regression indicates that important age effects exist separate from age effect on other demographic variables; they are clearly small but significant.

Our analysis has understated the more extensive help patterns among single-parent families by treating marital status and the presence of children separately. These differences, and those by race, are being studied more intensively by Sandra Hofferth.

Our focus on life-course differences and on composite patterns led to putting aside an analysis of racial differences, because blacks have similar age patterns and offsetting differences among the various types of help. If we run a series of regressions on dichotomous dependent variables reflecting the various kinds of help given and received or available, the coefficients of a dichotomous explanatory variable "whether black" will estimate black-white differences corrected for the other variables in the regression. This correction is important because giving or receiving money, particularly where a $500 cut-off is used, depends on income level as well as the importance of kinship networks. The adjusted estimates were that blacks were:

   3.6 percent more likely to have given time to
   help others in an emergency;

   insignificantly more likely to have given money
   (but less likely unadjusted);

   3.1 percent more likely to have received time
   help in an emergency;

   12.0 percent less likely to have had emergency
   money help;

Figure 1.18
GAVE HELP IN ONE OR MORE OF FOUR WAYS, BY AGE
(Unadjusted and adjusted by regression)

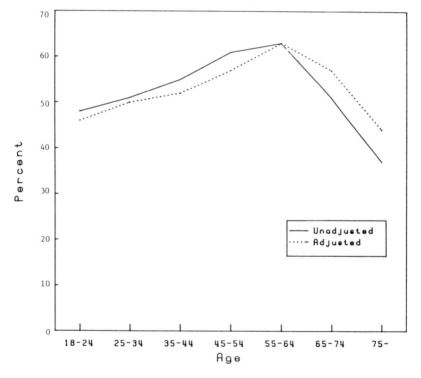

Figure 1.19
GAVE HELP IN ONE OR MORE OF FOUR WAYS, BY INCOME DECILE
(Unadjusted and adjusted by regression)

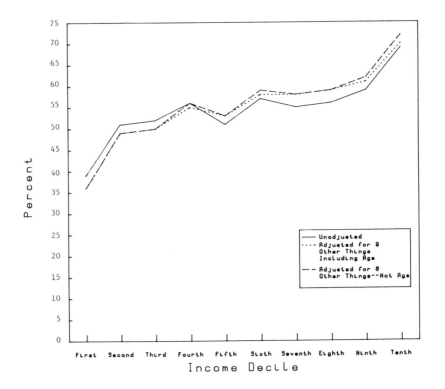

insignificantly less likely to report emergency
time help available nearby;

4.3 percent more likely to report emergency time
help available nearby;

4.3 percent more likely to report emergency help
available from distant relatives or friends;

7.6 percent less likely to report emergency money
help would be available;

and on a regular nonemergency basis:

3.5 percent more likely to report giving $500 or
more last year to outside relatives (but only
after adjustment for income/needs, etc.);

5.5 percent less likely to get $500 or more from
friends or relatives last year (again, only after
adjustment for income/needs, etc.);

10.4 percent more likely to provide housing for
others.

One stereotype appears true, that of more doubling up among
blacks, with or without adjustments for income, family size,
marital status, and the like. In general, blacks report more
time and less money given, received, and available, even after
adjusting for income/needs. Rational utility-maximizing models
could be introduced to support that pattern or the reverse, since
lower wage people commonly work longer hours to make up for low
wages, leaving less free time, and the tax advantages for extra
outside dependents are trivial for them; but unemployed or
underemployed people might have more time available.

A CHECK ON VARIABLES AVAILABLE ONLY FOR
STABLE FAMILIES SINCE 1972

If we take the 3,040 families with the same head and wife
since 1972, in order to make use of the richer set of background
information available at that time, we can scan for relationships
using only the two composite measures of giving and getting:

Giving
Whether gave time (emergency)
Whether gave money (emergency)
Regular support of others $500 a year
Housing others

Getting
Whether got emergency money
Whether got emergency time help
Got regular support $500 or more
Got free rent (neither owns nor rents)

The following were examined:

> Five-year trend in income/needs
> Five-year instability in income/needs
> Years in same residence
> Number of neighbors known in 1972
> Whether relatives near in 1972
> Church attendance in 1972
> 1972 report on whether ever refused to move and so
>   turned down a job
> 1972 "efficacy" scale
> 1972 trust-hostility scale
> 1972 scale on avoidance of undue risk
> 1972 scale on connectedness
> 1972 "test score" (sentence completion from Bellevue-
>   Wechsler)
> 1972 "feelings" achievement motivation index

There were no strong effects either on the number of ways people reported getting help in 1980 or on the number of ways they reported giving help. A weak negative effect of years in residence on getting help could easily be an age effect. Very weak, probably nonsignificant, tendencies appear for those with many connections to both give and receive more help, and for those who avoid risk to give more and get less help. Hence, it seems unlikely that any important effects would show up on the components of giving or receiving help.

We also looked at the same two measures of giving and getting, focusing on characteristics of the wife, including her attitudes in 1976, her education, religion, number of siblings, job experience, and perceptions of her husband's attitudes about more children and about his wife working. Again, there were no important factors associated with giving or getting emergency help among the 19 variables examined.

SUMMARY

There is extensive and varied help given and received between family members, both those living together and those living apart, most of it nonmoney help. Intrafamily transfers go to those at both ends of the age range, and to extra adults living doubled up. Interfamily help goes mostly from the middle aged or older to the young. Blacks help each other far more with time and housing, and less with money. An attempt to assess the effects of demands (siblings, children living away from home) and capacities (income, work hours, children under six) found only small and generally nonsignificant effects, except for the expected effect of income on giving help, while the age effects were strong and became even more systematic when adjusted for the other variables.

It is clear that people help other people in many ways other than with regular transfers of money, and that transfers within families living together are still an extremely important form of income maintenance.

44

References

Andrews, Frank et. al., Multiple Classification Analysis
Rev. Ed., Ann Arbor: Institute for Social Research, 1973.

Angel, Ronald, and Tienda, Marta. "Determinants of Extended
Household Structure: Cultural Pattern of Economic Need?"
American Journal of Sociology 87 (May 1982): 1360-1383.

Baerwaldt, Nancy, and Morgan, James N. "Trends in Intra-Family
Transfers." In Surveys of Consumers 1971-1972, Lewis Mandell
et al. Ann Arbor: Institute for Social Research, 1973.

Becker, Gary S. A Treatise on the Family. Cambridge, MA.: Harvard
University Press, 1981.

Caldwell, John C. "Mass Education as a Determinant of the Timing
of Fertility Decline." Population and Development Review 6
(June 1980): 225-55.

Hofferth, Sandra L. Trends in the Family Structure and Living
Arrangements of Children: A Cohort Approach. Paper given at
a workshop sponsored by the Life Course Committee of the
Social Science Research Council, Baltimore, November
1981. Revised January 1982. Washington, DC: Urban
Institute, 1982.

Lazear, Edward P., and Michael, Robert T. "Family Size and the
Distribution of Real per Capita Income." American Economic
Review 70 (March 1980): 91-107.

Menchik, Paul, and Weisbrod, Burton. "Volunteer Labor Supply in
the Provision of Collective Goods." In Nonprofit Firms in a
Three-Sector Economy, Michelle White. C.O.U.P.E. Papers on
Public Economics, Vol. 6. Washington, DC: The Urban
Institute, 1981.

Morgan, James N. "Occupational Disability and Its Economic
Correlates." In Five Thousand American Families--Patterns of
Economic Progress, Vol. VIII, ed. Greg J. Duncan and James
N. Morgan. Ann Arbor: Institute for Social Research, 1980.

Morgan, James N. "Intra-Family Transfers Revisited: The Support
of Dependents Inside the Family." In Five Thousand American
Families--Patterns of Economic Progress, Vol. VI, ed. Greg
J. Duncan and James N. Morgan. Ann Arbor: Institute for
Social Research, 1978.

Morgan, James N.; Dye, Richard; and Hybels, Judith. Results from
Two National Surveys of Philanthropic Activity. Research
Report Series. Ann Arbor: Institute for Social Research,
1979.

Shanas, Ethel. A National Survey of the Aging, 1975: Report to
the Administration on Aging. Washington, DC: Administration
on Aging, 1978.

Shanas, Ethel. "Family Help Patterns and Social Class in Three
    Countries." Journal of Marriage and the Family (May 1967):
    257-66.

Willis, Robert J. "The Direction of Intergenerational Transfers
    and Demographic Transition: The Caldwell Hypothesis Re-
    examined." Unpublished. Stony Brook: State University of
    New York, 1981.

Appendix A to Chapter 1

SOME MEASURES OF GIVING OR RECEIVING HELP
(With Weighted Percent of Sample)

Index of Family Giving
_____

Emergency (in last five years)
28   Gave time
 7   It was to a nonrelative
29   Gave or loaned money (several hundred dollars or more)
 7   It was to a nonrelative
16   No interest was paid on it
 9   It was a gift (counts double because it also means no interest)

Regular (last year)
12   Supported someone not living here
 5   Supported 2 or more
 4   One or more were dependent on R for more than half their total support
 2   Two or more were dependent for more than half their total support
 6   Extra adults live here--housed by the main family

Index of Family Getting
_____

Emergency (in last five years)
15   Got time
22   Got money (several hundred dollars or more)
10   No interest was paid on it
 8   It was a gift (counts double because it also means no interest)

Regular (last year)
 6   Received child support or help from relatives of $500 or more
 5   Neither owns nor rents (free housing)

Number of Different Types of Contribution
_____

Emergency
28   Gave time
29   Gave money
 9   Money was a gift

Regular
 6   Extra adults--houses others
10   Supports others elsewhere with $500 or more per year
 4   Provides more than half of someone else's support
 8   Pays income taxes net of any noncontributory transfers of $500 or more

Number of Different Types of Help Received

Emergency
15	Got time
22	Got money
8	Money was a gift

Regular
6	Received child support or help from relatives of $500 or more
7	Got food stamp subsidy of $100 or more
5	Neither own nor rent--free housing
7	Noncontributory transfers (AFDC + SSI + Welfare) of $500 or more

Whether Contributed in Any Way (1-0)

28	Gave time
29	Gave money
6	Houses others
10	Supports others elsewhere at $500 or more
7	Pays taxes beyond any noncontributory transfers received of $500 or more

Whether Got Any Kind of Help (1-0)

15	Got time
22	Got money
5	Neither owns nor rents
6	Child support or help from relatives of $500 or more
7	Noncontributory transfers (AFDC-SSI-Welfare) of $500 or more

Appendix B to Chapter 1

OVERALL ANSWERS TO THE MAIN QUESTIONS ON HELP
GIVEN OR RECEIVED, ACTUAL OR POTENTIAL
(With Weighted Percent of Sample)

Last year did you help support anyone who doesn't live here with you now?

11.9	Yes
88.1	No

How many?

6.9	One
2.7	Two
1.2	Three
0.6	Four
0.2	Five
0.1	Six
0.1	Eight or more
0.1	NA; DK

Were any of these people dependent on you for more than half of their total support?

4.4	Yes
7.4	No
0.1	NA; DK

How many?

2.6	One
1.0	Two
0.5	Three
0.1	Four

People sometimes have emergencies and need help from others--either time or money. Let's start by talking about time. In the last five years have you (or anyone living with you) spent a lot of time helping either a relative or friend in an emergency?

28.3	Yes
71.7	No

Is the person you helped a relative of (yours/anybody who lives here)?

21.0	Yes
7.1	No

What kind of help was that?

1st Mention	2nd Mention	
4.3	1.1	Transportation (people or property)
10.3	1.8	Looking after children; other people; babysitting
2.5	1.3	Looking after property; pets; plants
0.8	1.3	Running errands
1.6	0.4	Doing work (job) for them
1.7	0.4	Provide housing
4.0	1.1	Counseling; listening to troubles; giving advice, encouragement, affirmation
1.1	0.3	Other
1.6		DK; NA

Suppose there were a serious emergency in your household. Is there a friend or relative living nearby whom you could call on to spend a lot of time helping out?

78.1	Yes
21.9	No
2.0	DK; NA

Would that be a relative?

63.4	Yes
17.3	No

What is that person's relationship to you?

18.3	Parent(s)
15.0	Child; children; grandchildren
13.4	Brother; sister
2.1	Aunt; uncle
0.9	Niece; nephew
1.0	Cousin
0.7	Grandparent(s)
11.5	In-laws

How much would that person mind spending time helping you out--a lot, a little bit, or not at all?

4.5	A lot
11.9	A little bit
61.5	Not at all
2.7	DK; NA

Would you feel you had to repay that person in some way?

24.1	Yes
54.9	No
1.5	DK; NA

If that person were not available, is there someone else you could call on?

66.4	Yes
11.0	No
3.1	DK; NA

Do you have a relative or friend who <u>doesn't</u> live near you who could come to help you in an emergency?

69.9	Yes
29.7	No
0.4	DK; NA

Is that person a relative?

55.7	Yes
14.2	No

What is that person's relationship to you?

11.3	Parents
11.1	Child; children; grandchildren
16.6	Brother; sister
3.6	Aunt; uncle
1.0	Niece; nephew
1.8	Cousin
0.7	Grandparent(s)
9.1	In-laws
0.3	DK; NA

In the last five years has either a friend or a relative spent a lot of time helping you in an emergency?

15.2	Yes
84.8	No

What kind of help did you receive? (Did you receive any other kind(s) of help?)

1st Mention	2nd Mention	
1.8	0.6	Transportation (people or property)
7.3	1.5	Looking after children; other people; babysitting
1.4	0.9	Looking after property; pets; plants
0.5	0.8	Running errands
0.8	0.3	Doing work for R
0.9	0.5	Provide housing
1.9	0.8	Counseling; listening to troubles; giving advice, encouragement, affirmation
0.2	0.1	Other
0.5		DK; NA

Suppose in an emergency you needed several hundred dollars more than you had available or could borrow from an institution. Would you ask either a friend or a relative for it?

64.6	Yes

Is the person you would ask a relative?

60.0	Yes
8.9	No

What is that person's relationship to you?

25.6	Parent
10.6	Child; grandchild
11.8	Sibling
1.5	Aunt; uncle
0.4	Niece; nephew
0.7	Cousin
0.8	Grandparents
8.2	In-laws

How much would that person mind helping you out with money--a lot, a little bit, or not at all?

3.9	A lot
12.5	A little bit
49.3	Not at all
3.0	DK; NA

Would this money be a loan or a gift?

57.1	Loan
10.4	Gift
1.3	NA; DK

Would you expect to pay interest on it?

18.2	Yes
38.4	No
0.5	DK; NA

In the last five years have you received any amount such as several hundred dollars from either a friend or relative?

20.3	Yes
79.7	No

Was it a loan or a gift?

12.5	Loan
7.6	Gift
0.1	NA; DK

Did you pay interest on it?

  3.3   Yes
  9.1   No

In the last five years have you helped out either a friend or relative in an emergency by giving or loaning them several hundred dollars or more?

29.0   Yes
71.0   No

Was the person you helped a relative?

22.4   Yes
  6.5   No

What is that person's relationship to you?

  2.6   Parent(s)
  9.9   Child
  5.3   Sibling
  0.3   Aunt; uncle
  0.6   Niece; nephew
  0.4   Cousin
  0.1   Grandparent
  3.0   In-laws

Was that a loan or a gift?

19.1   Loan
  9.7   Gift

  0.2   NA; DK

Did (he/she) pay interest on it?

  2.7   Yes
16.2   No

  0.1   NA; DK

Appendix C to Chapter 1

ESTIMATION OF INTRAFAMILY TRANSFERS

Assumptions must be made about the benefit allocation of the
family income to its members and about allocation of some income
components as to who contributed them. A realistic estimate also
requires inclusion of the major nonmoney components of income.
We start by defining a more global concept of income that
consists of:

> Total family money income (before taxes)
>
> Imputed return (at 5 percent) on net equity in
> the house--free rent
>
> Value of housing received free for those who
> neither own nor rent
>
> Value of food stamp subsidy
>
> Government subsidy of heating costs (1979 only)
>
> Value of housework hours (at $6 in 1979; $5 in
> 1975)

It is assumed that the individual benefits from the family income
with everyone 14 or older counting as one, those 6 to 13 counting
.857, those 3 to 5 counting .571, and those under 3 counting
.286, the sum of these equivalent adult numbers being the base.
Thus, an only child aged 4 is assumed to benefit from .571/2.571
of the family income. This implicitly assumes that taxes paid
out of income purchase a benefit too.

As for the contribution attributed to individuals, we can
identify the earnings of the wife, and the wages, bonus,
professional practice, and market gardening labor income of the
husband. All taxable income of the head and wife beyond that is
divided equally between them, its being mostly asset income from
assets that they presumably both helped accumulate. The transfer
income of head and wife from contributory transfers--Social
Security, retirement, unemployment, workers compensation, child
support--is also divided equally between them. Noncontributory
transfers of head and wife are divided among the whole family in
the same proportions as their estimated share of the consumption
of income.

That leaves the income of "others," which appears in each
individual's record in two parts: taxable income and transfer
income. For the detail in the tables, other individuals'
transfer income is considered to be part of their income from

"contributory transfers or assets" if it is reported to be from
Social Security, retirement pay, unemployment compensation,
workers compensation, or child support; otherwise it is
considered income from noncontributory transfers. Notice that
the latter is attributed to the individual, even though
noncontributory transfers to head or wife are allocated as a
"contribution" by all family members. Taxable income of these
other individuals is allocated between labor income and "asset
income or contributory transfers" according to a code that
distinguishes those whose taxable income was only labor income,
only asset income, or both, with the "both" cases being assigned
half labor and half asset income.

Our estimates of the family total income come from
worksheets that lump the individuals other than the head and
wife, but the contributions attributed to those other individuals
come from individual records that contain the two figures for
taxable and transfer income of that individual. This probably
explains why the total net contribution across all family members
does not come out to zero, but the orders of magnitude of the
components are reasonable, and it is the age and gender patterns
we are concerned with.

For comparisons between 1975 and 1979, it is necessary to
include only individuals who were in some family both times,
leaving out the children born since 1975 and those who married
into the sample. The resulting families are all right for 1976,
but for 1980 are rather artificial; hence, the mean change in
relative net contribution for the subsample may be less realistic
than the change in the mean relative net contribution for the
same age-gender groups using the full 1980 sample.

In both years, in order to have complete families it is
necessary to include nonsample members who have been born in or
married into the sample. Since they have zero individual
weights, we use the family weights that are the same as the
individual weight in unchanged families, and that approximately
weight down all individuals in families where one spouse is
nonsample.

There is some selection bias in any dynamic analysis of a
population because people or families are entering it at young
ages and low incomes and leaving it at advanced ages. Selecting
even identical individuals who were in the population at two

dates even four years apart can exaggerate the increase in income from one point of view, though those individuals are indeed receiving those increases. Notice, for example, that the average labor earnings for the individuals who were in the sample families in both 1976 and 1980 was $6,328, compared with $5,967 for all the individuals in the 1980 sample. The latter includes people born in and marrying into the sample. For married men only, the average labor earnings were $15,509 for those in both samples, and $15,039 for those in the 1980 sample.

In order to have complete families, we had to retain nonsample individuals, which means that the weighting is not precise. Rather than give nonsample individuals zero weights, we used the family weight for all family members. The effect on the overall average net or absolute contribution should be very small.

Table C1.1

1979 CONTRIBUTIONS TO THE FAMILY, BY SEX-MARITAL STATUS-RELATION TO HEAD
(For 18,920 individuals in sample households in 1980)

	Labor Earnings	Housework @ $6/Hour	Asset Income plus Contributory Transfers	Total Contribution	Net Contribution	Relative Net Contribution	Absolute Net Contribution
Married men	$15,509	$2,291	$3,297	$21,241	$6,539	.13	$8,520
Single men	10,876	2,834	3,355	17,637	788	.02	1,901
Single women	4,895	5,149	3,540	14,203	1,785	.08	2,897
Wives	4,341	8,829	3,297	16,611	1,909	.07	5,715
Children	1,005	1,322	77	2,644	-6,027	-.14	7,035
Other	2,282	2,421	706	5,948	-3,325	-.11	5,001

Table C1.2

1979 CONTRIBUTIONS TO THE FAMILY LIVING TOGETHER BY AGE AND SEX

(18,920 individuals in sample households in 1980)

Age in 1980	Labor Earnings	Housework @$6/Hour	Asset Income Plus Contributory Transfers	Total Contribution to Family	Net Contribution	Relative Net Contribution	Absolute Net Contribution
Men							
0-2	$0	$25	$4	$158	$3,306	-.10	$3,306
3-5	0	168	2	337	-5,857	-.17	5,910
6-13	148	1,046	156	1,806	-6,811	-.15	8,245
14-17	461	1,494	13	2,123	-8,023	-.19	8,745
18-24	7,184	1,638	350	9,510	-2,164	-.04	4,758
25-29	13,836	2,243	1,001	17,362	3,122	.09	4,833
30-34	16,904	2,447	1,930	21,482	6,648	.16	7,646
35-44	18,696	1,989	3,297	24,158	10,255	.21	11,033
45-54	20,615	2,201	3,517	26,460	9,821	.17	11,078
55-64	14,547	2,339	3,837	20,884	4,134	.07	6,350
65-74	3,506	3,078	6,492	13,352	-1,152	-.06	3,842
75 or older	830	3,031	7,185	11,565	-3,260	-.08	4,456
Women							
0-2	0	9	0	117	-3,365	-.10	3,366
3-5	0	207	1	394	-5,359	-.16	5,401
6-13	4	1,254	11	1,489	-7,155	-.18	7,386
14-17	328	2,868	36	3,402	-7,516	-.15	8,331
18-24	4,199	4,972	293	9,885	-1,615	-.01	4,628
25-29	5,868	7,058	1,139	14,415	1,205	.05	4,312
30-34	6,114	8,108	2,069	16,535	3,672	.12	5,989
35-44	6,181	8,218	2,781	17,365	5,056	.15	7,137
45-54	5,692	8,081	3,394	17,394	1,384	.06	6,529
55-64	3,490	7,570	4,714	16,049	200	.02	3,986
65-74	781	7,264	6,387	14,901	145	.04	3,435
75 or older	108	5,485	5,821	11,918	-506	-.01	2,015
All Ages and Sexes	$5,967	$3,756	$2,097	$12,091	-$134	-.00	$6,248

Table C1.3

1975 AND 1979 CONTRIBUTIONS TO THE FAMILY BY AGE AND SEX

(For 15,152 individuals in sample households in 1976 and in 1980)

Age in 1980	Labor Earnings 1975	Labor Earnings 1979	Net Contribution 1975	Net Contribution 1979	Relative Net Contribution 1975	Relative Net Contribution 1979	Mean Change in Relative Net Contribution	Number
Men								
0-2								0
3-5	$0	$0	$-2,463	$-5,859	-.10	-.17	-.07	321
6-13	0	160	-4,686	-6,798	-.17	-.15	-.03	1,260
14-17	13	447	-5,086	-7,893	-.17	-.18	-.02	708
18-24	1,300	6,786	-4,579	-2,600	-.14	-.05	.09	1,022
25-29	6,815	14,460	307	3,612	.03	.10	.07	797
30-34	10,425	17,218	3,077	6,847	.13	.16	.04	687
35-44	13,077	18,618	7,245	10,252	.22	.21	.01	698
45-54	15,592	20,748	9,536	10,024	.23	.17	-.05	625
55-64	12,071	14,658	4,543	4,179	.12	.07	-.05	512
65-74	5,051	3,496	86	-1,130	-.02	-.06	-.04	305
75 or older	668	812	-1,041	-3,253	-.06	-.08	-.03	145
Women								
0-2								
3-5	$0	0	-2,361	-5,434	-.10	-.16	-.06	316
6-13	0	4	-4,664	-7,167	-.17	-.18	-.01	1,145
14-17	10	326	-4,608	-7,489	-.14	-.15	-.01	706
18-24	754	4,127	-3,027	-1,583	-.07	.00	.07	1,231
25-29	3,384	5,688	1,212	1,659	.08	.06	-.02	973
30-34	3,766	6,134	4,045	3,845	.18	.13	-.05	716
35-44	3,650	6,191	5,883	5,212	.22	.15	-.06	832
45-54	3,615	5,659	4,379	1,408	.16	.06	-.10	828
55-64	3,257	3,598	2,144	304	.10	.03	-.08	638
65-74	1,652	806	2,076	264	.14	.05	-.09	462
75 or older	99	64	1,393	-350	.10	.00	-.10	224
All	$4,087	$6,328	$776	$224	.03	.01	-.02	15,152

In 1975 prices. Price Index was 161 in 1975; 218 in 1979 (1967=100).

Table C1.4

1975 CONTRIBUTIONS TO THE FAMILY LIVING TOGETHER, BY SEX AND AGE IN 1980

Age in 1980	Labor Earnings	Housework @$5/Hour	Asset Income Plus Contributory Transfers	Total Contribution to Family Income	Relative Net Contribution	Absolute Net Contribution
Males						
3-5	0	15	0	85	-.10	2,466
6-13	0	200	0	334	-.17	4,473
14-17	23	753	0	878	-.17	5,100
18-24	1,430	1,064	39	2,670	-.15	5,286
25-29	6,838	1,409	361	8,845	.01	2,733
30-34	10,087	1,554	877	12,692	.10	3,913
35-44	13,093	1,241	1,722	16,149	.20	7,460
45-54	15,110	1,538	2,222	18,943	.20	9,488
55-64	12,143	1,427	2,404	16,116	.11	5,680
65-74	4,817	1,721	4,102	10,834	-.03	3,186
75 or older	455	2,199	4,979	7,843	-.10	2,789
Females						
3-5	0	4	0	92	-.10	2,266
6-13	0	220	0	343	-.17	4,651
14-17	10	1,360	0	1,486	-.14	4,747
18-24	820	2,955	57	4,009	-.09	4,179
25-29	3,526	5,118	389	9,304	.02	2,896
30-34	4,049	6,487	906	11,656	.11	4,031
35-44	3,904	7,162	1,830	13,011	.16	5,503
45-54	3,617	6,914	2,133	12,763	.11	5,156
55-64	3,299	6,373	2,081	12,506	.05	3,810
65-74	1,504	5,784	4,330	11,869	.05	2,847
75 or older	239	4,639	3,973	9,128	.02	2,036
All ages and sexes	4,036	2,875	3,234	8,353	-.00	4,563

Chapter 2

EFFECTS OF INFLATION ON ATTITUDES, STATUS, AND BEHAVIOR

James N. Morgan

INTRODUCTION

Inflation seldom means a uniform increase in all
prices. An oil cartel can produce exploding energy prices,
while rents rise more slowly and homeowners hardly notice
the rising "opportunity cost" of living in an ever more
expensive house. Indeed, homeowners may notice the capital
gains on their home more than they notice what this implies
for the real cost of their housing.

People also differ in their capacity to make
adjustments that reduce the impact of inflation--
substituting cheaper alternatives, working more hours, even
postponing having children. Just as there may be
organizational slack in business firms in good times, so
there may be economies a household can make under pressure,
such as eating out less or repairing things rather than
replacing them.

We report here three kinds of evidence on the impact of
inflation: (1) people's notions of how much they have been
hurt, by which prices, and what they are doing about it,
(2) changes in actual income and spending and work, which
reflect partly a changing environment and partly response to
it, and (3) an assessment of who has kept up best with
inflation in a recent five-year period (1975-1979), compared
with an earlier period, 1968-1972. We shall not attempt to
model supply shifts or estimate demand and substitution
elasticities but shall describe people's verbal responses to
questions about the impact of inflation, and their reported
behavioral responses to it. Repeated interviews reduce
reliance on memory, since people tend to remember the past
as differing less from the present than it often does. Some
of these changes reflect the impact of inflation, such as

60

changes in property taxes, some reflect response to
inflation, such as changes in work hours, and others reflect
mixtures, such as changes in utility bills that combine
rising prices of fuel with lowering of thermostats and
adding of insulation.

PERCEPTIONS OF INFLATION

People's notions of how much they have been hurt and
what they are doing about it can of course be subject to
biases of various sorts, but their perceptions are still
worth examining, particularly when the questions are
repeated as inflation accelerates.

Consumer prices rose by 7.5 percent in 1978, by 11.3
percent in 1979, and by 14.4 percent in 1980. At the same
time, per capita disposable income was rising by about 10 or
11 percent each year. In 1979 and again in 1980,
respondents were asked how these price increases affected
them, if some particular increases hit them especially
hard,' and if so what, if anything, they had been able to
do about it.

Of the 84 percent of respondents who said in 1979 that
they were hit especially hard by some facet of inflation,
more than 19 percent said they had found something to do
about it (Table 1). The next year, although the number of
people hard hit rose by only about 2 percent, the number of
families who said they had found ways to cope with rising
prices had increased to 26 percent. Table 2.1 shows that it
was the young, parents, and homeowners who increasingly
reported being able to do something about inflation.

The reaction of most respondents to inflation was to
cut consumption, primarily of those things whose prices had
risen most (the number of families who said they had cut
back on consumption rose from 12 percent in 1979 to 19
percent in 1980). A few people mentioned saving money by
shopping more carefully and even fewer reported that they
had increased home production and do-it-yourself activities.

'"Prices and costs have been rising generally--are there
some particular increases that have hit you especially
hard?"

Table 2.1

PERCENT REPORTING THEY WERE ABLE TO DO
SOMETHING ABOUT RISING PRICES
(5,950 families with unchanged head in 1979 and 1980.)

	Able to Do Something about Inflation	
	1979	1980
All	19%	26%
Female	19	21
Black	15	15
Homeowners	20	27
Parents	21	30
18 to 44	22	31
45 to 64	19	25
65 or older	13	16
75 or older	10	12

We went on to ask if inflation had caused people to change their ideas about retirement.[2] The question was asked of everyone, so some of the answers came from people who had already retired or were too young to have given it much thought. In both 1979 and 1980, almost a quarter of the respondents said their ideas about retirement had changed. Some retired people regretted their retirement, and quite a number of respondents reported that they were now thinking less about the pleasures of retirement and more about how they were going to survive it.

By limiting the sample to those aged 45 to 64 in 1980, people who were more immediately concerned with retirement, we got the following answers:

	1979	1980
Now planning to retire later	10.1	11.5
Now planning not to retire	3.3	4.0
Not sure when will/can retire	3.1	6.0
Total changed plans	16.5	21.5
Will save more	2.0	2.5
Retirement doesn't look so good	5.3	4.7

Depending on what one expected to find, these changes look large or small. Given the erosion of asset values, increasing unemployment, and an uncertain future, the fact that the largest change is in uncertainty seems reasonable. The amount of actual change was quite small.

WHERE DOES IT HURT?

While prices in general were going up at an increasing rate, food prices rose by 10.0 percent in 1978 and 10.9 percent in 1979, but went up only 6.9 percent in 1980. As the rate of increase in the price of food dropped, the Iranian oil embargo drove up the price of gasoline, so the shift, shown in Table 2.2, between transportation and food as the major price burden is understandable.

That people tend to travel less and get sick more as they get older is borne out by Table 2.2 and Figure 2.1,

[2]"Has inflation caused you to change your ideas about retirement?"

Table 2.2

FRACTION REPORTING PRICE INCREASES THAT HIT PARTICULARLY HARD
(Unchanged head 1979-1980, N=5,950)
(Two prices could be mentioned)

Percent of Each Group Mentioning Each Price

	Food		Housing		Utilities		Transportation		Medicine		Clothing	
	1979	1980	1979	1980	1979	1980	1979	1980	1979	1980	1979	1980
All	50	43	5	5	23	28	39	50	2	3	4	4
Female	52	47	9	7	25	29	24	31	4	4	7	7
Black	59	54	7	6	28	30	24	34	2	3	7	9
Homeowner	51	41	3	3	28	35	41	53	2	2	3	2
Parents	58	49	4	4	24	30	42	56	1	1	4	5
18 to 44	50	43	6	6	18	24	46	60	1	1	4	5
45 to 54	53	42	4	4	29	35	36	50	2	1	4	4
65 or older	48	43	6	4	26	27	24	28	5	8	5	4

Table reads: First column, second row: In 1979, 52 percent of female-headed families reported being hit particularly hard by food prices.

which show a dramatic reduction with age in the proportion feeling hurt by the cost of transportation but an increase in sensitivity to the cost of medical care. Since people have some choices to make about their transportation but very few about their medical care, price increases in the two have different meanings.

Table 2.2 also shows that it was the middle aged and homeowners who were feeling hurt by utility prices, particularly in 1980. And it was parents and homeowners who talked less about food in 1980 than they had in 1979.

ACTUAL RESPONSE: CHANGES IN BEHAVIOR AND
EXPERIENCE, 1978 TO 1979 AND 1975 TO 1979

Some changes, such as increases in property taxes or rent, can be considered to be exogenous—something that happened to people. Others, such as increases in utility bills or food expenditures, are a mixture of price increases and responses to those increases—demand elasticities. Still others, such as the fraction of food expenditure spent eating out, seem to be mostly under the control of individuals and respond to relative prices and changing real income.

Table 2.3 shows the proportions within age groups whose reports in 1979 and 1980 reveal various kinds of changes. In fact there appears to be very little age effect, except that those 65 or older were less likely to report substantial increases in food expenditures. The patterns are more interesting when we allow a longer period for changes to appear above the "noise," as in Table 2.4 and Figure 2.2: Younger people were full of activity— increasing their driving and moving, paying higher or lower rents, eating out more, and often increasing their work hours by 500 hours or more. Rising wages that offset inflation were also more likely among the young, and they are more mobile. Older people ate out less and were more likely to report food expenditures that, in real terms and in relation to their family food needs, fell by 20 percent or more. The elderly were also likely to have actual decreases in property taxes. However, it was the middle aged whose real taxable income relative to their needs was

Figure 2.1

PERCENT REPORTING IN 1980 BEING PARTICULARLY HARD HIT BY PRICE INCREASES OF FOUR TYPES, BY AGE
(Two Mentions)   (For all 6,533 families in 1980.)

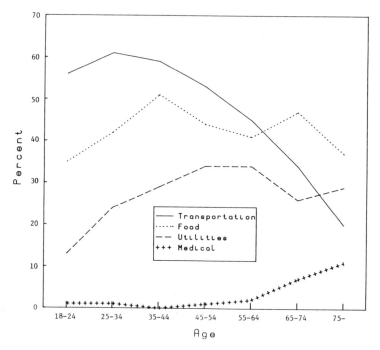

likely to fall--sometimes by 20 percent or more--presumably
this resulted from divorce, having children who still lived
with parents, or retiring.

MULTIVARIATE ANALYSIS OF PERCEIVED IMPACT OF INFLATION

We can summarize perceptions of the impact of inflation
by a series of multivariate analyses relating initial
states, changes in income, and demographic factors to
whether the respondent reported being hurt by inflation, and
to whether he or she reported being hit especially hard by
one of four particular prices. We are treating a
dichotomous yes-no as a dependent variable, but with such a
large sample and with proportions not near either extreme,
we lose little statistical efficiency and can estimate
effects on the probability of a particular response. Table
2.5 shows, in the first column, that older people, women,
and married men and those who started in a low income/needs
decile were more likely to report being hurt. More
interesting, however, are the factors associated with
feeling especially hit by particular prices.

Table 2.5 illustrates that there is a differential
sense of inflationary impact among different groups of the
population. Married people were more likely to feel price
increases in food and housing, less in utilities and
transportation. Blacks reported being hurt by price
increases in food and utilities, but seldom by
transportation (gasoline) prices. We have already noted the
convex age curve, except for utilities where it rose, and
transportation where it fell, with age. Homeowners
mentioned utilities and transportation and talked less often
about food or housing. The main increase in housing costs
for homeowners is, of course, in imputed rent, which they
neither see nor feel and which is in some sense offset by
unrealized capital gains. New second-generation respondents
were likely to focus their attention on the rising costs of
food and utilities, although the proportion of their income
that they spent initially on these things did not seem to
matter to them.

We have evidence from the actual reports on utility
bills in the interview on the actual percent increase in

Table 2.3

1978 TO 1979 CHANGES IN EXPENDITURES BY AGE
(For 4,757 families with unchanged head, 1976-1980.)

Age in 1980	Percent of Food Expenditure Used to Eat Out		Property Taxes Rose $1,000 or More	Utilities Rose $100 or More	Rent Rose $100 or More per year	Food Expenditures Rose:	
	Fell 10 Percent or More	Rose 10 Percent or More				$100 or More	$500 or More
18 to 24	40	20	11	37	34	46	36
25 to 34	27	19	20	48	23	58	39
35 to 44	16	15	19	44	11	57	39
45 to 54	18	16	23	45	10	54	36
55 to 64	15	13	18	48	9	49	33
65 to 74	18	13	13	36	12	49	26
75 or older	14	13	10	41	15	47	21
All	19	15	18	44	14	53	34

Table reads: Top left--"40 percent of families with head 18 to 24 years old in 1980 reported food expenditures in 1979 and 1980 in which the proportion spent eating out fell 10 percent or more."

Table 2.4

CHANGES IN EARNINGS AND PRICES AND RESPONSES IN WORK AND SPENDING, 1975-1979
(For 4,757 families with unchanged heads, 1978 to 1980)

Impacts

Age in 1980	Head's Real Hourly Earnings Fell 20% or More	Head's Real Hourly Earnings Increased 50% or More	Real Taxable Income/Needs Rose 50% or More	Utility Bills Went Up $500 or More	Rent Went Up $500 or More	Property Taxes Went Up $500 or More	Property Taxes Went Down
18 to 24	11	48	73	22	41	6	6
25 to 34	27	28	50	26	24	17	11
35 to 44	34	16	39	28	12	15	23
45 to 54	25	12	47	25	9	11	23
55 to 64	38	13	35	17	8	7	25
65 to 74	45	10	12	12	11	6	30
75 or older	25	6	12	16	15	3	37
All ages	32	16	36	22	15	10	23

Responses

	Total Miles Driven Fell 1,000+	Total Miles Driven Rose 1,000+	Real Food Expenditures Relative to Needs Fell 20%+	Real Food Expenditures Relative to Needs Rose 20%+	Percent of Paid Expenses Eating Out Fell 5%+	Percent of Paid Expenses Eating Out Rose 5%+	Work Hours per Adult Rose by 500+ Hours
18 to 20	33	47	37	39	40	42	49
25 to 34	40	43	41	37	39	36	35
35 to 44	37	44	38	35	26	33	30
45 to 54	39	45	34	45	23	39	25
55 to 64	48	33	36	44	23	35	19
65 to 74	46	22	49	32	26	27	15
75 or older	39	12	51	32	25	24	15
All ages	41	36	40	38	28	33	25

Table reads: Upper left--"11 percent of the young (18 to 24 in 1980) heads reported earnings in 1980 (for 1979) that were 20 percent or more below their 1976 report on 1975 earnings."

Figure 2.2

CHANGES 1975 TO 1979 FOR 4,757 FAMILIES WITH THE SAME HEAD ALL FIVE YEARS, BY AGE
(From two interviews)

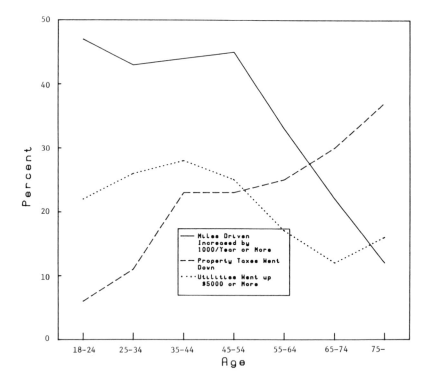

utility bills, and the last two columns of Table 2.5 show
how that is related to the same background factors. Younger
people, married, blacks, and homeowners had larger
increases, as did those with larger increases in income/
needs and those who reported being hurt by utility prices.
What we cannot tell is whether those who felt hurt would
have had larger increases in utility bills if they had not
done something about it. Blacks might well have had less
well insulated homes and/or landlords less able or willing
to improve insulation.

MULTIVARIATE ANALYSIS OF RESPONSES TO INFLATION

Changes which, at least in part, reflected responses to
price inflation are looked at in Table 2.6, where the food
expenditures are in constant (deflated) dollars. One-year
changes provide few significant effects except that families
with children increased their food expenditures less rapidly
than their needs would have warranted. Over the longer
period, the results were more interesting and significant.
Reports of being hurt by transportation costs were
associated with fewer miles driven. Changes in food
expenditures were clearly responsive to changes in ability
to pay and depressed by increasing numbers of mouths to
feed. Increases in food expenditures/needs and in the
fraction of food costs spent eating out were heavily age-
dependent and appeared to peak at about 50 years of age.
Feeling hurt by inflation went along with changed ideas and
plans about retirement. Surprisingly, reports of being hurt
by inflation were not associated with increases in work
hours. However, as we have reported elsewhere, many people
do not have choices about their work hours even in normal
times.

WHO KEEPS UP WITH INFLATION?

Duncan and Morgan (1981) analyzed the factors affecting
change in family economic status from 1971 to 1978, showing
the dominant importance of changes in family and marital
status and changes in labor force status. A substantial
amount of change, however, can result from environmental
forces beyond the control of individuals, and there have

Table 2.5

IMPACT OF INFLATION

(Regression coefficients for 4,756 families with unchanged heads 1976-1980)

| | Perceived Impact | | | | | Impact + Response Inferred from Two Reports | |
| | Reported Being Hurt | Especially by Prices of | | | | Percent Increase in Utility Bills. 1976-79 | |
		Food	Housing	Utilities	Transportation		
Income/needs decile, 1975	-0.49*	-1.94**	0.05	-0.73	1.69**	0.64*	0.59**
Annual percent increase in income/needs (1975-1979)	-4.30	-21.61**	-3.98	-1.66	9.61	15.18**	15.11**
Male	-5.50**	-12.55**	-3.80**	-7.13**	14.88**	-8.23**	-8.62**
Married	4.60*	9.65**	2.84**	-1.29	-1.26	6.53**	6.46**
Black	0.09	5.94**	0.32	6.33**	-11.21**	8.04**	8.39**
Education	-0.18	-1.17**	0.40**	0.55*	0.32	0.27	0.30
Age	0.80**	0.90**	0.06	1.06**	-0.19	-1.62**	-1.57**
Age squared/100	-0.99**	-0.81**	0.06	0.95**	-0.49	1.23**	1.18**
Number of children	2.82*	4.25*	-1.04	3.75**	-3.32	-1.57	-1.37
Owns home	2.36	-8.46**	-7.57**	21.05**	5.23*	12.48**	13.62**
1975 utilities/income	....	....	....	1.88	....	....	....
1975 food expenditures/income	....	-0.77	....	....	....	....	....
1975 food expenditures/food needs	....	0.11	....	....	....	....	....
Hurt by utility prices	....	....	....	....	....	5.40**	....
R^2 (adjusted)	.027	.064	.032	.048	.126	.061	.057

Significance levels: *.05 **.01

Table 2.6

RESPONSES TO INFLATION

(Regression coefficients for 4,756 families with unchanged heads, 1976-1980)

	1978-1979		1975-1979					
	Increase in Deflated Food/Needs	Increase in Percent Spent Eating Out	Increase in Percent Spent Eating Out	Annual Percent Increase in Real Food/ Food Needs	Change in Work Hours per Adult	Change in Miles Driven to Work	Changed Ideas about Retirement	Changed Retirement Plans
Income/needs decile, 1975	-1.17*	0.08	0.14	0.07	-36.61**	-2.64**	0.96**	0.60**
Annual percent increase in real income/needs, 1975-1979	-2.60	5.06*	13.78**	20.16**	†	75.81**	20.78**	11.88**
Male	-4.87	1.67*	4.12**	0.07	2.31	-16.89*	0.62	0.31
Married	0.29	-2.10*	-5.07**	-0.02	74.53	9.67	1.12	2.30
Black	-0.43	0.38	-1.64	-2.87**	63.34	7.70	3.40	6.39**
Education	0.35	0.06	0.08	0.25**	19.30**	1.06	0.81**	0.38*
Age	1.30**	0.31**	0.39**	0.18**	-20.13**	-1.18	1.76**	1.76**
Age squared/100	-1.36**	-0.27**	-0.39**	-0.20**	14.19**	0.01	-1.79**	-1.70**
Number of children	-8.76**	-0.28	-1.39*	-2.84**	45.97	28.06**	0.20	0.23
Owns home	-1.18	1.78**	1.87*	0.78	59.30	2.57	1.14	1.20
Hurt	4.16	-0.94	0.07	0.82	26.19	-11.20	7.48**	2.74*?
Did something	-0.93	0.73	-0.28	-0.02	-16.75	-4.10	2.74	-1.32
Annual percent increase in real hourly earnings	-12.64	-2.03	-4.95*	-1.56	1537.22**	....	-5.31	†
Hurt by transportation prices						-11.04*		
R² Adjusted	.003	.007	.021	.071	.121	.025	.048	.039
Mean of dependent variable	-.041	-.006	.013	.003	13.43	-.356	.252	.142
(Standard deviation)	(.809)	(.163)	(.178)	(.125)	(.871)	(13.367)	(.434)	(.349)

†Omitted as circular

Significance levels: *.05 **.01

been substantial changes in that environment. One change in particular is that, in response to increasing inflation, some protections have been built into union contracts. Hence, it seems useful to compare two historic periods, the recent five-year period we have been using, 1975-1979, and a period before inflation became an issue, 1968-1972.

We shall use individuals as the unit of analysis, since over such long periods the family becomes an elusive concept for counting. Family status remains useful as a measure, of course.

We examine four measures, each a percent annual real increase estimated by fitting logs to deflated family well-being measures. The measures are: total taxable income plus imputed rent (capacity to support self without transfers), family money income (the traditional measure), income/needs (taking account of family composition), and money income plus imputed rent plus food stamp subsidy relative to needs (an improved measure of well-being).

We can maximize comparability by looking at the same individuals in two historic periods, that is, by including individuals who were sample members, and head or wife, in 1969, 1973, 1976, and 1980. But this means that they are all older in the second period than the first, whereas two representative cross sections would be replacing older people with younger people, and even two five-year panels would avoid confounding differences in average age between the two periods with differences in the historic periods. In other words, by maximizing our ability to compare the same individuals' experiences in the two periods, we confound period differences with age differences. Of course, we use age as an explanatory variable in the analysis, so it is largely the means that are affected. The differences in means are not trivial, however. If we compare the 5,076 individuals in the sample for the whole period with 6,887 individuals for whom 1975-1979 data are available as heads or wives, we have the following average amounts of change in economic status:

Measure of Status	5,076 Heads or Wives in for the Whole Period Percent per Year Trend Over:		6,887 Heads or Wives in for 1975-1979 Percent Per Year Trend Over:
	1968-1972	1975-1979	1975-1979
Family money income	2.3%	0.8%	2.4%
Income/needs	2.2	1.7	2.6
Full income/needs	2.9	2.3	3.2
Taxable income + imputed rent	1.9	1.2	3.1

The dramatic differences in rates of change for the same historic period when we omit the young people (because they were not family heads or wives in the earlier period) show the importance of possible truncation (selection) biases, and the fact that the longer a panel period, the more selective the sample to represent any subperiod. The fact that rates of change of income drop rapidly with age means that omitting the new young families with their rapid increments depresses the average. However, to answer the question of which individuals did better in the later period than the first, we need to follow the same individuals.

We look first at the experience of the same 5,076 individuals in the two historic periods, remembering that the difference in the two periods can be slightly confounded with age differences not taken care of by the age variable in the regression.

One question, then, is who kept up with inflation better in the period 1975-1979 than they did during 1968-1972. Table 2.7 shows the values of the four measures at the midpoint of each of the five-year periods, the annual percentage increases in each of the two periods, the percentages who have a positive trend showing that they have kept up with inflation, and the percentages who did better in terms of trend in the second period than in the first. These averages cover up a wide diversity of individual experiences, with more than a third showing annual increases of more than 5 percent per year and more than a fourth showing annual decreases of more than 5 percent per year. While there were somewhat more who kept up in the earlier period, the proportions with substantial annual increases or decreases did not change much between periods. The standard deviations of the trends are 11 to 14 percent, more than four times their averages.

There were, of course, more with decreases among those in the age groups near retirement age, particularly if we look at taxable income, without transfers or adjustments for family size. The period just before retirement tends to be one where taxable income is more likely to fall in real terms--that is, not keep up with inflation--but where income/needs still rises because children are leaving home.

Tables 2.8 and 2.9 show multivariate analyses of the trends in two of the four measures for the two periods for the identical individuals, with emphasis on the effects of changing marital status and changing work status. The other two trend measures showed very similar patterns; the adding of imputed rent or omitting transfers merely changed the overall level. We have also left out a few explanatory factors that proved conclusively nonsignificant in explaining any of the changes: whether the household head was a skilled or semi-skilled blue-collar worker, whether he orshe belonged to a union. And we allow only a linear age effect; otherwise the effects of being retired are confounded with a flattening of the "age effect" after retirement.

We first summarize the findings for 1975-1979 and then compare them with the earlier period. The comparison group (excluded group) for the first nine lines in each table is made up of those who were married at both the beginning and end of the period. In effect, with dichotomous predictors the excluded group's coefficient is constrained to be zero, so the upper left number in Table 9 indicates that men who got divorced had 3.5 percent per year less increase in family money income than all people who stayed married even without deducting alimony or child support they paid. But (top of second column) they had 3.3 percent greater annual increase in income/needs, because they gave up more obligations than income.

The comparison groups for changes in work status are the cases where the family head was working more than 500 hours at both the first and fifth year, or where the wife was working more than 500 hours at both the first and fifth

Table 2.7

MEANS AND MIDPOINT LEVELS OF CRITERION VARIABLES
(For 5,076 individuals 15 or older in 1980 and in sample the
whole period and head or wife in 1969, 1973, 1976, and 1980.)

(In 1967 prices)

	1968-1972	1975-1979
Yearly Percent Increase in:		
Family income/needs	2.2	1.7
Family money income	2.3	0.8
Full income/needs[a]	2.9	2.3
Taxable income +		
imputed rent	1.9	1.2
Percent with Positive Trend in:		
Family money income	59.1	53.4
Full income/needs	61.9	58.5
Taxable income +		
imputed rent	57.7	55.2

Percent with a Better Trend in 1975 than 1968, in:	
Family money income	46.0
Full income/needs	49.6
Taxable income +	
imputed rent	46.5

Midpoint Levels:	1970	1977
Family money income	$10,363	$11,202
Family income/needs	3.00	3.37
Full income/needs	3.16	3.80
Taxable income +		
imputed rent	$10,114	$10,694

[a]Full income adds to money income: food stamp subsidy and
imputed rent (5 percent of house equity).

Table 2.8

TRENDS IN WELL-BEING, 1968-1972. EFFECTS OF CHANGES IN FAMILY AND IN WORK
(For 5,076 persons who were family head or wife in 1969, 1973, 1976, and
1980. Regression coefficients with standard errors in parentheses)

(Deflated to 1967 prices)

	Percent Increase per Year in		Mean and (Standard Deviation) of Explanatory Variable
	Family Money Income	Income/Needs	
Changes in Marital Status			
Man, got divorced	-.029* (.012)	.056** (.014)	.015 (.122)
Man, got married	.042** (.013)	-.034* (.015)	.013 (.011)
Man, stayed single	.008 (.010)	.009 (.012)	.021 (.144)
White woman, got divorced	-.073** (.008)	-.034** (.009)	.034 (.182)
White woman, got married	.112** (.012)	.069** (.013)	.017 (.130)
White woman, stayed single	-.001 (.006)	.013+ (.006)	.088 (.283)
Black woman, got divorced	-.048* (.022)	.004 (.025)	.004 (.066)
Black woman, got married	.076* (.030)	-.003 (.034)	.002 (.048)
Black woman, stayed single	.011 (.012)	.032* (.013)	.019 (.136)
All who remained married	0	0	
Changes in Work Status			
Family head stopped work	-.076** (.006)	-.118** (.009)	.174 (.262)
Family head started work	.078** (.009)	.095** (.012)	.026 (.160)
Family head stayed not working	.020** (.006)	.002 (.007)	.100 (.300)
Family head stayed working	0	0	
Wife stopped work	-.058** (.005)	-.072** (.006)	.128 (.335)
Wife started work	.056** (.006)	.047** (.007)	.104 (.305)
Wife stayed not working	-.003 (.004)	-.019** (.005)	.570 (.495)
Wife stayed working	0	0	

Table 2.8 (continued)

| | Percent Increase per year in | | Mean and (Standard Deviation) of Explanatory Variable |
	Family Money Income	Income/Needs	
Head worked in durables manufacturing, 1971,1973	.012 (.007)	.007 (.008)	.131 (.337)
Head not in durables 1971 or 1973	.021** (.006)	.017* (.007)	.808 (.394)
Background Factors			
Efficacy, 1969	-.002 (.002)	-.001 (.002)	2.08 (0.94)
Head a college graduate	.015** (.004)	.013** (.005)	.170 (.376)
Head a high school dropout	.009** (.003)	.010* (.004)	.387 (.487)
Age of head (years)	-.00161* (.00012)	-.00045** (.00014)	54.8 (14.4)
R^2 (adjusted)	.232	.164	
Mean of dependent variable	.023	.022	
(Standard Deviation)	(.116)	(.127)	

Table reads: Top left--"Men who got divorced had a rate of increase in their family money income 2.9 percent lower than all those who stayed married."

Significance levels: * .05 ** .01

Note: Work means more than 500 hours in the year.

Table 2.9

TRENDS IN WELL-BEING, 1975-1979, EFFECTS OF CHANGES IN FAMILY AND IN WORK
(For 5,076 persons who were family head or wife in 1969, 1973, 1976, and
1980. Regression coefficients with standard errors in parentheses)

(In 1967 Prices)

	Percent Increase per Year in		
	Family Money Income	Income/Needs	Mean and (Standard Deviation) of Explanatory Variable
Changes in Marital Status			
Man, got divorced	-.035** (.010)	.033** (.011)	.023 (.150)
Man, got married	.042** (.015)	-.035* (.018)	.009 (.094)
Man, stayed single	.002 (.008)	-.001 (.010)	.034 (.182)
White woman, got divorced	-.094** (.008)	-.050** (.010)	.033 (.179)
White woman, got married	.138** (.011)	.072** (.015)	.019 (.117)
White woman, stayed single	-.012* (.005)	.011 (.006)	.128 (.334)
Black woman, got divorced	-.086** (.028)	-.015 (.033)	.003 (.051)
Black woman, got married	.179** (.026)	.133** (.032)	.003 (.054)
Black woman, stayed single	.013 (.010)	.007 (.012)	.023 (.150)
All who remained married	0	0	
Changes in Work Status			
Family head stopped work	-.077** (.005)	-.114** (.006)	.101 (.301)
Family head started work	.081** (.009)	.073** (.010)	.028 (.160)
Family head stayed not working	-.004 (.005)	-.031** (.006)	.210 (.407)
Family head stayed working	0	0	
Wife stopped work	-.037** (.006)	-.041** (.007)	.087 (.282)
Wife started work	.035** (.005)	.028** (.006)	.105 (.307)
Wife stayed not working	-.000 (.004)	-.012* (.005)	.572 (.495)
Wife stayed working	0	0	
Head worked in durables manufacturing, 1975,1979	.019** (.007)	.023** (.008)	.109 (.312)
Head not in durables 1975 or 1979	-.006 (.005)	-.008 (.006)	.811 (.392)

Table 2.9 (continued)

| | Percent Increase per Year in | | |
Background Factors	Family Money Income	Income/Needs	Mean and (Standard Deviation) of Explanatory Variable
Efficacy, 1975	-.002	-.003	2.21
	(.002)	(.002)	(0.92)
Head a college graduate	.008	.001	.170
	(.004)	(.005)	(.376)
Head a high school dropout	.005	.012**	.387
	(.003)	(.004)	(.487)
Age of head (years)	-.00093	-.00006	54.8
	(.00014)	(.00016)	(14.4)
R² (adjusted)	.207	.143	
Mean of dependent variable	.008	.017	
(Standard Deviation)	(.112)	(.129)	

Significance levels: *.05 **.01
Note: Work means more than 500 hours in the year.

year. Using the traditional measure, family money income, it is clear that divorce hurts everyone and marriage benefits everyone, but staying single hurts only white women. And of course, being in a family where the head or wife started working (more than 500 hours per year) or stopped working had substantial effects in the expected direction. For the measure based on taxable income plus imputed rent (not shown), the results were similar to those for income, except for men, where marrying or divorcing had no effect, while those who stayed single had a less favorable trend in earnings. And when the head started or stopped working, the effect on taxable income was greater than the effect on total income.

When we use a measure that takes account of family composition, dividing income by a needs standard, the effects of marriage and divorce for men are reversed; they benefit from divorce, losing more dependents than income, and pay for getting married. This merely reflects that women usually keep the children and that they earn less than men. When black women divorce, they do not suffer differential trends in income/needs as white women do, implying that the departing husband was not earning much or that the transfer programs are more nearly adequate for blacks.

Adding food stamps and imputed rent to income before dividing by the needs standard had no effect on the pattern of effects but raised the average annual improvement rate substantially. In fact, adjusting for needs also raised the overall average trend appreciably, probably because the largest declines in income are often offset by declines in needs too, whether from death of a spouse, divorce, or a child with earnings leaving home.

The average trend values for the earlier period were higher (Table 2.8), not so much reflecting less inflation (these are deflated figures) and more real growth, but the aging of this group, which was in the sample for the whole period. But the patterns of effects remain very similar. An exception is the industry where the family head worked. In the 1975-1979 period (when the respondents were older), it clearly paid to be working in durables manufacturing,

compared with either working elsewhere or switching from one
to the other. But those working in anything but durables
manufacturing in the early period, 1968-1972 had a clear
advantage, rather than those who switched (the excluded
group).

College graduates did no better than the high school
dropouts in either period, and indeed the latter did better
than anyone else in the second period on the income/needs
measures. In the early period, both extremes, the college
graduates and the high school dropouts, did better than the
high school graduates and those with some college. Rates of
improvement decline with age in both periods and for almost
every measure, the only exception being the income/needs
measures in the later period.

Table 2.10 applies a similar analysis to the change in
the trend between the two periods, asking the question, who
was keeping up with inflation better in the second period
than in the first? An initial notion was that unions had
negotiated cost-of-living clauses so that union workers in
certain industries should show improved growth rates in the
second period. Union membership did not even qualify for
the table. As expected, the significant factors affecting
annual gains have negative effects if they happened in the
first period and positive effects if they happened in the
second period.

If we think of subtracting the equation accounting for
income trends in the early period from that accounting for
the later period, we have an accounting for the change in
the trend--the extent to which the family status was
improving at a better rate in the later period than in the
earlier period. Explanatory variables that do not change
should have no coefficient unless there was a change in
their effect or unless that factor directly affects change.
For explanatory variables that differ in the two periods,
one would expect their coefficients to be roughly equal in
size and opposite in sign; that is, if getting married
improves economic status, doing so in the second period
should mean an improvement in the rate of growth, while
doing so in the first period should mean relatively less
growth in the second period than the first. Table 2.10

Table 2.10

CHANGE IN TREND IN VARIOUS MEASURES OF WELL-BEING, 1968-1972 TO 1975-1979. EFFECTS OF CHANGES IN FAMILY AND IN WORK
(For 5,076 persons who were family head or wife in 1969, 1973, 1976, and 1980. Regression coefficients with standard errors in parentheses.)

(In 1967 Prices)

Family or Work Changes or Efficacy Measured in		Change from 1968-1972 to 1975-1979 in Annual Percent Increase in	
		Family Money Income	Income/Needs
Changes in Marital Status			
Man, got divorced	.028 (.018)	-.031* (.013)	.051** (.016)
Man, got married	-.040* (.018)	.027 (.022)	-.044 (.027)
Man, stayed single	-.012 (.018)	.003 (.015)	.017 (.018)
White woman, got divorced	.092** (.013)	-.086** (.011)	-.034* (.014)
White woman, got married	-.092** (.016)	-.074** (.018)	.028 (.022)
White woman, stayed single	.026* (.012)	-.039** (.011)	-.035** (.013)
Black woman, got divorced	.001 (.041)	.086* (.038)	.013 (.050)
Black woman, got married	-.095** (.042)	.156** (.044)	.124* (.052)
Black woman, stayed single	-.044 (.030)	.007 (.030)	.006 (.054)
All who stayed married	0	0	0
Changes in Work Status			
Family head stopped work	-.088** (.009)	-.073** (.007)	-.108** (.009)
Family head started work	-.049** (.012)	.084** (.012)	.081** (.015)
Family head stayed not working	-.002 (.009)	-.003 (.008)	-.026* (.010)
Family head stayed working	0	0	0
Wife stopped work	.086** (.008)	-.045** (.008)	-.053** (.010)
Wife started work	-.037** (.008)	.008 (.008)	.008 (.010)
Wife stayed not working	.024** (.006)	-.016* (.008)	-.029** (.008)
Wife stayed working	0	0	0
Head worked in durables manufacturing, 1971, 1973	-.016 (.010)	.034 (.009)	.037** (.012)
Head not in durables 1971 or 1973	-.017 (.009)	-.001 (.008)	.003 (.010)

Table 2.10 (continued)

Family or Work Changes or Efficacy Measured in	Change from 1968-1972 to 1975-1979 in Annual Percent Increase in			
	Family Money Income		Income/Needs	
Background Factors				
Efficacy, 1969, 1975	.004 (.002)	-.007** (.002)	.003 (.003)	-.009** (.003)
Head a college graduate	-.009 (.006)		-.011 (.007)	
Head a high school dropout	-.006 (.004)		-.001 (.006)	
Age of head (years)	.00048* (.00019)		.00024 (.00024)	
R^2 (adjusted)	.181		.141	
Mean of dependent variable	-1.4		-0.5	
(Standard Deviation)	(15.1)		(18.2)	

Significance levels: *.05 **.01
Note: Work means more than 500 hours in the year.

indeed shows that pattern. There are signs on the index of personal efficacy opposite to what would be expected if it had a positive effect. The coefficients on the sense-of-efficacy index are consistent with a model in which efficacy reflects current status and where there is some regression (negative autocorrelation) between the two trends. Those with large increases in the first period would have a high efficacy score in 1975 and a lower income trend in the second period. Those with small increases or even decreases in the first period might have low efficacy scores and higher rates of income increase in the second period, without any necessary causal connection. Indeed, the persistently negative, if nonsignificant, coefficients for efficacy in Tables 2.8 and 2.9 are consistent with the notion that there is some negative autocorrelation in economic status and a larger effect of changes in status on sense of efficacy than the effect of efficacy on subsequent changes in status. There does appear to be a barely significant positive effect of 1968 efficacy on the change in the trend of taxable income plus imputed rent, but even this could reflect long-term persistent interpersonal differences in economic advancement apparent to respondents even at the beginning of the period. On the other hand, those interpersonal differences could be in motivation as well as background, luck, or ability.

With large samples, anything worth looking at will be highly significant, but one must ask how much it matters. How much of the variance in income trends is accounted for by changes in marital status, and how much by changes in work status?

In Duncan and Morgan (1981) and in Duncan and Morgan (1976), we reported on the importance of changes in family composition in accounting for trends in well-being. It was much more important for women and children than for men. (We are looking here only at adult men and women together and at the change in the trend rather than the trend itself.) By reestimating the regressions, omitting whole sets of variables dealing with change in marital status or sets dealing with change in work status, we can assess their importance. However, we underestimate the importance of family composition changes since we are not looking at the children, and we combine men and women.

Changes in marital status accounted only for a few percent of the variance, and 1 to 7 percent of the variance unexplained by other factors. (Even 1 percent is highly significant with samples of this size.) Changes in work status, however, accounted for 7 to 20 percent of the variance, or 10 to 30 percent of the variance unaccounted for by other things. The reason lies in the more frequent occurrence of changes in work status rather than in the size of the effect of such a change on the trend in income.

Comparison with a More Representative, Second-Period Panel

For seeing who, which subgroups, did better in the second period than in the first, we needed to compare the same individuals, at the expense of confounding their age with the period difference. We can compare the periods for similar total age distributions by comparing Table 2.11 with Table 2.8. Table 2.11 is a more nearly representative sample of families in the second period, and can be compared with Table 2.9 to see what difference the omitting of the newly formed families (not in the sample in the earlier period) makes.

The only important difference between Table 2.11 and Table 2.8 is in the means of the dependent variable. However, having a family head who stayed not working did curiously appear to benefit the money income trend in the first period but visibly to impair the trend in income/needs in the second period.

The "selection bias" from using the restricted group instead of all heads and wives representing the population to examine 1975-1979 can be interpreted as age interactions combining with the underrepresentation of the younger people. (Of course, if the model were fully and properly specified, even those would not matter.) With the larger, more representative sample, men getting married no longer impair their income/needs trends, presumably because the younger men we have added to the sample are more likely to acquire an earning partner when they marry and are less likely to acquire children.

Table 2.11

EFFECTS OF CHANGES IN MARITAL STATUS AND WORK
STATUS ON INCOME TREND, 1975-1979
(For 6,887 who were head or wife in 1976 and 1980)

	Family Money Income	Income/ Needs	Mean and (Standard Deviation) of Explanatory Variable
Changes in Marital Status			
Men who got divorced	-.036**	.032**	.025
	(.010)	(.012)	(.055)
Men who got married	.066**	.015	.023
	(.011)	(.013)	(.148)
Men who stayed single	.006	.017	.045
	(.008)	(.009)	(.207)
White women who got divorced	-.089**	-.045**	.033
	(.009)	(.010)	(.179)
White women who got married	.127**	.063**	.024
	(.010)	(.012)	(.152)
White women who stayed single	-.007	-.003	.116
	(.005)	(.006)	(.320)
Black women who got divorced	-.095**	-.038	.004
	(.025)	(.030)	(.080)
Black women who got married	.160**	.107**	.004
	(.024)	(.030)	(.061)
Black women who stayed single	-.026**	-.006	.024
	(.010)	(.012)	(.153)
Changes in Work Status			
Head stopped working	-.073**	-.110**	.087
	(.006)	(.007)	(.282)
Head started working	.100**	.105**	.036
	(.008)	(.010)	(.187)
Head stayed not working	.005	-.023**	.168
	(.006)	(.007)	(.374)
Wife stopped working	-.037**	-.042**	.101
	(.006)	(.007)	(.302)
Wife started working	.047**	.044**	.125
	(.006)	(.007)	(.330)
Wife stayed not working	.003	-.010	.539
(or no wife)	(.004)	(.005)	(.498)

Table 2.11 (continued)

	Family Money Income	Income/ Needs	Mean and (Standard Deviation) of Explanatory Variable
Head in durables manufacturing, 1975 and 1979	.010 (.007)	.016* (.008)	.100 (.300)
Head not in durables 1975 or 1979	-.008 (.005)	-.005 (.006)	.804 (.397)
Background Factors			
Efficacy of head, 1975	-.004** (.002)	-.005* (.002)	2.18 (0.93)
Head a college graduate	.006 (.004)	-.002 (.005)	.184 (.387)
Head a high school dropout	.000 (.004)	.003 (.004)	.335 (.472)
Age of head (years)	-.00148** (.0001)	-.00046** (.00015)	48.9 (16.7)
R^2 (adjusted)	.261	.151	
Mean of dependent variable (Standard Deviation)	.024 (.123)	.026 (.139)	

Significance levels: *.05 **.01

Note: Work means more than 500 hours in the year.

The race difference between women who remained
unmarried is reversed for the larger group, which implies
that younger black women suffer more from staying single
than do younger white women. A significant effect of
education disappears: apparently it was only the older high
school dropouts whose trend on income/needs was actually
better. Having a family head working in durables
manufacturing was more consistently beneficial in the
restricted (older) sample, implying that only those with
seniority benefited.

In general, however, the pattern of highly significant
effects of changes in marital status and work status on
economic status persists and did not change much between
periods. Improvement trends do decline substantially with
age so that restricting the sample to those in the panel for
a long period--hence omitting younger families--can cause
distortions if there are age interactions with other
factors. This underscores the need to make careful
distinctions among the questions being asked, and to select
the data appropriately. Using a panel study as a series of
cross-sections is tricky, requiring the omission of any
families duplicated in early years as sources of several
present families, and adding newly formed families in later
years. Following individuals in a panel over time avoids
difficulties in defining which is the same family, and
allows us to see how individual life-course changes happen,
but it restricts the sample in terms of age. Part of our
analysis here was a compromise that compared two reasonably
representative panels to see whether the factors affecting
trends in well-being had changed.

SUMMARY

People are aware of inflation, are perceptive about
where it hurts most, and appear to make modest changes in
response. Those who said inflation hurt were more likely to
report changing their retirement plans. Those who reported
being hurt by transportation prices did significantly reduce
their driving. Different income experiences did account for
differences in eating, eating out, and driving, as expected.

Patterns of who kept up with inflation did not change much when we compare a recent period, 1975-1979, with an earlier one, 1968-1972. But vast differences in trends of income and of income/needs are produced by changes in marital status and in work status and not equally for the two measures. For men, divorce reduces the income trend but improves the trend in income/needs. They give up more dependents than income. Divorce leaves white women worse off on all measures, and marriage means improvement. Black women are helped less than white women by marriage, and hardly hurt at all by divorce. In general, the effects of family changes and work changes are different for the two measures, since undoubling or doubling will affect income/ needs more than income, but changing labor force status affects income more than needs.

References

Duncan, Greg J. and Morgan, James N. "Introduction, Overview, Summary, and Conclusions", in Five Thousand American Families - Patterns of Economic Progress, Vol. IV, ed. Greg J. Duncan and James N. Morgan, Ann Arbor: Institute for Social Research, 1976.

Duncan, Greg J. and Morgan, James N. "Persistance and Change in Economic Status and the role of Changing Family Combustion", in Five Thousand American Families - Patterns of Economic Progress, Vol. IX, ed. Martha Hill, et al., Ann Arbor: Institute for Social Research, 1981.

Chapter 3

PARTICIPATION IN THE SUPPLEMENTAL SECURITY
INCOME PROGRAM BY THE ELIGIBLE ELDERLY

Richard D. Coe[1]

INTRODUCTION

In 1974 the Supplemental Security Income (SSI) program was introduced as a replacement for the myriad of state programs aimed at aiding the elderly and the disabled. Under the provisions of the program, the federal government would guarantee a minimum monthly income to persons aged 65 or over and to the disabled. The individual states had the option[2] of supplementing the basic federal grant.

The basic intent of the program was to assist the elderly or disabled who either did not qualify for Social Security payments or qualified for benefits that were too low to prevent severe economic hardship. It was thought at the time that the various state programs were not adequately providing such assistance, as a result of either incomplete coverage or insufficient benefits. The sometimes cumbersome administrative apparatus of the states was also believed to be a barrier to participation for the needy. A streamlined, comprehensive federal program administered by the Social Security Administration was expected to eliminate many of these problems. Advocates of the program expected a considerable increase in participation in the federal program as compared to that in the state programs. In fact, the Social Security Administration estimated in 1973--the year before the program was implemented--that the participation rate of eligible elderly persons would be 90 percent (Menefer, Edwards, and Scheiber, 1981:5).

---

[1]The author wishes to thank David Boomsma for his assistance in this research.

[2]When the program was originally introduced, some states were required to supplement the basic federal grant at a level that would not reduce benefits received by recipients of state old age and disability (including blindness) payments. In other words, the law contained a "hold-harmless" provision.

93

It is now clear that such estimates were far off the mark. The participation rate in the SSI program by eligible elderly persons has been estimated to be approximately 55 percent (Menefee et al., 1981; Warlick, 1982). The reasons for this low participation rate are not well understood. The stigma associated with receiving welfare payments has been one factor often mentioned as crucial, as the elderly are thought to be particularly prone to such feelings. Low benefit levels, physical access problems, administrative hassles, and poor information have been other reasons advanced to explain why the eligible elderly do not receive SSI payments.

The purpose of this chapter is to analyze why eligible elderly persons do not participate in the SSI program. In Spring, 1980, the Panel Study of Income Dynamics (PSID) asked all households with an elderly head or spouse who did not report receiving any SSI income in 1979 why they did not participate in the program. By applying the SSI eligibility rules to this sample, it can be determined which of these elderly persons were eligible in 1979 to receive SSI payments. Analyzing the reasons given for nonparticipation by eligible persons should provide some insights into why the SSI program has experienced such low participation rates.

A DESCRIPTIVE ANALYSIS OF PARTICIPATION IN THE SSI-AGED PROGRAM

In 1979, 811 Panel Study households had either a head or a spouse aged 65 or over. Of these, 188 were estimated to be eligible for SSI payments at some time in 1979. (The procedures used for determining eligibility are detailed in Appendix A.) These eligible households represented 16 percent of all households containing an elderly head or spouse.

Table 3.1 provides the characteristics of this sample of eligible households. Almost three-quarters of the sample consisted of unmarried women, most living alone. Half of the eligible persons lived in a household in which the head was less than 75 years old. Seventy percent were white. Almost half of the eligible households lived in the South; 38 percent resided in rural areas. Three-quarters of the sample had less than a ninth grade education. Almost half owned their homes. More than half of the sample reported some health problems, not surprising given the age distribution of these people. Almost 90 percent of these

households reported receiving some Social Security income.
Finally, 57 percent of these eligibles had incomes below the
official federal poverty line in 1979. Over one-third had spent
the previous three years in poverty.

Participation Rates

The aggregate participation rate of these eligible elderly
households was 52.5 percent in 1979 (see Table 3.1), a figure
quite similar to other estimates of SSI participation. The
unadjusted participation rate was positively correlated with the
monthly benefit level and negatively correlated to a degree with
the age of the household head. Nonwhites were somewhat more
likely to participate than whites. Persons residing in the South
were more likely to participate than persons in other regions.
Homeowners were considerably less likely to participate than
nonhomeowners. Health problems apparently encouraged
participation, while the receipt of Social Security income
appeared to exert a negative influence on participation.

Reasons for Nonparticipation

Table 3.2 shows the distribution of reasons for
nonparticipation by those eligible elderly households that did
not receive SSI income in 1979. (Table 3.1 shows the
distribution of reasons by subgroups of the eligible sample.)
The reasons given in Table 3.2 represent a high degree of
aggregation, due to the small number of observations (N=76).
(For a more detailed breakdown of the responses, see Appendix
Table B3.1.)

As can be seen, informational barriers dominated as a reason
for nonparticipation, as almost three-fourths of the eligible
nonparticipants indicated that they did not think (or did not
know) that they were eligible to receive SSI payments. Slightly
more than one-half of those who did not think they were eligible
apparently were almost totally unaware of the rules and
procedures of the program. This group included those who replied
that they simply didn't know anything about the eligibility
requirements of the program (N=12), those who did not know how to
go about applying for benefits (N=4), and those who when asked
why they did not think they were eligible said they didn't know
(N=15).

Table 3.1

PARTICIPATION STATUS OF ELDERLY HOUSEHOLDS ELIGIBLE FOR SSI, 1979
BY SELECTED DEMOGRAPHIC AND PROGRAM CHARACTERISTICS

Household Characteristic	Number of Observations	Weighted Percent of Eligible Households	Participant	Nonparticipant, Thought Ineligible Because Knew Nothing about Program	Nonparticipant, Thought Ineligible, Gave Specific Reason Why	Thought Eligible, but Did Not Participate
All	188	100.0%	52.5%	18.2%	16.1%	13.2%
Household Status						
Married couple, both head and wife age 65 or more	32	16.8	53.7	20.9	14.1	11.4
Unmarried male	9	5.6	34.8	36.9	0.0	28.3
Unmarried female	129	72.3	55.6	15.1	18.3	11.0
Married couple, one person under age 65	18	5.2	23.7	34.0	9.2	32.9
Living Arrangements						
Head and wife only	147	85.4	50.9	18.2	17.6	13.2
Other members besides head and wife, total income of others $4,000 or less	28	8.5	55.9	31.7	0.0	12.3
Other members besides head and wife, total income of $4,000 or more	13	6.1	69.0	0.0	17.4	13.6
Monthly Benefit						
$1-24	31	19.2	26.3	20.6	26.9	26.2
$25-49	23	13.3	44.7	38.0	16.9	0.4
$50-99	52	26.9	51.3	17.5	14.1	14.0
$100-199	50	22.9	46.3	19.7	15.1	18.9
$200 or more	32	17.6	92.0	0.0	8.0	0.0

Table 3.1 (continued)

Household Characteristic	Number of Observations	Weighted Percent of Eligible Households Participant	Nonparticipant, Thought Ineligible Because Knew Nothing about Program	Nonparticipant, Thought Ineligible, Gave Specific Reason Why	Thought Eligible, but Did Not Participate
Age of Head					
Less than 70 years	89	29.1	63.8	11.4	7.3	17.4
70-74	44	21.8	49.6	22.4	19.5	8.5
75-79	20	14.9	52.8	21.3	19.6	6.2
80-84	20	20.2	49.3	23.7	14.7	12.3
85 years or more	15	14.0	37.4	14.8	27.3	20.4
Race					
Nonwhite	101	29.1	59.8	11.8	1.1	27.3
White	87	70.9	49.4	20.9	22.3	7.4
Region					
Northeast	21	14.4	39.3	29.6	14.8	16.3
North Central	24	17.1	36.1	23.0	29.1	11.8
South	109	47.9	61.5	15.9	11.3	11.3
West	34	20.7	54.1	11.8	17.4	16.6
Population of Largest City in County					
500,000 or more	65	29.1	46.1	28.4	8.8	16.7
100,000-499,999	33	17.0	69.2	1.1	15.1	14.5
25,000-99,999	28	15.5	46.9	13.2	20.3	19.6
Less than 25,000	62	38.3	52.1	20.2	20.4	7.3
Education of Head					
0-5 years	69	33.6	55.9	14.6	2.1	27.4
6-8 years	73	41.8	43.4	25.4	28.7	2.5
9-11 years	36	16.9	67.8	16.0	5.8	10.3
12 or more	10	7.8	53.1	0.2	31.2	15.5

Table 3.1 (continued)

Household Characteristic	Number of Observations	Weighted Percent of Eligible Households	Participant	Nonparticipant, Thought Ineligible, Because Knew Nothing about Program	Nonparticipant, Thought Ineligible, Gave Specific Reason Why	Thought Eligible, but Did Not Participate
Housing Status						
Owns	77	46.3	39.0	21.4	22.1	17.6
Rents	85	41.0	63.8	17.0	9.6	9.6
Neither owns nor rents	26	12.7	65.2	10.7	15.3	8.7
Whether State Supplementation						
No	127	58.0	56.4	17.7	13.1	12.8
Yes	61	42.0	47.0	19.1	20.2	13.8
Whether Health Problems, Head						
No	80	45.5	45.2	24.8	22.2	7.8
Yes	108	54.5	58.5	12.8	11.0	17.8
Non-SSI Monthly Income, Head and Wife						
$1-99	25	12.3	87.2	1.3	11.5	0.0
$100-199	75	38.3	71.5	13.7	7.6	7.2
$200-299	61	31.3	31.4	19.5	21.8	27.4
$300 or more	27	18.1	25.1	37.3	27.4	10.2
Whether Received Social Security						
No	28	12.4	80.9	11.4	0.5	7.2
Yes	160	87.6	48.4	19.2	18.3	14.0
Whether Owns Car						
No	123	65.9	58.1	21.4	10.8	9.8
Yes	65	34.1	41.6	12.2	26.4	19.8

Table 3.1 (continued)

Household Characteristic	Number of Observations	Weighted Percent of Eligible Households	Participant	Nonparticipant, Thought Ineligible Because Knew Nothing about Program	Nonparticipant, Thought Ineligible, Gave Specific Reason Why	Thought Eligible, but Did Not Participate
Whether Poor, 1979						
No	66	43.2	51.7	19.0	15.1	14.2
Yes	122	56.8	53.1	17.7	16.9	12.4
Number of Previous Years in Poverty						
None	46	33.3	48.3	19.6	21.8	10.3
One	37	15.7	43.1	16.9	18.8	21.1
Two	33	14.8	54.4	7.5	13.2	24.9
Three	72	36.2	59.5	22.0	10.9	7.7

Table 3.2

DISTRIBUTION OF REASONS FOR NONPARTICIPATION IN THE SUPPLEMENTAL
SECURITY INCOME PROGRAM, 1979, ELIGIBLE ELDERLY HOUSEHOLDS

Reason for Nonparticipation	Number of Observations	Weighted Percent of Observations
Did not think eligible because knew nothing about eligibility rules	31	38.3%
Did not think eligible, gave specific reason why	23	33.9
Thought eligible, but did not participate	22	27.8
Totals	76	100.0%

For a more detailed distribution of reasons, see Appendix
Table B3.1.

The remainder of those who did not believe they were eligible indicated that they had at least some awareness of the operation of the program, even if their actual understanding of how the program operated was mistaken. The most common response given by this group was that they thought their income or assets were too high to qualify for benefits (N=12).

Slightly over one-quarter of the eligible nonparticipants thought they were eligible for the program, but still did not receive benefits. The most common mentioned reason for not receiving benefits was that the person had been declared ineligible by local officials (N=7). The source of the discrepancy between this reason and the procedures used in this analysis to determine eligibility is not clear. The procedures documented in Appendix A contain room for error, but errors are also made by local officials.[3]

A MULTIVARIATE ANALYSIS OF PARTICIPATION

To obtain a clearer picture of the independent effect that certain demographic and program variables exert on participation, a multivariate approach must be employed. In addition, if a certain demographic or program variable is found to be a significant predictor of participation, it would be of interest to determine which factors account for the effect of this variable. A multiple-choice linear probability model can perform both of these tasks. Each eligible household will fall into one of four categories: it will either be a participant in the program, a nonparticipant because it knew virtually nothing about the program, a nonparticipant because it considered itself to be ineligible for a specific reason, or a nonparticipant even though it thought it was eligible for benefits. Based on this categorization, four equations can be estimated:

$$(1) \quad P_{1i} = a_1 + B_1X_i + e_1$$
$$(2) \quad P_{2i} = a_2 + B_2X_i + e_2$$
$$(3) \quad P_{3i} = a_3 + B_3X_i + e_3$$
$$(4) \quad P_{4i} = a_4 + B_4X_i + e_4$$

---

[3]It is also possible that both the procedures used in this study are accurate and that the official determination of ineligibility was correct <u>at the time that it was made</u>. This could result if a household's income fluctuated over the year, of if the official determination were made before 1979 and the eligible individual accepted this as applying to 1979 as well.

where P_{1i} = the probability that household i will be a participant,

P_{2i} = the probability that household i will be a nonparticipant because it knows nothing about the program,

P_{3i} = the probability that household i will be a nonparticipant because it considers itself ineligible for a specific reason,

P_{4i} = the probability that household i will be a nonparticipant even though it considers itself eligible for the program, and

X_i = the set of demographic and program variables.

The estimated probabilities P_{1i} - P_{4i} will sum to one as a result of the fact that each household can choose only one alternative. Furthermore, the estimated coefficients, B_1 through B_4, will sum to zero, or,

(5) $B_1 = - (B_2 + B_3 + B_4)$

The coefficient B_1 is an estimate of the effect of a particular demographic or program variable on participation. By equation (5), this effect can be decomposed into the individual effects that particular variable has on the probability of citing one of three reasons for nonparticipation. For example, assume it was found from estimating equation (1) that eligible elderly persons who were homeowners were 50 percentage points less likely to participate, that is, B_1 = -.50. The question now becomes, Why is homeowning status an important predictor of participation? The results from estimating equations (2) to (4) can aid us in this inquiry. Suppose it was found that B_3 = .25; that is, homeowners were 25 percentage points more likely than nonhomeowners to respond that they did not participate because they did not think they were eligible for a specific reason. The ratio B_3/B_1 indicates what percentage of the lower participation rate of homeowners can be accounted for by this reason, in this case 50 percent. The remaining 50 percent would be accounted for by the other two reasons for nonparticipation (B_2 + B_4 = .50). In this manner, the results from the multiple-choice linear probability model can aid us in understanding both which characteristics are important in predicting participation and why such characteristics are important.

The Determinants of Participation in the SSI Program

The first column of figures in Table 3.3 shows the results of regressing a set of demographic and program characteristics of the household on the household's participation status (equation (1) above). For the variables that are significant predictors of participation, the final three columns indicate how the effect of that variable can be accounted for by the different reasons given for nonparticipation. The figures entered in the last three columns equal B_i/B_1, where the B_i's are taken from the results of estimating equations (2) to (4). (The complete regression results for equations (2) to (4) are given in Appendix C.) Only the B_i's that were significant at the 10 percent level are presented in Table 3.3.

The fact that an eligible elderly person was married to a person under the age of 65 had a considerable negative impact on participation. (Note, however, that there were only 18 couples in this category.) The primary reason accounting for this negative influence was that these couples were more likely to respond that they didn't really know anything about the rules and procedures of the program. What is not clear is why this group is unaware of the program. One might speculate that a married couple in which one of the persons is nonelderly may not consider itself elderly and thus does not pay attention to programs aimed at the elderly. Unawareness of the program was not the only factor accounting for this group's low participation rate. Even if these households thought they were eligible to receive SSI benefits, they were less likely to participate. However, this factor was less important (and less significant) than the effect of a general lack of knowledge about the program.

Significant region differentials in participation rates were apparent even when other factors were controlled. Eligible elderly households residing in the North Central and Western regions of the country were less likely to receive SSI benefits than those residing in the South. These differences were not a result of differential informational barriers, as households in the North Central and West were no more likely than Southern households to respond that they thought they were ineligible. Instead, virtually the entire difference was attributable to other factors, such as no perceived need or administrative problems.

Table 3.3

REGRESSION RESULTS ON PARTICIPATION IN THE SSI PROGRAM AND ALLOCATION OF
REASONS FOR NONPARTICIPATION, ELIGIBLE ELDERLY HOUSEHOLDS, 1979
(N = 188)

Household Characteristic (Omitted Category)	Regression Coefficient on Whether Participant	Allocation of Reasons for Differential Participation Rate		
		Knew Nothing about Program	Thought Ineligible, Gave Specific Reason	Thought Eligible, but Did Not Participate
Sex-Marital Status				
Married couple, head and wife both age 65 or more	-.089 (.112)	....	....	....
Unmarried male	-.143 (.158)	....	....	....
(Unmarried female)	....	....	....	....
Married couple, one spouse under age 65	-.686** (.158)	-52.8**	....	-31.3†
Region				
Northeast	-.245 (.175)	....	....	....
North Central	-.272* (.106)	....	....	-87.5**
(South)	....	....	....	....
West	-.387** (.178)	....	....	-109.3**

Table 3.3 (continued)

Household Characteristic (Omitted Category)	Regression Coefficient on Whether Participant	Allocation of Reasons for Differential Participation Rate		
		Knew Nothing about Program	Thought Ineligible, Gave Specific Reason	Thought Eligible, but Did Not Participate
Size of Largest City in County (500,000 or more)				
100,000-499,999	.026 (.121)	. . . .	. . . .	. . . .
25,000-99,999	-.023 (.116)	. . . .	. . . .	. . . .
Less than 25,000	-.009 (.120)	. . . .	. . . .	. . . .
Education, Head (0-5 years)				
6-8 years	.040 (.084)	. . . .	. . . .	. . . .
9-11 years	.107 (.102)	. . . .	. . . .	. . . .
12 years or more	.076 (.139)	. . . .	. . . .	. . . .
Whether Homeowner	-.204** (.078)	-63.2†	. . . .	-63.7*
Age of Head	-.017†† (.005)	. . . .	-35.3†	-52.9**
Whether White	-.011 (.080)	. . . .	. . . .	. . . .
Monthly SSI Benefit ($10)	.030** (.005)	-38.5**	-21.1†	-40.1**

Table 3.3 (continued)

Household Characteristic (Omitted Category)	Regression Coefficient on Whether Participant	Allocation of Reasons for Differential Participation Rate		
		Knew Nothing about Program	Thought Ineligible, Gave Specific Reason	Thought Eligible, but Did Not Participate
Whether State Supplementation	-.002 (.146)	. . . .	. . . .	. . . .
Whether Health Problems, Head	.101 (.066)	. . . .	. . . .	. . . .
Whether Owns Car	-.007 (.090)	. . . .	. . . .	. . . .
Number of Previous Years Poor	.012 (.032)	. . . .	. . . .	. . . .
R² (adjusted)	.315	.191	.212	.262

Significance Levels: †.10   *.05   **.01

Eligible homeowners had an adjusted participation rate that was 20 percentage points lower than that of eligible nonhomeowners. Homeowners were significantly more likely both to be unaware of the workings of the program and, if possessing accurate information concerning eligibility, not to participate anyway. The SSI program in the past has been somewhat ambivalent in its treatment of low-income elderly homeowners. When the program was implemented, a $35,000 ceiling was placed on the value of the house a person could own and still be eligible. This was later replaced by "a reasonable value" standard. It is possible that the application of this standard has proved to be an administrative deterrence to participation by otherwise eligible households.

Participation was negatively correlated with the age of the household head, as each additional year of age reduced the probability of participation by 1.7 percentage points. (The mean age of household head was 75.6 years, with a range of 62 to 93 years.) Informational factors were not the primary reason accounting for this negative relationship, as age was not related to general awareness of the program.

Participation was positively correlated with the benefit level to which the household was entitled. This effect was not trivial, as each $10 increase in benefits increased the probability of participation by 3 percentage points. About 60 percent of the positive relationship could be accounted for by informational factors, in particular, that eligible households with lower benefit levels were more likely to be generally unaware of the program. The remaining 40 percent of the positive correlation between benefit level and participation was a result of low benefit households who thought they were eligible being more likely to have some reason for nonparticipation. (One might suggest that this reason was simply that the low benefit level was not worth the effort of applying for it. While this is an eminently reasonable suggestion, only one respondent explicitly mentioned too low a benefit as a reason for nonparticipation.) One might note that extremely low benefits are a reflection of incomes very close to the eligibility maximums. This group would be particularly prone to administrative misdetermination of eligibility status or changing status over the course of the year if income fluctuated (or, for that matter, to incorrect

assessment of eligibility by the procedures used in this study
if, for example, income was misreported.)

Finally, the variables that were not significant predictors
of participation should be noted. These include marital status
(unless one of the spouses was under age 65), sex, size of
largest city in the county of residence, education of head, race,
whether the state supplemented the basic federal benefit payment,
whether the head reported health problems, car ownership, and the
number of previous years that the person lived in poverty.

AN ASSESSMENT OF THE RESULTS

Perhaps the one conclusion that best summarizes the
empirical findings of this analysis is that, taken alone, they
offer few conclusions that one could rely on with a large measure
of confidence. It would seem that it can safely be concluded
that only about one-half of the elderly households eligible for
SSI benefits actually receive them, that there are significant
regional differences in participation, that eligible elderly
homeowners are considerably less likely to participate, and that
participation is negatively correlated with age and positively
correlated with the benefit level. But the combination of a
relatively small number of eligible nonparticipants and the
inherent ambiguity in coding and categorizing open-ended
responses to survey questions renders conclusions concerning why
these factors influence participation tentative at best. While
the answers of nonparticipants reveal a discernible lack of
accurate information about SSI, the distinction between those who
are generally unaware of the program and those who have specific,
but inaccurate, knowledge is clearly tenuous. While such a
distinction would be useful in designing strategies to overcome
the lack of proper information about the program, basing any
concrete policy proposals on the results of this analysis alone
would clearly be a dicey proposition.

And yet, despite the reservations, when the results of this
study are taken in conjunction with the results of other studies
concerning participation in the SSI program by eligible elderly
households, a consistent picture begins to emerge. Both Warlick
(1982) and Menefee (1981) estimated the aggregation participation
rate to be approximately 55 percent, equivalent to the results of
this analysis. Warlick found similar results with respect to

region, age of head, and the benefit level, although her interpretation of why these variables were significant was problematic. Menefee used a considerably more detailed set of demographic variables than were available from the PSID. Many of these more refined objective measures were insignificant in distinguishing eligible nonparticipants from participants. They concluded that: "Knowledge or information is an important determinant of nonparticipation in any type of public assistance program and may be especially important for the SSI target populations because of their limited exposure to and knowledge of public support programs" (Menefee et al., 1981:20). The results of this analysis are consistent with that assessment.[4]

---

[4]See also the results on participation in the food stamp program by eligible elderly households presented in Chapter 4.

References

Coe, Richard D. "Participation in the Food Stamp Program, 1979," Five Thousand American Families, Volume X, ed. Greg J. Duncan and James N. Morgan, Ann Arbor: Institute for Social Research, 1983.

Coe, Richard, D. "Participation in the Food Stamp Program." Working Paper Series, Institute for Social Research. Ann Arbor: Institute for Social Research, September 1979.

Menefee, John; Edwards, Bea; and Schieber, Sylvester. "Analysis of Nonparticipation in the SSI Program." Social Security Bulletin, June 1981.

Warlick, Jennifer. "An Empirical Analysis of Participation in the Supplemental Security Income Program Among Aged Eligible Persons." Journal of Human Resources, Summer 1982.

Appendix A to Chapter 3

DERIVATION OF SAMPLE OF HOUSEHOLDS
ELIGIBLE FOR THE SSI-ELDERLY PROGRAM

The Supplemental Security Income program for the elderly is
a means-tested, categorically eligible program for all persons
aged 65 or over. In this study, only those elderly persons who
were either the head or the wife of a household were included in
the sample. In 1979 there were 811 Panel Study households
residing in the contiguous United States in which either the head
or wife was age 65 or over. The SSI eligibility rules were
applied to this group in order to derive a sample of eligible
elderly households.

THE SSI ELIGIBILITY RULES

The SSI program in essence provides a minimum guaranteed
income to elderly households. As such, it is a means-tested
program. The income maximums for eligibility vary by the living
arrangements of the household. For an elderly individual living
independently (i.e., not a dependent of someone else), the basic
federal stipend (income ceiling) was $208 a month in 1979. For
an individual living in the household of another, the federal
income ceiling was $139 a month. A married couple living
independently was entitled to a maximum federal payment of $312
per month, while for a married couple living in the household of
another the ceiling was $209 per month. To be considered a
married couple for purposes of SSI eligibility determination,
both the head and the wife have to be age 65 or more. If an
elderly person is married to a nonelderly person, the elderly
person is considered to be an individual for purposes of SSI
eligibility. However, the nonelderly spouse's income is still
counted as part of household income.

The above figures refer to the basic federal eligibility
guidelines. The individual states have the option of
supplementing the basic federal benefit, and many do. Some
supplement the benefits for all four categories listed above;
others are more selective.

In determining countable income for purposes of SSI
eligibility, the first $60 of monthly earned income is excluded
plus one-half of the excess over $60. In addition, a flat $20

per month of household income is excluded, if it was not already excluded under the earned income provision.

The SSI program also has an asset test. For an individual, $1,500 is the asset maximum; for a married couple, the asset ceiling is $2,250. For nonliquid assets such as a house, a car, or personal property, a "reasonable value" exclusion is applied. For a car the reasonable value is set at $1,200; for personal property the exclusion is set at $1,500.

One additional point should be noted. The federal law provides for an increase of $104 in the monthly stipend of an eligible person if an "essential person" resided in the household. An essential person is someone who provides care to the eligible person. The provision was primarily aimed at allowing the nonelderly spouses of disabled eligibles to qualify for some payment. This provision was not accounted for in this analysis.

THE APPLICATION OF THE RULES TO THE PANEL STUDY DATA

The first issue to be addressed was how to determine whether the elderly person (or couple) was living independently or in the household of another. The procedure used in this study was to define a person or couple as living in the household of another if the total income of the other members of the household (as defined by the Panel Study) was greater than $4,000. The rationale behind this was that if the other members in the dwelling unit had incomes of $4,000 or less, they would not be able to contribute to the support of the elderly SSI eligible person. This would seem to be a conservative definition.

Panel Study income figures are reported on an annual basis, thus necessitating the use of average monthly household income (and earned income) for the purposes of determining eligibility (and the earned income exclusion).

The Panel Study does not report the asset holdings of the household. It does, however, report the annual "Rent, Dividend, and Interest" income received by the household. This variable was used to estimate liquid assets, assuming a 5 percent rate of return.

The application of these procedures resulted in 605 of the 811 households with an elderly head or spouse to be declared income-ineligible. An additional 18 households were estimated to fail the asset test, leaving 188 households as eligible for SSI benefits.

References

Public Law 92-603.

Rigby, Donald E., and Ponce, Elsa. The Supplemental Security Income Program for the Aged, Blind, and Disabled: Selected Characteristics of State Supplementation Programs as of October, 1979. Washington, DC: U.S. Government Printing Office, 1980.

Appendix B to Chapter 3

THE DETAILED DISTRIBUTION OF RESPONSES TO
THE NONPARTICIPATION QUESTIONS

Figure B3.1 shows the actual sequence of questions that were
asked elderly persons who reported receiving no SSI income in
1979. Table B3.2 presents the full distribution of responses to
these questions.

Figure B3.1

K15.   We are interested in the government's Supplemental Security Income Program.
(V7280)   Did you think you were eligible for Supplemental Security Income in 1979?

| 1.   YES | | 3.   MAYBE | | 5.   NO | | 8.   DON'T KNOW |

TURN TO P. 37, K19

K16.   Did you try to get SSI last year (1979)?
(V7281)

| 1.   YES | | 5.   NO | → TURN TO P. 37, K18

K17.   Can you tell me why you couldn't get SSI? (Any other reasons why?)
(V7282)

_____

_____

_____

TURN TO P. 37, K20

K18.   Can you tell me why you didn't try? (Any other reasons why?)

_____ (V7283 - First mention) _____

_____ (V7284 - Second mention) _____

_____

GO TO K20

K19.   Can you tell me why you thought you weren't eligible? (Any other reasons why?)

_____ (V7285 - First mention) _____

_____ (V7286 - Second mention) _____

_____

Table B3.1

DISTRIBUTION OF RESPONSES TO SSI NONPARTICIPATION
SEQUENCE, ELIGIBLE ELDERLY HOUSEHOLDS, 1979
(N=188)

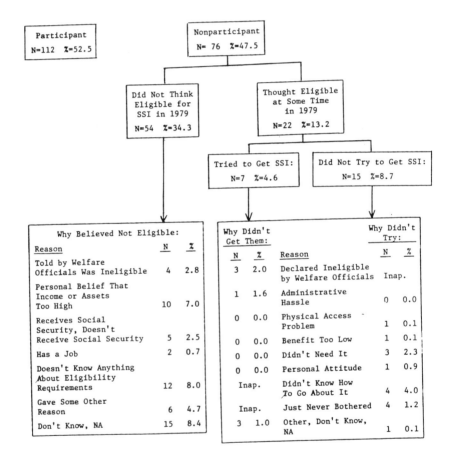

Participant	
N=112 %=52.5	

Nonparticipant	
N= 76 %=47.5	

Did Not Think Eligible for SSI in 1979	
N=54 %=34.3	

Thought Eligible at Some Time in 1979	
N=22 %=13.2	

Tried to Get SSI:	
N=7 %=4.6	

Did Not Try to Get SSI:	
N=15 %=8.7	

Why Believed Not Eligible:

Reason	N	%
Told by Welfare Officials Was Ineligible	4	2.8
Personal Belief That Income or Assets Too High	10	7.0
Receives Social Security, Doesn't Receive Social Security	5	2.5
Has a Job	2	0.7
Doesn't Know Anything About Eligibility Requirements	12	8.0
Gave Some Other Reason	6	4.7
Don't Know, NA	15	8.4

Why Didn't Get Them:			Why Didn't Try:		
N	%	Reason		N	%
3	2.0	Declared Ineligible by Welfare Officials		Inap.	
1	1.6	Administrative Hassle		0	0.0
0	0.0	Physical Access Problem		1	0.1
0	0.0	Benefit Too Low		1	0.1
0	0.0	Didn't Need It		3	2.3
0	0.0	Personal Attitude		1	0.9
Inap.		Didn't Know How To Go About It		4	4.0
Inap.		Just Never Bothered		4	1.2
3	1.0	Other, Don't Know, NA		1	0.1

Appendix C to Chapter 3

COMPLETE REGRESSION RESULTS

The full regression results for text equations (1) to (4) are presented in Table C3.1.

Table C3.1

COMPLETE REGRESSION RESULTS FOR PARTICIPATION IN THE SUPPLEMENTAL
SECURITY INCOME PROGRAM BY ELIGIBLE ELDERLY HOUSEHOLDS, 1979
(N = 188)

Independent Variable (Omitted Category)	Dependent Variable			
	Whether Participant	Whether Knew Nothing about Program	Whether Thought Ineligible, Gave Specific Reason	Whether Thought Eligible, but Did Not Participate
Sex-Marital Status				
Married couple, head and wife both age 65 or more	-.089 (.112)	.250** (.094)	-.128 (.086)	-.034 (.079)
Unmarried male	-.143 (.158)	.239† (.133)	-.124 (.122)	.028 (.112)
(Unmarried female)	....	....	....	....
Married couple, one spouse under age 65	-.686** (.158)	.362** (.134)	.109 (.122)	.215† (.112)
Region				
Northeast	-.245 (.175)	.111 (.147)	-.168 (.135)	.302* (.124)
North central	-.272* (.106)	.009 (.089)	.025 (.082)	.238** (.075)
(South)	....	....	....	....
West	-.387** (.178)	.048 (.150)	-.084 (.137)	.423** (.126)

Table C3.1 (continued)

Independent Variable (Omitted Category)	Dependent Variable			
	Whether Participant	Whether Knew Nothing about Program	Whether Thought Ineligible, Gave Specific Reason	Whether Thought Eligible, but Did Not Participate
Size of Largest City in County (500,000 or more)				
100,000-499,999	.026 (.121)	-.225* (.102)	.088 (.093)	.111 (.086)
25,000-99,999	-.023 (.116)	-.188† (.098)	.142 (.090)	.069 (.082)
Less than 25,000	-.009 (.120)	-.207† (.101)	.167† (.093)	.050 (.085)
Education, Head (0-5 years)				
6-8 years	.040 (.084)	.094 (.071)	.148* (.065)	-.283** (.059)
9-11 years	.107 (.102)	-.006 (.086)	.013 (.079)	-.115 (.072)
12 years or more	.076 (.139)	-.125 (.117)	.183† (.107)	-.134 (.098)
Whether Homeowner	-.204** (.078)	.129† (.066)	-.055 (.060)	.130† (.055)
Age of Head	-.017** (.005)	.002 (.004)	.006† (.004)	.009** (.003)
Whether White	-.011 (.080)	.138* (.067)	.127† (.062)	-.254** (.057)
Monthly SSI Benefit ($10)	.030** (.005)	-.012** (.004)	-.006† (.004)	-.012** (.003)

Table C3.1 (continued)

Independent Variable (Omitted Category)	Dependent Variable			
	Whether Participant	Whether Knew Nothing about Program	Whether Thought Ineligible, Gave Specific Reason	Whether Thought Eligible, but Did Not Participate
Whether State Supplementation	-.002 (.146)	-.056 (.123)	.184 (.113)	-.127 (.104)
Whether Health Problems, Head	.101 (.066)	-.120* (.056)	-.036 (.051)	.055 (.047)
Whether Owns Car	-.007 (.090)	-.238** (.076)	.201** (.069)	.089 (.064)
Number of Previous Years Poor	.012 (.032)	-.003 (.027)	-.046† (.025)	-.038† (.023)
R² (adjusted)	.315	.191	.212	.262

Significance levels: †.10   *.05   **.01

Chapter 4

PARTICIPATION IN THE FOOD STAMP PROGRAM, 1979

Richard D. Coe

INTRODUCTION

Over the past ten years it has become increasingly clear
that despite the rapid growth in the food stamp program only
about one-half of the households eligible to participate in the
program actually do. This conclusion has been confirmed by
several studies (U.S. Bureau of the Census, 1976; Coe 1977; 1979;
MacDonald, 1977). What is not so clear is why eligible
households do not participate. Previous research using the Panel
Study of Income Dynamics has indicated that the majority of
eligible nonparticipants do not believe that they are eligible
(Coe, 1979). This belief was particularly strong among the
single elderly and among household heads who worked. No other
factor, such as low bonus values or physical access problems, was
mentioned by more than 10 percent of the eligible participants.
However, data were not available to indicate why eligible
nonusers believed they were ineligible.

The purpose of this study is to update and extend the
previous research on participation in the food stamp program.
Coe's earlier analysis on the Panel Study data dealt with the
year 1976. The Food Stamp Act of 1977 subsequently changed the
eligibility rules, altered allowable deductions, and eliminated
the purchase requirement, factors which might be expected to
alter participation rates. This study analyzes data for the year
1979, after the major reforms had been implemented. Furthermore,
nonparticipants who did not believe they were eligible to receive
food stamps were asked why they thought they were ineligible.
The responses to this question should provide some insight into
the question left unanswered by the earlier study of why do so
many eligible household members believe themselves to be
ineligible?

DESCRIPTIVE ANALYSIS OF PARTICIPATION IN THE FOOD STAMP PROGRAM

In general, eligibility for the food stamp program is determined by a household's net monthly income and the number of people in the household. Table 4.1 shows the net income eligibility levels that were in effect for the first half of 1979.[1] Net income is determined by subtracting from a household's monthly gross income a standard deduction of $65 a month, a work expense deduction equal to 20 percent of earned income, a shelter expense deduction equal to the amount by which a household's expenses exceed 50 percent of its income (after taking account of other deductions), and a deduction for expenses involved in caring for a dependent person in the household (usually a child), if such expenses are necessary for employment or training for employment. The sum of the latter two deductions cannot exceed $85 in a given month. In addition to the income test for eligibility, there are other conditions that a household must meet in order to be eligible, such as the asset test and the work requirement. With regard to the asset test, if a household's countable assets exceeded $1,750, it would not be eligible to receive food stamps. In the case of a household with two or more persons, one of whom is age 60 or over, the asset ceiling equaled $3,000.

The procedures followed in this study in applying the program eligibility rules are detailed in Appendix A. In general a conservative approach was taken in determining eligibility in order to insure with a reasonably high degree of confidence that the households analyzed were indeed eligible for food stamps at some time in 1979. Based on these procedures, 993 households were estimated to be eligible. Forty-six percent received food stamps in 1979. Table 4.2 gives the breakdown of this sample by selected characteristics, as well as mean participation rates. Over 60 percent of the eligible households were headed by a woman. Nonelderly[2] women had well-above-average participation rates, while elderly women were less likely than average to use food stamps. Approximately 10 percent of the eligible households

---

[1] The income maximums are adjusted semi-annually to reflect changes in the Consumer Price Index. For this study the income maximums that were in effect for the first half of 1979 were used.

[2] Elderly is defined as 60 years old or over. "Young" is defined as under age 30, while "middle age" includes ages 30-59.

Table 4.1

INCOME ELIGIBILITY LIMITS BY HOUSEHOLD SIZE, 1979

Household Size	Maximum Allowable Monthly Income
One	$277
Two	365
Three	454
Four	542
Five	630
Six	719
Seven	807
Eight	895
Each additional member	+89

Source: Federal Register, Vol. 43, No. 225, November 21, 1978, p. 54203.

were headed by unmarried men, a group that was considerably less likely to participate in the program. This was especially true of elderly unmarried men, although the small number of observations in this category dictates some caution in accepting this conclusion.

One-quarter of the sample received income from the Aid to Families with Dependent Children Program (AFDC)[3] in either 1979 or 1978, and an additional 15 percent received Supplemental Security Income (SSI) payments. Both of these groups had above average participation rates, especially the AFDC recipients. One-quarter of the sample received neither AFDC nor SSI payments but did receive Social Security. The participation rate for this group was 21 percent, well below average. Finally, one-third of the sample received neither AFDC, SSI, nor Social Security; this segment was also considerably less likely to use food stamps.

Over 40 percent of the eligible households resided in the South, while only 10 percent lived in the Western region of the country. (Note that the sample is restricted to households residing in the contiguous United States.) In general, there were few regional differences in participation rates, although residents of the Northeast were somewhat more likely to use food stamps. The sample was roughly equally divided between households residing in counties with large cities and counties with small cities. No readily discernible pattern of participation by city size appeared.

One-third of the sample was nonwhite, and its participation rate was higher than that of whites. As a whole, the group of eligible households was relatively poorly educated, with participation being inversely related to the number of years of education. Almost one-fifth of the household heads worked at least 1,500 hours in 1979. This group was about half as likely to use food stamps as households headed by someone who worked less regularly. Almost 60 percent of the eligible households had no children; participation increased as the number of children in the household increased.

Sixty percent of the eligible households were officially in poverty in 1979, and the poor, with a 55 percent participation rate, were more likely to use food stamps than the nonpoor. One-

---

[3]For expository convenience, the term "AFDC" also includes General Assistance Income.

Table 4.2

DISTRIBUTION OF SAMPLE OF ELIGIBLE HOUSEHOLDS AND MEAN PARTICIPATION RATES, 1979

Household Characteristic	Number of Observations	Percent of Eligible Households	Mean Participation Rate
All	993	100.0%	46.1%
Age-Sex-Marital Status			
Young married couple	95	5.3	47.9
Middle-aged married couple	95	8.2	35.4
Elderly married couple	78	8.4	44.9
Young unmarried female	197	17.8	64.4
Middle-aged unmarried female	240	18.4	62.9
Elderly unmarried female	173	29.5	36.9
Young unmarried male	46	4.1	15.1
Middle-aged unmarried male	42	4.9	43.7
Elderly unmarried male	21	3.5	4.5
Whether Head Disabled			
No	610	57.3	45.4
Yes	383	42.7	46.9
City Size			
500,000 or more	404	31.8	50.9
100,000 - 499,999	219	20.7	44.2
25,000 - 99,999	140	16.3	52.3
Less than 25,000	230	31.2	39.1

Table 4.2 (continued)

Household Characteristic	Number of Observations	Percent of Eligible Households	Mean Participation Rate
Whether Public Transportation			
No	338	45.7	42.8
Yes	655	54.3	48.8
Race			
White	288	65.4	40.4
Nonwhite	705	34.6	56.7
Education of Head			
0-5 grades	147	16.2	54.4
6-8 grades	201	25.5	44.8
9-11 grades	330	26.5	50.0
12 grades	158	16.4	39.7
12 plus vocational	83	6.1	56.8
12 plus some college	62	7.5	27.2
BA, advanced degree	12	1.9	30.9
Number of Children, 0-17 Years			
None	435	59.8	35.3
One	165	14.7	55.9
Two	180	10.6	64.1
Three	100	6.1	73.5
Four or more	113	8.7	62.1
Whether Farmer			
No	984	98.5	46.7
Yes	9	1.5	0.0

Table 4.2 (continued)

Household Characteristic	Number of Observations	Percent of Eligible Households	Mean Participation Rate
Number of Previous Years Poor			
None	300	38.7	31.6
One	207	18.7	48.6
Two	201	17.5	58.0
Three	285	25.1	58.1
County Unemployment Rate			
Less than 4%	154	19.2	32.3
4 - 5.9%	337	33.2	47.8
6 - 8.9%	378	35.5	47.7
9.0% or more	48	8.4	55.6
NA	76	3.7	64.8
State Basic AFDC Allotment			
$150 - 199	52	3.3	32.3
$200 - 249	247	19.2	40.3
$250 - 299	135	15.4	44.8
$300 - 349	133	7.6	50.7
$350 - 399	157	26.3	42.4
$400 - 449	174	14.4	54.5
$450 or more	95	13.8	54.4
Welfare Use Status			
AFDC recipient	401	29.3	85.3
SSI recipient	135	17.3	59.1
Social Security recipient	161	26.2	20.6
No public transfers	296	27.2	20.0

Table 4.2 (continued)

Household Characteristic	Number of Observations	Percent of Eligible Households	Mean Participation Rate
Whether Head Employed 1,500 Hours or More			
No	777	82.3	50.6
Yes	216	17.7	24.8
Monthly Bonus Value			
$10	189	32.2	29.1
$11 – 25	118	14.9	43.4
$26 – 50	190	18.5	47.9
$51 – 100	280	20.8	54.2
$101 – 150	123	8.7	73.8
$151 or more	93	4.9	75.0
Region			
Northeast	119	22.5	48.9
North central	210	24.6	44.5
South	570	42.2	45.8
West	94	10.7	44.4

Table 4.2 (continued)

Household Characteristic	Number of Observations	Percent of Eligible Households	Mean Participation Rate
Food Needs/Income			
Less than .05	2	0.1	0.0
.05 - .099	0	0.0	0.0
.10 - .149	1	0.0	0.0
.15 - .199	58	11.8	12.4
.20 - .249	113	17.3	39.1
.25 - .299	143	17.4	37.7
.30 - .399	208	20.6	48.2
.40 - .499	170	14.5	51.5
.50 or more	298	18.4	75.6
Monthly Gross Income			
$0 - 299	411	44.2	50.8
$300 - 399	199	22.8	36.1
$400 - 499	135	14.0	52.3
$500 - 599	107	9.1	48.8
$600 - 699	66	6.1	44.9
$700 - 799	41	2.3	26.5
$800 - 899	16	0.8	22.8
$900 - 999	12	0.5	10.6
$1,000 or more	6	0.2	21.1

Table 4.2 (continued)

Household Characteristic	Number of Observations	Percent of Eligible Households	Mean Participation Rate
Whether Poor, 1979			
No	336	40.5	33.4
Yes	657	59.5	54.7
Whether Eligible Through Deductions			
No	653	59.5	57.8
Yes	340	40.5	28.7

quarter of the sample was poor in each of the three years preceding 1979. On the other hand, 40 percent of the sample had not been poor in any of the three previous years, and this group had below average participation rates. Sixty percent of the eligible households had incomes so low that they would have been eligible for food stamps even if no deductions were allowed. This group was twice as likely to participate as those households who were income-eligible as a result of deductions taken from gross household income.

REASONS FOR NONPARTICIPATION

In 1979 46.1 percent[4] of the eligible households used food stamps some time during the year; in 1976 the comparable figure was 41.3 percent. This 4.8 percentage point increase represents a 11.6 percent rise in the aggregate participation rate, a nontrivial gain but one that still leaves the majority of eligible households not using food stamps. Despite the continued low participation rate, it is possible that the reasons cited by eligible nonparticipants for not using food stamps may have changed substantially over the four-year period. Table 4.3 presents the distribution of reasons given for nonparticipation by households eligible in 1979[5] and households eligible in 1976. As can be seen, there is little change between the years. A belief of ineligibility still dominates as the major barrier to nonparticipation, accounting for more than half of the eligible nonparticipants. In 1979, as in 1976, no other specific reason was mentioned by more than 10 percent of nonusers.

The data available from 1979 enable us to gain further understanding of why eligible nonparticipants believed they were ineligible. In 1979 nonusers who replied that they did not think or did not know whether they were eligible were asked why they so thought so. Table 4.4 details the results. Beliefs of financial ineligibility were clearly crucial, as one-third of the households replied that they believed their income or assets were too high to qualify for eligibility. Seven percent of the

---

[4]The U.S. Department of Agriculture (1979) estimated that the participation rate for the contiguous United States was 47 percent in 1978.

[5]For a complete detailing of the responses to the 1979 nonparticipation questions, see Appendix B.

Table 4.3

DISTRIBUTION OF RESPONSES TO NONPARTICIPATION QUESTIONS, 1979 AND 1976

Reason for Nonparticipation	1979 (N=952)		1976 (N=1,201)[a]	
	Weighted Percent of All Eligibles	Weighted Percent of Nonparticipants	Weighted Percent of All Eligibles	Weighted Percent of Nonparticipants
Participant	46.1%	—	41.3%	—
Did not think eligible	29.0	53.8	34.9	59.4
Purchase price problems	—	—	3.3	5.7
Bonus value too low	0.4	0.7	1.8	3.1
Administrative hassle	4.4	8.2	2.3	4.0
Tried, but refused	4.0	7.4	4.9	8.4
Physical access problems	3.0	5.6	1.4	2.3
Don't know how to apply	0.3	0.6	0.8	1.4
Don't need them	4.7	8.7	1.8	3.1
Attitudinal factors	2.6	4.8	3.3	5.7
Don't know, other	5.5	10.2	4.1	6.9
Total	100.0%	100.0%	99.9%	100.0%

[a]From Coe (1979:22).

eligible nonparticipants who did not think they were eligible responded that they just did not know anything about the program eligibility requirements.

Approximately 20 percent of the households that did not believe they were eligible to participate responded in a manner that indicated that the real reason for nonparticipation was something other than poor information about the program. Slightly less than 10 percent reported that they had been declared ineligible by welfare officials, and this is why they considered themselves ineligible. One cannot tell whether this is a result of the estimation procedures used in this study or a mistake by local welfare officials--neither are perfect. It is also possible that although these households were eligible at some time during the year, they may have applied in a particular month when they were not eligible. Having been told once that they were ineligible, they believed that to be true of the entire year. Five percent of the households indicated that their personal attitudes toward food stamps, which presumably are negative, led them to believe in their ineligibility. It seems reasonable to assume that it was the adverse feelings toward welfare that were the actual reason for nonparticipation rather than a belief in ineligibility. Seven percent of the nonparticipants who believed they were ineligible indicated that the basis of that belief stemmed from a feeling that they did not need food stamps.

The remaining 37 percent of this group gave a hodgepodge of answers to the question on why they believed they were ineligible. The answers ranged from a simple "Don't know" to "Just never thought about it" to a specific reason other than the ones mentioned above.

AN ECONOMETRIC ANALYSIS OF
PARTICIPATION IN THE FOOD STAMP
PROGRAM

Most empirical analyses of participation in welfare programs have consisted of regressing a set of demographic and program variables (when available) on the participation status of households, that is, whether they participate or not. When program variables are included in the analysis, the interpretation is usually straightforward. For example, marginal tax rates on earned income might be found to be positively

Table 4.4

DISTRIBUTION OF RESPONSES OF ELIGIBLE NONPARTICIPANTS
CONCERNING WHY THEY DID NOT THINK THEY WERE ELIGIBLE, 1979

Reason Why Did Not Believe Eligible	Number of Observations	Weighted Percent of Responses
Declared ineligible by welfare officials	16	8.6%
Personal belief that income or assets too high	71	33.8
Didn't need them	15	6.9
Personal attitudes	7	5.5
Doesn't know anything about eligibility requirements	20	7.2
Some other reason, never thought about it, don't know	88	37.9
Total	217	99.9%

correlated with participation, implying that high marginal tax rates discourage work effort and lead to increased reliance on welfare income. The interpretation of demographic variables has been more problematic. Ascriptive variables, such as race and sex, are generally included in order to capture unmeasured informational and taste influences, including personal attitudes toward welfare income and individual assessment of need. Locational variables, such as region and urban-rural residence, are often justified to control for supply side characteristics (e.g., attitudes of local administrators), as well as taste and information factors. For policy purposes it is important to know more precisely what influences these variables are reflecting. Different approaches would be needed to alter informational factors as compared to attitudinal effects (if, indeed, it was deemed wise to tamper with attitudes at all).

Using the responses to the nonparticipation questions, it is possible to separate the individual importance of each of these factors in contributing to the overall effect on participation of a particular demographic variable (see Coe, 1979b). Each household in the sample must fall into one of the outcome categories: it is either a participant in the program, a nonparticipant because it had no information on the program, a nonparticipant because of a belief that its income or assets were too high, etc. The result is a system of nine equations of the following form:

$$(1) \quad P_{1i} = a_1 + B_1 X_i + e_1$$
$$(2) \quad P_{2i} = a_1 + B_1 X_i + e_2$$
$$\vdots$$
$$(9) \quad P_{9i} = a_9 + B_9 X_i + e_9 \, ,$$

where P_{1i} is the probability that household i will be a participant, P_{2i} the probability that it will be a nonparticipant due to a lack of information about the program, and so on. X_i represents the vector of demographic and program characteristics of the ith household. In a multiple choice linear probability model such as this, the estimated probabilities, P_{ji}, are constrained to sum to one as a result of the fact that each household can choose only one alternative. As a consequence, the estimated intercepts, a_i, sum to one, and, more important for the

purposes at hand, the estimated coefficients, B_i, sum to zero.[*]
As a result,

$$(10) \quad B_1 = - \sum_{j=2}^{9} B_i \quad .$$

Equation (10) states that B_1--the estimated effect on
participation of a particular demographic variable--will equal
(the negative of) the sum of the effects of that variable on the
various reasons given for nonparticipation. In other words, the
results of this series of regressions will enable us to allocate
the effect of a demographic variable (and other variables) on
participation across the different reasons given for
nonparticipation, thus allowing for conclusions concerning what
effects the demographic variable is actually capturing.

Empirical Results Regarding
Participation in the Food Stamp Program

Table 4.5 presents the results of regressing participation
status on a set of demographic and program variables. As
expected, the age-sex-marital status of the head of the household
exerted a strong effect on whether a household participated in
the program. Households headed by an unmarried elderly person
were considerably less likely to use food stamps, as were
households headed by an unmarried male of any age. On the other
hand, households headed by a young married couple were
significantly more likely to participate than the omitted
category of households headed by a middle-aged married couple.

Households residing in rural areas were less likely to
participate than households residing in or near a major
metropolitan area. Similarly, farm households were considerably
less likely to use food stamps, although it should be remembered
that only 9 of the 993 eligible households were farm households.
Participation was negatively correlated with the educational
level of the household head and with the income level of the
household. On the other hand, the ratio of food needs to
household income was not a significant predictor of
participation, and had the wrong sign. (This variable,
incidentally, was not highly correlated with household income,

---

[*]See Pindyck and Rubinfeld (1976) for a proof of these
properties.

Table 4.5

REGRESSION ON PARTICIPATION IN THE FOOD STAMP
PROGRAM BY ELIGIBLE HOUSEHOLDS, 1979 (N=952)

Dependent Variable: Whether Used Food
Stamps in 1979. Mean: .461

Independent Variable (Omitted Category)	Regression Coefficient (Standard Error)
Age-Sex-Marital Status	
Married couple, head age less than 30	.258** (.069)
(Married couple, head age 30-59)	....
Married couple, head age 60 or over	-.071 (.073)
Unmarried female, age less than 30	-.052 (.067)
Unmarried female, age 30-59	-.035 (.061)
Unmarried female, age 60 or over	-.208** (.071)
Unmarried male, age less than 30	-.219* (.090)
Unmarried male, age 30-59	-.201* (.080)
Unmarried male, age 60 or over	-.613** (.095)
Whether Head Disabled	-.041 (.031)

Table 4.5 (continued)

Independent Variable (Omitted Category)	Regression Coefficient (Standard Error)
Population of Largest City in County	
(500,000 or more)	....
100,000 - 499,999	-.057 (.038)
25,000 - 99,999	-.027 (.041)
Under 25,000	-.137** (.042)
Whether Public Transportation Available	-.048 (.034)
Whether Nonwhite	.003 (.029)
Years of Education, Head	-.022** (.005)
Number of Children, Age 0-17	.086** (.026)
Whether Farmer	-.301** (.110)
Number of Previous Years in Poverty	-.001 (.012)
County Unemployment Rate	.009 (.007)
Level of State Basic AFDC Allowance ($100)	.014 (.017)
Food Needs/Income	-.00015 (.00009)

Table 4.5 (continued)

Independent Variable (Omitted Category)	Regression Coefficient (Standard Error)
Transfer Income Status	
Received AFDC or other welfare in 1978 or 1979	.538** (.041)
No AFDC or other welfare, but received SSI in 1978 or 1979	.355** (.055)
No AFDC or SSI, but received Social Security in 1978 or 1979	.031 (.051)
(No AFDC, SSI, or Social Security in 1978 or 1979)	....
Whether Head Employed 1,500 Hours or more in 1979	-.103* (.044)
Monthly Household Income ($100)	-.070** (.018)
Monthly Bonus Value ($10)	-.012† (.006)
R^2 (Adjusted)	.418

Significance levels: †.10   *.05   **.01

with the correlation coefficient equaling -.15.) Households in
which the head worked virtually full time for the entire year
were significantly less likely to participate, while
participation was positively correlated with the number of
children in the household.

A connection with other parts of the welfare system exerted
a powerful positive effect on participation in the food stamp
program. Households that were currently receiving AFDC or had
received it in the previous year had adjusted participation rates
that were 50 percentage points higher than the omitted category
of households that received no AFDC, SSI, or Social Security in
either the current or previous year. Supplemental Security
Income recipients had adjusted participation rates that were 33
percentage points higher than those of the omitted group. In
contrast, Social Security recipients did not differ significantly
from the no-public-transfer group.

Several variables entered into the equation to control for
various factors were not significant in predicting participation
status. These included race, the availability of public
transportation, number of previous years in poverty, the county
unemployment rate, and the level of the state's basic AFDC
allowance for a family of four. Most notable among the
insignificant variables, however, was the bonus value to which
the household was entitled. One would expect that higher bonus
values would increase participation, and the unadjusted results
from Table 2 would seem to confirm this. But not only was the
regression coefficient on this variable insignificant, the sign
was wrong also. The problem is that bonus value is highly
correlated with number of children in the household (r = .73).
When the number of children variable is omitted from the
equation, the coefficient of bonus value becomes positive and
significant. The fact that when both variables are entered bonus
value loses its effect implies that bonus value has no
independent effect on participation, but rather is a proxy for
the effect of children in the household. Whether this makes
sense from a theoretical and policy point of view is an issue
discussed later in this chapter.

A Comparison of the Results for 1979 and 1976

Despite some differences in detail, the results for 1979 discussed above are very similar to the results found for 1976 (see Coe, 1979a). The age-sex-marital status of the household head was a crucial variable in predicting participation in both years, with corresponding findings that households headed by elderly unmarried persons and households headed by unmarried males had below average participation rates. Recipients of AFDC income had considerably higher participation rates in both years. Households with working heads and those with no children were both less likely to participate in the two years. Race, past poverty status, and bonus value were insignificant predictors of food stamp participation in both 1979 and 1976.

Results for some other variables did not show such consistency across years. Participation was positively and significantly related to the county unemployment rate in 1976. In 1979 the coefficient, although positive, was insignificant. In 1976 the availability of public transportation led to increased participation, a relationship that did not hold up in 1979. This is perhaps not surprising, since in 1976 the apparent reason for the significance of public transportation was that it was negatively associated with eligible households citing purchase price and bonus value problems (Coe, 1979a:35). There was no readily apparent reason why such a relationship should exist.

Other variables that exhibited some inconsistency in results between 1979 and 1976 were the educational level of the household head, family money income, and region of residence. While part of these differences stem from a different specification of the regression equation (e.g., substituting the state basic AFDC allowance for region in an attempt to measure more precisely the prevailing attitude toward redistribution to lower income households[7]), the others cannot be explained away so easily. As with other research, results that have not been confirmed by other studies or are inconsistent with other studies should be treated with considerably more caution than results that have been duplicated.

---

[7]The state basic AFDC allowance is for a family of four.

Allocation of Reasons for Differences in Participation

As discussed earlier, interpreting significant coefficients on demographic variables is often a matter of speculation. For example, are households headed by elderly unmarried women less likely to use food stamps because they are less well-informed about the program, because they have more adverse attitudes toward receiving welfare, because they have less need for food, or for some other reason? With the aid of the multiple-choice linear regression model, we can identify which of these reasons actually accounts for the estimated negative effect. Table 4.6 has been constructed to assist in this procedure. In this table we focus only on those variables that were found in Table 4.5 to be significant at the 5 percent level in predicting participation. An example of how the entries in the table were derived will be illustrative.

From Table 4.5 we know that households headed by a young married couple were 25.8 percentage points more likely to use food stamps than households headed by a middle-aged married couple. The coefficient was significant at the 1 percent level. The issue now is what accounts for this effect. From Appendix Table C4.1 it is found that young married couples were 12.8 percent *less* likely than middle-aged married couples to cite administrative hassles or physical access problems as a barrier to participation. This implies that differences in (perceived) administrative difficulties or physical access problems accounted for 49.6 percent (12.8/25.8) of the difference in participation rates between the two groups. Alternatively, this result implies that if the two groups viewed the administrative hassles and physical access problems equally, the difference in their participation rates would be reduced by 49.6 percent.[*] This,

---

[*]Statements such as this should be interpreted with some caution. It is accurate to state that if young married couples faced the same perceived administrative difficulties as middle-aged married couples, their participation rate would be lowered by 11.2 percentage points, resulting in a 54.5 percent reduction in the difference. It is more problematic to argue that if middle-aged married couples viewed their administrative difficulties in the same manner as young married couples do, their participation rates would be increased by 11.2 percentage points, thus reducing the difference in participation rates by 54.5 percent. The catch is that we do not know with any degree of certainty whether middle-aged married couples would cite another barrier to participation if the administrative hassles were removed. It can be stated with greater confidence that

Table 4.6

ALLOCATION OF REASONS FOR DIFFERENCES IN PARTICIPATION RATES AMONG ELIGIBLE HOUSEHOLDS, 1979
(N=993)

Independent Variable (Omitted Category)	No Information on Eligibility Rules or How to Apply	Belief That Income or Assets Too High	Believed Ineligible for Some Other Reason	Declared Ineligible by Welfare Officials	Administrative Hassle, Physical Access Problems	Didn't Need Them	Personal Attitudes	Just Didn't Bother, Other
Age-Sex-Marital Status								
Young married couple (Middle-aged married couple)	-7.7	+9.2	-17.9	-13.3	-49.6**	-27.4	-2.0	+8.8
Elderly unmarried woman	+25.0	-44.7†	-50.0†	....	....	....	....	....
Young unmarried male	....	....	....	....	+17.4†	....	....	-39.7†
Middle-aged unmarried male	+14.5*	....	-25.4**	-105.4**	+48.9†	-43.6†	-56.4**	-48.3*
Elderly unmarried male	....	-50.3*	....	....	....	....	-32.0**	....
Population of Largest City in County								
(500,000 or more)	....	....	....	....	....	....	-	....
Less than 25,000	-24.8*	-45.5**	-50.3*	....	+64.7**	-79.1**	-50.5**	....
Years of Education, Head	+22.7**	-37.2†	-31.6*	+33.7†	....	....	+32.4*	....
Number of Children	....	....	-47.2*	....	....	....	-54.3*	....
Whether Farmer	-87.7**	....	....	....	....	....	....	....
Transfer Income Status								
AFDC recipient	....	....	-32.1**	-12.4**	-13.6**	-11.2*	-10.5*	-8.9†
SSI recipient (No AFDC, SSI, or Social Security in 1979 or 1978)	....	....	-59.6**	....	....	-23.0*	-23.0*	....
Whether Head Employed 1,500 Hours or More	....	-90.3**	....	....	....	....	....	....
Monthly Household Income	....	-55.1**	....	....	....	....	....	....

Significance levels: † .10   * .05   ** .01

then, is the entry in Table 4.6 under the Administrative Hassle column and the Young Married Couple row.

Some additional interpretational comments are in order. A negative sign before an entry in the table indicates that equalizing this factor will reduce the differences in participation rates. A positive sign on an entry implies that differences in participation rates would be increased if the factor in question were equalized. Because it is possible to have such offsetting influences, it is also possible that the entries in a particular row will sum to greater than 100 percent, or that any single variable can account for more than 100 percent of the difference. If all the potential entries in a given row were shown on the table, the total would sum to 100 percent as a result of the property that $B_1 = - \sum_{j=2}^{9} B_j$. To illustrate this point, all of the entries for the group of young married couples are presented in the first row of Table 4.6. For the remaining variables, only the results that were statistically significant at the 10 percent level are shown. If these results sum to more than 100 percent, then there are some omitted offsetting influences that were not statistically significant. The interested reader can calculate these omitted entries from the results given in Appendix Table C4.1.

We can now turn to the substantive results. In Table 4.5 it was found that households headed by elderly unmarried women had an adjusted participation rate that was 20.8 percentage points lower than the omitted category. As can be seen in Table 4.6, informational factors were of particular importance in accounting for this differential. Elderly unmarried women were significantly (at the 10 percent level) more likely to respond that they did not believe they were eligible for food stamps both for financial reasons and for other reasons not related to their financial position. These two information factors accounted for 95 percent of the difference in their participation rate. The effect of this type of misinformation is offset to a degree by the fact that households headed by an elderly unmarried woman

---

other measures taken to increase participation of this group will not be effective until the perceived administrative difficulties are removed.

were _less_ likely to respond that they know nothing about the eligibility rules or how to apply. In other words, they knew about the program, but their knowledge was faulty. Finally, elderly unmarried women were more likely to respond that they just had not bothered to get food stamps or did not get them for some other, miscellaneous reason. This accounted for 40 percent of the difference in participation rates.

The situation of elderly unmarried men was similar to that of elderly unmarried women. Although better informed than middle-aged married couples about the program in general, they were more likely to believe that they were ineligible for both financial and nonfinancial reasons. The net effect of these informational factors was to account for approximately 60 percent of the difference in adjusted participation rates. In addition to differences in information, elderly unmarried men were also more likely to cite adverse attitudes toward receiving food stamps as a reason for nonparticipation. This factor accounted for one-third of the lower participation rate of this group.

Households headed by middle-aged unmarried men had adjusted participation rates that were 20 percentage points below those of households headed by a middle-aged married man. Three factors contributed to this difference. The single most important factor was that these men were more likely to be declared ineligible for food stamps by local welfare officials. This accounted for approximately 105 percent of the difference in participation rates. In other words, if middle-aged unmarried men had not been denied eligibility by welfare officials, their (adjusted) participation rate would have been virtually identical to that of middle-aged married couples. This is a potentially disturbing finding. The implication is that local welfare officials are using their discretionary ability to deny certification to this group, presumably to enforce some belief that these men should be self-supporting. This empirical finding is not proof that this is actually what is occurring. Given the inaccuracy of the eligibility estimation procedure, these people might indeed have been ineligible. But the result is suggestive that this income-eligible group is under greater scrutiny by local welfare officials.

The other two significant factors that accounted for the lower participation rate of middle-aged unmarried men reflect a tendency among this group for self-selection with respect to participation. If it is indeed true that local welfare officials applied stricter standards to these men, it also appears that this group applied stricter standards to itself, perhaps also reflecting society's belief that these men are less entitled to welfare. Members of this group were significantly more likely to say they didn't need food stamps, and also to cite adverse personal attitudes toward the receipt of welfare as a reason for nonparticipation. If middle-aged married couples had the same attitudes toward using food stamps and viewed their need in the same manner as the unmarried men, the adjusted participation rates of the two groups would have been virtually equal.

The results in Table 4.5 show that eligible households located in or near small towns had adjusted participation rates almost 14 percentage points lower than eligible households located in or near large cities. Several factors were at work here. In the first place, eligible respondents in small towns were more likely to answer that they didn't need food stamps, a factor accounting for 80 percent of the difference in participation rates. This variable may reflect differences in interfamily networks of support that exist in small and large cities (i.e., people in small towns may rely more on relatives or neighbors for assistance than do people in large cities), or it may reflect differences in feelings about self-reliance. However, the equalizing effect of this variable was partially offset by the fact that people in large cities were more likely to complain of administrative hassles and physical access problems. The notorious long lines at big city welfare offices apparently did have a significant effect in deterring eligible households from participating, a factor that did not appear to be present (at least to as great an extent) in small towns. Finally, people in small towns were more likely to be uninformed about the food stamp program. They were less likely to know anything about the rules for eligibility or how to go about applying for food stamps. They were more likely to believe they were ineligible for some nonfinancial reason. These factors accounted for about three-fourths of the difference in participation rates between eligible households in large cities and those in small towns.

These results are supported by the findings regarding the low participation rate of farmers. Almost 90 percent of their lower probability of using food stamps was accounted for by the fact that they were considerably more likely to know nothing about the rules or procedures of the program. In addition, farmers were significantly more likely to respond that they have negative personal attitudes toward receiving food stamps. Again, however, the reader is reminded that in the sample there were only nine farm families estimated to be eligible for food stamps in 1979, a dangerously small number from which to draw firm conclusions.

Table 4.5 reveals that household heads with higher levels of education were less likely to participate in the food stamp program. Most researchers on participation in welfare programs include education of the household head in the estimation equation as a proxy for information about the program (see MacDonald, 1977; Warlick, 1982). The argument is that more educated people will be more informed about the program because of their greater ability to read and comprehend items in the media. Thus, an insignificant finding for the education variable (MacDonald) or a significantly negative result (Warlick) has led to the conclusion that lack of information is not an important factor in explaining nonparticipation. The results in Table 4.6 indicate that this reasoning behind including education as an explanatory variable was plausible, but the conclusion drawn from it was not valid. Household heads with lower educational levels were indeed less likely to possess general information about the food stamp program. While better educated household heads had better general information, this positive effect on participation was more than outweighed by the negative effect of a belief that they could not meet the eligibility criteria, both financial and otherwise, of the program. Two factors may be at work here. The better educated presumably earn higher wages, and they may not realize that, given their family size and allowable deductions, they still would qualify for food stamps. In other words, the better-educated households are basing their beliefs concerning eligibility on gross income, unadjusted for family size and deductions. The other possibility is that the better educated have been more able to accumulate assets from past working experiences, and they believe that these assets render them ineligible to participate. Given that asset holdings are imperfectly measured in the Panel Study, they would not necessarily be wrong in this belief. However, given the estimation procedure used in this study, it would have to be true that whatever assets they hold are in an extremely low cash-income earning portfolio. Perhaps a more plausible explanation is that their assets are held in the form of a house, which unknown to them, is exempt for purposes of determining food stamp eligibility.

The other significant factor that explains the negative relationship between participation and education is the fact that the more educated household heads were more likely to hold adverse personal attitudes toward receiving food stamps. This accounted for approximately one-half of the lower participation rate of the more educated eligibles. Perhaps this reflects a feeling among the more educated that, given their education and resultant expected wage, they should be more able to provide for their own needs without the support of public assistance.

Each additional child in the household increased the probability of participation by 8.6 percentage points. As the number of children in the household increased, the probability of a belief in ineligibility, for either financial or nonfinancial reasons, decreases. In other words, with other factors held constant, households with more children were more likely to believe they were eligible to participate. This factor accounted for 85 percent of the higher probability of participation. However, these informational influences, which seem intuitively plausible, were offset by two factors that operated in an unexpected direction. As the number of children in the household increased, the probability of being declared ineligible by local welfare officials and the probability of citing personal attitudes as a reason for nonparticipation both increased. These results are contrary to a priori expectations and do not lend themselves to any readily apparent explanation.

A consistent finding in previous research regarding food stamp participation has been that households which receive other forms of public assistance are more likely to use food stamps. Various hypotheses have been advanced to explain this result. Welfare recipients are better informed about the rules of the food stamp program; streamlined application procedures reduce the administrative hassle of being certified for eligibility; welfare recipients are more needy than nonrecipients; recipients have less adverse attitudes toward receiving food stamps, as evidenced by the fact that they are receiving welfare; and so forth. As seen in Table 4.6, all of these factors are significant in explaining the substantially higher participation rate of AFDC or General Assistance recipients. Differences in beliefs concerning eligibility account for about one-third of the difference between welfare recipients and nonrecipients in the propensity to use food stamps. It is interesting to note the source of the differences in beliefs about eligibility. It is not a consequence of welfare recipients being better informed in general about the nature of the food stamp program, nor is it a result of nonwelfare recipients being more likely to believe that their income or assets are too high to qualify for eligibility. The difference arises from welfare recipients being less likely to cite some other specific reason for ineligibility. This factor is likewise of major importance in explaining the higher participation rate of SSI recipients, accounting for nearly 60 percent of the difference in their propensity to use food stamps. A probable explanation of the importance of this factor is that non-welfare recipients believe that eligibility for food stamps is categorically based, as is eligibility for the other major welfare programs. For example, non-welfare recipients may believe that they must have a dependent child in the home in order to be eligible, as is the case with the AFDC program. Without a more detailed coding of the responses, we cannot say for sure what these reasons actually are, but it is clear that they are not related to means-based aspects of eligibility. On the other hand, welfare recipients, who may initially have had the same beliefs about the food stamp program, upon being declared eligible for welfare are informed of their potential eligibility for food stamps. Any misconceptions that they may have held concerning food stamp eligibility would be straightened out by the welfare caseworker.

Several other factors were significant in explaining the higher participation rate of AFDC recipients, each factor individually accounting for 10 to 15 percent of the difference in participation rates. Welfare recipients were less likely to be declared ineligible for food stamps. This may reflect a belief among local welfare officials that if a family is needy enough to qualify for welfare, it is needy enough to qualify for food stamps. (This belief was a legislated mandate until the 1977 amendments to the Food Stamp Act, which eliminated the automatic food stamp eligibility for AFDC recipients.) Welfare recipients were also less likely to cite administrative hassles or physical access problems as a barrier to participation. Having gone through the process of applying for and receiving AFDC, there is probably little additional hassle involved in applying for food stamps, especially with a caseworker to aid in the process. AFDC recipients, as well as SSI recipients, were less likely to respond that they did not need food stamps. Non-welfare recipients, even after controlling for the level of household income, apparently felt they were able to make ends meet without public assistance. Finally, AFDC recipients not surprisingly were less likely to respond that adverse personal attitudes toward receiving food stamps were a reason for nonparticipation.

Eligible households in which the head worked at least 1,500 hours in 1979 were significantly less likely to use food stamps. Most (90 percent) of this lower participation rate was accounted for by the fact that such respondents were significantly more likely to believe that their income or assets were too high. This may reflect unawareness on the part of working eligibles of the earned income deduction, which allows 20 percent of earned income to be subtracted from household income in order to determine income eligibility.

Finally, Table 4.5 shows that participation was negatively correlated with the level of household gross income. The major factor that accounted for this negative relationship was that the probability of believing that one's income was too high to qualify for eligibility increased as household income increased, a reasonable finding.

A Comparison of Results across Years

In both 1979 and 1976 differences in beliefs about eligibility were the single most important influence in accounting for subgroup differentials in participation. These differences accounted for 60 to 70 percent of the lower participation rate in both years of elderly unmarried persons, both male and female. Informational differences were the most powerful factor in accounting for the higher participation rate of AFDC recipients in both years. Differing beliefs with respect to eligibility accounted for approximately 80 percent of the higher probability of participation associated with additional children in the household. Finally, in both 1979 and 1976 the lower participation rate of households with working heads was accounted for primarily by differences in information concerning eligibility.

Other results explaining subgroup differences in participation were also consistent across years. Middle-aged unmarried men were significantly more likely in both years to report that they had been declared ineligible by local welfare officials. This factor was the most important in both years in accounting for their low participation. AFDC recipients were significantly less likely in both years to report that they had been denied eligibility by welfare officials or that adverse attitudes toward receiving welfare were a reason for nonparticipation. Each of these factors individually accounted for 10 to 20 percent of their higher participation rate.

Other results were not consistent across years, thus casting doubt on the stability of the purported effect on participation. Most notable among these inconsistencies are the results concerning the low participation rate of elderly unmarried women. In 1976 this group was significantly more likely to cite physical access problems as a reason for nonparticipation, a factor accounting for 10 percent of its lower participation rate. This result was not confirmed for 1979. Another difference between the two years concerned working heads. In 1976 eligible employed heads listed administrative hassles as significant reasons for nonparticipation, a result that may be attributed to the fact that employed heads might have to take time off work to apply for eligibility at the cost of foregone wages. This factor was not significant in 1979.

The Relationship between Number of Children and Bonus Value

Economic theory would indicate that, other factors being equal, larger bonus values will lead to increased probability of participation by eligible households, for the simple reason that the payoff to participation is greater. And, in fact, unadjusted mean participation rates appear to be highly correlated, positively, with bonus value (see Table 4.4). One might conclude from this that a straightforward policy prescription for low participation rates would be to increase the bonus value to which households were entitled.

However, when other factors are controlled for in the regression equation, bonus value is not a significant predictor of participation. This result held up for both 1976 and 1979. (In 1979 bonus value was significant at the 10 percent level with a negative coefficient.) The conclusion from the regression results is that increasing bonus values would not have a major impact on participation rates. Virtually no eligible respondent mentioned too low a bonus value as a reason for nonparticipation further buttresses this conclusion.

The reason for these contrasting results is not difficult to pinpoint, at least from an econometric point of view. Bonus value and the number of children in the household are highly correlated variables, with a correlation coefficient of .727. When number of children is omitted from the regression equation, bonus value becomes a significant (at confidence level 94.45 percent) and positive predictor of participation. (The size of the effect is not large however. Each $10 increase in bonus value would result in a .6 percentage point increase in participation. See Table 4.7.) What independent effects might we expect the number of children in the household to exert on the participation decision? A priori, it was thought that the existence of children in the household would alter a person's attitudes toward receiving food stamps. Simply put, adults might prefer to cut back on the nutritional adequacy of their own diets rather than receive food stamps but would not make the same decision for their children. Empirically, within the framework of this analysis, such an effect would show up as number of children being a negative predictor of "no need" or "personal attitude" reasons for nonparticipation.

As seen in Table 4.6, however, these were not the reasons that accounted for the positive relationship between number of

Table 4.7

THE RELATIONSHIP BETWEEN NUMBER OF CHILDREN AND
BONUS VALUE AND THE EFFECT ON PARTICIPATION

Variable	Coefficient (Standard Error)	Coefficient (Standard Error)	Coefficient (Standard Error)
Monthly Bonus Value ($10)	-.010† (.006)	.006† (.003)	---
Number of Children	.086** (.026)	---	.045** (.014)
R^2 (adjusted)	.418	.413	.417

Significance levels: †.10 *.05 **.01

children and participation.' The primary reason was
informational factors, in particular, the nonfinancial factors.
A probable interpretation of this result, mentioned earlier, is
that households without children believe they are categorically
ineligible for food stamps, as would be the case for the Aid to
Families with Dependent Children Program.

What can one conclude regarding the possibility of
increasing participation rates by making bonus values more
generous? The conclusion suggested by the evidence discussed
above is that marginal increases in bonus values would have only
a negligible impact on the aggregate participation rate of
eligible households. This does not rule out the possibility that
the participation rates of certain subgroups of the eligible
population would be positively affected by an increase in the
bonus value or that a more selective benefit increase (say, for
example, a tripling of the minimum benefit from $10 to $30 a
month) could have a significant effect on participation. Neither
of these proposals was specifically addressed in the above
analysis. But until informational barriers are broken down,
marginal adjustments to the benefit schedule would not seem to be
an effective method of increasing overall participation by
eligible households in the food stamp program.

The Level of Need and Participation

The question of the effect of bonus value raises another
important issue regarding the determinants of participation. It
has been suggested that the primary factor in determining
participation in welfare programs by eligible households is the
"level of need" of the household, with more needy families being
more likely to participate. MacDonald, who found bonus value to

---

'When bonus value is omitted from the regression equations,
less negative personal attitudes toward receiving food stamps is
a significant factor accounting for the positive relationship
between number of children and participation. When bonus value
is included, the direction of the effect changes, as shown in
Table 6. This illustrates that although the inclusion of number
of children in the participation regression is the primary reason
why bonus value does not operate in the expected direction, the
two variables are not measuring the same influences on
participation. This shows up in the equations predicting the
reasons for nonparticipation, the results for which change
noticeably if either number of children or bonus value is
omitted.

be a significant positive predictor of participation (he did not have number of children in his estimation equation), concluded that "We also find substantial evidence that participation does increase with the household's need for assistance, as determined by the patterns of adjusted means for annual food stamp bonus" (MacDonald, 1977:103). Because bonus values are indeed based on the need level of the household, as measured by the difference between the food needs of the household and available income, this conclusion is not implausible.

However, a direct attempt to test this argument yielded insignificant results. A food needs/gross income variable was entered into the regression equation to capture the need effect. The coefficient was insignificant and had the wrong sign.[10] Combined with the fact that bonus value was also an insignificant predictor, little support is provided for the idea that need determines participation. One might go further and argue that the proposition that some eligible households do not participate because they are less needy is inherently unbelievable. While it may be true that there are variations in the level of need among the eligible population, we should not forget that to be eligible for food stamps implies considerable need in the first place. Few would argue that the food needs standard or the income eligibility rules are generous. In short, although some food stamp eligible households are more needy than others, all are under severe financial constraints.

But there is a catch. There is a subjective element involved in the concept of need. Some eligible households with high food needs/income ratios may not feel that they are particularly needy. Perhaps their view of their food needs is lower than the objectively determined needs level. Perhaps they have lower desires for nonfood consumption. Or, not improbably, they may be experiencing a short-run decline in economic level that they believe will be corrected in the near future.[11] Given that, they may feel that a temporary belt-tightening does not qualify them as "needy."

---

[10]This result did not change when either bonus value or number of children were omitted from the equation.

[11]On an unadjusted basis, the number of previous years poor was positively correlated with participation. However, this relationship was not significant in the multivariate analysis.

All of this is just another way of saying that tastes vary, and after all objective factors are measured and taken into account, preferences will still affect the participation decision. But there are important policy implications of the need argument, particularly with regard to the results of this study. What does the policy maker do if he or she is convinced that the primary factor that distinguishes eligible nonparticipants from participants is differences in need? Presumably nothing. One certainly would not want to undertake any programs that increased need as objectively measured. Perhaps there would be some role for educational programs that pointed out to people the nutritional deficiencies of their current diets in an attempt to overcome subjective feelings of no need. But one hesitates to recommend widespread programs aimed at making people feel more needy than they currently feel. There are no policy recommendations flowing from the need explanation of low participation because that explanation implies that current policies are successful in funneling aid to those who really need it. Put another way, eligible nonparticipants don't get food stamps for the simple reason that they don't need them, and thus should not be a concern for policy makers.

The empirical results of this analysis showed that poor information concerning eligibility was the major reason for the low participation rate in the food stamp program. A significant portion of eligible nonparticipants believe they are ineligible because either their income or assets are too high. Might this reflect that certain eligible nonparticipants have income or assets sufficiently high that they feel they can provide for their nutritional needs without food stamps, and thus believe that they must be financially ineligible? In other words, is it possible to interpret at least part of the empirical results of this analysis as a needs explanation? Without additional direct inquiry concerning why respondents considered themselves financially ineligible, this possibility cannot be ruled out. But it does not seem likely. Respondents who replied that they did not think they were eligible to receive food stamps were asked an open-ended question concerning why they thought so. Two mentions were coded. Only 15 of the 217 households who did not think they were eligible mentioned no need as a reason. Thus it would seem that although the needs-based explanation cannot be

conclusively rejected, the available evidence points to poor
information as the major barrier to participation in the food
stamp program by eligible households.

SUMMARY OF RESULTS

The major results of this analysis can be summarized as
follows:

1. In 1979 the aggregate participation rate in the food
stamp program by eligible households was 46.1 percent. In 1976
the comparable figure was 41.3 percent. This represents an
increase in excess of 10 percent in the participation rate, but
still resulted in a majority of eligible households not receiving
food stamps.

2. Participation rates varied considerably across subgroups
of the eligible population. The unmarried elderly, unmarried men
of all ages, the working eligible, and those residing in small
towns were less likely to participate. Eligible households
receiving other public assistance income, those with children,
the less-educated, and those with lower incomes were more likely
to receive food stamps.

3. A belief that they were not eligible to receive food
stamps is the dominant reason given by eligible nonparticipants
for not participating in the program. In 1979, 54 percent of the
eligible nonparticipants cited this reason. In 1976 the
comparable figure was 59 percent. Approximately one-half of the
eligible nonparticipants who did not believe they were eligible
cited financial reasons as the source of their belief, while the
remainder mentioned nonfinancial reasons. Slightly less than 10
percent of these households replied that they simply did not know
anything about the eligibility requirements of the program.

4. Differing beliefs concerning eligibility were a primary
determinant accounting for subgroup differences in participation.
The unmarried elderly, the more-educated, the childless, the
employed, those residing in small towns, and non-public
assistance households were all more likely to believe they were
not eligible to receive food stamps. Other reasons for
nonparticipation were important for certain subgroups, but no
other reason had the pervasive effect that poor information
exhibited.

The major conclusion to be drawn from this analysis is that the food stamp program will continue to be characterized by a low aggregate participation rate until informational barriers to participation are significantly reduced. The program reforms enacted by the Food Stamp Act of 1977--most notably, the elimination of purchase requirement--while apparently having some beneficial effects on participation, still failed to induce the vast majority of eligible nonparticipants to receive food stamps. This author concluded from his analysis of food stamp participation in 1976 that:

> The overriding conclusion which emerges from this analysis is that if the government wishes to increase participation in the food stamp program among eligible households, it must devote its energies to informing such households that they are eligible for food stamps. Changes in other parameters of the program, such as lowering the purchase price or increasing the physical accessibility of obtaining the stamps, would have only a marginal impact on increasing aggregate participation... . But these reforms cannot hope to have much impact on participation until eligible households realize that they do indeed qualify for food stamps. (Coe, 1979a:44)

This conclusion still stands today.

References

Coe, Richard D. "Participation in the Food Stamp Program." Working Paper Series, Institute for Social Research. Ann Arbor: Institute for Social Research, September 1979a.

Coe, Richard D. "Participation in the Food Stamp Program among the Poverty Population, 1976." In Five Thousand American Families--Patterns of Economic Progress, Vol. VII, ed. Greg J. Duncan and James N. Morgan. Ann Arbor: Institute for Social Research, 1979b.

Coe, Richard D. "Participation in the Food Stamp Program among the Poverty Population." Five Thousand American Families--Patterns of Economic Progress, Vol. V, ed. Greg J. Duncan and James N. Morgan. Ann Arbor: Institute for Social Research, 1977.

Federal Register, Vol. 43, No. 225, November 21, 1978.

MacDonald, Maurice. Food Stamps and Income Maintenance. Institute for Research on Poverty: Poverty Policy Analysis Series. New York: Academic Press, 1977.

Pindyck, Robert S., and Rubinfeld, Daniel L. Econometric Models and Economic Forecasts. New York: McGraw-Hill, 1976.

Public Law 95-113. "Food Stamp Act of 1977." Washington, DC: U.S. Government Printing Office, 1977.

U.S. Bureau of the Census. Characteristics of Households Purchasing Food Stamps. Current Population Reports, Series P-23, No. 61. Washington, DC: U.S. Department of Commerce, 1976.

U.S. Department of Agriculture. "Annual Food Stamp Program Evaluation, Fiscal Year 1978." Washington, D.C.: U.S. Department of Agriculture, September 1979.

Warlick, Jennifer L. "An Empirical Analysis of Participation in the Supplemental Security Income Program Among Aged Eligible Persons." Journal of Human Resources, Summer 1982.

Appendix A to Chapter 4

DERIVATION OF SAMPLE OF ELIGIBLE HOUSEHOLDS

The Panel Study of Income Dynamics is not designed to estimate whether a household is eligible for the food stamp program; consequently, procedures must be developed to handle those situations when the data do not conform exactly to the administrative requirements of the program. Those procedures are detailed in this appendix. One overriding principle guided the choice of appropriate procedures. Because this is a study aimed at determining why eligible households do not participate in the food stamp program, a conservative approach was taken in determining eligibility. The goal was to insure that the households deemed eligible to participate were, to a high degree of probability, indeed eligible for food stamps at some time in 1979. Clearly, some households that were possibly eligible at some time are not included in the sample. But it was thought that the conclusions drawn from the analysis would rest on firmer ground if they pertained to a sample of clearly eligible households rather than relating to a larger sample that contained more eligible households, but also contained a nontrivial number of ineligible households.

HOUSEHOLDS RESIDING OUTSIDE OF THE CONTIGUOUS UNITED STATES

The Panel Study is designed to be a representative sample of the population of the lower 48 states and the District of Columbia. The initial sample of households all resided in this area. Over the life of the Panel Study, some of these households have moved outside the contiguous United States. The Panel Study has continued to follow these households, but they cannot be considered representative of the population of those areas. Consequently, they were eliminated from the sample. Sixty-three of the aggregate 6,752 Panel Study households were removed for this reason. Ten of those households received food stamps in 1979.

FAMILY COMPOSITION CHANGE

Interviews for the Panel Study are conducted in the spring (April-June) of a particular year. At that time, certain questions are asked concerning the present situation of the household, most importantly marital status and current composition of the household, and other questions are asked concerning the previous year's experience of the household, most notably the household's income and food stamp experience. If the composition of the household did not undergo any radical change between the two interviewing periods, the matching of a point-in-time status with an entire year's experience does not produce any interpretational difficulties. However, if a radical change in the composition of the household occurred between the two interviewing periods, severe analytical problems arise. Take the case of a woman who became divorced between the two interviewing periods. In the spring of 1980 she would be the head of her own household; in the spring of 1979 she would have been the wife of a household headed by her husband. It is unknown whether the divorce occurred during 1979 or early in 1980; consequently, it is impossible to categorize her marital status for the 1979 year. (Previous research has found marital status to be a key variable in predicting participation.) It is difficult to ascertain her economic position for the year as a whole, since it is quite likely that it changed dramatically upon divorce. Furthermore, it is impossible to determine her actual food stamp experience of the previous year. The interview in spring 1980 would ask if anyone in the current household had received food stamps in 1979. If, for example, her husband had received food stamps but she stopped receiving them upon divorce (an improbable occurrence but useful for illustrative purposes), she would be recorded as not receiving food stamps in 1979.

Given these problems, the decision was to eliminate from the analysis all households in which the head or wife changed between the 1979 and 1980 interview. While this eliminates some of the more interesting households with respect to food stamp participation (i.e., divorced women, children leaving home to form their own households), it does not mean that the effect of these types of changes is totally eliminated from the analysis. For example, the sample still contains households headed by divorced women, but the divorces occurred before the spring of

1979. Only the transitional cases are eliminated. This does not seem inappropriate for a one-year analysis; a more dynamic year-to-year change in food stamp status would be more appropriate to capture the immediate change resulting from a dramatic change in the composition of the household.

Restricting the sample to households in which the head and wife (if appropriate) did not change between the two interviewing periods resulted in the elimination of 777 households, accounting for 9.3 percent of the original 6,752 households. The breakdown of these households by type of family composition change is given in Table A4.1. One hundred thirty-three of these households received food stamps at some time in 1979, 68 of them for at least nine months during the year.

TWO-FAMILY HOUSEHOLDS

The Panel Study defines a household as including all persons residing in the designated dwelling unit. This does not necessarily correspond to the definition of a household under the food stamp program. Under the rules of the program, a household must also be an economic unit, which is defined as a group of people sharing common living expenses, regardless of who earns the income. Thus it might be possible to have more than one food stamp household within a dwelling unit.

Table A4.2 provides information on the possible magnitude of this problem. Households that passed the family composition test were grouped into four categories based on two variables: whether the income of family members other than the head or wife was greater than $3,000 and whether family size equalled the head and wife (if appropriate) plus the number of children under the age of 18. The rationale for this division was that if there were adult members of the household other than the head and wife and if the income of these other members exceeded $3,000, then there existed a prima facie case for a two-family household. The actual food stamp experience of these households was then compared to their estimated income eligibility status, using two measures of income: total family money income and income of the head and wife only. Of particular concern was how many long-term food stamp users (nine months or more) were misclassified.

As can be seen from Table A4.2, the potential for misclassification was particularly high for the suspect group of

Table A4.1

DERIVATION OF SAMPLE OF ELIGIBLE HOUSEHOLDS

Classification	Number of Observations	Percent of All Households	Number of Short-Term Food Stamp Users	Number of Long-Term Food Stamp Users	Running Total of Households
All	6,752	100.0%	391	690	6,752
Minus					
(1) Residing outside contiguous United States	63	0.7	3	7	6,689
(2) Different head or wife					
(a) Head same, but change in wife	197	2.5	19	12	6,492
(b) Wife now head	115	1.9	13	11	6,377
(c) Female head married	114	0.8	9	16	6,263
(d) Splitoff household	351	4.1	24	29	5,912
(3) Net income too high	4,768	78.0	173	144	1,144
(4) Asset income too high	61	1.4	3	3	1,083

Table A4.1 (continued)

Classification	Number of Observations	Percent of All Households	Number of Short-Term Food Stamp Users	Number of Long-Term Food Stamp Users	Running Total of Households
(5) Supplemental Security Income recipient residing in Wisconsin or Massachusetts	1	0.0	0	0	1,082
(6) No home food expenditures	31	0.2	1	4	1,051
(7) Two-family households	58	0.4	9	32	993
Total Number of Eligible Households	993	9.8	137	432	993

[a]"Short-term food stamp user" is defined as a household that reported receiving food stamps for less than nine months in 1980.

Table A4.2

COMPARISON OF USER-ELIGIBILITY STATUS BASED ON TOTAL HOUSEHOLD INCOME AND HEAD AND WIFE INCOME ONLY, 1979

Household Category	Household User-Eligibility Status					
	Ineligible, Nonparticipant	Ineligible, Short-Term User	Ineligible, Long-Term User	Eligible, Nonparticipant	Eligible, Short-Term User	Eligible, Long-Term User
Others' income less than or equal $3,000, family size equals adjusted family size	3,529	113	49	431	122	358
Others' income less than or equal $3,000, family size not equal adjusted family size	250	8	14	74	19	80
Others' income greater than $3,000, family size equals adjusted family size	76	1	5	0	0	1
Others' income greater than $3,000, family size not equal adjusted family size	596	51	76	18	9	32
Totals	4,451	173	144	523	150	471

Table A4.2

Household Category	Head and Wife User–Eligibility Status					
	Ineligible, Non-participant	Ineligible, Short-Term User	Ineligible, Long-Term User	Eligible, Non-participant	Eligible, Short-Term User	Eligible, Long-Term User
Others' income less than $3,000, family size equal adjusted family size	3,533	114	46	427	121	361
Others' income less than $3,000, family size not equal adjusted family size	246	10	15	78	17	79
Others' income greater than $3,000, family size equal adjusted family size	66	0	1	10	1	5
Others' income greater than $3,000, family size not equal adjusted family size	503	30	21	111	30	87
Totals	4,348	154	83	626	169	532

"Household Eligibility Status" is based on total household income and family size equal to the total of all members in the household.

"Short-Term User" is a household that reported receiving food stamps for less than nine months.

"Long-Term User" is a household that reported receiving food stamps for nine months or more.

"Head and Wife Eligibility Status" is based on head and wife income only and family size equal to adjusted family size, which equals head and wife (if applicable) plus the number of children less than 18 years old.

households. When eligibility was based on total household income and family size equal to the total number of members in the household unit, 144 long-term food stamp users were classified as ineligible. Seventy-six of these households were in the category of households in which others' income exceeded $3,000 and family size did not equal the head and wife (if applicable) plus the number of children under the age of 18. (There were 596 such households.) As can be seen in the bottom half of Table A4.2, this misclassification can be greatly reduced if eligibility is based on head and wife's income only and family size is adjusted to include only the head and wife plus children. Fifty-five of the 76 misclassified households were then properly classified. Unfortunately, the number of eligible nonparticipants increases from 18 to 111. Given the size of these changes and the inherent inability to ascertain the true food stamp status of these households, the decision was made to eliminate from the analysis all households in which the income of members other than the head and wife exceeded $3,000. This restriction alone resulted in the elimination of 865 households; however, only 58 would have been deemed eligible by the procedures used in this study (see bottom line of Table A4.2).

DETERMINING COUNTABLE FOOD STAMP INCOME

Eligibility for the food stamp program is based on the monthly income of the household. Certain deductions are allowable from total monthly income of the household. A standard deduction of $65 per month was in effect in the first half of 1979. In addition, a work-related deduction equal to 20 percent of earned income is allowed (P.L. 95-113, Title XIII, Sec. 5(e)). Finally, deductions are allowed for housing expenses and expenses necessary to care for a dependent person in the household if necessary for employment. The housing expense deduction is equal to the amount of such expense (i.e., rent, utilities, etc.) which exceeds 50 percent of income after the other allowable deductions are subtracted. Table A4.3 shows the effect of such deductions on the eligibility status of households. As can be seen, almost 60 percent of the households estimated to be eligible for food stamps had income that was below the eligibility levels before any deductions were taken into account. An additional 20 percent became eligible once the standard deduction was subtracted from income. It should be noted that the shelter deduction has a surprisingly small effect on eligibility. This could be partially due to the ordering of the deductions as presented in Table A4.3. But it may also indicate that the restrictions on the shelter deduction incorporated in the Food Stamp Act of 1977 had their intended effect.

With regard to the full sample, 4,768 households had net incomes that were in excess of the food stamp maximums for the appropriate family size.

THE ASSET TEST

In addition to the income test, the food stamp program also employs an asset test for eligibility. In 1979 the limitation on countable assets for a household was $1,750; the limit increased to $3,000 for families that included a person aged 60 or over. (In January 1981, the limit for households containing no elderly person was lowered to its pre-1979 level of $1,500.) Not all assets are counted. The value of a home and the first car (up to $4,500) are excluded, as are personal effects and income-producing real property. All liquid assets are counted.

The Panel Study does not contain a direct measure of household assets. However, it does contain information on income from "rent, interest, and dividends." The amount of liquid assets a household possessed was estimated based on this variable, assuming a modest 5 percent rate of return. Thus, if a household that contained no elderly persons had rent, dividend, and interest income in 1979 in excess of $87 ($150 for a household containing a person aged 60 or more), the household was deemed asset ineligible. Sixty-one income-eligible households, six of which received food stamps in 1979, failed to pass this asset test.

OTHER ELIGIBILITY RESTRICTIONS

Individual states have an option of cashing out food stamp benefits to Supplemental Security Income recipients. In 1979 two states, Massachusetts and Wisconsin, had this provision. One household in the sample was eliminated for this reason.

In order to qualify for food stamps, a household must have access to cooking facilities. The Panel Study does not contain

Table A4.3

EFFECT OF DEDUCTIONS ON FOOD STAMP ELIGIBILITY, 1980

Classification	Number of Observations	Percent of All Eligibles	Participation Rate
Gross income too low	653	59.5	57.9%
Gross income minus ___ too low:			
(1) Standard deduction	158	21.0	32.4
(2) Earned income deduction	128	10.7	32.1
(3) Shelter deduction	39	6.7	18.9
(4) Dependent care deduction	15	2.0	4.1
Totals	993	100.0	46.1%

this information. However, it does have information on the
amount of expenditures a household made for food to be eaten at
home. If this figure (which included the annual bonus value of
any food stamps actually received) was less than $100, the
household was deemed not to have home-cooking facilities.
Thirty-one otherwise eligible households, five of which received
food stamps at some time in 1979, were eliminated by this
procedure.

Appendix B to Chapter 4

DISTRIBUTION OF RESPONSES TO NONPARTICIPATION
QUESTIONS BY ELIGIBLE HOUSEHOLDS

Figure B4.1 reproduces the sequence of questions used to
generate the data analyzed in this chapter. Table B4.1 gives the
distribution of responses to this sequence. Table B4.2 shows the
consolidated distribution of these responses into a set of
analytically useful categories.

Figure B4.1

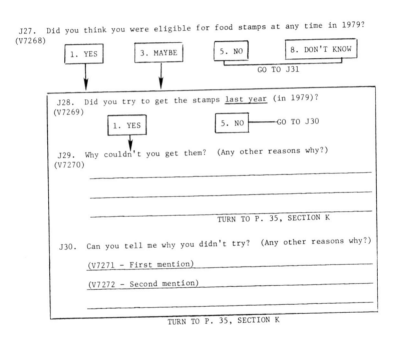

J27. Did you think you were eligible for food stamps at any time in 1979?
(V7268)

| 1. YES | 3. MAYBE | 5. NO | 8. DON'T KNOW |

GO TO J31

J28. Did you try to get the stamps last year (in 1979)?
(V7269)

| 1. YES | 5. NO ——GO TO J30 |

J29. Why couldn't you get them? (Any other reasons why?)
(V7270)

_____

_____

_____ TURN TO P. 35, SECTION K

J30. Can you tell me why you didn't try? (Any other reasons why?)

(V7271 - First mention) _____

(V7272 - Second mention) _____

_____

TURN TO P. 35, SECTION K

J31. Can you tell me why you thought you weren't eligible? (Any other reasons why?)

(V7273 - First mention) _____

(V7274 - Second mention) _____

_____

Table B4.1

DISTRIBUTION OF RESPONSES TO FOOD STAMP
NONPARTICIPATION SEQUENCE, ELIGIBLE HOUSEHOLDS, 1979
(N=993)

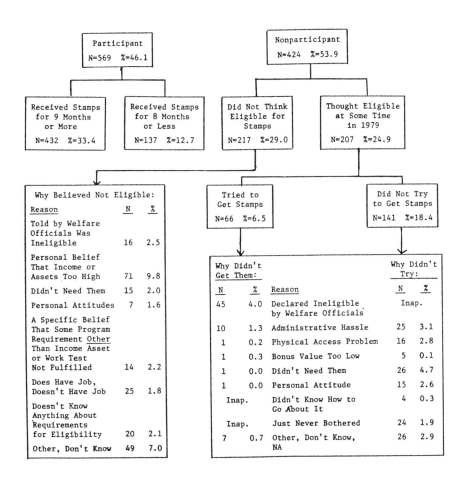

Table B4.2

CONSOLIDATED REASONS FOR NONPARTICIPATION
BY ELIGIBLE HOUSEHOLDS, 1979
(N=952)

Reason	Number of Observations	Weighted Percent of All Eligibles	Percent of Eligible Nonparticipants
Participant	569	46.1%	. . . . . .
Didn't know anything about eligibility or how to apply	24	2.4	4.5%
Thought income or assets too high	71	9.8	18.2
Thought ineligible for some other reason	88	11.0	20.4
Told by welfare officials was ineligible	61	6.5	12.1
Administrative hassle	35	4.4	8.2
Bonus value too low	6	0.4	0.7
Physical access problem	17	3.0	5.6
Didn't need them	42	6.7	12.4
Personal attitude	23	4.2	7.8
Other, don't know	57	5.5	10.2
Totals	993	100.0%	100.1%

From Table B4.1.

Appendix C to Chapter 4

COMPLETE REGRESSION RESULTS

The full set of regression results used in this analysis are presented in Appendix Table C4.1.

Table C4.1

COMPLETE REGRESSION RESULTS FOR PARTICIPATION IN THE FOOD STAMP PROGRAM BY ELIGIBLE HOUSEHOLDS, 1979
(N=952)

Independent Variable (Omitted Category)	Dependent Variable								
	Participant How to Apply	No Information on Eligibility Rules or How to Apply	Belief That Income or Assets Too High	Believed Ineligible for Some Other Reason	Declared Ineligible by Welfare Officials	Administrative Hassle. Physical Access Problem	Didn't Need Them	Personal Attitudes	Just Didn't Bother. Other
Age-Sex-Marital Status									
Married couple, head age less than 30	.258** (.069)	-.020 (.027)	.024 (.051)	-.046 (.055)	-.034 (.042)	-.128** (.046)	-.071 (.044)	-.005 (.035)	.022 (.042)
(Married couple, head age 30-59)	--	--	--	--	--	--	--	--	--
Married couple, head age 60 or over	-.071 (.073)	-.055* (.028)	.083 (.054)	.049 (.058)	.005 (.045)	.027 (.048)	-.001 (.046)	.017 (.037)	.045 (.044)
Unmarried female, age less than 30	-.052 (.067)	-.032 (.026)	.079 (.049)	.030 (.053)	.016 (.041)	-.095* (.044)	-.028 (.042)	.056† (.034)	.027 (.041)
Unmarried female, age 30-59	-.035 (.061)	-.001 (.023)	.065 (.045)	-.018 (.048)	.022 (.037)	.009 (.040)	.009 (.039)	.077† (.031)	-.010 (.037)
Unmarried female, age 60 or over	-.208** (.071)	-.052† (.027)	.094† (.053)	.104† (.056)	-.071 (.044)	-.034 (.047)	.063 (.045)	.021 (.036)	.083† (.043)
Unmarried male, age less than 30	-.219* (.090)	-.024 (.035)	.103 (.066)	.065 (.071)	.072 (.055)	-.104† (.059)	.061 (.057)	.072 (.045)	.106† (.055)
Unmarried male, Age 30-59	-.201* (.080)	-.042 (.031)	-.022 (.059)	-.025 (.063)	.212** (.049)	-.098† (.053)	.088† (.051)	.113** (.040)	-.025 (.049)
Unmarried male, age 60 or over	-.613** (.095)	-.089* (.037)	.308** (.071)	.156* (.075)	-.090 (.058)	.093 (.063)	.047 (.061)	.196** (.048)	-.008 (.058)
Whether Head Disabled	-.041 (.031)	-.002 (.012)	.031 (.023)	.006 (.025)	.067** (.019)	-.005 (.021)	-.041* (.020)	-.022 (.016)	.005 (.019)
Population of Largest City in County									
(500,000 or more)	--	--	--	--	--	--	--	--	--
100,000-499,999	-.057 (.038)	.030* (.015)	.074** (.028)	.013 (.030)	-.010 (.023)	-.046† (.025)	.053* (.024)	-.009 (.019)	-.049* (.023)
25,000-99,999	.027 (.041)	.033* (.016)	.022 (.031)	.010 (.033)	-.005 (.025)	-.063† (.027)	.060† (.026)	-.053† (.021)	-.031 (.025)
Under 25,000	-.137** (.042)	.034* (.016)	.025 (.031)	.069† (.033)	-.011 (.026)	-.089* (.027)	.108** (.026)	-.006 (.021)	.007 (.025)
Whether Public Transportation Available	-.048 (.034)	.030* (.013)	-.072* (.025)	.028 (.027)	-.041† (.021)	.040† (.022)	.033 (.021)	-.001 (.017)	-.030 (.021)
Whether Nonwhite	.003 (.029)	-.005 (.011)	-.026 (.026)	-.017 (.023)	.057** (.018)	-.056** (.019)	-.042* (.018)	-.043** (.015)	.017 (.018)
Years of	-.022** (.031)	-.005** (.012)	.010** (.023)	.007† (.007)	-.003 (.019)	.000	.001	.011** (.011)	.001

Table C4.1 (continued)

Independent Variable (Omitted Category)	Dependent Variable: Participant	No Information on Eligibility Rules or How to Apply	Belief That Income or Assets Too High	Believed Ineligible for Some Other Reason	Declared Ineligible by Welfare Officials	Administrative Hassle. Physical Access Problem	Didn't Need Them	Personal Attitudes	Just Didn't Bother. Other
Education, Head	(.005)	(.002)	(.003)	(.004)	(.003)	(.003)	(.003)	(.002)	(.003)
Number of Children, Age 0–17	.086** (.026)	-.011 (.010)	-.032† (.020)	-.041* (.021)	.029† (.016)	.005 (.017)	.025 (.017)	-.028* (.013)	.015 (.016)
Whether Farmer	-.301** (.110)	.265** (.042)	.113 (.082)	.055 (.087)	-.074 (.067)	-.036 (.073)	.113 (.070)	.163** (.055)	-.073 (.067)
Number of Previous Years in Poverty	-.001 (.012)	-.004 (.005)	-.017† (.009)	-.002 (.010)	.021** (.007)	.007 (.008)	.021** (.008)	.020** (.006)	.011 (.007)
County Unemployment Rate	.009 (.007)	-.001 (.003)	.006 (.005)	.005 (.005)	.004 (.004)	-.004 (.004)	-.004 (.004)	-.003 (.003)	-.005 (.004)
Level of State Basic AFDC Allowance ($100)	.014 (.017)	.016* (.006)	-.012 (.012)	.010 (.013)	.001 (.010)	-.000 (.011)	-.004 (.011)	-.001 (.008)	-.005 (.010)
Food Needs/Income	.00015 (.00009)	-.00007† (.00004)	-.00001 (.00007)	.00025** (.00007)	.00002 (.00006)	.00001 (.00006)	.00004 (.00006)	-.00002 (.00005)	.00002 (.00006)
Transfer Income Status									
Received AFDC or other welfare in 1978 or 1979	.538** (.041)	-.019 (.016)	-.046 (.030)	-.173** (.033)	-.068** (.025)	-.073** (.027)	-.060* (.026)	-.057** (.021)	-.044† (.025)
No AFDC or other welfare, but received SSI in 1978 or 1979	.355** (.055)	-.021 (.021)	-.018 (.041)	-.211** (.044)	.022 (.034)	-.004 (.036)	-.082* (.035)	-.019 (.028)	-.023 (.034)
No AFDC or SSI, but received Social Security in 1978 or 1979	.031 (.051)	.023 (.019)	.045 (.037)	-.128** (.040)	.036 (.031)	-.047 (.033)	-.034 (.032)	.025 (.025)	.018 (.031)
(No AFDC, SSI, or Social Security in 1978 or 1979)	--	--	--	--	--	--	--	--	--
Whether Head Employed 1,500 Hours or More in 1979	-.103* (.044)	.000 (.017)	.093** (.032)	-.042 (.034)	.029 (.027)	.002 (.029)	-.033 (.028)	.030 (.022)	.024 (.027)
Monthly Household Income ($100)	-.070** (.018)	.003 (.007)	.039** (.013)	.002 (.014)	.000 (.011)	.002 (.018)	.015 (.011)	.011 (.009)	.001 (.011)
Monthly Bonus Value ($10)	-.012† (.006)	.001 (.002)	.008† (.005)	-.011* (.005)	-.008* (.004)	-.005 (.004)	.003 (.004)	.003 (.003)	.000 (.004)
R^2 (adjusted)	.418	.072	.106	.089	.106	.079	.079	.108	.032

Significance Levels: † .10   * .05   ** .01

Chapter 5

THE IMPACT OF NATURAL GAS DEREGULATION ON AMERICAN FAMILIES

Daniel H. Hill

Increasing energy prices to levels which cover full resource
costs is the keystone of recent American energy policy. During
the Carter administration, legislation to accomplish this through
phased deregulation of petroleum and natural gas prices was
passed. One of President Reagan's first executive acts was to
accelerate the deregulation process by ending domestic oil price
controls eight months ahead of schedule. The economic shock of
this sudden move was relatively short-lived and not nearly as
severe as many economists and most liberal politicians had
anticipated. The present administration is now considering a
similar acceleration in decontrolling natural gas prices.

In this series of volumes we have periodically used
information collected from panel study respondents to assess the
economic impact of changes in energy prices on American families
(see, e.g., Duncan, 1974; Holmes, 1976; Morgan, 1978; Coe, 1980;
Hill, 1980). The present chapter presents yet another look at
the issue. That policy makers are currently considering radical
changes in the existing laws governing natural gas pricing is but
one of three reasons such a reexamination of the data is in
order. A second reason is that conditions change. Since Coe
last examined utility expenditure burdens, for instance, more
than 1.2 million households switched from heating their homes
with fuel oil to natural gas or wood, largely in response to the
sharp increases in oil prices that followed the Iranian embargo
(see U.S. Department of Energy, 1981). Thus, the increased
burden that would result from rapid decontrol of natural gas
prices is greater now than it was estimated to be when, for
instance, policy makers were drafting the Natural Gas Policy Act
of 1978 (NGPA). The third reason that another look at the impact
of rising energy prices is warranted is that both the quantity
and quality of the data have been improved. While we have been

178

collecting data on total utility expenditures since 1968, it was not until the 1980 interviewing year that type of fuel used to heat the home was obtained. This new information is essential if we wish to examine the impact of increases in natural gas prices as distinct from increases in utility prices in general. Outside data have also improved and we can now validate our results by making comparisons with data from the Department of Energy's National Residential Energy Consumption Survey (NRECS).

The chapter is organized in three major sections and a summary. In the first section, the recent legislative history and research issues of natural gas price regulation are discussed. In the second, the new Panel Study of Income Dynamics (PSID) data are analyzed and the results validated by comparison with the data from the NRECS. Finally, in the third section, the impact on household utility burdens of the proposed policy changes are estimated and compared with Coe's earlier findings on utility burdens and with Hill's on gasoline expenditure burdens.

RECENT LEGISLATIVE HISTORY AND RELATED RESEARCH ISSUES

Many of the policy makers involved in the current move to accelerate the decontrol of natural gas prices point to successful decontrol of oil prices as evidence that natural gas decontrol will be relatively painless. There are, however, some important differences in the markets for these two major energy sources that must be recognized in analysis. Before going on to a discussion of these differences, it is worthwhile reviewing some of the similarities of the two policies as well as the rationale for the current natural gas legislation.

The situations are similar in that regulations that maintain prices below true resource costs invariably lead to inefficiencies in both production and consumption. Examples of inefficient use of oil and natural gas are plentiful. A national average automobile fuel economy of less than 14 miles per gallon in 1976 is an obvious example of persisting inefficient use of petroleum resulting from regulated prices. Furthermore, such inefficiencies are not easily remedied by legislation. For instance, the fuel economy standards of the Vehicle Information and Cost Savings Act of 1974 were being thwarted by the tendency of American consumers to purchase light trucks and vans for commuting purposes as late as the 1976-1978 model years (see,

e.g., Hill and Hill, 1979). This did not change until after the
Iranian revolution in late 1979 when real gasoline prices began
to increase rapidly. Similarly, the fact that natural gas is the
dominant heating fuel throughout much of the deep South and
Southwest despite the fact that electric heat pumps are roughly
1.5 times as efficient on a primary energy BTU input basis in
these climates is a clear illustration of the sort of
inefficiency being caused by continued regulation of natural gas
prices. Regulation-induced inefficiencies in production result
also and primarily from the fact that low prices call forth too
little investment in domestic exploration and field development.

Past/Present Legislative Responses

To eliminate these inefficiencies, the Carter administration
mounted a major legislative drive that resulted, in the case of
natural gas, in the Natural Gas Policy Act of 1978. This law was
designed to provide domestic producers strong incentives to
search for natural gas while gradually increasing conservation
incentives to consumers. The supply incentives were accomplished
by allowing greatly increased wellhead prices for new gas
beginning in 1980. Conservation incentives would increase, via
higher retail prices, as a larger and larger fraction of all gas
sold became "new" gas and as the allowable price of this gas
increased. The allowable price of new gas was designed to
increase at a rate that would place it at the 1978 BTU equivalent
price of world oil by 1985, when most gas would be deregulated
entirely. Despite its complicated nature, there is much to be
said for the act. It maximized supply response while minimizing
price shocks of the sort that contributed to the recessions of
1975 and 1980. Furthermore, efficiency of use was encouraged
without transferring huge amounts of wealth to owners of gas
wells that were profitable even under old (controlled) prices.
Unfortunately, when the NGPA was passed, it was assumed that oil
prices would remain approximately constant in real terms until
1985. The radical increases in world oil prices following the
Iranian revolution and boycott were not anticipated, and the
allowable price schedule under the existing law will not result
in a smooth transition of prices in 1985. The Department of
Energy (DOE) now estimates a sudden 40 percent increase in retail
natural gas prices in 1985. Fortunately, the law has been rather

successful to date both in increasing supply and reducing demand, and it is reasonable to consider modifying the legislation to accelerate decontrol now while supplies are good.[1]

There are three major research issues that need to be addressed in the course of this reconsideration. The first is the issue of how responsive is natural gas (and substitutes for natural gas) supply to price increases. If these supplies are highly responsive to prices, then any policy that holds prices too low will result in large losses to society in the form of losses to consumers who would like to use the fuel but cannot obtain it. Household-level data such as that collected in the Panel Study of Income Dynamics are not well suited to analysis of this issue.

The second research issue that needs addressing during the reconsideration of natural gas legislation is the extent to which demand responds to price. Again, ceteris paribus, the more responsive demand is to price, the larger are societal losses due to policies that set prices too low. Household-level data are potentially quite useful in addressing this issue, and while the author is currently conducting such a study with PSID data, this research is not sufficiently advanced to be reported here.

---

[1]Patching up the NGPA to insure a smooth transition to decontrolled new gas prices in 1985 is, however, the least radical (and popular) proposal being considered by the present administration. The most favored proposals involve complete decontrol of natural gas in 1982 along with repealing the Fuel Use Act (FUA), which limits the use of natural gas as a boiler fuel by industry and electric utilities. This proposal would, according to the DOE, result in roughly a 50 percent increase in retail natural gas prices during the first year and a transfer of $100 billion (net present value) from gas consumers to producers in the form of "increased producer surpluses" (formerly known as windfall profits) over and above that implied by the original legislation.

Normally, eliminating restrictions on the use of inputs such as natural gas leads to unambiguous improvements in economic efficiency. The Fuel Use Act, in combination with the Clean Air Act, however, may be approximating the most efficient long-run market outcome. The reason is that market-determined fuel prices fail to reflect the true societal costs of effluents produced in the combustion process. If users were charged the appropriate fee for effluents released to the environment, then natural gas prices would be bid up as users of dirtier fuels converted to the cheaper-to-use fuel. If the resulting "cleanliness premium" of natural gas were high enough, then large users would find it cheaper to use dirtier fuels and clean up the pollutants--taking advantage of the very large economies of scale that exist in cleaning up combustion products.

At the time of this writing, data from the 1981 interviewing wave are being merged with previous years' data. This new data will allow analysis of change in natural gas demand over the 1979-1980 period. Differencing expenditures for the two periods will improve parameter estimates by removing from the error term time-invariant, household-specific effects, such as structural thermal efficiency, which might bias price and income coefficients due to their spurious correlation with region, prices, and income. Relatively few houses in the Southern states (where gas prices are relatively low) have basements, for instance, and because houses with crawl spaces or houses built on slabs are less efficient from a thermal standpoint, estimation of expenditure level without measures of such thermal characteristics would overstate the effects of price. Differencing expenditures for the same house over two periods will remove such biases.[2]

The third and final research issue to be addressed in considering changes to existing natural gas pricing legislation regards the evenness of the initial impact of various changes across all consumers. If only a few consumers are seriously affected by a change, then they can be easily compensated. It is this third issue discussed in the third section of this chapter for which PSID data are uniquely suited. Before going on to that discussion, however, the burden is upon us to demonstrate that PSID data on energy expenditures are sufficiently accurate to warrant our confidence in drawing conclusions about the equity of the impact of changes in energy prices.

VALIDATION OF PSID ENERGY CONSUMPTION DATA

The average utility expenditure of Panel households in calendar year 1979 was, in then-current dollars, $818.[3] This compares to an $815 average energy expenditure as measured by the

---

[2]Some might argue that building houses with basements is a response to high energy prices and requirements, and thus, the correlation is not spurious. We consider the correlation to be noncausal in the sense that if energy prices in the South were to rise to the levels of the Northeast, we would not expect Southern homeowners to dig basements under their existing houses. If there is a causal link, it operates only in the very long run.

[3]This includes all PSID households except split-off households who had subsequently recombined with their original sample families.

NRECS survey for the 12-month period beginning April 1, 1979.
While the virtual identity of these two estimates does indicate
general agreement of the two techniques, it should not be taken
too seriously. If nothing more, both studies are subject to
sampling error that would make this close a correspondence
extremely fortuitous. The NRECS average total expenditure figure
has an estimated standard deviation of about $18.

To see just how lucky this result is, it is necessary to
disaggregate the data. Figure 5.1 plots the average expenditure
from the two studies by geographic region. Although rank
orderings of region by expenditure are identical for the two
studies, the PSID expenditure averages are significantly higher
than the NRECS's for both the Southern and Western regions of the
country. The identity of the overall national estimates comes
about because their difference is almost exactly offset by higher
(although not significantly higher) NRECS estimates in the
Northeast and North Central regions.

A possible explanation of these regional differences is
provided by the data in Table 5.1, which lists the Heating Degree
Days (HDD) experienced in selected PSUs for the winters (January
through March) of 1979 and 1980. The winter of 1980 (the "DOE
winter") was much milder than that of 1979 (the "PSID winter") in
all the Southern and Western cities, while the opposite held, for
the most part, in Northern cities. Thus, the regional
differences shown in Figure 5.1 may merely be a reflection of
these regional weather differences and the fact that expenditures
are positively affected by the severity of winter weather.

Figure 5.2 presents average utility expenditures by home
ownership status and illustrates that regional weather
differences between the two study periods are clearly not the
only important differences in study procedures. Homeowners in
the Panel Study report annual expenditures $125 higher than those
in the NRECS: a difference sufficiently large as to make it
unlikely that the inclusion of water and sewage in the former
total is its sole cause. Another reason is, of course, that, as
mentioned above, the winter of 1979 was more severe overall than
was the winter of 1980.

The significantly lower utility payments of PSID renters
when compared to NRECS renters is an artifact of an even more
important difference in study designs than period of coverage or

Figure 5.1 ,
UTILITY EXPENDITURES BY REGION

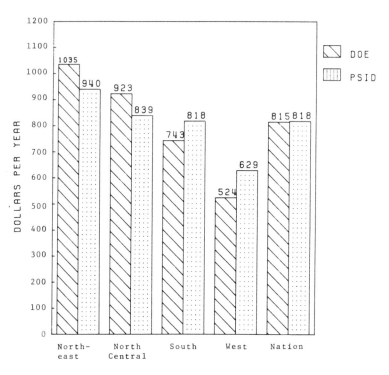

GEOGRAPHIC REGION

Table 5.1

HEATING DEGREE DAYS FOR SELECTED CITIES
FOR THE WINTERS OF 1979 AND 1980

City	Winter of 1979 (Covered by PSID)	Winter of 1980 (Covered by NRECS)	
Los Angeles	848	477	43.8%
San Francisco	1,261	664	47.3
Atlanta	1,778	1,683	5.3
Dallas	1,807	1,466	18.9
Detroit	3,518	3,630	5.2
Dayton	3,287	3,262	0.8
Boston	2,862	3,033	6.0
New York	2,696	2,863	6.2

Figure 5.2

UTILITY EXPENDITURES BY HOME OWNERSHIP

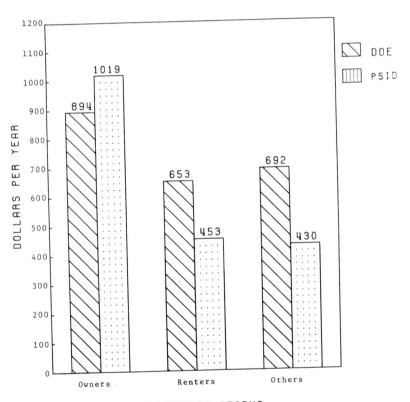

inclusion of water and sewage payments. In the NRECS study, imputations were made for missing or incomplete monthly observations or when households did not pay directly for heat or other utilities. The NRECS study does not, therefore, allow for any "legitimate zero" payments. In the PSID, on the other hand, only direct payments are considered, and it is quite legitimate for some households to have zero utility payments if someone outside the family unit pays the bills. If we exclude from the PSID data all households where either utility payments are zero or where heat is included in the rent, then the average payments for renters rises from $453 to $720, the latter figure being some $67 more than NRECS--a figure nearly twice the standard deviation of the NRECS average. Again, we see PSID averages being somewhat higher than NRECS. This time, however, we cannot cite the inclusion of sewage and water in the total because these bills are most often sent to the registered owner by the municipal utilities--that is, to the landlord. The observed overstatement of PSID expenditures for renters who pay directly for utilities, including heat, is probably the result of the weather differences during the two study periods but might also reflect the fact that when one excludes renters whose heating payments are part of the rent, one ends up with a subsample of all renters that is biased toward renters of single-family and/or electrically heated units.[4]

While up to this point we have been concentrating on the differences between the two studies, the overall impression we get when we look at the data presented in Table 5.2 (and in Appendix Figures A5.1 through A5.4), is that the data are remarkably similar both in overall level and in their relation to other variables. In both studies, utility expenditures increase monotonically with family size from roughly $500 per year for one-person households to more than $1,000 for households with five or more family members. Similarly, utility payments in each sample increase monotonically with income and house size and exhibit an inverted-U, age-expenditure profile.

---

[4]This exclusion removes 29 percent of all rental units in multi-unit structures but only 7 percent of single-family rentals. Similarly, only 8 percent of electrically heated homes are removed.

Table 5.2

UTILITY EXPENDITURES AS MEASURED BY DEPARTMENT OF
ENERGY AND PSID, BY DEMOGRAPHIC CHARACTERISTICS

	NRECS	PSID
Income		
$0-$ 4,999	$604	$439
$5,000-$ 9,999	657	576
$10,000-$14,999	763	668
$15,000-$19,999	812	752
$20,000-$24,999	919	964
$25,000-$34,999	929	1,011
$35,000 or more	1,180	1,231
Age of Head		
18-29	677	526
30-44	899	971
45-59	915	1,018
60 or older	743	731
Family Size		
One	539	454
Two	765	810
Three	827	926
Four	1,009	1,055
Five or more	1,069	1,218
Number of Rooms		
1-3	483	282
4	646	576
5	760	789
6	892	937
7	989	1,116
8 or more	1,237	1,311

Given these similarities, we can be fairly confident that PSID data are sufficiently accurate to allow analysis of the impact of pricing policy. Some care is warranted in interpreting utility expenditure burdens while using PSID data. Specifically, the PSID data will tend to overstate slightly the burdens for homeowners due to inclusion of water and sewage payments while understating those of renters due to the failure to include utility payments that are indirectly made through rent.

With these differences in mind, we can now proceed to an analysis of the impact of natural gas price deregulation on American families.

THE RELATIVE IMPACTS OF NATURAL GAS AND OIL
PRICE DECONTROL ON AMERICAN FAMILIES

The DOE projections of first year retail price increases of 50 percent leads to the first major difference between the natural gas and petroleum decontrol situations. When oil was decontrolled in February 1981, retail prices did not increase appreciably at the retail level. The timing of the move was excellent. Primarily because of recessions in western industrial countries there was a glut of crude oil on the world market. Oil refiners found themselves in a buyer's market for crude. Increases in domestic oil prices were largely offset by decreasing reliance on higher priced OPEC oil and proportionately increasing reliance on lower priced Saudi oil. An even more important factor in the failure of oil decontrol to increase retail prices is that there were no effective controls on demand before decontrol, nor were any needed. Oil was already the most expensive boiler fuel available; natural gas users were not about to shift to oil. But if the Fuel Use Act is done away with in the process of natural gas deregulation, there will be a very strong increase in the demand for natural gas as large boilers are switched from oil to gas.

The second major difference in oil and natural gas decontrol has to do with the nature of demand for these fuels in the household sector. Natural gas is used as a primary stationary fuel in residences for space and water heating and to a lesser extent cooking, while petroleum products are used primarily as

mobile fuels for transportation.[5] Home-based energy consumption
is less of a luxury good than is personal transportation--a fact
confirmed by its much lower income elasticity.[6]

The data in the first two columns of Table 5.3 illustrate
the point quite dramatically. In 1977 household utility
expenditures (including water but dominated by energy) accounted
for 5.9 percent of total family income overall. Because of the
low income elasticity, however, this fraction decreased sharply
with income level: for households with incomes low enough to
place them in the bottom 10 percent of the income distribution
the fraction of income devoted to utility payments was 15 percent
or six times the fraction (15/2.5=6) of income expended by
households in the top 10 percent of the income distribution. The
burden of motor fuel expenditures is far less disproportionate as
well as being only three-quarters as large overall. The high
income elasticities of both automobile ownership and annual miles
traveled is reflected by the fact that the fraction of income
devoted to gasoline actually increases with income as one moves
from the second to third and fourth income deciles (column 2).
The burden of gasoline prices is, even so, greater for the
poorest of households (4.9 percent of total income) than for the
richest (2.7 percent).

The implication of these patterns of expenditures is that
policies which increase the cost of home energy fuels are far
more regressive than those which affect motor fuel prices--
utility price increases hit those least able to pay much harder
than do gasoline price increases, while each have only minor
impacts on more affluent households. In addition to this
vertical inequity of increased utility fuel price increases there
is considerable variation in the impact of price increases within
narrowly defined income groups (horizontal inequities),

---

[5]This is not to say that no one uses petroleum products for
heating. In 1979 roughly 16 percent of all United States
households used fuel oil as the primary heating fuel and were
severely burdened by the 60 percent increase in fuel oil prices
experienced after the Iranian revolution in the year preceding
decontrol. Nationwide, however, there are three and a half homes
heated with gas for each one heated with fuel oil.

[6]In similar analyses of data from the PSID, Richard Coe
estimated an income elasticity of utility expenditure one half
the size of that estimated by Hill for gasoline demand (see,
respectively, Coe, 1980; Hill, 1980).

Table 5.3

UTILITY AND GASOLINE PAYMENTS AS A PERCENT OF INCOME VARIOUSLY DEFINED, 1977 AND 1979

Income Decile	1977		1979			
	Utilities ÷ Income	Gasoline[a] ÷ Income	Utilities ÷ Income	Utilities Less Subsidy ÷ Income Less Income Taxes	Utilities Less Subsidy ÷ Two-Year Average Disposable Income	Utilities Less Subsidy ÷ Disposable Income Plus Imputed Assets
Lowest	15.0	4.9	11.5	10.3	10.3	8.8
Second	9.1	3.5	7.1	7.0	7.4	6.3
Third	7.1	5.2	5.4	5.5	5.6	5.1
Fourth	5.8	5.2	4.3	5.0	4.7	4.7
Fifth	5.2	4.6	4.2	4.5	4.8	4.2
Sixth	4.6	4.8	4.2	4.7	4.9	4.4
Seventh	4.0	4.2	3.8	4.3	4.4	4.0
Eighth	3.7	3.9	3.4	3.9	4.0	3.6
Ninth	3.2	4.8	2.9	3.4	3.7	3.2
Highest	2.5	2.7	2.3	2.9	3.1	2.7
All	5.9	4.3	5.6	5.7	5.8	5.1

[a] These estimates are based on the household's reported total miles driven in 1977, state gasoline prices, and an assumed average fuel economy of 14.5 miles per gallon.

especially at the bottom of the income distribution. Sixty-two percent of the households in the bottom decile do not own automobiles and are therefore not directly burdened by increased gasoline prices. This means that the remaining 38 percent of the households in the bottom decile have gasoline expenditures that average 12.9 percent (4.9/.38) of their total income. Only 2 percent of the richest households do not own cars, and thus the gasoline burden of the richest car owners increases but slightly, from 2.7 to 2.8 percent. Similarly, roughly one-third of the households in the lowest income decile do not directly pay for utilities (primarily because they rent small apartments with centralized heating and master metering). Thus, those poorest households who do pay directly for their utilities expend more than 22 percent of their incomes on utilities.

The data in column 3 of the table are derived from the most current available year of the Panel Study of Income Dynamics and indicate that the burden of utility payments actually decreased between 1977 and 1979. This reduction is partly the result of a milder winter in the latter year but also reflects price-induced conservation and, more important, increased real incomes. Despite the reduced burdens when one looks at lowest-decile households which paid utilities, the average burden remains at 16 percent as compared to only 2.3 percent for those in the highest decile. This method of examining the regressivity is subject to the criticism that it overstates the actual problem because it ignores the progressive nature of our income tax system and the existence of low-income energy assistance programs. For this reason we recalculated the burden as a fraction of after tax income and subtracted out any government subsidies for heating (see column 4). In 1979 the newly instituted government heating assistance programs had the effect of reducing the utility burden from 11.5 percent to 10.3 percent for households in the lowest income decile (7.1 percent to 7.0 percent in the second decile), while the larger tax bite at higher incomes has the effect of raising the burden of the very richest households from 2.3 percent to 2.9 percent. Again, the burden of utility payments for households in the lowest decile actually paying them remains high at 15.9 percent.

One further plausible explanation of the extreme burden which utility payments represent for the very poorest families is that their incomes are only temporarily low while their utility consumption expenditures are based on their higher permanent income. The fifth column of figures in Table 5.3 shows, however, that this consideration has little effect on the results. When we average utility expenditures and incomes for 1978 and 1976 (for households with the same heads), virtually nothing changes. The burden for households in the lowest (1979) income decile remains 10.3, although the two-year average income for these households is higher than one-year income. The reason is that the winter of 1978 was even more extreme than that of 1979.

A final criticism of using disposable money income as the basis upon which to compute burdens is that it exaggerates vertical inequities because it ignores the imputed "free" rent enjoyed by homeowners, and homeowners have the highest utility payments. The final column of figures in Table 5.3, therefore, adds to disposable income an estimate of imputed rent equal to 5 percent of homeowners' current net equity in their house. The result is, of course, a reduction in burdens at all income levels. Overall, this reduction in burden amounts to 10.5 percent ((5.7 - 5.1)/5.7) but is more extreme at the lower end of the income distribution (14.6 percent). Nevertheless, the utility burden of low-income households remains more than three times as great as that of the most affluent households. Thus, we can conclude with considerable confidence that, as of 1979, the regressivity of policies that increased utility prices is real, substantial, and not eliminated by taxes or government assistance programs.

Another difference in the nature of the demand for natural gas and petroleum products which must be considered when comparing oil price and natural gas price decontrol is that natural gas demand is far more sensitive to weather conditions than is oil demand. Coe (1980) estimated a heating degree day expenditure elasticity of unity. Thus, a 10 percent increase in the severity of the winter results in a 10 percent increase in utility expenditures. There is no such sensitivity of driving to this sort of vagary of nature. The initial impact of deregulation of natural gas prices will depend to a large extent on the severity of weather conditions during the first years--a factor which can neither be anticipated nor controlled by the administration.

The sensitivity of utility expenditures to weather conditions combined with the fact that older people are more prone to hypothermia has raised the concern that increasing fuel prices will result in the most extreme hardships for the elderly. Table 5.4 presents the utility burdens for the population household heads over age 55 under two income definitions. While on average the utility burdens of elderly households are 25 to 30 percent higher than those of the population as a whole, this result is due more to the fact that the elderly are concentrated at the lower end of the income distribution than it is due to any intrinsically greater propensity for them to use utilities. As the first column of numbers in Table 5.4 indicates, nearly 50 percent of the elderly have incomes placing them in the bottom two deciles of the money income distribution (this compares to, of course, 20 percent exactly and definitionally, of the general population). Thus, the elderly will suffer more as a result of policies such as accelerated natural gas price decontrol, not because they consume more (Table 5.2 shows they consume less) but because they have lower incomes. Indeed, a careful comparison of Tables 5.3 and 5.4 indicates that the 32.8 percent most affluent elderly, those in the top six deciles of the income distribution, are actually _less_ severely burdened by energy prices than are comparable members of the general population. This result is important because it implies that subsidies based solely on age, such as mandated in the Public Utility Regulatory Policy Act of 1978, are inherently inefficient in the sense that more than half of the households receiving them would not be judged sufficiently needy if a means test were applied.

In summary, the equity difficulty with policies that result in higher in-home energy prices is illustrated in Figure 5.3, which presents the cumulative fractions of after tax money income devoted to utilities and other household necessities for households who rely on natural gas as the primary heating fuel. After meeting expenses for these necessities most households still have at least half their after tax incomes unencumbered on average. Households in the lowest income decile, however, are left with only 18 percent of their after-tax income to pay for such "nonessentials" as clothing, medical bills, transportation and all other commodities. Presuming a winter no more severe than that of 1979 (upon which these figures are based),

Table 5.4

DIRECT UTILITY PAYMENTS AS A PERCENT OF DISPOSABLE INCOME AND
DISPOSABLE INCOME PLUS IMPUTED RENT FOR THE ELDERLY POPULATION

Income Decile	Percent Elderly	Utilities Less Subsidy÷ Income Less Income Taxes	Utilities Less Subsidy÷ Disposable Income Plus Imputed Rent
Lowest	28.3	12.1[a]	10.0[b]
Second	17.2	8.3	7.2
Third	12.4	6.4	5.6
Fourth	9.3	5.7	5.3
Fifth	6.4	4.1	3.9
Sixth	5.8	4.1	3.9
Seventh	5.3	3.9	4.1
Eighth	5.1	3.0	3.1
Ninth	5.1	2.8	3.1
Highest	5.1	2.1	2.4
All	100.0	7.3	6.4

[a]As a percent of after-tax income.

[b]As a percent of after-tax income plus imputed rent.

Figure 5.3

FRACTION OF AFTER TAX INCOME DEVOTED TO BASIC NECESSITIES
(Households who pay for gas heat)

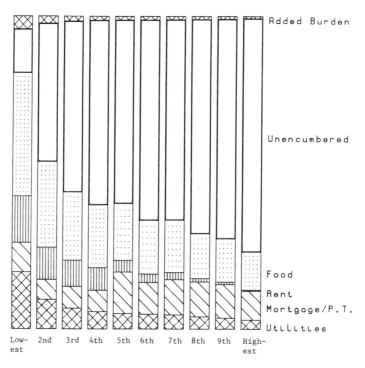

Income Decile

deregulation of natural gas would have the effect of removing
one-third of this surplus for the lowest income households.[7]
For more affluent households, however, the direct impact of
increased gas prices is a trivial fraction of unencumbered after-
tax income.

SUMMARY

This chapter has reviewed the recent legislative history of
natural gas regulation and identified three areas where economic
analysis is needed for more informed policy. These areas are to
provide estimates of the price elasticity of supply, the price
elasticity of demand, and the equity of 'policy-induced increased
burdens on the population. The analysis has concentrated on the
third area--taking advantage of the PSID's rich income data to
estimate the vertical equity of burdens under various definitions
of income.

While the PSID's income data are unquestionably superior to
that of other data bases for this purpose, the quality of the
utility expenditure study was questionable. To validate the data
we used information from the Department of Energy's National
Residential Energy Consumption Surveys to compare with PSID data.
The data from the two surveys are remarkably similar--both in
overall level and in terms of their relation to basic demographic
and income variables. The major differences in the data are the
result of a slightly different period of account and, hence,
slightly different weather conditions, and of the fact that the
PSID does not inpute utility expenditures for households not
paying their utilities directly.

The basic finding of the analysis is that the demand for
natural gas is far less income-elastic than the demand for
gasoline, and, therefore, the impact of policies that result in
increased prices is far more regressive. This regressivity is
substantial, with households in the lowest income decile
expending a fraction of their income three times greater than
those in the upper 10 percent of the income distribution under

---

[7]These figures are based on the assumption of a 50 percent
first year increase in prices and on DOE data indicating that the
fraction of total utilities made up of natural gas payments (for
households using natural gas as the primary heating fuel)
averages 58.5 percent in the Northeast, 52.5 percent in the North
Central, 41.7 percent in the South, and 48.5 percent in the West.

even the most stringent definition of income. We have also seen
that as of 1979 the regressivity of policies resulting in
increased energy prices is not offset either by the progressivity
of the income tax laws or by government subsidies for heating.
It is also not qualitatively altered by computing burdens in
terms of two-year average income and expenditures or by including
imputations for the free rent enjoyed by homeowners in the income
measure.

Finally, we have shown that while the elderly are more
heavily burdened by utility payments and hence will be more
severely affected by policies that increase energy prices, their
higher burdens are due to their lower incomes and to higher
expenditures. Thus, assistance programs based solely on age will
be poorly targeted, as compared to needs-tested assistance
programs.

Although much of this discussion has concentrated on the
problems implied by accelerated decontrol of natural gas prices,
the reader should not infer that decontrol is unnecessary. The
present pricing structure results in large and real losses to our
country. Loury (1981) estimates these efficiency losses at
roughly four and a half billion dollars annually as long as
controls stay in effect. These losses, which amount to more than
$20 per person in the U.S., are "dead weight losses"--meaning
they are losses to both potential consumers and producers.
Current regulation of domestic gas also leads to excessively high
energy imports. Loury estimates the reduction in oil imports
resulting from immediate decontrol of natural gas demand (i.e.,
repealing the FUA) at roughly $41 billion over the next four
years.

All in all, natural gas price decontrol is probably in the
national interest. As Figure 5.3 indicates, there is room in the
budgets of the majority of households to handle the direct
impacts of increased natural gas prices. Furthermore, most
households can still improve the thermal efficiency of their
homes as well as make other adjustments to the increased prices.
Nevertheless, a significant number of households who will be
severely burdened by the increase, and improvements in emergency
energy assistance programs rather than their immediate
elimination may be necessary. Future analysis should concentrate
on identifying program changes that efficiently alleviate excess

burdens while maintaining incentives for conservation. The PSID data are well suited for this analysis.

References

Coe, Richard D. "A Comparison of Utility Payments and Burdens Between 1971 and 1977." In Five Thousand American Families--Patterns of Economic Progress, Vol. VIII, ed. Greg J. Duncan and James N. Morgan. Ann Arbor: Institute for Social Research, 1980.

Duncan, Greg J. "Non-pecuniary Work Rewards." In Five Thousand American Families--Patterns of Economic Progress, Vol. II, ed. James N. Morgan. Ann Arbor: Institute for Social Research, 1974.

Hill, Daniel H. "The Relative Burden of Higher Gasoline Prices." In Five Thousand American Families--Patterns of Economic Progress, Vol. VIII, ed. Greg J. Duncan and James N. Morgan. Ann Arbor: Institute for Social Research, 1980.

Hill, Daniel H., and Hill, Martha S. Consumer Attitudes toward Fuel-Efficient Vehicles. Cambridge, MA: Cambridge Systematics, 1979.

Holmes, John. "The Relative Burden of Higher Gasoline Prices." In Five Thousand American Families--Patterns of Economic Progress, Vol. IV, ed. Greg J. Duncan and James N. Morgan. Ann Arbor: Institute for Social Research, 1976.

Loury, Glen C. "An Analysis of the Efficiency and Inflationary Impact of the Decontrol of Natural Gas Prices." Natural Gas Supply Association, April 1981.

Morgan, James N. "Trends in Driving and Commuting." In Five Thousand American Families--Patterns of Economic Progress, Vol. VI, ed. Greg J. Duncan and James N. Morgan. Ann arbor: Institute for Social Research, 1978.

U.S. Department of Energy. Residential Energy Consumption Survey: 1979-1980 Consumption and Expenditures (Part 1: National Data). DOE/EIA-0262/1. Washington, DC: Energy Information Administration, April 1981.

Appendix A to Chapter 5

GRAPHICAL COMPARISONS OF PSID AND DOE
UTILITY EXPENDITURE ESTIMATES

Figure A5.1

UTILITY EXPENDITURES BY FAMILY SIZE

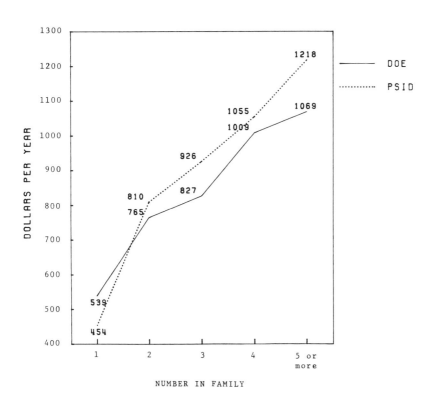

NUMBER IN FAMILY

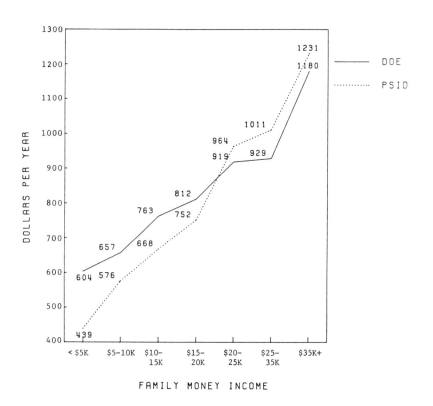

Figure A5.2

UTILITY EXPENDITURES BY INCOME

Figure A5.3

UTILITY EXPENDITURES BY AGE

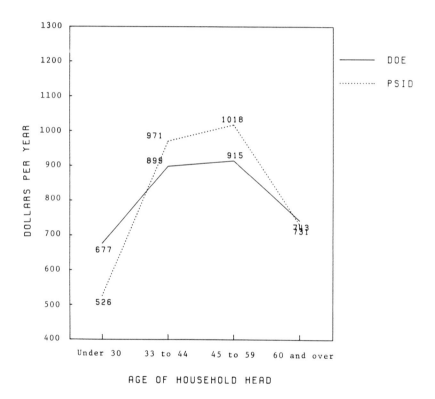

Figure A5.4

UTILITY EXPENDITURES BY NUMBER OF ROOMS

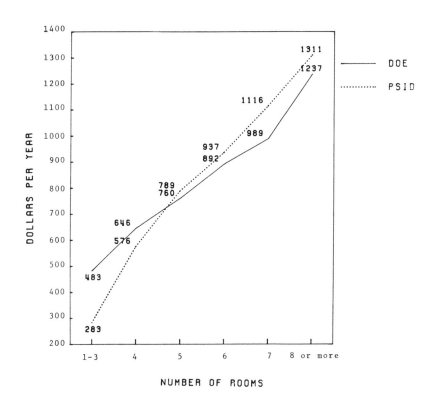

Chapter 6

RACIAL DIFFERENCES IN THE PERSISTENCE OF AFFLUENCE

Linda Datcher

INTRODUCTION

In recent years, many analysts have concluded that racial earnings differentials among men have declined significantly since 1960. For example, according to Freeman (1978), black college men aged 25 to 29 earned 93 percent as much as their white peers in 1975. Such findings are echoed by Smith and Welch (1978), who attribute most of the change to convergence in human capital characteristics rather than a decline in labor market discrimination.

While the general thrust of this view has been widely accepted, critics have questioned whether analyses such as these overstate the degree of similarity between the races. Darity and Myers (1979) have suggested that looking at all men in the young cohorts, both with and without earnings, dramatically alters the picture of narrowing racial differentials in economic status. Lazear (1979) argues that the smaller gap in current earnings for young cohorts is due to a wage measurement problem. Although the observed wages for young blacks and whites are much closer than for older cohorts, total compensation has not converged nearly as much because blacks receive less on-the-job training. Lillard and Willis (1978) have demonstrated that the current black poor are worse off than current white poor because their status is longer lasting.

The purpose of this chapter is to extend the work of Lillard and Willis to examine whether blacks and whites differ in the stability of earnings affluence among men by focusing on the extent to which contemporaneous earnings affluence at a given moment in time is a good measure of permanent affluence. If the ratio of the fraction of earners permanently affluent to the fraction affluent in any given year is smaller for blacks than whites, then cross-section estimates of black/white earnings ratios overstate the degree of similarity between the races. This chapter is divided into three sections. The first outlines the methodology, the second presents the empirical results, and the third summarizes the conclusions.

EMPIRICAL EARNINGS MODEL

The basic model used to distinguish between current and permanent earnings was developed by Hause (1980). In this model, the log of real earnings for the ith worker in year t (Y_{it}) is given by:

(1) $\quad Y_{it} \ = \ X_{it}\beta \ + \ \delta_i \ + \ v_{it} \qquad \delta_i \ = \ \phi_{i1} \ + \ \phi_{i2}t$

where X_{it} is the vector of observed personal characteristics of person i in year t,

ϕ_{i1} and ϕ_{i2} are, respectively, the individual's own intercept and slope parameters,

v_{it} are random errors.

It is assumed that $E(v_{it}|X_{it},Z, \phi_i)=0$, that the ϕ_i is uncorrelated across the sample, and that the error structure takes on the following form:

$\quad v_{it} \ = \ \rho_t v_{it-1} \ + \ \eta_{it} \qquad \eta_{it} \sim N(0,\sigma_{tt})$.

As indicated, first-order autoregressive parameters, ρ_t, and the variances of $\eta_{it}(\sigma_{tt})$ are allowed to take on period-specific values. This model is a very general specification of the determination of earnings and is consistent with a wide variety of theoretical models including human capital theory, institutional models of the labor markets such as Piore and Thurow, and more radical treatments.

The variance of the individual component of earnings, δ_i, equals $\theta_{11} + 2t\theta_{12} + t^2\theta_{22}$, where θ_{11} is the variance of the individual constant, θ_{22} is the variance of the individual slope, and θ_{12} is the covariance of the two. The variance of v_{it} equals

$$\sigma_{tt} + \sum_{k=1}^{t-1} (\prod_{m=1}^{k} \rho_{t-m}^2) \ \sigma_{t-k,t-k} \ .$$

In order to examine whether black and white men differ in the stability of earnings affluence, it is first necessary to distinguish between contemporaneous affluence (i.e., affluence at a given moment in time) and permanent affluence. Contemporaneous affluence can be defined as the expected proportion of a group that is affluent in any given year t. It equals the probability (P_{it}) that a random person in that group has earnings above a given threshold value, $Y*$. Let $\mu_{it} = \delta_{it} + \nu_{it}$, then

$$P_{it} = \text{Prob} \frac{\mu_{it}}{\sigma_{\mu t}} > \frac{Y*-X_{it}\beta}{\sigma_{\mu t}} = 1 - F\left(\frac{Y*-X_{it}\beta}{\sigma_{\mu t}}\right)$$

where $\sigma_{\mu t}$ is the standard deviation of μ_{it}, and F denotes the cumulative standard normal function.

In contrast, permanent affluence can be defined as the proportion of the group, $\hat{P}_{it}$, whose _expected_ or _permanent_ earnings are above the threshold value. For the purposes of this chapter, expected or permanent earnings $(\hat{Y}_{it})$ is defined to be all components of earnings excluding the purely random element, ν_{it} and therefore equals $E(Y_{it})$. Thus, the expected proportion of the group that is permanently affluent is given by:

$$\hat{P}_{it} = \text{Prob}\left(\frac{\delta_i}{\sigma_\delta} > \frac{Y*-X_{it}\beta}{\sigma_\delta}\right) = 1-F\left(\frac{Y*-X_{it}\beta}{\sigma_\delta}\right) \text{ where}$$

σ_δ is the standard deviation of δ.

Another measure of affluence that reflects the stability of the attainment is the expected proportion of the group that is affluent in year t and year τ $(P_{it,\tau})$. This term is given by:

$$P_{it,\tau} = \text{Prob}(Y_{it}>Y^* \text{ and } Y_{i\tau}>Y^*) = 1-G\left(\frac{Y*_t-X_{it}\beta}{\sigma_{\mu t}}, \frac{Y*-X_{i\tau}\beta}{\sigma_{\mu\tau}}, \gamma\right)$$

where G is the cumulative standardized bivariate normal with correlation, γ.

In order to determine whether there are racial differences in the stability of earnings affluence, it is useful to compare $\hat{P}_{it}/P_{it}$ and $P_{it,\tau}/P_{it}$ for blacks to $\hat{P}_{it}/P_{it}$ and $P_{it,\tau}/P_{it}$, respectively, for whites. If the white figures were significantly higher, the results would suggest that the number of permanently affluent relative to contemporaneously affluent is smaller for blacks than for whites. This would imply that black affluence status is a much more fragile phenomenon and that it occurs more frequently because of transitory luck or changes in general economic conditions rather than because of the individual's own enduring circumstances or characteristics.

ESTIMATION AND RESULTS

In order to ascertain the relative sizes of these ratios, earnings functions using the log of annual earnings were estimated with the six years of Panel Study data from 1974 to

1979. The sample was restricted to men ages 25 to 49 in 1974 who worked at least 250 hours each year. In future analysis the parameters β will be estimated by ordinary least squares (OLS) on data pooled over individuals and years, while the variances of δ_i and ν_{it} will be estimated by maximum likelihood from the OLS residuals. Parameter estimates for the residual structure will be reported when (1) no independent variables are used, and (2) education, work experience, occupation, union status, and location variables are included in the regressions. The preliminary results described here are limited to the first analysis. In this work, the impact of features that change little, if any, over time such as education, background, aptitude, and attitudes are captured by ϕ_{i1}. Characteristics such as work experience and on-the-job training, which cause earnings to rise over time, are reflected in ϕ_{i2}.

Parameter estimates of the covariance structure with no explanatory variables included are given in Table 6.1 for hourly earnings and in Table 6.2 for annual earnings. In Table 6.1, the variances of the individual constant are virtually the same across all groups except for blacks with 12 or more years of schooling. Similarly, the variances of the individual slopes are not significantly different except for less educated whites. The covariance of the two items were almost identical across groups and so were constrained to be the same.' The covariance term implies that the level of earnings and the rate of growth are negatively correlated. The autoregression parameters and innovation variances vary considerably across groups within a given year and across years within a given group.² Chi-square tests to determine whether the model could be simplified by across- or within-group constraints indicated that the alternative models could be rejected at a 5 percent level of significance.

The findings for annual earnings in Table 6.2 are similar to the hourly earnings results in that there is a substantial amount

---

'This constraint could not be rejected even at the 10 percent level.

²The only anomalous result was that the original estimate of σ_{66} for whites with less than high school was negative. Imposing the constraint that σ_{66} equal .001 could not be rejected at the 10 percent level because the standard error of the original estimate was quite large.

Table 6.1

ESTIMATED HOURLY EARNINGS COVARIANCE
STRUCTURE BY RACE AND EDUCATION

	Blacks		Whites	
	Less Than 12 Years	12 Years or More	Less Than 12 Years	12 Years or More
Individual constant variance ($\theta_{11} \times 10^{-2}$)	22.048 (2.475)	16.937 (2.099)	23.268 (2.452)	23.000 (1.561)
Individual slope variance ($\theta_{22} \times 10^{-2}$)	.265 (.093)	.234 (.110)	.372 (.055)	.203 (.070)
Covariance ($\theta_{12} \times 10^{-2}$)	-.882 (.239)	-.882 (.239)	-.882 (.239)	-.882 (.239)
Autoregression parameters				
ρ_1	-.101 (.284)	-.106 (.159)	-.322 (.342)	.132 (.077)
ρ_2	.202 (.090)	.255 (.191)	.372 (.077)	.191 (.071)
ρ_3	.123 (.114)	.155 (.084)	.204 (.057)	.277 (.049)
ρ_4	.591 (.126)	.280 (.149)	.046 (.069)	.468 (.064)
ρ_5	.095 (.096)	.138 (.517)	-.696 (.155)	.419 (.059)
Variances of innovations ($\times 10^{-2}$)				
σ_{11}	3.807 (1.244)	6.221 (1.430)	3.587 (1.166)	7.469 (.905)
σ_{22}	7.582 (1.486)	2.788 (1.023)	7.202 (1.661)	5.227 (.547)
σ_{33}	5.634 (.776)	6.819 (.870)	8.446 (.801)	7.167 (.505)
σ_{44}	7.041 (.925)	5.016 (.829)	6.477 (.615)	6.457 (.438)
σ_{55}	11.656 (1.385)	2.432 (.950)	4.311 (.788)	9.285 (.599)
σ_{66}	5.062 (1.479)	4.736 (1.780)	.100 --	7.400 (.620)
N	184	163	232	900

Note: Standard errors are in parentheses.

Table 6.2

ESTIMATED ANNUAL EARNINGS COVARIANCE
STRUCTURE BY RACE AND EDUCATION

	Blacks		Whites	
	Less Than 12 Years	12 Years or More	Less Than 12 Years	12 Years or More
Individual constant variance ($\theta_{11} \times 10^{-2}$)	23.706 (3.706)	17.427 (4.252)	19.366 (4.629)	25.690 (2.290)
Individual slope variance ($\theta_{22} \times 10^{-2}$)	.034 (.152)	.294 (.258)	.342 (.125)	.219 (.094)
Covariance ($\theta_{12} \times 10^{-2}$)	.118 (.620)	-1.131 (.829)	.061 (.712)	-.967 (.387)
Autoregression parameters				
ρ_1	.599 (.108)	.119 (.226)	.176 (.214)	.413 (.070)
ρ_2	-.034 (.081)	.840 (.193)	.364 (.074)	.272 (.054)
ρ_3	-.317 (.417)	.045 (.077)	.511 (.065)	.304 (.042)
ρ_4	.491 (.154)	.213 (.569)	.283 (.078)	.416 (.076)
ρ_5	.389 (.075)	1.236 (.118)	-.131 (.091)	.388 (.086)
Variances of innovations ($\times 10^{-2}$)				
σ_{11}	6.713 (1.630)	7.210 (2.410)	8.984 (2.908)	8.124 (19311
σ_{22}	6.489 (.737)	7.935 (1.542)	12.814 (1.726)	7.237 (.460)
σ_{33}	2.671 (1.101)	9.151 (1.049)	10.689 (1.032)	8.641 (.553)
σ_{44}	6.089 (1.628)	3.758 (2.100)	10.395 (.993)	5.262 (.398)
σ_{55}	17.890 (1.981)	5.330 (2.414)	9.100 (1.299)	6.886 (.594)
σ_{66}	11.474 (1.547)	6.910 (.786)	.100 --	6.295 (.686)
N	184	163	232	900

Note: Standard errors are in parentheses.

of within- and across-group variation in the autoregression parameters and innovation variances. Again, chi-square tests of imposing constraints were rejected at the 5 percent level. There are, however, noticeable differences in the patterns of the variances and covariance of the individual slopes and constants for annual earnings compared to hourly earnings. Table 6.2 shows that there is no significant difference among blacks in the growth of annual earnings over time and, correspondingly, that there is no systematic relationship between the level of earnings and the rate of growth. While the variance in the individual slopes for whites with less than high school is significantly different from zero, the rate of growth of earnings again does not depend on the initial level. Only in the case of more educated whites is the hourly earnings pattern of significant variance in individual constants and individual slopes, along with a large negative covariance between the two, repeated.

Table 6.3 reports the sample variance in earnings ($\sigma^2_{\mu t}$) and estimated values of the permanent component of the variance in earnings ($\hat{\sigma}^2_{\delta}$) using the figures from Tables 6.1 and 6.2. While $\hat{\sigma}^2_{\delta}$ and $\sigma^2_{\mu t}$ for blacks with at least 12 years of schooling are uniformly smaller than that of their white peers, this is true only in the case of hourly earnings for blacks with less schooling. The annual earnings figures vary across years.

Tables 6.4 and 6.5 list the findings concerning differences in the persistence of affluence. The first two columns for each education group in Table 6.4 show the estimated proportion of the population with current earnings above the threshold levels in 1976 and 1978. The next two columns list the estimated proportion of the population with expected or permanent earnings above the threshold level, while the last two columns show the ratio of the expected proportion to the current proportion. As indicated earlier, a higher ratio for whites would imply that white affluence is more stable than black affluence.

Looking at the annual earnings figures shows that over 80 percent of all more educated whites affluent in any given year were permanently affluent. In contrast, at most two-thirds of blacks affluent in any given year achieved that status. The annual earnings gap was smaller for the more educated group in 1978 than in 1976. This change results primarily from a drop in the variance of the log of current black earnings from .228 to

Table 6.3

SAMPLE VARIANCE IN EARNINGS (σ_μ^2) AND ESTIMATED PERMANENT COMPONENT OF VARIANCE IN EARNINGS $(\hat{\sigma}_\delta^2)$

| | Blacks | | | | Whites | | | |
| | Less Than 12 Years | | 12 Years or More | | Less Than 12 Years | | 12 Years or More | |
	$\sigma_{\mu t}^2$	$\hat{\sigma}_\delta^2$	$\sigma_{\mu t}^2$	$\hat{\sigma}_\delta^2$	$\sigma_{\mu t}^2$	$\hat{\sigma}_\delta^2$	$\sigma_{\mu t}^2$	$\hat{\sigma}_\delta^2$
Hourly Earnings								
1974	.233	.206	.225	.154	.262	.219	.283	.214
1975	.300	.196	.168	.143	.263	.212	.258	.203
1976	.252	.191	.228	.138	.300	.213	.278	.195
1977	.264	.192	.172	.136	.296	.222	.268	.192
1978	.353	.199	.161	.140	.298	.237	.291	.193
1979	.257	.210	.204	.148	.274	.261	.285	.197
Annual Earnings								
1974	.310	.242	.238	.154	.294	.198	.320	.240
1975	.375	.245	.203	.141	.311	.210	.310	.227
1976	.267	.249	.266	.133	.359	.228	.316	.219
1977	.323	.254	.162	.131	.410	.253	.280	.215
1978	.482	.260	.199	.135	.412	.285	.283	.125
1979	.402	.266	.305	.144	.324	.324	.296	.220

Table 6.4

ESTIMATED PROBABILITIES ABOVE SELECTED THRESHOLD VALUES BY RACE AND EDUCATION

	Years of Schooling: 1-11						Years of Schooling: 12 or More					
	Actual Earnings Proportion of Population		Expected Earnings Proportion of Population		Expected Proportion/ Actual Proportion		Current Earnings Proportion of Population		Expected Earnings Proportion of Population		Expected Proportion/ Current Proportion	
	Black	White	Black	White	Black	White	Black	White	Black	White	Black	White
1978 real annual earnings greater than												
$29,000	9.0	16.2	3.4	11.8	.38	.73	9.9	26.0	5.9	23.0	.60	.89
$28,000	9.9	17.6	4.0	13.2	.40	.75	11.3	28.2	7.1	25.4	.63	.90
$27,000	10.8	19.1	4.6	14.7	.43	.77	13.0	30.6	8.5	28.0	.66	.92
$26,000	11.9	20.8	5.4	16.4	.45	.79	14.8	33.1	10.3	30.8	.69	.93
$25,000	13.0	22.6	6.3	18.3	.48	.81	17.0	35.8	12.3	33.8	.73	.94
1976 real annual earnings greater than												
$29,000	7.4	13.2	3.8	8.1	.52	.61	11.7	23.7	4.6	19.4	.39	.82
$28,000	8.3	14.5	4.5	9.2	.54	.64	13.0	25.7	5.6	21.6	.43	.84
$27,000	9.2	15.9	5.2	10.5	.56	.66	14.6	27.8	6.8	23.9	.47	.86
$26,000	10.3	17.5	6.0	12.1	.59	.69	16.3	30.1	8.3	26.5	.51	.88
$25,000	11.5	19.3	7.0	13.8	.61	.76	18.3	32.5	10.1	29.3	.55	.90
1978 real hourly wages greater than												
$14.00	6.8	11.0	2.3	8.5	.34	.77	6.5	21.5	5.2	16.6	.80	.77
$13.50	7.6	12.3	2.8	9.7	.37	.79	7.8	23.6	6.4	18.8	.82	.80
$13.00	8.5	13.8	3.4	11.1	.40	.80	9.2	25.8	7.7	21.2	.84	.82
$12.50	9.6	15.4	4.1	12.7	.43	.82	10.9	28.2	9.4	23.9	.86	.85
$12.00	10.8	17.3	5.0	14.5	.46	.84	13.0	30.8	11.3	26.9	.87	.87
1976 real hourly wages greater than												
$14.00	3.2	10.3	1.7	6.6	.53	.65	9.5	19.2	4.6	15.0	.48	.78
$13.50	3.8	11.5	2.1	7.7	.55	.67	10.8	21.2	5.6	17.0	.52	.80
$13.00	4.5	12.9	2.6	9.0	.58	.69	12.4	23.2	6.8	19.3	.55	.83
$12.50	5.3	14.5	3.2	10.4	.60	.72	14.1	25.6	8.3	21.8	.59	.85
$12.00	6.2	16.2	3.9	12.1	.63	.75	16.1	28.2	10.2	24.6	.63	.87

Table 6.5

ESTIMATED PROBABILITIES OF TWO-YEAR SEQUENCES ABOVE SELECTED THRESHOLD VALUES BY RACE AND EDUCATION

| | Years of Schooling: 1-11 | | | | | | Years of Schooling: 12 or More | | | | | |
| | Proportion of Population | | 1978, 1976 Proportion/ 1976 Proportion | | 1978, 1976 Proportion/ 1978 Proportion | | Proportion of Population | | 1978, 1976 Proportion/ 1976 Proportion | | 1978, 1976 Proportion/ 1978 Proportion | |
	Black	White	Black	White	Black	White	Black	White	Black	White	Black	White
1978 and 1976 real hourly wages greater than												
$14.00	1.7	5.3	.53	.51	.25	.48	3.6	11.4	.38	.59	.55	.53
$13.50	2.0	6.1	.53	.53	.26	.50	4.4	12.8	.41	.60	.56	.54
$13.00	2.4	7.0	.53	.54	.28	.51	5.3	14.5	.43	.63	.58	.56
$12.50	2.9	8.1	.53	.56	.30	.53	6.4	16.3	.45	.64	.59	.58
$12.00	3.5	9.3	.56	.57	.32	.54	7.7	18.4	.48	.65	.59	.60
1978 and 1976 real annual earnings greater than												
$29,000	2.9	8.1	.39	.61	.32	.50	4.1	14.6	.35	.62	.41	.56
$28,000	3.4	9.1	.41	.63	.34	.52	5.0	16.1	.38	.63	.41	.57
$27,000	3.8	10.1	.41	.64	.35	.53	5.8	17.8	.40	.64	.45	.58
$26,000	4.4	11.3	.43	.65	.37	.54	6.8	19.7	.42	.65	.46	.60
$25,000	5.0	12.6	.43	.65	.38	.56	8.1	21.8	.41	.67	.48	.61

.161. Therefore, even though mean earnings rose, the fractions with current earnings above the threshold levels declined.

The annual earnings gap for the less educated group was higher in 1978 than in 1976. Although there was little change in the proportions of blacks with expected earnings above the threshold levels, the current earnings proportions grew by about 20 percent. This suggests that a number of black men experienced a relatively good earnings year in 1978 but that this change did not continue permanently. In 1978, about three-fourths of white men who were affluent in any given year were permanently affluent. Less than half of blacks affluent in any given year were as stable.

The hourly earnings figures in Table 6.4 are qualitatively similar to annual earnings ratios. However, the differences between blacks and whites are typically smaller. For example, in 1978 there is little difference in the stability of blacks and whites with at least 12 years of schooling. Such comparisons between the hourly and annual earnings ratios suggest that racial differences in the stability of hours worked explains at least part of the observed disparity in annual earnings.

The first two columns for each education group in Table 6.5 show the proportion of the population with earnings above the threshold levels in both 1978 and 1976. The third and fourth columns divide this proportion by the fraction affluent in 1976, and the fifth and sixth columns divide by the fraction affluent in 1978. It again shows that, in the case of annual earnings, affluence is a much more stable phenomenon for whites than for blacks. For example, about two-thirds of whites affluent in 1976 were also affluent in 1978, while only about 40 percent of blacks were as successful. As in the case of Table 6.4, the hourly earnings figures are much closer than the annual earnings estimates. They show that, at best, blacks are comparable to whites, and in many circumstances, are much less well off.

CONCLUSION

While blacks have made indisputable gains in economic status in recent years, many analysts have cautioned against overstating the degree of progress. The preliminary results of this analysis suggest that cross-section comparisons of black and white affluence may result in an overly favorable picture of black gains because affluence is a much less stable phenomenon for blacks than whites.

References

Darity, William A., and Myers, Samuel L. "Changes in Black-White Income Inequality, 1968-1978." Paper presented at the American Economics Association meetings in Atlanta, Georgia, December 1979.

Freeman, Richard. "Black Economic Progress Since 1964." Public Interest (1978): 52-68.

Hause, John C. "The Fine Structure of Earnings and the On-the-Job Training Hypothesis." Econometrica (May 1980): 1013-29.

Lazear, Edward. "The Narrowing of Black-White Wage Differentials Is Illusory." American Economic Review (1979): 553-64.

Lillard, Lee A., and Willis, Robert J. "Dynamic Aspects of Earnings Mobility." Econometrica (September 1978): 985-1012.

Smith, James P., and Welch, Finis. "Race Differences in Earnings: A Survey and New Evidence." Rand Corporation Report No. R-2295-NSF. Santa Monica, CA: Rand Corporation, 1978.

Chapter 7

DISENTANGLING THE EFFICACY-EARNINGS RELATIONSHIP AMONG WHITE MEN

Greg J. Duncan and Jeffrey Liker

INTRODUCTION

That successful people have more "positive" attitudes is confirmed by both casual observation and numerous scholarly studies. Much of the formal work has been conducted with data from cross-sectional studies that gather information on a population at a point in time. It is exceedingly difficult to disentangle cause and effect from such cross-sectional information--did the attitudes cause the success or did the success cause the positive attitudes?[1] The availability of several large scale longitudinal data sets adds greatly to one's ability to sort out the patterns of causation. Andrisani (1977, 1978) provides good examples of this by using the National Longitudinal Studies (NLS) of young men and older men to test models in which feelings of personal control observed at an initial point in time are related to subsequent changes in labor market status.

A complete understanding of the relationships between attitudes and economic status requires modelling both the effects of attitudes on economic status and the effects of level of and changes in status on attitudes.[2] In this chapter, we propose a set of such models and estimate them with data from the Panel Study on Income Dynamics (PSID) on white men, aged 25-54, who were continuous labor force participants. We pay particular attention to the interpretation of two-wave panel models and to the restrictions needed to identify such models. We find weak support for the causal link between initial feelings of personal control (efficacy) and subsequent changes in economic status but

---

[1] A third possibility is that some other factor caused both the attitudes and the success.

[2] Andrisani (1978) also estimates models of attitude change. Data limitations forced him to estimate them only for the older men in the NLS.

218

substantial support for the reverse path running from level and changes in economic status to changes in feelings of control. The results are sensitive to the length of time over which the changes may occur, to the measure of economic status, and to the treatment of a handful of cases with extremely large changes in earnings.

THE NATURE OF EARNINGS-EFFICACY RELATIONSHIP

As Andrisani (1977) notes, there are several reasons to expect that those who feel that their personal actions are effective will be more likely to take positive actions and improve their subsequent economic status. Theories of achievement motivation suggest that people will be motivated if two conditions hold (Gurin and Gurin, 1970; Parsons and Goff, 1980). First, they must value advancement or the rewards associated with advancement. Second, they must believe that their personal initiative will help them advance. Their expectancy of success in achieving work-related goals depends on their perceptions of their own general effectiveness in performing (efficacy), as well as perceptions of whether or not there are opportunities for advancement.[3]

To be sure, the ability to translate personal initiative into higher earnings may be constrained by existing opportunities. Higher paying jobs may simply not be available, supervisors may not recognize or reward personal initiative with higher pay, or there may be few opportunities for working extra hours. Hence, disadvantaged groups with fewer opportunities for advancement or persons otherwise constrained by their jobs or the

---

[3]Gurin et al. (1970), using factor analysis, show empirically that the concept of "personal control" is distinct from the concept of "control ideology." The former refers to beliefs about one's own ability to control life outcomes while the latter refers to beliefs about how society operates. As Andrisani (1977) notes, we would expect feelings of personal control to be more sensitive to and predictive of changes in earnings, and indeed Andrisani (1977) finds support for this view using the NLS data. For a discussion of the comparability of the PSID and NLS measures, see Duncan and Morgan (1981) and Andrisani (1981). In personal communication subsequent to this interchange, Gerald Gurin indicated that conceptual differences between personal control items such as used by Andrisani and efficacy items in the PSID are trivial and empirical differences between them are small, particularly in comparison to the inter-item reliabilities within each measure.

labor market in which they work are less likely than the advantaged or unconstrained to find outlets for translating feelings of efficacy into higher earnings. Moreover, to the extent that they perceive that few opportunities exist, there will be less incentive for them to show initiative (Gurin and Gurin, 1970). Note that the same arguments can be made to explain the ways in which a low sense of personal efficacy can lead to demotions and/or reduced earnings.

In this view, then, a greater sense of personal efficacy can be expected to lead to greater subsequent economic success. It is tempting to conceive of efficacy as a form of human capital. Several aspects of this analogy should be noted. First is the substantive question, as yet unanswered, of whether higher levels of efficacy can be acquired systematically and at some cost. A second set of considerations is statistical, and rests on the assertion that the primary effect of higher levels of efficacy is to produce larger subsequent _increases_ in earnings. In a typical cross-sectional human capital earnings equation, the natural logarithm of earnings is taken to be a function of such human capital measures as years of education and work experience. It is easily shown that unchanging measures such as education with similar wage effects at two points in time do not appear in a wage change equation.' To the extent that education does affect earnings change, it is thought to operate indirectly by facilitating on-the-job training. Although the level of efficacy may well affect the level of earnings, psychological theory of

---

'Suppose that X has the following effects on log earnings at times t=1 and t=2:

$$\ln Y_{1i} = A_1 + B_1 X_{1i} + \varepsilon_{1i} \text{ and}$$

$$\ln Y_{2i} = A_2 + B_2 X_{2i} + \varepsilon_{2i}$$

where $\ln Y_{ti}$ is the natural logarithm of the ith individual's earnings at time t and X_{ti} is the ith individual's level of X at time t. Suppressing the subscript i, the earnings change equation can be written as follows:

$$\ln Y_2 - \ln Y_1 = (A_2 - A_1) + (B_2 - B_1) X_1 + B_2 (X_2 - X_1) + (\varepsilon_2 - \varepsilon_1)$$

If neither the level of X nor its effects on ln Y changes between the two points in time, then the variable X does not enter into the change equation. Clearly, efficacy is not an X variable of this type, although more conventional human capital variables may not be either. Many of the empirical estimates of wage change models (e.g., Andrisani, 1978; Lazear, 1976, and this chapter) find that the level of education has a positive and significant effect on wage change.

expectancy leads us to expect that the level of efficacy affects earnings change as well and, implicitly, that the earnings advantage enjoyed by those with higher levels of efficacy increases over time. This assertion is stronger than the ones typically made for stocks of human capital.

On the other side of the causal picture, there are as many reasons to expect that level and change in economic status may produce concurrent and subsequent change in sense of efficacy. Research on the psychological consequences of "stressful life events" (Dohrenwend and Dohrenwend, 1974) has shown that many clinical symptoms previously assumed to be an outgrowth of early childhood experiences can be caused by current situational changes such as divorce, job loss, or an unexpected residential move. One explanation for the detrimental consequences of undesirable life changes is that these experiences challenge the individual's sense of being able to control life outcomes (Pearlin et al., 1981; Antonovsky, 1979).

There are a number of ways in which changes in economic status can influence personal efficacy. First, changing economic status can operate indirectly through changing life circumstances. For example, a fall in earnings can create tensions in family relationships (Straus et al., 1980) which, in turn, reduce feelings of efficacy. Second, changing economic circumstances are events in their own right. For example, a raise may provide a breadwinner with an enhanced sense that he or she can perform well on the job and hence continue to experience success, while a reduction in earnings might be interpreted as personal failure. Note that the influence of experiences on efficacy will depend upon a person's cognitive appraisal of those experiences. Cohn (1978) finds that persons who believe that the opportunity structure is responsible for their job loss are less likely to feel personally ineffective than those who feel personally responsible.

Thus far, we have been discussing how <u>changes</u> in economic circumstances can produce changes in efficacy. Enduring economic advantages and disadvantages can influence personal efficacy in much the same way (Pearlin et al., 1981). Persons with relatively low earnings are generally more susceptible to adverse life experiences and may lack the assets to adapt effectively to them. To the extent that lower income persons blame their inability to compete effectively in the labor market on personal inadequacies, the problems they face because of their low income will diminish feelings of mastery. Similarly, higher income persons who attribute their achievement to personal prowess will feel a reinforced sense of efficacy at their success in dealing with daily economic challenges.

We have identified a number of ways in which the level of and changes in economic resources could influence efficacy. These effects depend on cognitive appraisals; events will have their greatest effects when they are thought to reflect personal competency and achievement (Bem, 1967). As a result, personal' earnings for which the individual can take credit may be more important to efficacy than other family income, even though in a practical sense $100 is $100 no matter how acquired. For male household heads, we would expect personal earnings to be particularly important for personal efficacy since it is traditionally their role to provide economically for their families (Cohn, 1978; Elder,1974).

A MODEL RELATING EARNINGS AND EFFICACY

The model suggested by the discussion above suggests two patterns of possible causation between efficacy and earnings. First, that initial level of efficacy may affect subsequent change in earnings and second, that both prior level and concurrent change in earnings may produce a change in efficacy. This recursive model, depicted in Figure 7.1, is just identified.

It is important to note that we ruled out one key causal path a priori. We assume that efficacy changes do not influence concurrent earnings changes. As discussed above, personal initiative must be recognized by firms, and opportunities must be available before initiative can lead to earnings changes. This can take years, particularly if the pathway from efficacy to increased earnings involves completion of a training or educational program.[5] On the other hand, it is possible that

---

[5] That personality traits take time to effect work outcomes is demonstrated in the work of Kohn and Schooler (1978). They find that intellectual flexibility is translated into a shift to more complex jobs over a 10-year period, while there is no concurrent effect of intellectual flexibility on job complexity. By contrast, changes in job complexity are found to influence concurrent changes in intellectual flexibility.

Figure 7.1

A MODEL OF THE RELATIONSHIP BETWEEN EFFICACY AND EARNINGS

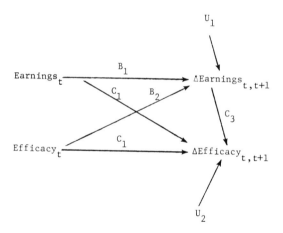

changes in monthly or annual earnings may be more immediate than changes in hourly earnings if workers are in a position to adjust their labor supply with overtime or extra jobs. Consistent with the assumption that changes take time is evidence that longer-term (four-year) changes in earnings are more sensitive to efficacy levels than changes from one year to the next (Duncan and Morgan, 1981). To test for the sensitivity of the earnings-efficacy relationship to the time period over which the change in each factor is observed, we looked at both two-year and four-year changes.

In addition to these causal paths, we include direct paths from initial level of efficacy to subsequent efficacy change and from initial level of earnings to subsequent earnings change (see Appendix A for a discussion of how this model, which focuses on change scores as dependent variables controlling for initial level, compares to models which predict subsequent level with initial level). Negative associations between initial level and changes in both measures were found to be quite strong in the empirical work of Andrisani (1978).[*]

With the addition of background control variables, the model in Figure 7.1 can be represented in equation form as:

(1) $\Delta Earnings_{t,t+1} = B_0 + B_1\,Earnings_t + B_2\,Efficacy_t$
$+ B_3\,Human\,Capital + U_1$

(2) $\Delta Efficacy_{t,t+1} = C_0 + C_1\,Efficacy_t + C_2\,Earnings_t$
$+ C_3\,\Delta Earnings_{t,t+1} + C_4\,Other$
$Resources_t + U_2,$

where B_3 is a vector of parameters representing the effects of various human capital measures on earnings change (i.e., cognitive ability, education, work experience, and physical health), and C_4 is a vector of parameters representing the effects of resources other than earnings which may have a bearing on personal efficacy (i.e., cognitive ability, education, age, physical health, nonlabor income, and family needs).

We begin with the assumption that efficacy is measured perfectly and there are no correlated measurement errors over

---

[*]Further work has convinced us that the inclusion of initial level in a change equation is rarely justified on statistical grounds but may be justified by theory. Our inclusion of it here probably leads to an <u>overstatement</u> of one earnings change effect of efficacy. See Augustyniak, Duncan, and Liker (forthcoming).

time. We then relax this assumption and estimate models allowing for correlated errors using techniques for the analysis of covariance structures (Joreskog and Sorbom, 1979).

A final variant of these models includes other life events, such as divorce and involuntary residential moves, which may be related to earnings changes. These life events may help to explain how earnings are translated into efficacy or, alternatively, may reveal that an apparent earnings effect is spurious. For example, a reduction in earnings may be created by a job loss and thus loss of work rather than the earnings change per se may be the true cause of reduced efficacy. Loss of a job means more than a loss of income; work provides extra-economic benefits such as social status and an interpersonal context (Kasl, 1979).[7]

In sum, we estimate panel models using annual and hourly earnings over two-year and four-year periods for white male household heads. We then examine the sensitivity of these models to the inclusion of life events related to earnings and assumptions about measurement error in efficacy and earnings.

DATA

The sample is restricted to white, male heads of households between the ages of 25 and 54 in 1969, who worked at least 500 hours in each of the years between 1969 and 1975 and who were respondents in each of the 1969-1972 and 1975 interviewing waves.[8] The lower age restriction was placed to avoid sample selection problems stemming from the fact that most men do not become heads of their own households until their early twenties. The upper age restriction was placed to avoid confounding the analysis with retirement decisions.[9] Taken together, the

---

[7]Similarly, job loss generally produces a drop in income, a point which is not taken into account in the models of Kasl (1979) and Cohn (1978), who are interested in the noneconomic effects of job loss.

[8]Each year a number of interviews were taken with the spouses of household heads if the head was unwilling to respond himself. The restrictions apply to the years in which the attitudinal information was asked.

[9]The hours restriction eliminated less than 10 percent of otherwise eligible white male household heads and was used because wage rate information calculated from annual earnings and hours appears to become relatively unreliable when work hours fall short of the 500 hour mark (Morgan, 1981).

restrictions left us with a fairly homogeneous sample of white, male, prime age, continuous labor force participants. Thus the results should not be taken as indicative of what would be found for youth, older men, or minorities, or in any way as a test of the culture of poverty hypothesis regarding attitudes and economic status.

The variables used in this analysis along with their mean values and standard deviations are listed in Table 7.1. Two time periods were chosen: the two-year span from 1971 to 1972 and the four years from 1972 to 1975. The measures of level and change in efficacy are constructed from three separate items: whether the respondent usually thinks that his life is working out the way he wants it to, whether the respondent usually carries out plans the way he had expected, and whether the respondent usually finishes things once he has started them. Exploratory factor analyses of many PSID attitudinal items by Dickinson (1972) show that these three items loaded on a single "efficacy" factor. Confirmatory factor analyses (described below) also suggest that these items share a common underlying factor. Responses to these questions were originally coded on a five-point scale but have been collapsed in this analysis to three points: 0, .5, 1, with very few respondents receiving the middle value. These items were then summed to form indices of efficacy ranging from 0 to 3. Identical questions were asked in each of the three years. Missing observations were slightly more prevalent in 1971 than in either 1972 or 1975, producing the smaller sample size for the two-year analysis. The case counts are not identical for the two four-year analyses since missing data cases on the 1975 efficacy measure had to be eliminated from the analysis of efficacy change but could be retained in the analysis of earnings change.

Two earnings measures were used in the analysis--the respondent's total labor income from all jobs (Annual Earnings) and that income divided by annual hours worked on all jobs (Hourly Earnings). Cases in which hourly earnings were less than $.50 per hour were set equal to $.50 and cases with earnings greater than $25 per hour were set equal to $25 per hour. Cases in which reported annual earnings were less than $500 were set equal to $500. All earnings measures have been transformed into natural logarithmic units. Two-year change was defined as the difference in the natural logarithm of the earnings levels at the

Table 7.1

MEANS AND STANDARD DEVIATIONS OF VARIABLES USED IN ANALYSIS

	Two Year Change Analysis t_1=1971 t_2=1972	Four Year Change Analysis t_1=1972 t_2=1975	
		Earnings Change	Efficacy Change
Level of efficacy in t_1	2.39 (0.82)	2.37 (0.83)	2.38 (0.82)
Change in efficacy (t_2-t_1)	-0.01 (0.77)	-- --	0.08 (0.79)
Level of ln annual earnings in t_1	9.09 (0.51)	9.14 (0.52)	9.15 (0.51)
Change in ln annual earnings (t_2-t_1)	0.06 (0.25)	-- --	-- --
Trend in ln annual earnings from t_1 to t_2	-- --	-.026 (.127)	-.028 (.124)
Level of ln hourly earnings in t_1	1.39 (0.49)	1.43 (0.51)	1.44 (0.50)
Change in ln hourly earnings (t_2-t_1)	0.05 (0.26)	-- --	-- --
Trend in hourly earnings from t_1 to t_2	-- --	-.007 (.110)	-.009 (.108)
Years of education	12.48 (3.25)	12.48 (3.22)	12.49 (3.20)
Test score	10.18 (1.88)	10.16 (1.90)	10.17 (1.89)
Years of work experience	18.98 (8.70)	19.12 (8.66)	-- --
Health limitation in t_1	0.08 (0.28)	0.07 (0.25)	0.07 (0.25)
Age	38.43 (8.30)	-- --	38.53 (8.27)
Level of ln family needs in t_1	8.30 (0.31)	-- --	-- --
Level of ln nonlabor income in t_1	6.86 (2.30)	-- --	-- --
Efficacy in t_1 times years of work experience	44.98 (26.70)	44.64 (26.13)	-- --
Unemployment in t_1 (hundreds of hours)	0.37 (1.60)	-- --	-- --
Change in unemployment (t_2-t_1) hundreds of hours	-0.16 (1.79)	-- --	-- --

Table 7.1 (continued)

	Two Year Change Analysis t_1=1971 t_2=1972	Four Year Change Analysis t_1=1972 t_2=1975	
		Earnings Change	Efficacy Change
Change in ln family needs (t_2-t_1)	0.00 (0.12)	-- --	-- --
Changes in ln nonlabor income t_2-t_1	-0.01 (1.69)	-- --	-- --
Evicted between t_1 and t_2	0.02 (0.14)	-- --	-- --
Moved for job reason between t_1 and t_2	0.04 (0.19)	-- --	-- --
Divorced between t_1 and t_2	0.01 (0.11)	-- --	-- --
Change in work hours between t_1 and t_2	0.01 (0.22)	-- --	-- --
Number of observations	696	739	715

Note: Standard deviations are in parentheses.
Source: Panel Study of Income Dynamics

two points. Four-year trends in earnings were defined as the
slope of a bivariate regression of the natural logarithm of each
respondent's earnings on time.[10] Six cases in which the
differences in log hourly or annual earnings were greater than
1.5 or less than -1.5 were eliminated from the analysis.[11]
Background measures include respondent's reported years of
education, age, a score from a 13-question sentence completion
test designed to measure cognitive ability,[12] years of work
experience (computed as current age minus either 18 or years of
formal education plus five, whichever is larger), whether the
respondent reported any condition that limited the amount or type
of work he could do, the natural logarithm of nonlabor family
income, and the natural logarithm of an Orshansky-type standard
of family needs based on its size and composition. The mean
values shown in Table 7.1 for the basic demographic variables
confirm the representativeness of this group of prime-aged white
household heads.

Several event measures were constructed from the data. For
the two-year change models, we have measures of hours spent
unemployed, the change in those reported unemployment hours
between the two years, changes in the natural logarithm of both
family needs and nonlabor income, whether the respondent reported
an involuntary residential move between the two years, whether
the respondent reported a voluntary move for job-related reasons,
whether the respondent was divorced between the two years, and
change in reported work hours between the two years. Similar
measures were constructed for the four-year period between 1972
and 1975, but since the regression results for the effects of
events on four-year changes in efficacy are only summarized in
this chapter, none of the four-year event measures appears on
Table 7.1.

---

[10]The earnings measures are flows for the entire calendar
year while the efficacy reports come from the time of the
interview (usually between the months of April and June of that
same year). This raises the possibility of mismatches between
the timing of change in the two sets of variables, but our
treatment seemed to be the most reasonable.

[11]As reported below, results were somewhat sensitive to this
latter sample restriction.

[12]Veroff and McClelland (1971) document the development of
this measure.

EFFECTS OF EFFICACY ON EARNINGS CHANGE

Results from the ordinary least squares (OLS) estimation of
the earnings change models are presented in Table 7.2. The
models are estimated over both two- and four-year time periods
and separately for the annual and hourly earnings measures. The
results indicate little support for the hypothesis that initial
efficacy affects subsequent change in economic status. When
efficacy is entered additively with the rest of the variables in
the model (columns 1, 3, 5, and 7), none of the estimated
coefficients on efficacy approaches conventional levels of
statistical significance.[13]

These results are at odds with findings of significant
positive effects by Andrisani (1977) using NLS data and are
somewhat at odds with the replication of Andrisani's work by
Duncan and Morgan (1981) using Panel Study information. One
reason for the difference may be our treatment of extreme cases.
Six observations had two-year earnings changes that fell outside
the interval from -1.5 to +1.5. They have been excluded from the
regression results reported in Table 7.2, although regressions in
which these extreme cases were recoded to more modest levels
(e.g., $\pm$ .75) produced results similar to those shown in Table
7.2. When the equation presented in column (1) was reestimated
with these outliers included but not recoded, the efficacy
coefficient rose to .026 with a standard error of .014. None of
the other coefficients changed appreciably. Although the
earnings changes for these outliers may have been measured
accurately, we chose not to have the substantive conclusions of
the effects of efficacy on earnings change rest on six
observations. There were no such outliers in the analysis of
four-year change. Another possible reason for the difference is
that there is little overlap between the age ranges used in the
previous work and the range selected for this analysis.
Andrisani's estimates were for 16-26 year olds and 48-62 year
olds in the first year of his analysis. The Duncan and Morgan

---

[13]The "conventional" levels of statistical significance
denoted in Table 7.2 use critical t-values for two-tailed tests
at the 1, 5, and 10 percent probability levels assuming simple
random sampling. Use of a one-tailed test would make these t-
values conservative. The clustered nature of the PSID sample
raise these critical t-values, making these tests
nonconservative. See Hill (1981).

replication selected Panel Study household heads aged 18-24. The current analysis is limited to household heads in the age range between 25 and 54 in the first year of the analysis (1969).

There is some indication in Andrisani's work that the effect of initial efficacy on earnings depended on age. He found that efficacy had a significant impact on change in hourly earnings for young but not older men and a significant effect on changes in annual earnings for the older men but not the younger ones. We tested for the possibility that the effects of efficacy on earnings change depended upon the experience of the worker by entering a multiplicative interaction term between level of initial efficacy and years of work experience. The results, shown in the even numbered columns of Table 7.2, provide some support for the contention that efficacy effects are stronger for older workers. The coefficient on the interaction term is positive in all cases but statistically significant in only two—for two-year change in annual earnings and for four-year trends in hourly earnings. That higher efficacy should add more to the annual earnings of experienced versus inexperienced workers is plausible, since the former are in a better position to control the number of hours they work, especially overtime hours. Why the longer-term trend in hourly earnings is more responsive to the level of efficacy of older workers is less clear and runs contrary to Andrisani's findings. The significance of the interaction terms for annual earnings provides a partial reconciliation with Andrisani's results for older workers.

Among the control variables entered into these earnings changes equations, only education had consistently significant effects. Additional years of education were associated with between .5 and 1 percent higher growth rates, controlling for initial level of earnings. The test score measure had significant effects on two-year hourly earnings change, and the experience variable was significant only when the experience-efficacy interaction variable was added in.

EFFECTS OF EARNINGS ON EFFICACY CHANGE

Social-psychological theories discussed above suggest a role for both prior level and concurrent change in economic status in producing changes in efficacy. The level of economic status as a measure of resources is presumably associated with a host of both

Table 7.2

ESTIMATES FROM ALTERNATIVE MODELS OF EARNINGS CHANGE

	One Year Change t_1=1971 t_2=1972				Four Year Change t_1=1972 t_2=1975			
	Annual Earnings		Hourly Earnings		Annual Earnings		Hourly Earnings	
	(1)	(2)	(3)	(4)	(5)	(6)	(7)	(8)
Efficacy in t_1	-.004 (.011)	-.056* (.028)	.002 (.012)	-.013 (.030)	.006 (.006)	-.013 (.014)	.004 (.005)	-.021† (.012)
Efficacy in t_1 times years of experience	-- --	.0026* (.0013)	-- --	.0007 (.0014)	-- --	.0010 (.0006)	-- --	.0012* (.0005)
Level of ln hourly earnings in t_1	-- --	-- --	-.170** (.022)	-.170** (.022)	-- --	-- --	-.089** (.008)	-.088** (.008)
Level of ln annual earnings in t_1	-.172** (.021)	-.173** (.021)	-- --	-- --	-.097** (.010)	-.098** (.010)	-- --	-- --
Years of education	.008* (.004)	.008* (.004)	.011** (.004)	.011** (.004)	.008** (.002)	.008** (.002)	.005** (.002)	.005** (.002)
Test score	.006 (.005)	.006 (.005)	.011† (.006)	.011† (.006)	.004 (.003)	.004 (.003)	.000 (.002)	.000 (.002)
Years of work experience	-.001 (.001)	-.008* (.003)	-.000 (.001)	-.002 (.004)	.000 (.001)	-.002 (.002)	.000 (.000)	-.003* (.001)
Health limitation in t_1	.020 (.033)	.022 (.033)	.003 (.035)	.004 (.035)	-.012 (.017)	-.010 (.018)	.002 (.015)	.005 (.015)
Constant	1.509	1.635	0.039	0.073	0.708	0.756	0.038	0.096
R^2 (adjusted)	.093	.097	.078	.077	.118	.120	.129	.134
Standard error of estimate	.238	.237	.251	.251	.119	.119	.103	.102
Number of observations	696	696	696	696	739	739	739	739

Significance levels: +.10 *.05 **.01, assuming simple random sampling
"--"indicates variable not included in the regression Source: Panel Study of Income Dynamics.   Note: Four-year earning change measures are calculated as the slope of a simple regression of ln (earnings) on time. Standard errors are given in parentheses.

favorable and unfavorable events that may lead to attitudinal changes as well as the resources needed to cope with unfavorable events. Changes in earnings are events in and of themselves that might be expected to produce an efficacy change.

Our simplest model of two-year efficacy change has as predictors the level and change in earnings and a set of control variables that includes age, personal resources (education, test score, health limitation), financial resources (nonlabor income), and family needs. These results are presented in columns 1 and 3 of Table 7.3, using measures of annual and hourly earnings, respectively. Both level and change in annual earnings are found to have positive and highly significant effects on efficacy change, and while the estimated effects of hourly earnings level and change are positive, they are considerably below or, in one case, just at the conventional levels of statistical significance.[14] This greater explanatory power of the annual earnings measure suggests that it is the total financial reward from the job that affects efficacy (perhaps indirectly through its stronger association with important events) and not just the potential earnings power for each hour worked.

The estimated effects of the control variables included in these two regressions are often in the expected direction but are rarely statistically significant. The test score measure of cognitive skills is the only resource measure with a positive and significant effect on efficacy change, but this effect disappears when the time horizon is extended to four years (columns 6 and 7). The effect of nonlabor income is positive but insignificant, indicating that dollars of unearned family income for these breadwinners have a much smaller effect on efficacy change than do dollars of earned income. This result supports Bem's self-perception theory. Both age and family needs have negative effects, but only for the age variable are the coefficients close to being twice the size of their respective standard errors.

The sizeable effects of level and change in annual earnings on efficacy change raise important questions about the process by which these two measures produce their effects. As Ehrlich

---

[14] These results were also affected by the treatment of cases with very large changes in earnings. When the equation presented in column (1) was reestimated with the six outliers included, the coefficient on annual earnings change fell to -.005 with a standard error of .093. The other coefficients were unaffected.

TABLE 7.3

ESTIMATES OF ALTERNATIVE MODELS OF EFFICACY CHANGE

	Two-Year Change: $t_1=1971$ $t_2=1972$					Four-Year Change $t_1=1972$ $t_2=1975$	
	(1)	(2)	(3)	(4)	(5)	(6)	(7)
Change in ln annual earnings (t_2-t_1)	.324* (.107)	.379** (.111)	-- --	-- --	-- --	.283 (.205)	-- --
Level of ln annual earnings in t_1	.175** (.064)	.137* (.066)	-- --	-- --	.184** (.064)	.168** (.059)	-- --
Change in ln hourly earnings (t_2-t_1)	-- --	-- --	.123 (.103)	.124 (.103)	.299** (.116)	-- --	.157 (.238)
Level of ln hourly earnings in t_1	-- --	-- --	.105† (.063)	.093 (.063)	-- --	-- --	.142* (.058)
Efficacy in t_1	-.486** (.033)	-.493** (.033)	-.483** (.033)	-.492** (.033)	-.486** (.033)	-.569** (.031)	-.564** (.031)
Years of education	-.006 (.010)	-.002 (.010)	-.001 (.010)	.001 (.010)	-.006 (.010)	.014 (.010)	.017† (.010)
Test score	.042** (.015)	.044** (.015)	.044** (.015)	.046** (.016)	.042** (.015)	-.000 (.015)	.001 (.015)
Age (in years)	-.006† (.003)	-.006† (.003)	-.006† (.003)	-.007† (.003)	-.007* (.003)	-.007* (.003)	-.007* (.003)
ln Family needs in t_1	-.092 (.086)	-.107 (.088)	-.081 (.086)	-.098 (.088)	-.100 (.087)	-- --	-- --
ln Nonlabor income in t_1	.014 (.012)	.017 (.013)	.012 (.012)	.015 (.013)	.017 (.013)	-- --	-- --
Health limitation in t_1	-.136 (.093)	-.131 (.093)	-.143 (.093)	-.129 (.093)	-.137 (.093)	-.230* (.099)	-.239* (.099)

Table 7.3 (continued)

	Two-Year Change: t₁=1971 t₂=1972					Four-Year Change t₁=1972 t₂=1975	
	(1)	(2)	(3)	(4)	(5)	(6)	(7)
Unemployment in t_1 (100s of hours)[1]	-- --	.005 (.020)	-- --	.004 (.019)	-- --	-- --	-- --
Change in unemployment t_2-t_1 (100s of hours)	-- --	-.042* (.016)	-- --	-.043** (.016)	-- --	-- --	-- --
Change in ln family needs t_2-t_1	-- --	.090 (.222)	-- --	.136 (.223)	-- --	-- --	-- --
Change in ln nonlabor income t_2-t_1	-- --	.008 (.016)	-- --	.006 (.016)	.012 (.016)	-- --	-- --
Evicted between t_1 and t_2	-- --	-.499* (.192)	-- --	-.407* (.194)	-- --	-- --	-- --
Moved for job reason between t_1 and t_2	-- --	-.089 (.137)	-- --	-.097 (.138)	-- --	-- --	-- --
Divorced between t_1 and t_2	-- --	-.088 (.228)	-- --	-.102 (.230)	-- --	-- --	-- --
Change in work hours between t_1 and t_2	-- --	-- --	-- --	-- --	.441** (.139)	-- --	-- --
Constant	0.107	0.509	1.404	1.533	0.086	-0.522	0.754
R^2 (adjusted)	.250	.258	.240	.247	.251	.324	.329

Table 7.3 (continued)

| | Two-Year Change: t_1=1971 t_2=1972 | | | | Four-Year Change t_1=1972 t_2=1975 | |
	(1)	(2)	(3)	(4)	(5)	(6)	(7)
Standard error of estimation	.668	.664	.672	.669	.668	.648	.650
Number of observations	696	696	696	696	696	715	715

Significance levels: +.10 *.05 **.01, assuming simple random sampling.
"--" indicates variable not included in the regression

Note: Four-year earning change measures are calculated as the slope of a simple regression of earnings on time. Standard errors are given in parentheses.
Source: Panel Study of Income Dynamics.

(1975) has shown, workers in relatively low paying jobs are much
more likely to experience a host of untoward events, both those
associated with the job (e.g., unemployment) and outside of it
(e.g., eviction). Changes in annual earnings may themselves be
produced by job-related events (e.g., unemployment). In our
attempt to discover some of the ways in which the annual earnings
measures may operate to produce a change in efficacy, a set of
events was added into the model, with the results shown in the
second column of Table 7.3. Many of these events were quite rare
in our sample during this two-year period of change (see Table 1
for the mean values), perhaps because of the sample restrictions
which left us with a relatively stable and advantaged group of
men. Despite this, two have statistically significant effects--
change in unemployment hours and involuntary residential moves.

Although both the amount of unemployment in the first year
and the change in the amount of unemployment between the two
years were included in the expanded model, only the latter
measure had statistically significant effects. Note that this
significant effect of change in unemployment on efficacy change
was obtained in a regression that controlled for annual earnings
changes that may have accompanied the unemployment, so that this
unemployment effect cannot be attributed to its financial
consequences. By the same token, the estimated effects of annual
earnings change on efficacy change, shown in the second column of
Table 7.3, cannot be attributed to noneconomic factors associated
with changes in unemployment experience.

The estimated effects of prior level of annual earnings on
efficacy change falls with the inclusion of the events,
supporting the contention that lower levels of annual earnings
may be associated with relative loss of efficacy by
distinguishing those workers who are more likely to experience
untoward events that they cannot control. But by no means does
the coefficient become so small that we can claim to have
included all of the individual level events with which earnings
change may be associated. Surprisingly, the estimated effect of
annual earnings change increases when the events are included in
the model. The estimated effects of level and change in hourly
earnings, shown in the third and fourth columns of Table 7.3,
change little when the set of events is included in the model.

Results from one interesting variation of the model are shown in the fifth column of Table 7.3. In it, efficacy change is regressed on the level of annual earnings and on changes in the components of annual earnings--work hours and hourly earnings. The effects of these two components of economic status are conceptually quite distinct and the relative sizes of their effects indicate, for example, whether getting a raise does more to influence one's efficacy than working more hours. The results show that changes in both of the components of annual earnings have highly significant effects. Changes in nonlabor income continue to have insignificant effects on efficacy change, again indicating the importance of the distinction between changes in economic status derived from one's own job versus family income from other sources.

The results from the four-year models of efficacy change showed less evidence of earnings effects. Although the initial level of both annual and hourly earnings has a positive and significant effect on four-year change in efficacy, neither of the measures of change in economic status was significant.[15] Interestingly, many of the background measures began to show stronger effects. Although the test score variable lost its significant effect in going from two- to four-year change, the measures of age and health limitations became significant and the education effects approached the point of statistical significance. None of the events measures had significant coefficients when they were added into the model (results not shown), suggesting that efficacy is more responsive to recent events than to longer-term processes.

---

[15]We also estimated the four-year efficacy change model with earnings changes measured as the simple difference between 1972 and 1975 earnings rather than as the slope of the trend line. Although both of the coefficients on these earnings change measures were positive, neither was significant at conventional levels. Four-year earnings patterns could be measured in other ways, as with counts of the number of earnings increases and decreases or as the number of consecutive increases and decreases.

The coefficients on the earnings trend variables can be interpreted as the change in efficacy associated with a 1 percent higher annual growth rate, controlling for the initial level of efficacy.

MEASUREMENT CONSIDERATIONS

The OLS regressions assumed perfect measurement of the independent variables--an obviously poor assumption that may be especially dangerous in models with lagged dependent variables. Several measurement issues can be distinguished. First is the question of whether the repeated indicators of efficacy are measuring the same phenomenon across time. That is, are the measure-construct relationships invariant over time? If the answer is no, we are not dealing with a repeated measures design in the strict sense. The second issue is the problem of correlated measurement errors. For example, if some respondents consistently overstate their efficacy across interviews while others do not, the effects of efficacy at time 1 on efficacy at time 2 will be overstated. The third issue is the reliability of measurement. Measurement errors in independent variables will generally attenuate their effects on dependent variables; for example, random noise will understate the temporal stability of a characteristic.

The sensitivity of the regression results to these measurement issues was tested using a maximum likelihood procedure which analyzes latent unmeasured variables (LISREL, see Joreskog and Sorbom, 1979). Because of the expense of the iterative maximum likelihood procedure for complex models, we chose not to reestimate all the regression equations presented here. In cases where there are clearly no effects in the OLS regression results, it is highly unlikely that they will be found in more sophisticated LISREL models. However, because of the issues involved in the measurement of the repeated earnings and efficacy measures, there were reasons to expect that the regression results overstated the effects of earnings on efficacy. Hence, we reestimated the two-year annual earnings-efficacy model, since annual earnings showed the largest effects. All life event measures and background variables were eliminated from the LISREL analyses to simplify the model, since these variables appear to have a very modest effect on the earnings-efficacy relationship. These results are compared to regression results with all control variables removed.

Our LISREL model treated personal efficacy as an unmeasured variable indicated by the three efficacy items which were all assumed to be measured with error. The error (i.e. specific component of variance) in each efficacy item at time 1 was assumed to be correlated with the error in its corresponding item at time 2 (i.e., three correlated errors in all). The measure-construct relationships for efficacy (i.e., unstandardized factor loadings) were assumed to be constant across interviews, although error variances and the variance in true efficacy were not constrained over time. Model estimates are shown in Figure 7.2. The model had an acceptable fit to the data (X^2 = 24.8, df = 15, p = .05) and this fit was not significantly improved in a model with the factor loadings free to vary over time. The fit was significantly worse for a model with the error variances of corresponding items constrained to be equal over time (X^2 = 41.0, df = 18, p = .001). For all three efficacy items, the error variance was greater in 1972 than in 1971.

The LISREL results confirmed our suspicions that efficacy was poorly measured. The validities for the three efficacy measures (i.e., the squared correlations between each item and the latent efficacy construct) ranged from .10 to .41. The item asking whether respondents generally finished things that they started had a considerably lower validity than the other two items. Taking into account the poor measurement of efficacy, the estimated correlation between 1971 annual earnings and 1971 efficacy was raised from .21 to .34.

There were also significant correlated errors over time ranging from .19 to .26. With these correlated errors and measurement error in the efficacy items taken into account, the stability of efficacy (unstandardized regression coefficient for 1971 efficacy predicting 1972 efficacy) was raised from .54 to .78. Hence, efficacy is a much more stable personality trait than we would expect on the basis of the OLS regression results.

These differences in the estimated correlates and stability of 1971 efficacy influence estimates of other coefficients in the efficacy-earnings model. The biggest difference was in the effect of 1971 annual earnings on efficacy change, which was reduced from b = .20, t = 3.7 in OLS regression results to b =

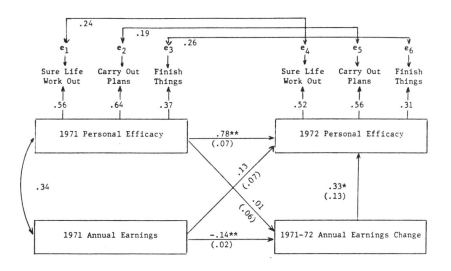

Figure 7.2
1971-1972 EARNINGS-EFFICACY MODEL USING LISREL
(Whites Only)

*significant at .05 level, two-tailed test.
**significant at .01 level, two-tailed test.
$\chi^2 = 24.8$, df = 15, p = .05, N = 696

Note: Unstandardized coefficients are shown for causal paths, while factor loadings are standardized. The unstandardized factor loadings are constrained equal over time, although the standardized loadings vary slightly because of the different variances over time.

.13 t = 1.8 using LISREL.'ᶜ By contrast, effects of annual
earnings change on personal efficacy change were almost identical
(b = .34, t = 3.2 and b = .33, t = 2.6 for the regression and
LISREL results, respectively).

The effect of efficacy in 1971 on earnings change between
1971 and 1972 was not affected by this alternative estimation
procedure. Even with measurement error in efficacy taken into
account, there was no evidence that persons with higher efficacy
were particularly successful in improving their economic status.

PERSONAL INITIATIVE AND THE STRUCTURE OF OPPORTUNITY

The lack of effects of efficacy on subsequent earnings
change could be interpreted in several ways. On the one hand,
they may suggest that persons with more positive attitudes about
their abilities show no more personal initiative than those who
doubt their abilities to carry through on intentions. On the
other hand, they may indicate that the labor market does not
consistently reward high personal initiative, or punish low
initiative. These interpretations begin to address the process
by which personal efficacy does or does not get translated into
earnings change. Unfortunately, we had no indicators of personal
initiative.

We could, however, construct two opportunity structure
measures: a single item asking whether the respondents could
have worked more hours on any of their jobs in 1971 if they had
chosen to, and a measure of the unemployment rate in their county

---

ᶜThese OLS results do not correspond exactly to those shown
in Table 7.3 because they do not control for the effects of the
background variables.

Since we did not have multiple indicators of annual
earnings, we could not take into account any unreliability in
this measure. Hence, this is a conservative estimate of the
effects of level of earnings on efficacy change. We did try
replacing the measure of annual earnings with an instrument to
take into account any correlated errors between earnings in 1971
and 1972. The instrument was constructed from a number of
correlates of 1971 annual earnings including education, work
hours, union status, region of the country, test scores,
occupational classification, and experience. In total, we
explained about 50 percent of the variance in 1971 annual
earnings. The LISREL model was reestimated using this earnings
instrument and the results were virtually unchanged, although the
standard error for the estimate of 1971 annual earnings on
efficacy change was increased, reducing the significance of this
coefficient below acceptable levels.

(dichotomized at the median). These opportunity structure measures were entered into the earnings change regression equations both additively and in interaction with 1971 efficacy. The 1972 measures were used to estimate comparable four-year earnings change equations. None of the interactions were even close to significant in the two-year earnings change model; however, in the four-year model all the efficacy-opportunity interactions were in the right direction and the 1972 efficacy-work available interaction was significant on the basis of a one-tailed test (p<.10).

Two other indirect indicators of opportunity structure are work experience and race. As described above, more experienced workers who generally have more opportunities than younger workers appear to be able to translate efficacy into earnings change. We also estimated models for blacks and there was no evidence that blacks were able to translate efficacy into earnings regardless of their experience level (indeed the signs were generally negative). This is consistent with the interpretation that the opportunity structure is more constraining for blacks, although it can be explained in many other ways as well.[17]

SUMMARY

Two national longitudinal studies which include repeated measures of economic status and personal efficacy yield contradictory results. Analyses by Andrisani (1977, 1978) using the National Longitudinal Studies of younger and older men have found considerable evidence that level of efficacy affects changes in earnings over a two-year period. The analyses reported here using the Panel Study of Income Dynamics provided very limited evidence that efficacy influences earnings changes of prime-aged white men. If at all, these effects show up only for more experienced workers.

In contrast, the effects of earnings level and change on efficacy change are stronger and more robust, although it appears that efficacy is more responsive to short-term fluctuations in

---

[17]A proper treatment of black-white differences should include direct tests of the difference in regression coefficients by race, as well as any difference in the reliability of measurement by race.

earnings than to longer-term trends. It also appears that earnings are more important than other sources of family income in influencing a male household head's efficacy.

It is important to stress that these results were obtained from a fairly homogeneous group of prime-aged white men. This group is clearly the easiest to work with, since its labor force participation is continuous and measurement of its economic status is fairly accurate. Nonetheless, of greater interest for questions of public policy are those groups for whom labor force participation is more erratic--young men and women of both races and female heads of households in particular. Research in progress focusses on these groups and consider intergenerational effects of parent's attitudes on mobility patterns of their offspring.

Appendix A to Chapter 7

In estimating models of change in a given variable, Y, with panel data, at least three formulations of change are possible: (a) final level of Y on the left-hand side with initial level of Y on the right-hand side, (b) a direct measure of change in Y on the left-hand side <u>with</u> initial level of Y on the right-hand side, and (c) a direct measure of change in Y on the left-hand side <u>without</u> controlling for initial level of Y on the right-hand side.[a] The conventional formulation of cross-lagged two-wave panel models takes the form of (a). Arguments supporting the superiority of (b) over (c), (e.g., controlling for regression to the mean or for "floor and ceiling effects" from using a Y measure with a restricted range) are beyond the scope of this appendix and usually can be evaluated only in the context of a specific substantive model. It is important to note, however, that models (a) and (b) are algebraically equivalent. This can easily be shown for the models considered in this chapter by comparing equations (1) and (2) with corresponding models which use the <u>level</u> of earnings and efficacy exclusively. Ignoring the Human Capital and Resource variables, models with levels can be written as:

(1') $\text{Earnings}_{t+1} = B_0' + B_1' \text{ Earnings}_t + B_2' \text{ Efficacy}_t + U_1'$

and (2') $\text{Efficacy}_{t+1} = C_0' + C_1' \text{ Efficacy}_t + C_2' \text{ Earnings}_t + C_3 \text{ Earnings}_{t+1} + U_2'$.

Simple algebra shows that (1') can be rewritten as:

(1") $\Delta\text{Earnings}_{t,t+1} = B' + (B_1' - 1) \text{ Earnings}_t + B_2' \text{ Efficacy}_t + U_1'$.

A comparison of (1) and (1') shows that $B_0 = B_0'$, $B_1 = (B_1'-1)$ and $B_2 = B_2'$.

Thus, the effect of efficacy on <u>changes</u> in earnings with initial level of earnings included as a control variable is identical to the effect of efficacy on final <u>level</u> of earnings with initial level of earnings included as a control.

---

[a] An additional formulation takes the final level of Y on the left-hand side and the initial levels of explanatory variables (<u>not including</u> the initial level of Y) on the right-hand side. The interpretation of this equation is difficult. It may be best to think of this model as a special case of (a)-(c) with an omitted variable or with certain parameters constrained to equal zero.

Manipulation of equation (2') gives

(2") $\Delta \text{Efficacy}_{t,t+1} = C_0' + (C_1' - 1) \text{Efficacy}_t + (C_2' + C_3') \text{Earnings}_t + C_3' \Delta\text{Earnings}_{t,t+1} + U_2'.$

Comparing (2") with (2) shows that:

$C_0 = C_0'$, $C_1 = (C_1' - 1)$, $C_2 = (C_2' + C_3')$, and $C_3 = C_3'$

This shows that the estimated effects of the time t+1 values of Earnings on Efficacy_{t+1} in model (2') are identical to the effects of <u>changes</u> in earnings between time t and t+1 on <u>changes</u> in efficacy between t and t+1 in model (2).

References

Andrisani, Paul J. "Internal-External Attitudes, Sense of Efficacy, and Labor Market Experience: A Reply to Duncan and Morgan." Journal of Human Resources, 16, no. 4 (Fall 1981): 658-66.

Andrisani, Paul J. Work Attitudes and Labor Market Experience. New York: Praeger, 1978.

Andrisani, Paul J. "Internal-External Attitudes, Personal Initiative, and the Labor Market Experience of Black and White Men." Journal of Human Resources, 12, no. 3 (Summer 1977): 308-28.

Antonovsky, Aaron. Health, Stress and Coping. San Francisco: Jossey-Bass, 1979.

Augustyniak, Sue, Duncan, Greg J., and Liker, Jeffrey, "Income Dynamics and Self-Conceptions." In Life Course Dynamics From 1968-80, ed. Glen H. Elder, forthcoming.

Bem, Daryl J. "Self-Perception: An Alternative Interpretation of Cognitive Dissonance Phenomena." Psychological Review 74, no. 3 (1967): 183-200.

Cohn, Richard M. "The Effect of Employment Status Change on Self-Attitudes." Social Psychology Quarterly. 41, (1978): 81-93.

Dickinson, Katherine. "Investigation of the Attitudinal and Behavioral Indexes." O.E.O. Working Paper (Project No. 4180). Ann Arbor: University of Michigan, Survey Research Center, 1972.

Dohrenwend, Bruce P., and Dohrenwend, Barbara S., ed. Stressful Life Events: Their Nature and Effects. New York: Wiley, 1974.

Duncan, Greg J., and Morgan, James N. "Sense of Efficacy and Subsequent Change in Earnings." Journal of Human Resources 16, no. 4 (Fall 1981): 649-57.

Ehrlich, Everett. "Involuntary Disruptions of 'Life Cycle' Plans." In Five Thousand American Families--Patterns of Economic Progress, Vol. III., ed. Greg J. Duncan and James N. Morgan, pp. 189-220. Ann Arbor: Institute for Social Research, 1975.

Elder, Glen H., Jr. Children of the Great Depression. Chicago: University of Chicago Press, 1974.

Gurin, Gerald, and Gurin, Patricia. "Expectancy Theory in the Study of Poverty," Journal of Social Issues 26, no. 2 (1970): 83-104.

Gurin, Patricia; Gurin, Gerald; and Morrison, Betty M. "Personal and Ideological Aspects of Internal and External Control." Social Psychology Quarterly 41 (1970): 275-96.

Hill, Martha S. "Some Illustrative Design Effects: Proper Sampling Errors Versus Simple Random Sample Assumptions." In Five Thousand American Families--Patterns of Economic Progress, Vol. IX. ed. Martha S. Hill, Daniel H. Hill, and James N. Morgan, Ann Arbor: Institute for Social Research, 1981.

Joreskog, Karl G. and Sorbom, Dug. Advances in Factor Analysis and Structural Equation Models. Cambridge, MA: Abt Books, 1979.

Kasl, Stanislav V. "Changes in Mental Health Status Associated with Job Loss and Retirement." In Stress and Mental Disorder, ed. J.E. Barrett, R.M. Rose, and G.L. Klerman. New York: Raven Press, 1979.

Kohn, Melvin L. and Schooler, Carmi. "The Reciprocal Effects of the Substantive Complexity of Work and Intellectual Flexibility: A Longitudinal Assessment." American Journal of Sociology 84 (July 1978): 24-52.

Lazear, Edward. "Age, Experience, and Wage Growth," American Economic Review 66 (September 1976): 548-58.

Morgan, James N. "Consistency of Reports of Hourly Earnings." In Five Thousand American Families--Patterns of Economic Progress, Vol. IX, ed. Martha S. Hill, Daniel H. Hill, and James N. Morgan. Ann Arbor: Institute for Social Research, 1981.

Morgan, James N. A Panel Study of Income Dynamics, Procedures and Tape Codes, Waves I-V, two volumes. Ann Arbor: Institute for Social Research, 1973.

Parsons, Jacquelynne E., and Goff, Susan B. "Achievement Motivation and Values: An Alternative Perspective." In Achievement Motivation: Recent Trends in Theory and Research, ed. L.L. Faynes Jr. New York: Plenum Press, 1980.

Pearlin, Leonard I.; Lieberman, Morton A.; Menaghan, Elizabeth G.; and Mullan, Joseph T. "The Stress Process." Journal of Health and Social Behavior 22 (1981): 337-56.

Straus, Murray A.; Gelles, Richard J.; and Steinmetz, Susan K. Behind Closed Doors. New York: Anchor Books, 1980.

Veroff, Joseph; McClelland, Lou; and Marquis, Kent. Measuring Intelligence and Achievement Motivation in Surveys. Ann Arbor: Institute for Social Research, 1971.

Chapter 8

WORK EXPERIENCE AND WAGE GROWTH OF WOMEN WORKERS

Mary Corcoran, Greg J. Duncan, and Michael Ponza

INTRODUCTION AND BACKGROUND

Women are a vital part of today's labor force, and work is clearly an important part of their lives. Women comprised more than two-fifths of the labor force in 1978, and almost 60 percent of women aged 18 to 64 years were employed in 1978. Almost all women work at some point in their lives and their earnings are often necessary to insure adequate family support. In 1978, nearly two-thirds of working women were either presently unmarried or married to men earning less than $10,000 per year (in 1977) (U.S. Department of Labor, 1979).

There is considerable evidence that women's and men's work participation patterns differ--with men working continuously after completing school, while women move in and out of the labor force to accommodate family and child-rearing duties. Women earn considerably less than men do. Since 1930, the median salary of full-time, full-year women workers has been about 60 percent of the median salary of men who work full time, full year. Women and men also have very different occupations. Treiman and Hartmann (1981) show that 70 percent of the men and 54 percent of the women in the labor force are concentrated in occupations dominated by their own sex. Women, unlike men, are heavily concentrated into a few job categories--secretarial work, sales, teaching, nursing, and various service occupations.

The most prominent economic explanation linking labor supply patterns and wages is human capital theory.[1] Human capital itself is defined as worker skills or qualifications, such as education or training. An individual worker's stock of human capital can be increased by the process of investment. This

[1] Human capital theory is quite similar to the functionalist theory of Davis and Moore. It has been argued that this theory underlies much of the empirical work in social stratification (see Horan, 1978).

investment has an opportunity cost (in terms of foregone earnings as well as the direct costs of training) and a return (in the form of higher subsequent earnings). Human capital theory particularly emphasizes investment in formal schooling (Becker, 1975) and in on-the-job training (Mincer, 1974). Workers are presumed to choose freely among jobs providing different amounts of training, and wages are presumed to reward past investments in education and training in a similar way for all workers.

In recent years, human capital theory has been expanded to deal with the structure of female wages. Some of its proponents have argued that the sex division of labor within the home generates sex differences in patterns of investment in work-related human capital, and this in turn generates sex differences in wages and the sex segregation of occupations (Mincer and Polachek, 1974; Polachek, 1976, 1979, 1981; Mincer and Ofek, 1982; Mincer and Polachek, 1978). These arguments have focused particularly on how sex differences in patterns of labor force participation affect economic advancement.

Proponents of segmented labor market models take issue with several of the assumptions of the human capital model. Segmented market models assume that the labor market can be broken down into several sectors--and within each sector wages are determined by very different processes. Thus, segmented labor market models focus on characteristics of jobs and of job markets rather than on characteristics of individuals. The relationship between an individual's experience and earnings is thought to be largely determined by the labor market in which he or she works. In these models, a person acquires training by first gaining access to a job within a sector that provides training; that is, jobs and job markets intervene between an individual and investment in on-the-job training.

Segmented labor market theories explain sex differences in acquired on-the-job training very differently than do human capital models. According to these theories, women are "crowded" into a relatively narrow range of jobs, and these "female" jobs offer fewer promotion and on-the-job training opportunities than do other jobs. Women acquire less training than men because they have been restricted to these "female" jobs--either because of employer discrimination in hiring and promotion or because of sex role socialization. Since the human capital models treat sex role socialization as exogenous, the sex segregation argument is not necessarily inconsistent with the human capital model.

In this chapter, we use the longitudinal nature of the Panel Study of Income Dynamics (PSID) to explore several of the issues surrounding the labor supply, earnings, and occupations of women workers. Most of the prior work in this area has been conducted with point-in-time, cross-sectional data. While such information is valuable for portraying the status of workers at a point in time or, if more than one cross section is available, in comparing the overall position of workers at several points in time, it is necessarily silent on the dynamics of _individual_ changes in labor supply, earnings, or jobs. Finding in two cross sections that one-half of the women were working at each time is consistent with the view that the same individual women worked at both points in time and that there is little movement into and out of the labor force among women workers. But it is also consistent with _complete_ labor force turnover among women, where _none_ of the women working at the first point in time were working at the second time. While it is possible to ask retrospective work history questions of a cross-section of women, the reported patterns of work and nonwork are much more prone to measurement error than if those same women were followed year after year and asked about work hours in the previous year only.

Information from successive cross-sections on the numbers of women in "female" and "male" jobs could give a very misleading picture of the dynamics of occupational segregation. If successive cross sections show that equal fractions of women work in a set of female-dominated jobs, it is tempting to conclude that women who begin in such jobs tend to get locked into them. But equal fractions in successive cross sections are also consistent with a picture of substantial mobility from one sector to another, as long as equal numbers of women leave and take these kinds of jobs. Segmented market models presume _individual_ immobility between sectors, and only longitudinal data can provide the necessary information to test this presumption.

Longitudinal data also provide a much better picture of the individual dynamics of the earnings of women workers than do data from single or multiple cross sections. Similar aggregate wage distributions at two points in time are consistent with either complete wage immobility or substantial wage mobility.[2] More important, longitudinal data provide much greater statistical leverage in analyzing the determinants of wage growth. Typical cross-sectional wage equations relate wages at a point in time to productivity-related factors such as education and labor force experience and, in testing segmented market models, to a set of measures about the job. Unmeasured and unchanging characteristics, such as motivation, may bias the estimated effects of the measured characteristics in such a cross-sectional analysis. But longitudinal models of wage change can be formulated to avoid such biases.

Our analysis of these issues is grouped into three sections. In the first, we present simple descriptive information on the patterns of labor supply for adult men and women in the PSID over the 13-year period from 1967 to 1979. We found the expected differences between the sexes in their total amount of market work during this period, with men, on average, working twice as many of the years as women and nearly three times as many total hours. Black women worked somewhat more than white women and black men somewhat less than white men, but racial differences were small relative to the huge differences between the sexes. We found that fewer than one-sixth of the women failed to work a minimum number of hours in at least one of the 13 years, but only about 1 woman in 15 worked full time for the entire time.

In the second section, we describe the human capital model in greater detail and use it to develop a model of wage growth for women workers. We built upon and extended the work of Mincer and Ofek (1982). They used longitudinal data from the National Longitudinal Surveys (NLS) and found that women who dropped out of the labor force were penalized with a drop in wages but experienced a relatively rapid initial growth in wages after returning to work, which, after as many years as the length of the interruption, erased much of the wage loss. We found a similar pattern of wage loss (depreciation) followed by wage rebound when we replicated their model on a comparably aged group of women in the PSID, and this pattern persisted when the sample was extended beyond the fairly narrow age range used in the

---

[2]Furthermore, age differences in a cross section can reflect permanent differences among age cohorts (generations), since at any point age designates year of birth.

replication. These findings of wage loss and rebound provide a reconciliation of apparently disparate findings of depreciation estimated from cross-sectional data.

The detailed reports on work hours given annually in the PSID allow us to explore the wage consequences of part- versus full-time work for women. Our results show clearly that full-time work is rewarded more than part-time work--a fact with important implications for women contemplating a labor supply strategy to accompany their household responsibilities.

Past empirical work has used the self-reported "intentions" of female respondents to test the human capital prediction that workers will invest less if they anticipate labor market withdrawals than if they do not. Since we know which women in the PSID sample were not working at the end of the 13 year period, we can directly test whether such workers' jobs provided them lower wage growth and lower depreciation. We found, for both white and black women, that those who did not work in 1979 had the same wage increment for additional years of experience as women who did work in 1979. However, while white women who did not work in 1979 had similar wage loss with time out as did otherwise similar white women who were working in 1979, black women who were not working in 1979 exhibited no wage loss during previous labor force withdrawals.

In the third section, we present and examine propositions advanced by Polachek that explain the sex segregation of jobs in the context of a human capital model. He argues that if work skills do atrophy during withdrawals from the labor force, then it is rational for married women who expect to take time out from the labor force to work in fields where there is less chance of atrophy of work skills, i.e., in fields with low returns to experience and low depreciation rates. By selecting jobs that are easy to leave and reenter, women can combine more easily the dual demands of career and family. The least atrophy is supposedly found in typically "female" jobs, and so the human capital explanation explains job segregation as well as low female wages.

We found little evidence to support these contentions. We looked first at the patterns of job changes over the five-year period 1975-1979 and found a surprising amount of movement between female-dominated and male-dominated jobs. Many women were clearly not unalterably locked into the jobs in which they began, casting doubt on segmented market models that presume extensive immobility into and out of jobs of this kind. We next examined the consequences of the type of job held on subsequent wage growth. We found few differences in the amount of wage growth associated with female-dominated work and male-dominated work; a much more important factor is whether the work performed in a particular kind of job was part or full time. Finally, we found that women with extensive time out between 1967 and 1979 were no more likely to work at "female" jobs than women who had worked continuously over that period.

PATTERNS OF LABOR SUPPLY, 1967-1979

The amounts and types of labor market experience acquired by adult men and women are revealed in the 13 consecutive annual reports of work hours in the PSID. Various measures of labor supply are given in Table 8.1 for adult men and women, aged 23 to 47, in the first year of the panel, who lived in their own households throughout the period.[3] The lower age restriction was imposed to avoid sample selection problems associated with the decision to leave the parental home and form one's own household. The upper age restriction eliminates from the sample individuals who would have reached the early retirement age of 62 by the end of the panel period.

The results presented in Table 8.1 confirm the dramatic differences between the sexes in the frequency and regularity of work and in the extent of part-time or part-year work. Differences between the races are much less dramatic within the groups of men and women. Black women do acquire more experience than white women, while black men acquire less of it than white men.

---

[3] In terms of the PSID sample, this group consists of all individuals who were household heads or wives in each of the 13 years. Eliminated from this analysis are children and the small group of other relatives of the household head (e.g., brother or sister).

Table 8.1

WORK HISTORY MEASURES: 1967-1979

(Male heads, female heads, or wives aged 23 to 47 in 1968)

Work History Measures	Men			Women		
	White	Black	All	White	Black	All
Experience (years)	12.7 (1.3)	12.4 (1.7)	12.7 (1.4)	6.6 (4.9)	7.6 (4.8)	6.7 (4.9)
Part-time experience (years)	0.7 (1.4)	0.9 (1.5)	0.7 (1.5)	2.9 (3.1)	3.3 (3.2)	2.9 (3.1)
Full-time experience (years)	12.0 (2.0)	11.6 (2.4)	12.0 (2.2)	4.1 (4.5)	4.9 (4.6)	4.2 (4.5)
Whether at least one year with hours less than 250	10.3	16.1	10.7	77.5	70.5	76.7
Whether at least one year with hours 250-1,499	32.5	48.2	33.6	74.1	75.2	74.2
Whether 13 years with hours greater than 1,500	64.9	49.5	63.8	6.3	7.9	6.5
Experience (weeks)	600 (79)	587 (99)	600 (80)	311 (225)	345 (222)	315 (220)
Experience (hours)	29,329 (6,403)	27,603 (7,012)	29,211 (6,891)	11,157 (9,359)	12,692 (9,139)	11,334 (9,309)
Number of nonwork spells[a]	1.2 (0.4)	1.5 (.04)	1.2 (0.4)	1.5 (0.7)	1.5 (0.7)	1.5 (0.7)
Duration of	2.5	3.7	2.6	6.8	5.9	6.7

Table 8.1 (continued)

Work History Measures	Men			Women		
	White	Black	All	White	Black	All
nonwork spells[a]	(2.7)	(2.5)	(2.7)	(4.4)	(4.4)	(4.4)
Hours/year during work spells[b]	2,177 (390)	2,037 (345)	2,166 (479)	1,513 (448)	1,506 (380)	1,512 (981)
Weeks/year during work spells[b]	47 (3.2)	47 (3.3)	47 (4.7)	42 (7.6)	42 (7.5)	42 (7.6)
Hours/week during work spells[b]	46 (6.9)	43 (5.6)	46 (7.3)	36 (8.0)	36 (6.0)	36 (8.0)
Whether Number of Nonwork Spells Were:						
Zero	89.7%	83.9%	89.3%	22.5%	29.5%	23.3%
One	8.5	14.3	8.9	47.1	44.4	46.8
Two	1.7	1.6	1.7	23.3	18.6	22.8
Three or more	0.1	0.2	0.1	7.1	7.5	7.1
Total	100.0	100.0	100.0	100.0	100.0	100.0
Number of cases	890	262	1,152	951	572	1,523

[a]Calculated for only those persons with nonwork spells.

[b]Calculated for only those persons with work spells.

Note: Standard deviations are given in parentheses.

Source: Panel Study of Income Dynamics

Between 70 and 80 percent of the two groups of women were absent from the labor force for at least 1 of the 13 years.[4] The comparable fractions for white and black men were about 10 and 16 percent, respectively. Even when they did work, women were much less likely to work full time. Less than one-tenth of these adult women worked full time during the entire 13 year period. Somewhat surprisingly, the stereotype of men as continuous, full-time workers is not entirely accurate. Fewer than two-thirds of white men and fewer than half of the black men worked for 1,500 hours in each of the 13 years under investigation.

Despite this, the total volume of work experience acquired by men was much higher than that for women. On average, men worked in almost twice as many of the years as women, in nearly twice as many weeks as women, and for nearly three times as many hours as women during this period. Compared to these huge differences between men and women, racial distinctions within the groups of men and women are small. These various measures of labor supply were between 10 and 15 percent higher for black women compared to white women and were less than 10 percent higher for white men than black men.

The part-time nature of the work of women is highlighted when the nonwork spells are removed from consideration and the

---

[4]Throughout this chapter, we use 250 hours during a calendar year to define whether an individual was in or out of the labor force during that year, and we use 1,500 hours to separate part- from full-time workers. This procedure has its disadvantages. An individual with a 40-hour per week job who drops out of the labor force altogether for six months out of a calendar year will be classified as a part-time worker during that year without having a spell of nonwork. In one sense this individual was a full-time worker and in another sense this individual experienced a spell of nonwork during that year. Our measure considers part-time workers to be those either working a limited number of hours per week or those working during only part of the year. Our measure of nonwork spells requires that such spells be long enough to take an individual away from work for virtually an entire year.

labor supply measures are recomputed during the work spells.[5]
The average work week of men exceeds 40 hours, amounting to 46
hours for white men and 43 hours for black men. In contrast,
white and black women averaged 36 hours per week during work
spells. Similar differences show up in the number of weeks
worked per year, with men averaging 47 weeks and women averaging
42 weeks. As a result, the total number of hours averaged by men
during their work spells is almost twice as high as for women
during their spells.

The _intermittency_ of work is also greater for women than
men, although these differences are not as great as the
differences in the volume of work. About three-quarters of the
women did spend at least one of the 13 years out of the labor
force, but of the group taking time out, nearly two-thirds did so
only once.

---

[5]Hours per year, weeks per year, and hours per week were
recalculated for those individuals who had at least one work
spell (i.e., worked 250 or more hours at least once) between 1967
and 1979. The derivation of these measures is as follows: if
the individual worked 250 or more hours in the "t"th year, his or
her total hours (total weeks, or hours per week) for that year
were entered; otherwise they were given a zero entry. This was
done for each year 1967-1979. These values were summed and then
divided by the number of years the individual worked 250 or more
hours between 1967 and 1979. Formally, the measures are:

$$\text{Hours per year during work spells} = \sum_{t=1967}^{1979} \left(\frac{\text{hours}_t}{\text{\# years worked 250 or more hours 1967-79}} \right)$$

where hours_t = actual hours, if worked 250 hours or more
0, otherwise

$$\text{Weeks per year during work spells} = \sum_{t=1967}^{1979} \left(\frac{\text{weeks}_t}{\text{\# years worked 250 or more hours 1967-79}} \right)$$

where weeks_t = actual weeks, if worked 250 hours or more
0, otherwise

$$\text{Hours per week during work spells} = \sum_{t=1967}^{1979} \left(\frac{\text{hours/week}_t}{\text{\# years worked 250 or more hours 1967-79}} \right)$$

where hours_t = actual hours/week, if worked 250
hours or more
0, otherwise.

WORK HISTORY AND WAGES: HUMAN CAPITAL MODELS

Work Experience and Wages

In the human capital model, investments in on-the-job training are considered to be critical determinants of wages (see Becker, 1975; Ben-Porath, 1967; Mincer, 1974; and Rosen, 1972). On-the-job training has a cost since time spent training is assumed to be time diverted from production, and production presumably determines earnings. On-the-job training also has a return in the form of higher later earnings. The following function describes this hypothetical relationship:

$$(1)\quad E_t = E_s + \sum_{i=s+1}^{t-1} rC_i = Y_t + C_t$$

where E_t = earnings capacity in year t;

E_s = earnings that would be received in the absence of any postschool training;

C_i = the dollar cost of investments in human capital in the ith year;

Y_t = earnings in the tth year;

C_t = dollar cost of investments in the tth year; and

r = rate of return to investments in human capital.

If we assume that total benefits of an investment increase as the payoff period increases and that the marginal costs of investments are upwardly sloping in a single time period, it can be shown that a declining profile of investment ratios (C_i/E_i) maximizes the present value of expected lifetime earnings (see Ben-Porath, 1967). That is, the proportion of one's earning capacity invested in on-the-job training will be high in the early years and then decline.

The human capital model assumes that workers freely choose among a variety of jobs--each with a different combination of training and productive work. It generally views training and productive work as mutually exclusive activities, and because of that, employers will pay less for jobs with training than for similar jobs that are not providing training. An implication of the model is that wages grow with experience because workers are acquiring additional skills as they increase their experience and not just because of seniority.

Labor Force Withdrawals and Wages

Mincer and Polachek (1974) extend the human capital model to account for the possible depreciation of human capital that may result from the discontinuity of women's work experience. They argue that periods of labor force withdrawal for childbearing and rearing may cause the skills acquired at school and work to become less valuable. Implicit in their discussion is the assumption that intermittency (frequent exits and entries) will lower female wages.

The following function adjusts the basic human capital wage model to account for depreciation or obsolescence effects:

$$(2) \quad E_t = E_s + \sum_{i=s+1}^{t-1} (rC_i - \sigma_i E_i)$$

where E_t, E_s, r, C_i are defined as in equation (1);

σ_i = the depreciation rate of human capital in year i; and

E_i = earnings capacity in year i.

The total benefits of investments in on-the-job training increase with the length of the payoff period and decline with the length of periods of nonparticipation that follow investments. This suggests that optimal investment patterns will differ depending on the continuity of market activities. Continuously employed workers should concentrate investments early in their careers. Workers who interrupt their work careers will defer investments in on-the-job training until they reenter the labor market after completing these activities so as to minimize the loss from depreciation. Since such workers have a shorter payoff period, their overall volume of investment should be lower than that of workers who remain continuously in the labor force.

Mincer and Ofek (1982) have since revised this initial model to account for "restoration" or "repair" of depreciated human capital. They argue that the "reconstruction of [previously eroded] occupational skills is more efficient than the construction of new human capital" (Mincer and Ofek, 1982: 4).

That is, it costs less to repair human capital than to build it. The following model reflects this:

$$(3) \quad E_t = E_s + \sum_{i=s+1}^{t-1} ((rC_i + r^*R_i) - \sigma_i E_i)$$

where E_t, E_s, r, C_i, σ_i, and E_i are defined as in equations (1) and (2);

R_i = the dollar cost of investments in restoration of human capital in the ith year.

r^* = rate of return to a dollar invested in restored human capital.

Here the return to restoring one unit of human capital (r^*) would be greater than the return to investments in new human capital (r). This "restoration" phenomenon leads Mincer and Ofek to distinguish the short-run and long-run consequences of nonparticipation. In the short run (say, the first year following an interruption), one would expect sharply lower wages than just before the interruption followed by a period of rapid wage growth during which human capital is restored. Thus, the long-run effects on wages of nonwork time may be considerably smaller than the short-run effects.[*]

Since the empirical work of Mincer and Ofek and our own replication of it show that wage "rebound" following an interruption is an important phenomenon, it is useful to consider alternative explanations of it. Corcoran (1979) and Corcoran and Duncan (1979) suggest that time out may lead to a temporary reduction in wages because of temporary mismatches between worker skills and jobs. Women workers lack complete information about job opportunities when they do return to the labor force, and it takes time for them to discover jobs that are best matched to

---

[*]Note that this restoration effect is different from the faster wage growth that would be expected to follow the completion of the final work interruption. Compare two individuals, both 35 years of age and both expecting to work continuously until the same retirement age. That one of them did not work in the years just prior to age 35 may well affect the relative wage levels of the two workers, but it ought not to affect the incentives for future investment and hence future wage growth, if the accumulated stock of human capital does not affect the marginal cost of subsequent investment. The Mincer-Ofek formulation with restoration of human capital will lead to expectations of more rapid wage growth for the intermittent worker in the years following the return to the labor market than for the continuous worker.

their skills. Employers also have imperfect information about the productivity of their new employees, and the learning process for them is a time-consuming one.[7] One common mechanism for this sorting process is to hire new workers at low wages but then rapidly promote them as they successfully complete their probationary periods. In neither of these cases are the workers "restoring" depreciated skills in the Mincer-Ofek sense. Wage increases accompany improved information of employees about their job opportunities or improved information of employers about the productivity of their employees.[8]

Note that Mincer and Ofek have considerably revised the original Mincer and Polachek model. Since depreciated human capital can be restored, it no longer follows that intermittent workers will necessarily defer investments in on-the-job training until all interruptions are over. This decision will depend on the relative sizes of the "depreciation" and "restoration"

---

[7]Mortensen (1978), Jovanovic (1979), and Prescott and Visscher (1980), for example, explain that earnings rise with experience with a firm because firms learn about worker productivities in various jobs (instead of workers acquiring skills through experience). This learning process results in the more senior workers being matched more accurately to jobs commensurate with their skills than less experienced workers. Better job matches allow the senior workers to exhibit higher productivity on average, and if the market rewards productivity, these differences may account for their higher average earnings.

[8]Mincer and Ofek (1982, Table 1) find (and our replication confirms) that the wage loss due to work interruption depends on the length of interruption. They argue that this finding is inconsistent with the "job-matching" hypothesis: "while losses of general capital increase with the duration of absence from work, the loss of specific capital is a once-and-for-all phenomenon due to separation from the job. This means that, if the losses were only in specific capital, the correctly estimated marginal depreciation rates would be zero. Consequently, we may reject the notion that observed depreciation rates are restricted to specific capital" (1982: 17). But finding that wage loss due to interruption depends on interruption length is fully consistent with the job-matching explanation of wage loss and rebound precisely because the value of the information could depreciate with length of interruption. That is, the longer the interruption, the longer the worker is likely to be away from information about the labor market, and the greater will be the likelihood of a worse job match upon return to work.

effects.' Similarly, the relative sizes of these two effects
will also determine the long-run costs of labor force
withdrawals. If these long-run costs are small, then
depreciation may account for little of the wage gap between men
and women.

WORK HISTORY AND WAGES: EMPIRICAL EVIDENCE

The "Depreciation" Effect

Empirical evidence on whether depreciation lowers wages
consists mostly of cross-sectional data comparing earnings of
workers with different work histories, after statistical
adjustment to make the individuals as similar as possible. An
equation of this type is the following cross-sectional
relationship between hourly earnings, prior labor force history,
and other productivity-related characteristics:

$$(4) \quad \ln W_{it} = \alpha_{0t} + \alpha_{1t}S_{it} + \alpha_{2t}e_{0it} + \alpha_{3t}e_{1it} + \alpha_{4t}h_{0it} + \alpha_{5t}h_{1it} + \mu_t X_{it} + \pi_t Z_{it} + \theta_{it}$$

where: W_{it} is the wage rate of the ith individual in time t.

α_{0t} is a constant in time t.

S_{it} is the education level of the ith individual in time t.

e_{0it} is years of experience prior to the most recent interruption for the ith individual in time t.

e_{1it} is years of experience since the most recent interruption for the ith individual in time t.

h_{0it} is years of nonwork prior to the most recent interruption for the ith individual in time t.

'A qualification, suggested to us by Jacob Mincer, is
necessary here: For the intermittent worker, each interruption
carries with it a positive probability of not returning to the
labor market. Thus, the expected payoff period is diminished by
more than the interruption each time it looms. So although wage
loss due to depreciation can be made up, the intermittent
worker's decision whether and when to invest will depend jointly
on the relative sizes of the depreciation and restoration effects
and the probability of returning to work.

h_{1it} is years of nonwork during most recent interruption for the ith individual in time t.

X_{it} is a vector of <u>observed</u> productivity-related characteristics for the ith individual in time t.

Z_{it} is a vector of <u>unobservable</u> individual-specific productivity-related characteristics, workplace characteristics, and labor market differences for the ith individual in time t.

θ_{it} is the stochastic disturbance term for the ith individual in time t.

The coefficients α_2 and α_3 are interpreted as the long-run and short-run effects of participation, and α_4 and α_5 as the long-run and short-run effects of nonparticipation. Human capital theory suggests α_2 and α_3 are both positive, and α_3 should exceed α_2, while α_4 and α_5 are negative, and α_5 should exceed α_4 in absolute value.

The evidence obtained using variations on (4) has produced contradictory results about the size of the "depreciation" effect, i.e., about the extent to which wages decline with time out of the labor force once one controls for differences in labor market experience and job tenure. Mincer and Polachek reported that 1967 wages dropped by 1.2 percent per year out of work for white married women aged 30 to 44 with children. Sandell and Shapiro (1978) replicated the Mincer-Polachek analysis after correcting for coding errors in women's reports of employment behavior. They reported that wages declined only .4 percent per year of nonparticipation and that this effect was insignificant. Corcoran (1979) replicated the Mincer-Polachek analysis for a national sample of wives aged 30 to 44 with children, taken from the 1976 wave of the Panel Study of Income Dynamics and obtained similar results to Mincer and Polachek. But Corcoran (1979) and Corcoran and Duncan (1979) also reported that the decline in wages was much smaller (.6 percent per year out of work) for working women in a broader age range (18 to 64 years). These results suggest that wages of married women aged 30 to 44 are more affected by labor force withdrawals than are wages of women in a broader age range. Corcoran further showed that timing affected these penalties. Wages declined .9 percent per year out of work for white women who dropped out of the labor force after school completion, but there was no wage penalty for women who began work after school completion and later interrupted their work careers.

It is likely that some of these inconsistencies in past research arise because past cross-sectional analyses have tended to confound the short-run and long-run effects of nonparticipation. For example, married working women aged 30 to 44 who have interrupted work are likely to have recently returned to the labor force, so short-run effects may have a large weight in analyses run on this group (e.g., in Mincer and Polachek). Cross-sectional analyses run on women in a broader age range (e.g., Corcoran, 1979; Corcoran and Duncan, 1979) are likely to put more weight on the long-run effect and so will provide lower estimates of the depreciation effect. Mincer and Ofek use eight years of data to explore how time out of the labor force affected wages on a sample of white women aged 30 to 44 in 1967 who were married sometime during 1967-1974. They estimate equation (4) at the time (T) of the most recent labor force reentry for an intermittent worker to mitigate confounding the short- and long-run effects of nonparticipation. At the time of reentry, years of participation after the most recent spell of nonparticipation (e_{1iT}) equals zero. Using their notation, this yields the following equation:

$$(5) \quad \ln W_{iT} = \alpha_{0T} + \alpha_1 S_{iT} + \beta e_{0iT} + \delta h_{0iT} + \varepsilon h_{1iT} + \mu X_{iT} + \theta_{iT}.$$

Note that while the longitudinal component of the NLS is used to measure work history more accurately, this wage level equation is still essentially a cross-sectional one. Mincer and Ofek report that there is a large short-run loss in wages immediately following an interruption (ranging from 3.3 and 7.6 percent per year depending on the specification and sample used), followed by a period of rapid wage growth and resulting in a moderate long-run wage loss (.4 to 1.1 percent per year out of work).

The first two columns of Table 8.2 reproduce the Mincer-Ofek NLS estimates of equation (5) for the combined group of continuous and intermittent workers and for intermittent workers by themselves, respectively. We replicated the Mincer-Ofek analysis for a national sample of wives aged 30 to 44 in 1967 using 13 years of data from PSID (see Table 8.2, column 3) and

obtained strikingly similar results. Our estimate based on a
wider age range (23 to 47 in 1967) and without the marriage
restriction (see column 4) produced a slightly lower estimate of
the short-run depreciation effect (3.5 versus 4.5 percent per
year) and a slightly larger long-run depreciation effect (1.5
versus 1.0 percent per year).

Estimation of wage equations like (4) and (5) with cross-
sectional data poses three types of problems. First, the
experience and nonexperience variables are constructed from
retrospective reports, raising the likelihood of substantial
measurement error. Second, despite the greater availability of
detailed microeconomic data concerning characteristics of
individual workers, one cannot completely control for all worker-
specific differences in productivity, characteristics of the
workplace, and labor market differences that might give rise to
wage differentials. When one attempts to estimate a wage level
equation using a single cross section, these unobserved effects,
Z_{it}, will be included in the disturbance term. To the extent
that these are correlated with the included measured explanatory
variables, biased estimates of the measured explanatory variables
as well as biased estimates of their standard errors will result.
Third, the cross-sectional wage equation is prone to selection
bias. In any single year only 50 percent of the female
population will be working and therefore have an observable wage
rate. Cross-sectional estimates of the relationship between wage
rates, prior labor force history, and other characteristics will
be based on this group of working women, and, to the extent that
these women differ from those omitted from the analysis, biased
parameter estimates can result. This selection problem is also
present in the Mincer-Ofek equation (and our replication) since
those women who did not have a completed labor force interruption
followed by a gainful spell of employment during 1967-1974 were
excluded from their analysis.

A refinement to the single-equation estimation procedure
developed to overcome the statistical problems introduced by
unobservable and time-invariant influences, as well as
retrospective reports, is the estimation of wage change using
longitudinal data. Mincer and Ofek (1982) also used the NLS data
to obtain longitudinal estimates of the wage effects of nonwork
time for adult married white women. Their basic wage change

Table 8.2

REPLICATION OF MINCER-OFEK WAGE LEVEL EQUATION

Sample	NLS Sample of Continuous and Intermittent Working Women[a,c] Age 30-44	NLS Sample of Intermittent Working Women[b,c] Age 30-44	PSID Sample of Intermittent Working Women[d] Age 30-44	PSID Sample of Intermittent Working Women[e] Age 23-47
Dependent Variable	Natural Log of Reentry Wage (1)	Natural Log of Reentry Wage (2)	Natural Log of Reentry Wage (3)	Natural Log of Reentry Wage (4)
S	.052 (7.85)	.037 (2.74)	.059 (3.07)	.059 (4.41)
h_1	-.060 (6.95)	-.045 (2.39)	-.048 (1.81)	-.035 (1.97)
h_0	-.006 (1.90)	-.010 (1.75)	-.011 (1.04)	-.015 (3.11)
e_0	.018 (2.42)	.022 (1.62)	.036 (1.24)	.014 (.84)
e_0^2	-.00038 (1.59)	-.00096 (1.72)	-.001 (1.49)	-.0007 (1.35)
Married	-.048 (.63)	-.135 (.80)	.094 (.33)	-.150 (.88)
Divorced	.033 (.64)	.001 (.00)	-.119 (.46)	-.052 (.36)
Birth	.033 (.77)	-.00 (.00)	-.161 (.63)	-.085 (.67)
Migrated	-.032 (.92)	-.091 (1.45)	-.093 (.41)	-.045 (.38)
Constant	4.56	4.79	.492	.703
R^2	.24	.08	.11	.12
Number of cases	1,485	612	200	360

[a]The sample includes all <u>white</u> women aged 30 to 44 in 1967, spouse present (at least in part of the survey period), who were either intermittent workers or continuous workers and, in addition, satisfied the following conditions: only those intermittent workers are included who have experienced a complete spell of labor force interruption within the survey period (1967-1974) followed by a spell of-gainful employment for which reported wage rates are available in the data. Continuous workers are included provided their 1972 wage rates are reported in the data.

[b]The sample is a subsample of that used to obtain estimates in the first column and includes only intermittent workers and excludes continuous workers.

[c]Other explanatory variables in the Mincer-Ofek specification were: tenure at reentry, dummies for whether laid-off, whether unemployed, and whether health impairment occurred just prior to or during the most recent interruption. These are not included for the

PSID replications because such information is generally only complete for heads of households and not spouses.

[d]The sample includes <u>white women</u> aged 30 to 44 in 1967, spouse present (at least in part of the survey period), who were intermittent workers, where intermittent workers are included only if they have experienced a complete spell of labor force interruption within the survey period (1968-1980) followed by a spell of employment for which wage rates are available in the data. Continuous workers were excluded.

[e]The sample includes white women aged 23 to 47 in 1967 who were intermittent workers, where intermittent workers are included only if they have experienced a complete spell of labor force interruption within the survey period (1968-1980) followed by a spell of employment for which wage rates are available in the data. Continuous workers were excluded.

Note: t-statistics are in parentheses.

equation comes from differencing the cross-sectional equation in
(4) at the time of labor force withdrawal (V) and reentry (T):

(6) $\ln W_{iV} = \alpha_{0V} + \alpha_{1V}S_{iV} + \alpha_{2V}e_{0iV} + \alpha_{4V}h_{0iV} + \mu_V X_{iV} + \pi_V Z_{iV} + \theta_{iV};$

(7) $\ln W_{iT} = \alpha_{0T} + \alpha_{1T}S_{iT} + \alpha_{2T}e_{0iT} + \alpha_{4T}h_{0iT} + \alpha_{5T}h_{1iT} + \mu_T X_{iT} + \pi_T Z_{iT} + \theta_{iT}.$

Note that h_{1i} and e_{1i} do not appear in (6) since, at the time of
withdrawal, both equal zero. Similarly, at the time of reentry,
e_{1i} in (7) will have a value of zero. Subtracting (6) from (7),
suppressing the subscript i, denoting changes between V and T as
"Δ," and assuming all parameters and the unobservable
characteristics Z_i do not change between V and T results in:

(8) $\Delta \ln W = \alpha_1 \Delta S + \alpha_5 h_1 + \mu \Delta X + \Delta \theta.$

Estimates of the short-run depreciation effect, α_5, in (8) are
not biased by the possible effects of unmeasured, unchanging
characteristics Z_i; they have been differenced out of (8).[10]
This bias will also be removed from estimates of the effects of
schooling (S_i) and other observed characteristics (X_i), but
estimates of these effects can be obtained only if those
characteristics change from point of withdrawal to point of
reentry. The level of schooling and other characteristics do not
enter equation (8) as long as their parameters do not change over
time.[11]

   Mincer and Ofek estimate the short-run depreciation effect
to range between 6 and 9 percent per year depending on the sample
and specification used. We found it to be 2 to 4 percent per
year in a comparable longitudinal analysis with data from the
PSID (see Table 8.3). One reason for the smaller depreciation
estimate in the PSID is that the reentry wage rate is calculated
over the entire year following the interruption. Thus, PSID
wages may reflect some of the wage restoration that follows a
period of nonwork (see below). An additional reason is that PSID
information on hours of wives is reported by husbands, while
information in the NLS is reported directly by the wives. If

---

[10]Note that while h_1 is an independent variable in both the
level equation (7) and in the change equation (8), its parameter
(α_5) is identical in both. In other words, the change equation
provides an alternative and, in most cases, statistically
superior estimate of the parameters of the level equation.

[11]Hausman and Taylor (1981) develop a method for estimating
the parameters of level variables in a change equation.

Table 8.3

REPLICATION OF MINCER-OFEK WAGE CHANGE EQUATION

Sample	NLS Sample of Continuous and Intermittent Working Women[a],[c] Age 30-44	NLS Sample of Intermittent Working Women[b],[c] Age 30-44	PSID Sample of Intermittent Working Women[d] Age 30-44	PSID Sample of Intermittent Working Women[e] Age 23-47
Dependent Variable	$\ln(w_T) - \ln(w_V)$	$\ln(w_T) - \ln(w_V)$	$\ln(w_T) - \ln(w_V)$	$\ln(w_T) - \ln(w_V)$
S	.006 (1.19)	.008 (.659)	-.007 (.30)	-.024 (1.52)
h_1	-.056 (7.81)	-.060 (3.60)	-.029 (.98)	-.035 (1.44)
Marriage	-.038 (.64)	-.063 (.50)	.167 (.50)	.055 (.301)
Divorce	-.004 (.08)	.009 (.077)	.035 (.12)	.066 (.37)
Birth	-.050 (1.33)	-.030 (.46)	.069 (.23)	.055 (.359)
Migrated	-.051 (1.62)	-.071 (1.19)	-.033 (.13)	-.006 (.038)
Constant	-.028	.162	.005	.254
R^2	.06	.05	.008	.013
Number of cases	1304	373	200	360

[a] The sample includes all white women, married, spouse present (at least in part of the survey period), who were either intermittent workers reporting wages before and after at least one

complete spell of labor interruption within the survey period, or, alternatively, were continuous workers reporting wages in both years, 1971 and 1972.

[b] The sample is a subsample of that used to obtain estimates given in the first column and includes only intermittent workers and excludes continuous workers.

[c] Other explanatory variables in the Mincer-Ofek specification were: dummies for whether laid-off, whether unemployed, and whether health impairment occurred just prior to or during the most recent interruption. These are not included for the PSID replications because such information is generally only complete for heads of households and not spouses.

[d] The sample includes all white women aged 30 to 44 in 1967, spouse present (at least in part of the survey period), who were intermittent workers, where intermittent workers are included only if they have experienced a complete spell of labor force interruption within the survey period (1968-80) followed by a spell of employment for which wage rates are available in the data. Continuous workers were excluded.

[e] The sample includes all white women aged 23 to 47 in 1967 who were intermittent workers, where intermittent workers are included only if they have experienced a complete spell of labor force interruption within the survey period (1968-1980) followed by a spell of employment for which wage rates are available in the data. Continuous workers were excluded.

Note: t-statistics are in parentheses.

this difference leads to greater measurement error in the PSID,
then coefficients may be biased downward (in absolute value).
Taken together, these results suggest that there are substantial
short-run penalties to labor force withdrawals and modest long-
run penalties. Mincer and Ofek interpret these short-run
penalties as a depreciation effect, but such penalties are also
consistent with the argument that women's wages are depressed
upon labor market reentry because of temporary mismatches between
skills and jobs.

The "Rebound" Effect

In their original paper, Mincer and Polachek suggested that
the optimal timing of investment in on-the-job training would
differ depending on the continuity of market activities. In
particular, workers who interrupt their work careers for
nonmarket activities will defer investments in on-the-job
training until they reenter the labor market after completing
these activities so as to minimize the loss from depreciation.
Mincer and Ofek have considerably revised this hypothesis by
arguing that "depreciated" or "eroded" human capital can be
cheaply and rapidly "restored" soon after labor market entry.
They show that post-interruption wages grow at roughly 2.5
percent per year of experience, on average, and that growth rates
in the first year following an interruption range from 5.8 to 6.4
percent per year. This growth rapidly erases estimated short-
term losses from depreciation. They demonstrate further that
amount of job tenure with the current employer accounts for less
than half of this wage growth and interpret this to mean that the
remainder is due to growth (repair) of general training.
However, these conclusions are based on estimates obtained from a
cross-sectional wage equation like (4) rather than a change
equation like (8) and are therefore subject to the same
criticisms outlined above under the depreciation effect. A
preferred method for estimating restoration effects would be
through a wage change equation, the development of which is given
in the following section.

Basic Wage Change Equation

The comparative advantage of the Panel Study of Income
Dynamics data for analyzing earnings lies in the 13 consecutive

annual reports of work hours and earnings of adult women between 1967 and 1979. Women who were heads of their own households reported this information directly; women who were married had this information reported by their husbands. We wish to develop a wage change equation that makes maximal use of this rich information to provide estimates of short-run wage penalties from dropping out of the labor force, patterns of wage rebound following interruptions, and the wage growth consequences of part- versus full-time work and sex typing of work experience.

We have seen the diverse patterns of labor force participation among women. In any given period of time, some will not be working at the beginning, some not working at the end, and some will have spells of work and nonwork interspersed throughout the period. Suppose we select the adult women in the PSID sample, examine the 13 years of work history we have for them, and identify the first (F) and last (L) wage observation for each of them. A Mincer-Ofek type cross-sectional equation at time F would be of the form:

$$(9) \quad \ln W_{iF} = \alpha_{0F} + \alpha_{1F}S_{iF} + \alpha_{2F}e_{0iF} + \alpha_{3F}e_{1iF} + \alpha_{4F}h_{0iF} + \alpha_{5F}h_{1iF} + \mu_F X_{iF} + \pi_F Z_{iF} + \theta_{iF}.$$

PSID information on the work history between F and L allows us to distinguish:

e_L: years of work experience accumulated between F and L <u>since</u> the last completed interruption.

$e*$: years of work experience accumulated between F and L <u>prior to</u> the most recent completed interruption.

h_L: years of nonwork between F and L <u>during</u> most recent completed interruption.

$h*$: years of nonwork accumulated between F and L <u>prior to</u> most recent completed interruption.

The cross-sectional wage relationship at time L (allowing the parameters to change) is given by:

$$(10) \quad \ln W_{iL} = \alpha_{0L} + \alpha_{1L}S_{iL} + \alpha_{2L}e_{0iF} + \alpha_{3L}e_{1iF} + \alpha_{4L}h_{0iF} + \alpha_{5L}h_{1iF} + \alpha_6 e_i^* + \alpha_7 e_{Li} + \alpha_8 h_i^* + \alpha_9 h_{Li} + \mu_L X_{iL} + \pi_L Z_{iL} + \theta_{iL}.$$

Subtracting (9) from (10), suppressing the subscript i, denoting changes from F to L as "Δ," and adding and subtracting $\alpha_{1L}S_F$, $\mu_L X_F$, and $\pi_L Z_F$ results in the following general equation for wage change:

$$(11) \quad \Delta lnW = \Delta\alpha_0 + \alpha_{1L}\Delta S + \Delta\alpha_1 S_F + \Delta\alpha_2 e_{0F} + \Delta\alpha_3 e_{1F} +$$
$$\Delta\alpha_4 h_{0F} + \Delta\alpha_5 h_{1F} + \alpha_6 e^* + \alpha_7 e_L + \alpha_8 h^* + \alpha_9 h_L +$$
$$\mu_L\Delta X + \Delta\mu X_F + \pi_L\Delta Z + \Delta\pi Z_F + \Delta\theta.$$

If one assumes that the cross-sectional effects of the
explanatory variables are invariant between F and L and, further,
that the unmeasured characteristics remain constant for the same
individual, then the wage change equation simplifies to:

$$(12) \quad \Delta ln W = \alpha_{1L}\Delta S + \alpha_6 e^* + \alpha_7 e_L + \alpha_8 h^* + \alpha_9 h_L + \mu_L\Delta X +$$
$$\Delta\theta.$$

The parameter estimates of short-run human capital depreciation
(h_L) and restoration (e_L) obtained by wage change equation (12)
using panel data are free from the statistical problems caused by
retrospective reports and by unmeasured variables correlated with
the included (measured) explanatory variables.[12] An additional
advantage is that many more women meet the requirements of
working at least 2 of the 13 years than work in a single year,
and, therefore, selection bias problems are much less severe in
estimating change equation (12) than in estimating a cross-
sectional equation or a Mincer-Ofek type of change equation.[13]

Equation (12) is the simplest version of the wage change
model we wish to estimate. Wage rebound following a spell of

---

[12]It may be possible that certain personal characteristics may
change or that wage effects of both measured and unmeasured
characteristics may change even for wage change as short as a
year or two. So although the wage change technique better
handles the statistical problems posed by unobserved measures
better than wage level equations, it may not be free from
possible bias itself. Although the wage change equation
represents an improvement over wage level specifications, it
causes two further statistical problems: (1) it is impossible to
estimate time-invariant variables since they do not have an
impact on wage change as specified in the model; (2) serial
correlation is now present in the error term. This leads to
biased estimates of standard errors, although parameter estimates
will be unbiased and consistent.
  It may seem that the inclusion of variables measuring time
in and out of the labor force will produce a singular matrix
because these variables sum to the same number for all sample
individuals. This would be the case if the length of time
between F and L were identical for all individuals. That is not
the case here, however, since F is not necessarily the first year
of the 13-year period nor is L necessarily the 13th year.

[13]At any point in time only about half of all adult women are
in the labor force. Requiring that women work at least two out
of thirteen years eliminates only about one-fifth of the sample.
Below, sample-selection adjustments are made for white women.
The sample-selection-bias correction is detailed in Appendix C.

nonwork may be nonlinear, and we can allow for that with a different functional form for e_L. Years of e* and e_L spent in part- versus full-time work can be distinguished to estimate wage growth corresponding to each type of experience.

Empirical Results

Table 8.4 shows the basic wage change equation for various subgroups of black, and white female workers. The results are fairly robust to changes in the definition of the number of hours it takes to be "in" or "out" of the labor force, to restricting the sample to workers with at least one interruption and therefore with a "clean" measure of e_L, and to adjustments for sample selection bias.[14] Estimates of depreciation for the most recent spell out of the labor force are consistently negative and generally range from 3 to 5 percent per year out. The statistical significance of the e_L coefficients (length of work spell since the most recent interruption) shows a wage "rebound" following spells out of the labor force that ranges between 4 and 8 percent per year. Taken together, these results suggest that women who dropped out of the labor force were penalized with a drop in wages but experienced a relatively rapid growth in wages upon returning to work so that, on average, it took slightly fewer years than the length of the interruption to erase the wage loss strictly due to depreciation.[15] Adjustments to the equation

---

[14]The method used to adjust for sample selection bias is detailed in Appendix C. The adjustments were made for white women but not black women.

[15]Wage restoration after reentry never fully erases wage loss due to interruption because of lost wages attributed to foregone experience.

With measures of both e_L and e_L^2 in the regression equation, the estimated coefficients trace out a parabola $y=a+b_1e_L+b_2e_L^2$. The coefficient on e_L can be interpreted as the wage growth rate immediately following a withdrawal. That the coefficient on e_L^2 is negative indicates that the parabola is an inverted "u," peaking at $(-b_1/2b_2)$ years following a withdrawal. For the estimates on Table 8.4, the parabola peaks at around ten years following a withdrawal.

That work experience is entered quadratically in wage equations has implications for the appropriate functional form for the e* and e_L variables in our wage change equation if either of these work segments began prior to 1967. Few sample individuals have e_L segments that began prior to 1967, but a substantial proportion have e* segments that do. To see the implications of this, consider the case where the wage-experience relationship is of the following functional form:

Table 8.4

VARIOUS WAGE GROWTH REGRESSIONS FOR WHITE AND BLACK WOMEN

Independent Variable	Full Sample, Using 250 Hours to Define Labor Force Participation			Full Sample, Using 500 Hours to Define Labor Force Participation		Subsample With at Least One Interruption Between First and Last Wage Observation	
	White	White[a]	Black	White	Black	White	Black
h^*: Years out of the labor force during 1967–1979 prior to most recent interruption	.016 (.029)	.015 (.029)	−.016 (.030)	.006 (.028)	−.016 (.030)	.023 (.033)	−.029 (.033)
h_L: Years out of the labor force during most recent interruption	−.039** (.013)	−.038** (.013)	−.046** (.016)	−.038** (.013)	−.035** (.015)	−.020 (.016)	−.063** (.022)
e^*: Years in the labor force prior to most recent reentry	.012† (.007)	.016* (.008)	.030** (.008)	.012† (.007)	.019* (.008)	−.004 (.013)	−.037* (.016)
e_L: Years in the labor force during most recent	.052*	.051*	.080**	.042†	.050*	.049	.077

Table 8.4 (continued)

Independent Variable	Full Sample, Using 250 Hours to Define Labor Force Participation			Full Sample, Using 500 Hours to Define Labor Force Participation		Subsample With at Least One Interruption Between First and Last Wage Observation	
	White	White[a]	Black	White	Black	White	Black
spell	(.023)	(.024)	(.026)	(.022)	(.025)	(.034)	(.050)
e_L^2	-.0027† (.0016)	-.0024 (.0016)	-.0041* (.0019)	-.0018 (.0016)	-.0021 (.0019)	-.0017 (.0029)	-.0064 (.0044)
$\hat{\rho}-1$		-.454** (.0016)					
Number of observations	837	821	521	809	500	569	266
R^2 (adjusted)	.021	.026	.057	.020	.033	.020	.064

Significance levels: +.10 *.05 **.01
[a] Corrected for sample selection bias (see Appendix C).
Note: Standard errors are in parentheses. Source: Panel Study of Income Dynamics

for white women for sample selection bias do not change these conclusions.

Effects of Prospective Interruptions on Wage Growth

Since the profitability of investments are affected by the length of time over which benefits are received, the human capital model predicts that otherwise identical workers will invest less if they anticipate labor market withdrawals than if they do not. Sandell and Shapiro (1980) test this proposition by estimating whether NLS women who expected to be out of the labor force at age 35 had flatter experience-earnings profiles before then than women who expected to be working at age 35. Although most of their key parameter estimates are in the expected direction, none are significant at the 5 percent level for white or black women. Corcoran (1979) and Corcoran and Duncan (1979) use two variables, "plan to stop work for nontraining reasons" and "expect more children," to test the hypothesis that, for women workers, expectations of employment continuity affect

---

(i) $W = a+b_1 exp+b_2 exp^2$.

When evaluated at time F, the equation has the form:

(ii) $W_F = a_F+b_1 exp_F+b_2 exp_F^2$.

At time L, assuming all experience is e_L, the equation becomes:

(iii) $W_L = a_L+b_1(exp_F+e_L)+b_2(exp_f+e_L)^2$.

Differencing these two equations gives:

(iv) $W_L-W_F = \Delta a+b_1 e_L+b_2(e_L^2+2exp_F \cdot e_L)$.

This suggests that any quadratic treatment of e^* and e_L requires an adjustment for experience in those segments acquired prior to 1967. There are two problems with such adjustments. The first is that work experience acquired prior to 1967 is reported retrospectively in 1976. Adjustments for pre-1967 experience are likely to be more prone to measurement error than experience between 1967 and 1979, which is reported annually. The imprecise reporting should bias estimates of b_2 in equation (iv) downward.

The second problem is of the appropriate functional form for e_L. If observations on e_L are at most 13 years in length, then a parabola is an appropriate functional form to model the short-term wage rebound. If observations on e_L extend beyond 13 years, then a more appropriate functional form would allow for rapid rebound followed by slower long-term growth. A parabola is inappropriate for this because it forces wages to decline at an increasing rate after its peak. The addition of variables like $2exp_F \cdot e_L$ to equation (12) did not change the coefficients of e_L and e_L^2 term appreciably.

investment decisions. If workers who expect discontinuous work careers have invested less intensively than other workers with similar work experience, then these variables should pick up this negative effect. Black women who expected to stop work for nontraining purposes were currently earning less (24 percent less) than otherwise similar black women workers. For white women, the effect was in the expected direction but was insignificant. Signs of coefficients on "expecting to have children" were the opposite of expectations and insignificant for both groups.

This hypothesis is an important one for the human capital model and deserves testing in the context of the wage change models developed here. Since we know which women in the PSID sample were not working at the end of the 13-year period, we can test directly whether such workers' jobs provided them lower wage growth and lower depreciation. In contrast to the self-reported intentions of respondents used in the articles listed above, this procedure tests for the effects of actual labor force behavior in period t+1 on wage profiles in period t. We did this by creating a dummy variable (NT79) for whether did not work in 1979, interacting this dummy with h_L, e_L, and e_L^2, and adding these four variables to the basic wage change equation (12). The results of this analysis are reported in Table 8.5. In general, white women who did not work in 1979 had the same wage increment for additional years of experience as women who did work in 1979 and similar wage loss with time out as did otherwise similar white women who were working in 1979. But one result for black women does conform with Polachek's predictions. Black women who were not working in 1979 exhibited no wage loss during prior labor force withdrawals.[14] Their past wage return to experience, however, did not differ from otherwise similar black women who were working in 1979.

Labor Supply and Wage Growth

Women are considerably more likely than men to work in part-time jobs, a fact that may lead to considerable differences in the amount of on-the-job training they acquire and, therefore, in

---

[14]The depreciation estimate for black women who did not work in 1979 is the sum of the coefficient on the h_L term (-.070) and the coefficient on the NT79*h_L term (+.059).

Table 8.5

EFFECT OF A PROSPECTIVE WORK INTERRUPTION
ON WAGE GROWTH AND DEPRECIATION

Independent Variables	Wage Growth		
	White	White[a]	Black
$h*$: Years out of the labor force during 1967-1979 prior to most recent interruption	.013 (.029)	.013 (.019)	-.015 (.030)
h_L: Years out of the labor force during most recent interruption	-.035* (.015)	-.031* (.015)	-.070** (.020)
$e*$: Years in the labor force prior to most recent reentry	.012 (.009)	.016† (.009)	.023* (.011)
e_L: Years in the labor force during most recent spell	.051† (.027)	.050† (.027)	.077* (.032)
e_L^2	-.0025 (.0015)	-.0022 (.0018)	-.0045* (.0022)
NT79: Did not work in 1979	-.017 (.099)	.002 (.101)	-.124 (.103)
NT79*h_L	-.030 (.029)	-.038 (.029)	.059† (.032)
NT79*e_L	.043 (.056)	.049 (.057)	-.006 (.068)
NT79*e_L^2	-.0081 (.0056)	-.0081 (.0057)	.0009 (.0090)
$\hat{\rho}-1$		-.451** (.183)	
R^2 adjusted	.024	.030	.035
Number of observations	837	821	521

Significance levels: +.10 *.05 **.01
[a]Corrected for sample selection bias (see Appendix C).
Note: Standard errors are in parentheses. Source: Panel Study of Income Dynamics

their relative wage growth. The most general human capital theories (Heckman, 1976; Blinder and Weiss, 1976) do not make unambiguous predictions on the effect of part-time work upon human capital investment and wages, but there are reasons for believing that less training is acquired in part-time work than in full-time work. First, because part-time work means fewer hours in the labor market than full-time work, women who expect to work part time in the future have a shorter expected work life and hence less incentive to invest in on-the-job training. In this case, both the overall volume of investment and the rate of investment would be lower for those who plan to work part time than for those who plan to work full time. If current part-time work patterns are associated with the likelihood of future part-time work, then current part-time workers will be making fewer investments. Second, if employers suspect that part-time workers are more likely to leave than full-time workers, they might restrict training opportunities in part-time work. Employers would be most likely to restrict opportunities for firm-specific training. Finally, just as it is argued that skills depreciate during periods of nonwork, skills could depreciate more (or appreciate less) during part-time work than during full-time work, since part-time work involves fewer hours of work (i.e., more hours of nonwork). The depreciation from nonuse would be greater if the nature of part-time work precluded workers from maintaining their market skills. If formal training is scheduled when part-time workers are not at work, then there will be less wage growth due to the acquisition of new skills for them.

Two sources of data with crude direct measures of on-the-job training do show a positive relationship between work hours and training. Duncan and Hoffman (1978) found with the 1976 wave of the PSID that adult workers aged 18 to 64 who worked less than 20 hours per week reported training periods attached to their jobs that were only about half as long as workers working between 40 and 50 hours. Those working more than 50 hours per week reported considerably longer training periods than any other group of workers. All in all, the work hours variable accounted for more than 5 percent of the variance of the training time measure--a highly significant amount. They also found that part-time workers were considerably less likely to be engaged in on-the-job training.'' Only about one-tenth of those working less than 20 hours per week were currently engaged in training, compared to nearly 20 percent of those working between 40 and 50 hours per week and more than one-quarter of those working more than 50 hours per week. Stafford and Duncan (1979) found qualitatively similar, although less statistically significant, differences in training by labor supply for workers in the 1975-1976 Time Use Study. The average amounts of time workers spent learning skills that were part of their regular job or spent learning skills that were not part of their regular jobs were least for those working less than 30 hours per week and greatest for those working more than 50 hours per week.

Corcoran and Duncan (1978) included a retrospective measure of the composition of past work experience in a cross-sectional wage equation and found significant effects for all four of the race-sex subgroups under investigation. They took reports of part- and full-time years worked since age 18 and calculated the fraction of total working years that were full time. (The respondents supplied their own definition of part- versus full-time work.) After controlling for a host of other experience and labor force attachment measures, they found that the wages of white women with entirely full-time work histories were 26.2 percent higher than otherwise similar white women with entirely part-time work histories. The comparable differences for black women and white and black men were 12.5 percent, 30.7 percent, and 55.1 percent, respectively. Virtually no men had completely part-time work histories, however, so their estimates were beyond the range of observations.

Jones and Long (1979) used data from the NLS to estimate two cross-sectional wage equations that included interactions between work experience segments and whether the work was part-week. Although the signs of the coefficients they estimated were consistent with the hypothesis that part-time work leads to slower wage growth, only 2 of the 12 coefficients were statistically significant at conventional levels. Their measures of the part-time nature of the work segments were very rough, however, and may have biased some of the coefficient estimates.

''A worker was considered to be engaged in on-the-job training if current job tenure was less than the reported time needed to become fully trained and qualified for the job.

We can investigate the effects of part- and full-time work on the wage growth of women workers with a simple modification to our basic wage growth equation. In (12), we did not distinguish between years in the e* and e_L segments that were full and part time. Since the volume of work hours was ascertained for each of the 13 years under investigation, we can use that information to classify years of experience that involved part-time work (less than 1,500 hours) and full-time work (1,500 hours or more). Four variables were formed with this information: (1) the number of years of e* that were part-time (e*-part), (2) the number of years of e* that were full-time (e*-full), (3) the number of years of e_L that were part-time (e_L-part), and (4) the number of years of e_L that were full-time (e_L-full). Substituting these variables for e* and e_L in (12) yields the following equation:

(13) $\Delta \ln W = \alpha_{1L} \Delta S + \alpha_8 h* + \alpha_9 h_L + \alpha_{10} e*\text{-part} + \alpha_{11} e*\text{-full} + \alpha_{12} e_L\text{-part} + \alpha_{13} e_L\text{-full} + \mu_L \Delta X + \Delta \theta.$

As with the more basic measures of e* and e_L, all four of these new variables are obtained in each of the annual interviews and do not rely on retrospective reports by either women workers or their husbands.

The results of the estimation of the augmented wage growth equation are shown in Table 8.6. Full-time work does indeed appear to be associated with significant wage growth, while part-time work does not. When the two measures of e_L are entered linearly, the wage growth associated with full-time experience is positive and significant for both white and black women, while the wage growth associated with years of part-time work in the most recent spell of employment was insignificant for both groups of workers. With years of experience prior to the most recent spell of nonwork (e*), the full-time work variables have larger coefficient than the part-time variables, although these differences were not significant at conventional levels. A parabolic specification for the e_L measure gives expected results for white women--there is a parabolic rebound for full-time but not part-time work that changes little with adjustments for sample selection bias. For black women, there is a parabolic wage rebound for part-time work--a result for which we have no ready explanation.

Table 8.6

EFFECTS OF PART- AND FULL-TIME WORK ON WAGE GROWTH

Independent Variable	Wage Growth					
	White	White[a]	Black	White	White[a]	Black
h*: Years out of the labor force during 1967-1979 prior to most recent interruption	.023 (.029)	.023 (.029)	-.005 (.030)	.022 (.029)	.022 (.029)	-.026 (.029)
h$_L$: Years out of the labor force during most recent interruption	-.034** (.013)	-.033** (.013)	-.037* (.015)	-.035** (.013)	-.034 (.013)	-.049** (.015)
Years of full-time e* (experience prior to most recent reentry)	.007 (.007)	.012 (.008)	.024* (.008)	.007 (.008)	.012 (.008)	.034** (.008)
Years of part-time e*	-.002 (.011)	-.0008 (.011)	.018 (.011)	-.002 (.011)	-.008 (.011)	.023* (.011)
Years of full-time e$_L$ (experience during most recent spell)	.028** (.008)	.026** (.008)	.030** (.010)	.062** (.021)	.062** (.021)	.037 (.024)
Full time e$_L$-squared	....	....	....	-.0036* (.0018)	-.0034* (.0018)	-.0008 (.0021)
Years of part-time e$_L$	-.003 (.010)	-.003 (.010)	.017 (.013)	-.021 (.026)	-.023 (.027)	.150** (.029)
Years of part-time e$_L$-squared	....	....	....	.0016 (.0025)	.0016 (.002)	-.014** (.003)
$\hat{\rho}$-1	....	-.557** (.183)	....	....	-.544** (.183)	....
R^2 adjusted	.025	.035	.049	.028	.036	.096

Table 8.6 (continued)

Independent Variable	Wage Growth					
	White	White[a]	Black	White	White[a]	Black
Number of observations	837	821	521	837	821	521

Significance levels: +.10 *.05 **.01
[a] Corrected for sample selection bias (see Appendix C).
Note: Standard errors are in parentheses. Source: Panel Study of Income Dynamics

LABOR FORCE WITHDRAWALS AND JOB
SEGREGATION: HUMAN CAPITAL EXPLANATIONS

The 1974 Economic Report of the President speculated that sex differences in patterns of work participation may be the cause of the sex segregation of jobs. This line of reasoning has been extensively developed by Zellner (1975) and Polachek (1976, 1979, 1981).[18] Since Polachek's explanation subsumes Zellner's model, we will concentrate on his model in the following discussion. Polachek (1981) defines atrophy as the loss of earnings potential that occurs when skills are not continuously used. He shows that if the cost of labor force withdrawals (the atrophy rate) varies across occupations, and if lifetime labor force participation differs among individuals, then a worker will choose "that occupation which imposes the smallest penalty, given his desired lifetime participation." This model treats the "lifetime as a unit." Interperiod occupational mobility is ignored (i.e., there is no mobility between occupations),[19] and lifetime work participation is assumed to be exogenously determined. Thus, this model implicitly assumes that workers tend to work in the same sort of occupation throughout their lives or at least over long periods of time.

This model provides a human capital explanation for the sex segregation of the labor market. If work skills do atrophy during withdrawals from the labor force, then it is rational for women who expect to take time out from the labor force to work in fields where there is less chance of atrophy, i.e., in fields with low depreciation rates but also with low returns to experience. By selecting jobs that are easy to leave and reenter, women can thus more easily combine the dual demands of career and family. Typically "female" jobs will be those in which there is the least atrophy, and so the human capital explanation explains job segregation as well as low female wages. Note that if depreciated skills can be restored rapidly (as

---

[18]England (1981, 1982) provides an extensive discussion of these models. The discussion in this section draws heavily from her work.

[19]Polachek notes that "this assumption can be relaxed by posing the problem within a dynamic control framework" but goes on to say that "even within such a framework the same conclusions hold for occupations chosen at a given stage of the life cycle" (Polachek, 1981:64). Note that this relaxation still implies occupational immobility within a life-cycle stage.

Mincer and Ofek and we show), this weakens the force of Polachek's arguments.

Webster's Third New International Dictionary defines atrophy as "a wasting away or progressive decline." Thus, the casual reader might assume that Polachek's atrophy rate is equivalent to Mincer's and Polachek's depreciation rate. But atrophy, as defined by Polachek, picks up two things--depreciation (i.e., reduction in work skills due to nonuse) and the loss in expected earnings growth due to missing a year of work.[20] Polachek's atrophy might be more appropriately called the "opportunity cost" of a year out of the labor force.[21]

The difference between depreciation and atrophy is best illustrated by comparing how the two effects are calculated. Mincer and Polachek calculate depreciation rates with work experience controlled. Their measure picks up only the depreciation of work skills--not the loss of a year of experience. This is analogous to comparing a woman with ten years of experience and a 2 year labor force withdrawal to a woman who has worked continuously for 10 years. Polachek calculated atrophy rates by controlling for potential work experience (in fact, years since school completion). This atrophy rate estimate picks up both a depreciation effect and the effect of fewer years of experience.[22] This is analogous to comparing two women who left school 12 years ago, one who has worked 10 years and one who has worked 12 years.

Depreciation and the growth of earnings with experience are quite different processes. The first implies that the level of work skills is lower following an interruption than just prior to

---

[20]Zellner's explanation of the sex segregation of occupations rests solely on this second effect. To paraphrase England (1981), "Zellner assumes that occupations can be divided into those that offer high initial salaries and flat earnings profiles and into those with low initial salaries and steep earnings profiles. Women, because of their shorter expected work lives, will be more likely to maximize lifetime earnings in the occupations with high initial salaries and flat wage growth-- i.e., in 'female' occupations."

[21]We are grateful to Siv Gustafson for first pointing this out to us in a personal conversation in 1978. England (1981; 1982) is the first author who clearly makes this distinction in a published paper.

[22]England (1981, 1982) refers to this latter effect as "foregone appreciation," and provides an excellent discussion of Polachek's models.

that interruption. If this earnings loss is long lasting, it is obvious why women who expect prolonged labor force withdrawals should enter fields with low depreciation rates. Polachek's model also implies that women who expect prolonged withdrawals should enter fields with high initial salaries but fairly flat earnings growth rates. This second decision only makes sense if we assume that, all else being equal, jobs with high earnings growth pay less initially than jobs without such earnings growth.[23]

To summarize, Polachek's explanation is an ingenious attempt to provide a human capital explanation for job segregation. If this explanation were correct, we would expect the following: First, since women's choice of a "female" or "male" occupation reflects lifetime participation plans, we would expect that the sex typing of women's occupations changes little over a prolonged period of time. Second, depreciation and/or earnings growth will be lower in "female" occupations. Third, women who expect discontinuous careers will choose "female" rather than "male" occupations because discontinuity is penalized less. Because of this choice, women with discontinuous work careers will be concentrated in "female" occupations. The first two implications of Polachek's argument are also predicted by any job-segregation model that presumes that women are locked into a set of female-dominated jobs that do not provide productivity-enhancing experience.

What Do Women's Occupational Histories Look Like?-- Patterns of Occupational Mobility, 1975-1979

There is some evidence that Polachek's assumption of little mobility between "male" and "female" occupations over a prolonged period of time is wrong. England (1982) reports that the correlation between percent female in 1967 detailed Census occupation and percent female in first detailed Census occupation is only .39 for women aged 30 to 44 years in 1967. This suggests there may be considerable mobility between "male" and "female" job sectors.

We further tested the assumption of intersectoral immobility by calculating patterns of occupational segregation over the years 1975-1979. Coding of the occupation and industry of

---

[23]England (1981) makes this point quite clearly.

workers in the Panel Study was sufficiently detailed during the years 1975-1979 to permit an analysis of the dynamics of job segregation during that period. Our procedure for determining whether a given job was "female dominated" or "male dominated" is detailed in Appendix A. Briefly, we took a single year of data (1975) and computed the fraction of Panel Study adult workers who were women in all possible combinations of occupations and industries.[24] After combining together homogeneous occupations with fewer than 25 observations, we arrived at a set of estimates of the fraction of adult workers who were women in 74 combinations of occupation and industries. In some of the analysis below, we use those fractions directly, naming that measure "percent female dominated." In most of the analysis, however, we group all jobs into only two categories: those with more than 50 percent women workers and those with fewer than 50 percent women workers. These jobs are termed "female dominated" and "male dominated," respectively.

The actual patterns of occupational segregation are shown first for a single year only, 1975, in Table 8.7. The sample is restricted to men and women workers between the ages of 23 and 57 who worked at least 250 hours in 1975.[25] The table shows, not unexpectedly, that both men and women work at jobs dominated by members of their own sex. Three-quarters of the women in the Panel Study sample worked in female-dominated jobs--a fact that applies equally well to both full- and part-time women workers and to white and black women as well. That part-time workers are not more likely to hold female-dominated jobs than are full-time workers is somewhat surprising. White men are even more heavily concentrated in jobs dominated by men than are women in jobs dominated by women. The relatively small number of part-time white male workers are less likely to be in male-dominated jobs, as are full-time black male workers.

---

[24]There were 429 combinations of occupations and industries formed from a two-digit occupation code and a two-digit industry code.

[25]As before, the sample consists of household heads and wives in this age range and thus excludes a small number of adults who relate to the head of the household in some other way. The age restriction is kept throughout this entire section, and includes workers who are younger than 62 by the end of the five-year period under study.

Table 8.7

OCCUPATIONAL SEGREGATION AND LABOR SUPPLY IN 1975
(All household heads or wives aged 23 to 57 who
worked 250 hours or more in 1975)

Fraction in Female-Dominated Jobs[a]	Women			Men		
	White	Black	All	White	Black	All
All workers	.74 (1,366)	.78 (766)	.74 (2,142)	.13 (2,058)	.26 (857)	.14 (2,915)
Part-time workers[b]	.77 (611)	.76 (296)	.76 (907)	.22 (223)	.15 (152)	.21 (375)
Full-time workers[b]	.72 (755)	.79 (480)	.73 (1,235)	.12 (1,835)	.29 (705)	.14 (2,540)

Table reads: 74 percent of the 1,366 white women who worked in
1975 were in female-dominated jobs.

[a]A job is designated as female dominated if the percentage of
women workers equals or exceeds 50 (see Appendix A).

[b]Full- and part-time workers are defined by whether 1975 work
hours were greater than or less than 1,500, respectively.

Note: Number of observations are given in parentheses below
each estimate.

Source: Panel Study of Income Dynamics

These figures on occupational segregation at a point in time are well known and can be estimated more reliably with larger data sets such as the decennial census. The Panel Study is unique in its ability to characterize the year-to-year change in the occupational position of a broad range of male and female workers. Such data on change can shed a great deal of light on whether women find themselves locked into certain kinds of jobs, as models of job segregation argue, at least implicitly.

To investigate the dynamics of occupational segregation over the period 1975-1979, we selected a sample of women who worked in the first and last years of that period and who may or may not have worked during the three years in between. Further limiting of the sample to continuous workers would have been unduly restrictive. The resulting figures on occupational position, shown in Table 8.8, are computed only for the years in which work hours exceeded 250.

The single-year figures shown in Table 8.7 revealed that about three-quarters of white women workers held female-dominated jobs at a point in time. If occupational segregation were completely rigid, then we would expect to observe that same fraction spending all of its working years in jobs dominated by women. Table 8.8 shows that this is clearly not the case. Only half of the white women spent all of their working years in the five years 1975-1979 in jobs dominated by women. Less than one-sixth of these white women spent all of their working years in jobs dominated by men, leaving more than one-third who switched sectors at least once. Switches between sectors for black women were almost as common—31 percent of the black women were coded as switching from a female-dominated job to a male-dominated one or vice versa.

These figures on the extent of switching between sectors mix together both kinds of changes. A more relevant statistic on the issue of whether women who take female-dominated jobs get stuck in them is the fraction of women who began in female-dominated jobs but switched out of them. That fraction is 31 percent for white women and 25 percent for black women. Both sets of figures would appear too high to be consistent with a model of occupational segregation based on impenetrable barriers.

These figures on switches between sectors deserve careful scrutiny. On the one hand, they are likely to understate the

Table 8.8

DYNAMICS OF OCCUPATIONAL SEGREGATION

| | Subgroup | | | | | |
| | Women Who Worked at Least 250 Hours in 1975 and 1979 | | | Men | | |
	White	Black	All	White	Black	All
Occupational Change						
Fraction spending <u>all</u> working years in female-dominated jobs	.51 (871)	.61 (538)	.52 (1,409)	.07 (1,563)	.18 (606)	.08 (2,169)
Fraction spending <u>all</u> working years in male-dominated jobs	.15 (871)	.09 (538)	.14 (1,409)	.79 (1,563)	.67 (606)	.78 (2,169)
Fraction switching at least once in either direction	.34 (871)	.31 (538)	.34 (1,409)	.15 (1,563)	.18 (606)	.16 (2,169)
Fraction of those in female-dominated jobs initially who switched to male-dominated jobs	.31 (647)	.25 (423)	.30 (1,070)	.60 (207)	.37 (106)	.56 (313)
Fraction of those in male-dominated jobs initially who switched to	.44	.55	.45	.09	.13	.09

Table 8.8 (continued)

	Subgroup					
	Women Who Worked at Least 250 Hours in 1975 and 1979			Men		
	White	Black	All	White	Black	All
female-dominated jobs	(224)	(115)	(339)	(1,300)	(456)	(1,756)

Table reads: The 871 white women who worked at least 250 hours in 1975 and 1979 spent 74 percent of their working time in female-dominated jobs.

[a] A job is designated as female dominated if the percentage of women workers is greater than or equal to 50. Otherwise, it is designated as male dominated.

[b] Full-time and part-time workers are defined by the number of years work hours equals or exceeds 1,500. If the ratio of years with work hours greater than or equal to 1,500 to the "total number" of years worked was greater than or equal to .50, then the worker is designated as "full time"; if not, the worker is designated part time.

Note: The number of observations are given in parentheses below each estimate.

true amount of movement between sectors because the time span over which such changes can be observed is limited to only five years.[26] In addition, our classification procedure for identifying female- and male-dominated occupations is a crude one and undoubtedly misses some true switches that would be caught with a more refined set of occupational and industrial codes. On the other hand, errors in the coding of occupation and industry may create the appearance of a switch when in fact there was none.[27] It is impossible to say whether the net effect of these considerations is to increase or decrease the estimated extent of switching between job sectors. It is almost certainly true that the extent of switching is substantial, however, a fact which is inconsistent with Polachek's assumption of occupational immobility and with any other labor market model based on rigid segmentation by sex. This result also suggests that analysts should be wary of using a woman's current occupation as a measure of her past occupational history.

Work History Wage Growth and Occupational Segregation: Empirical Evidence

Polachek (1981) presents a variety of empirical evidence to support his arguments about the effects of work history on occupational choice. He has shown that the probability of currently working in a given occupation (defined by one-digit Census categories) is affected by years out of the labor force and that the size of this effect differs by occupation. He has also demonstrated that the relationship between wage growth and years out of the labor force (home time) differs across occupations (i.e., occupations have different atrophy rates). And he has shown that there is a negative correlation between the

---

[26] Women who work continuously in the same sector between 1975 and 1979 but switch in 1980 or had switched in 1974 are classified here as persistent residents in one sector. Also, while most of the women in this sample worked in every one of the five years, some did not work in some of the middle three years, giving them fewer than five years in which a switch can be observed.

[27] Appendix Table 8B.1 sheds some light on this by showing comparable mobility figures for the case when male-dominated jobs are defined as less than 40 percent female, and female-dominated jobs are defined as greater than 60 percent female. Less mobility is found with this more restrictive definition, but the extent of mobility is still substantial.

effect of years out of the labor force on the probability of
working in an occupation and the atrophy rate in that occupation.

Even if we ignore the issue of mobility across occupations,
Polachek's evidence does not unambiguously support his
hypothesis. Take Polachek's first finding--that home time
affects the probabilities of currently being in a particular
occupation. This finding can only explain sex segregation cf
jobs if women with extensive home time were more likely to work
in female-dominated occupations than were otherwise similar women
without extensive home time. Polachek used his estimates of
these effects to obtain a projected population-wide occupational
distribution for women 30 to 44 who had worked continuously since
school completion. He reported that the proportion of women
professionals and managers (currently male-dominated fields)
would increase and that the proportion of women in household and
service work (currently female-dominated fields) would decrease.
On the other hand, his figures indicated an increase in the
proportion of women employed in clerical work (a female-dominated
field), a decrease in women employed in crafts (a male-dominated
field), and a decrease in the proportion of women in sales (an
integrated field).[28]

England (1982) investigated the effect of home time on sex
typing of current occupation more directly. She reports that the
sex composition of most recent occupation and the sex composition
of first occupation were uncorrelated with the proportion of
total time employed since school completion for white women aged

---

[28]Probably the best way to evaluate the quantitative
importance of this evidence is to estimate the extent to which
occupational sex segregation would be reduced if women's home
time were zero--i.e., if men and women had the same work
participation patterns. We estimated this by applying Duncan and
Duncan's (1955) segregation index to Polachek's sample. This
index measures "the minimum proportion of one group that would
have to be shifted for its occupational distribution to be equal
to that of the other." The segregation index for Polachek's
sample is .50. Then we calculated this segregation index on the
projected occupational distribution calculated by Polachek under
the assumption that women worked continuously. If his theory
were correct, occupational sex segregation should be considerably
reduced. Under the assumption that women do not withdraw from
the labor force, the segregation index is .48--a reduction of
only 2 percent.

36 to 50 years in 1973.[29] This result does not suggest a strong link between labor force discontinuity and the sex typing of current or first job.

Now we turn to Polachek's second finding--that the detrimental wage effects of home time vary across occupations. He calculated this by regressing the difference between 1972 and 1967 wages on home time and other variables expected to affect wages. Unlike most economic studies of wage differentials based on the human capital model, Polachek examines dollar changes in wages rather than percentage changes. If all occupations had identical percentage wage decreases per year out of the labor force, Polachek would likely obtain differences in dollar wage change with highly paid occupations showing greater decline. Indeed, in Polachek's analysis, dollar wage changes are most negative for professionals, crafts people, and managers--the three most highly paid occupations.

In order to study wage change between 1967 and 1972, Polachek must restrict analysis to women who reported a wage in 1967 and in 1972. Thus, Polachek's sample is chosen on the basis of work behavior. This could possibly lead to selection bias problems when estimating effects of work behavior on wage change.[30]

A further problem is that Polachek's estimate of effects of home time will be dominated by short-run effects, since he restricts analysis to a five-year period and only examines the effects of withdrawals during that period. If lost skills were rapidly restored (as Mincer and Ofek's and our results suggest), then Polachek's estimates will considerably exaggerate the lifetime costs of time out. Finally, note that Polachek's atrophy estimates pick up both "depreciation" and effects of fewer years of experience.

---

[29] England reports that Wolf and Rosenfeld (1978) present some evidence that suggests a weak link between home time and sex composition of occupation.

[30] As discussed above, this sample selection bias is a general problem for analysts of women's wages. At any point in time only about half of all adult women are in the labor force. Restricting the sample to women who worked in two specific years as Polachek does eliminates even more women from the sample. When we replicated our wage change model for women who worked in 1975 and 1979, the results were inconsistent with results from the larger and less restricted sample.

Even if Polachek's evidence that occupations differ in atrophy rates were correct, this would only explain sex segregation if there were less depreciation of skills and lower returns to experience in female-dominated occupations. England (1981, 1982) tested this assumption using both the NLS sample of mature women and a sample of women in a wider age range from the PSID. England's analyses have two advantages over Polachek's analysis. She looks directly at the relationship between home time and sex typing of current job, and she examines depreciation and returns to experience separately. England regressed the natural logarithm of wages on experience, education, time out, and percent female in current occupation (coded at three-digit Census level), and tested for significant interactions between experience and percent female and between time out and percent female. She reports that neither the depreciation rate nor returns to experience were affected by percent female in current occupation.

Both Polachek's and England's empirical tests of the Polachek argument presume considerable immobility between occupations over time. Whether their use of current occupation as a measure of occupational history is appropriate depends upon the validity of this presumption. As we have demonstrated, there is extensive mobility between "male" and "female" job categories. This in itself is inconsistent with Polachek's model. But it also suggests that the use of current occupation as a proxy for occupational history is inappropriate and may provide misleading information about whether job choice is conditioned by expectations about future work or whether experience garnered in "female" jobs results in lower wage growth and less depreciation than experience garnered in "male" jobs.

We used the longitudinal nature of the PSID to develop more direct tests of the following two predictions of the human capital model concerning occupational segregation:

1. Wage growth and depreciation are lower for work experience gathered in "female" jobs than in "male" jobs.

2. Women workers with extensive time out and frequent interruptions are more likely to have concentrated their work experience in "female" jobs.

We find virtually no support for either prediction for black and white women.

We used a simple modification of our basic wage growth equation to investigate the extent to which sex typing of experience influences the wage growth of women workers. In (13) we did not distinguish whether years in the e_L segment involved work in male-dominated or female-dominated jobs. Since both industry and occupation were reported for 9 of the 13 years under investigation, we could classify years in e_L that involved work in "female" and "male" jobs.[31] We combined this with the information on work hours to create four new variables:

1. the number of years of e_L that were full-time in male dominated jobs (e_L-full-md);

2. the numbers of years of e_L that were part-time in male-dominated jobs (e_L-part-md);

3. the number of years of e_L that were full-time in female-dominated jobs (e_L-full-fd); and

4. the numbers of years of e_L that were part-time in female-dominated jobs (e_L-part-fd).

This decomposition of e_L yields the following equation:

(14) $\quad \Delta \ln W = \alpha_{1L} \Delta S + \alpha_{10} e^*\text{-part} + \alpha_{11} e^*\text{-full} + \alpha_{14} e_L\text{-full-md} + \alpha_{15} e_L\text{-part-md} + \alpha_{16} e_L\text{-full-fd} + \alpha_{17} e_L\text{-part-fd} + \Delta \theta$

As with the basic measures of e_L, these four new variables are obtained in each of the annual interviews and do not rely on retrospective reports by either women workers or their husbands. These variables also provide more complete measures of the extent to which work experience was acquired in "female" jobs than do measures of occupation that are taken at a single point in time.

The results of estimating (14), shown in Table 8.9, provide little support for the argument that wage growth is much higher for male-dominated work than for female-dominated work,

---

[31] Industry is coded into two-digit categories for 1971-1979. Occupation is coded into one-digit Census categories for the years 1971-1974 and into two-digit categories for all the years thereafter. In Appendix A we describe how the original 429 two-digit occupation/two-digit industry groups for years 1975-1979 were collapsed into 74 subgroups. For each occupation-industry subgroup, we calculated a measure of percent female. If there were more than 50 percent women in that subgroup, we called it a "female-dominated" job. We used a similar procedure to collapse the 191 one-digit occupation/two-digit industry groups into 69 subgroups. Since we have only measures of occupation and industry for the last nine years of the study, we do not break experience in e* (which tended to occur early on in 1967-1979) into "male" and "female" components.

Table 8.9

EFFECTS OF "MALE-DOMINATED" AND "FEMALE-
DOMINATED" WORK EXPERIENCE ON WAGE GROWTH

Independent Variable	Wage Growth		
	White	White[a]	Black
$h*$: Years out of the labor force during 1967-1979 prior to most recent interruption	.0210 (.0293)	.023 (.0291)	-.0176 (.0292)
h_L: Years out of the labor force during most recent interruption	-.0359** (.0132)	-.033** (.0131)	-.0476* (.0153)
Years of full time e*	.0052 (.0077)	.0125 (.0084)	.0152† (.0809)
Years of part time e*	-.0031 (.0115)	-.0006 (.0115)	.0084 (.0113)
Years of full time e_L in male-dominated jobs	.0260* (.0124)	.0302** (.0124)	.0081 (.0159)
Years of part time e_L in male-dominated jobs	-.0092 (.0189)	-.0103 (.0188)	.0243 (.0282)
Years of full time e_L in female-dominated jobs	.0195* (.0090)	.0245** (.0091)	.0205* (.0107)
Years of part time e_L in female-dominated jobs	-.0036 (.0116)	-.0013 (.0115)	-.0030 (.0141)
$\hat{\rho}-1$		-.5614** (.1843)	
R^2 adjusted	.0230	.0329	.0438
Number of observations	837	821	510

Significance levels: +.01 *.05 **.01
[a]Corrected for sample selection bias (see Appendix C).
Note: Standard errors are in parentheses.
Source: Panel Study of Income Dynamics

especially for white women. A much more important factor was whether the work performed in a particular kind of job was part time or full time. For white women, a year of full-time, male-dominated work was associated with a 2.6 percent increase in hourly wages, while a year of full-time, female-dominated work was associated with a 1.9 percent increase in hourly wages. The differences between these two coefficients were not significant. For black women, a year of female-dominated, full-time work was associated with a 2.1 percent increase in wages. This compares to a .8 percent increase for a year of full-time, male-dominated work. Again, the difference was not significant. Part-time work experience, whether in "male" or "female" jobs had no significant effects on wages for either blacks or whites.[32]

We examined whether the sex typing of women's work experience affected the rate of depreciation during labor force withdrawals by interacting the two labor force withdrawals measures ($h*$ and h_L) with a measure of the average percent female in each woman's occupation-industry combination over the 13-year period.[33] These interaction terms were always insignificant when added to the wage change equation. This suggests that depreciation does not differ for "male" and "female" jobs.

The 13 years of PSID data allow a direct test of the hypothesis that workers who expect discontinuous labor force careers will concentrate in "female" jobs. If this hypothesis were correct, then the sex typing of work experience over the years 1967-1979 ought to be positively related to time out of the labor force 1967-1979, intermittency of work participation

---

[32]The .0243 coefficient estimated for years of part-time, male-dominated work for black women appears to be out of line with the other results. This estimate is based on a small number of observations, as reflected in its large standard error.

[33]This measure was estimated as follows:

$$\text{AVG \% FEM} = \frac{\sum_{t=1971}^{1979} (\text{WORK HOURS})_t * (\text{PROP-FEM})_t}{\sum_{t=1971}^{1979} (\text{WORK HOURS})_t}$$

where WORK HOURS_t = hours worked in year t;

PROP-FEM_t = proportion female in occupation-industry category in year t.

Table 8.10

DETERMINANTS OF THE SEX-TYPING OF WORK EXPERIENCE, 1967-1979

Independent Variables[a]	Sex-Typing of Work Experience 1967-1979[b]	
	White	Black
Total time out out 1967-1979 ($h*+h_L$)	-.0001 (.0026)	-.0061† (.0036)
Number of nonwork spells 1967-1979	.0070 (.0094)	.0000 (.0122)
NT79: Whether not working in 1979	-.0072 (.0192)	.0310 (.0249)
Number of observations	837	510
R^2 (adjusted)	.0047	.0192

† Significant at .10 level.
[a]Also included as controls were education, pre-1967 work experience, and pre-1967 time out.

[b]This measure is described in footnote 3.

Note: Standard errors are in parentheses.

Source: Panel Study of Income Dynamics

1967-1979 (measured by number of labor force withdrawals), and whether not working in 1979. Results of this exercise, shown in Table 8.10, confirm England's finding of no relationship between discontinuity of work and sex typing of concurrent occupation. None of these three measures of labor force discontinuity over 1967-1979 had a significant, positive relation to the sex typing of work experience over that period.

SUMMARY AND CONCLUSIONS

The wage change models of Mincer and Ofek and those from our own work yield similar results. Women who drop out of the labor force have lower real wages when they return to work than they had when they left work. However, the period following the return is characterized by rapid wage growth, and the net long-run loss in wages from dropping out is much smaller than the short-run loss. This result reconciles the apparently contradictory findings from cross-sectional studies about the size of the depreciation effect.

How does this empirical evidence affect our understanding of the process of female wage determination? The observed wage loss and rebound pattern is certainly consistent with the Mincer-Ofek story of human capital depreciation and restoration. This pattern is consistent with other accounts as well--the "job mismatch" argument and the "probationary period" argument. We do not have the necessary data to disentangle these arguments. Regardless of the reason, the rapid rebound after labor force withdrawals means that the wage losses associated with these withdrawals cannot explain much of the male/female wage gap.[34]

Women are often urged to choose part-time work rather than stopping work altogether to keep their "hands in." We find little evidence that the wage consequences of these two

_____

[34]That women work fewer years and more part-time years than men work does explain a substantial (one-third to two-fifths) part of the wage gap between men and women workers in a broad age range (Corcoran and Duncan, 1979). Note, however, that the bulk of the sex-based wage gap differences is still unexplained by male/female work history differences.

Figure 8.1

EFFECTS OF VARIOUS WORK PATTERNS ON WAGES

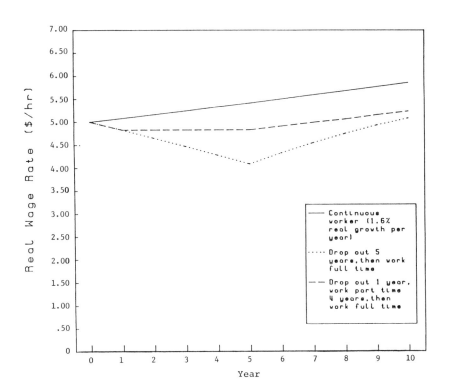

alternatives differ for white women workers taken as a whole.[35] An example of the quantitative importance of the estimated payoffs and penalties to work and nonwork spells for various strategies is shown in Figure 8.1. Three workers are assumed to begin a ten-year period with hourly earnings of $5.00 per hour. One is assumed to work continuously over the period, a second is assumed to drop out one year, work part time for four years, and then work full time for the remaining five years, and the third is assumed to drop out for five years and then return to full-time work. The real earnings growth rate for the continuous worker is taken to be 1.6 percent.[36] Depreciation and wage rebound estimates are taken from the second column of Table 8.4.[37]

Wage differences among these three workers are clearly maximized at the beginning of the fifth year, with the earnings of the full-time worker 32.3 percent higher than the five-year dropout, and 12.0 percent higher than the person who drops out for one year and works part time for the next four. The wage rebound associated with full-time work following a work interruption is sufficiently rapid to reduce the earnings

---

[35]Carolyn Shaw Bell has pointed out that it would seem that, at least for technical and professional workers, the returns to part-time work rather than dropping out completely might differ from the impact of such part-time work on future wage growth in other occupations. For example, the professional CPA, attorney, architect, or physician can limit her clients, and therefore her practice, to a part-time basis, and the management executive in advertising, marketing, finance, and other fields can become a consultant or free-lance worker. Both mechanisms enable a woman to go beyond keeping her hand in by permitting herself from being forgotten by potential future employers, whether they be clients or organizations. Insufficient data exists to explore this and related possibilities fully.

[36]This figure is the sample-selection-adjusted estimate of wage growth associated with the e* variable (column 2 of Table 8.4), but it is also insignificantly smaller than the estimated long-run payoff to experience for white men between their 30th and 40th birthdays (Duncan and Hoffman, 1979), and than Mincer and Ofek's estimate of the payoff to experience in their cross-sectional equation.

[37]Depreciation is assumed to be 3.4 percent per year, part-time work following time out is assumed to have a zero real wage growth associated with it, and the parabolic wage rebound that accompanies full-time experience is given by the coefficients on full-time e_r and e_r-squared. A final assumption is that the payoff to full-time experience that follows part-time experience is the long-run 1.6 percent figure.

advantage of the continuous worker over the five-year dropout from 32.3 percent to 15.4 percent by the end of the ten-year period. This 15.4 percent figure can be further decomposed into components of depreciation and foregone appreciation. If the five-year dropout had experienced neither depreciation nor unusual wage rebound, then her wage rate would have been $5.00 per hour upon returning and would have grown to $5.41 by the tenth year if the growth rate had been 1.6 percent per year. In fact, the net result of depreciation and rebound is to give her a predicted real wage rate of $5.08, so the net depreciation associated with the five years out is 6.1 percent altogether, or about 1.2 percent per year. The foregone appreciation component, of course, equals the long-run growth rate of 1.6 percent per year, which in this case is quantitatively more important than the net depreciation.

We also investigated the human capital models that explain job segregation as the result of women's discontinuous work history patterns. Such models emphasize two costs of discontinuous work participation: depreciation and foregone wage growth. The rapid restoration of wage losses in the period immediately following labor force withdrawals suggests that the first cost might be quite small. For these human capital explanations to hold, three things must occur. There should be considerable immobility between "male" and "female" job sectors, wage growth and depreciation should be lower for work in "female" jobs than for work in "male" jobs, and women with discontinuous work careers will be more likely to choose "female" jobs than women with continuous work careers.

We find little evidence for any of these propositions. First, there is considerable mobility between "male" and "female" job sectors. We found some evidence that the depreciation of work was lower for black women who were about to leave the labor force. Black women who dropped out of the labor force in 1979 had lower depreciation rates between 1967 and 1979 than other black women. But we did not find that result for white women, nor did we find that either wage growth or depreciation varied significantly with the sex typing of work experience. These results are consistent with England's cross-sectional work. Finally, women with discontinuous work careers were no more likely to have worked at "female" jobs than were women with more continuous work experience.

These results also have implications for models of job segregation other than the human capital model. Many models of job segregation either implicitly or explicitly assume that there is rigid segmentation between "male" and "female" job sectors and that there are fewer promotion and/or training opportunities in the "female" job sector than in the "male" job sector. The analyses reviewed in this chapter suggest that these assumptions are likely wrong.

References

Appelbaum, Eileen. Back to Work: Determinants of Women's Successful Re-entry. Boston: Auburn House Publishing Co., 1981.

Arrow, K. "Economic Dimensions of Occupational Segregation: Comment I." Signs 1, 3, Part 2 (Spring 1976):233-37.

Arrow, K. "Models of Job Discrimination." In Racial Discrimination in Economic Life, A.H. Pascal, pp. 83-102. Lexington, MA: D.C. Heath, 1972.

Beck, E.M.; Horan, P.M.; and Tolbertm L.M. "Industrial Segmentation and Labor Market Discrimination." Social Problems 28 (December 1980a):113-30.

Beck, E.M.; Horan, P.M.; and Tolbert, C.M. "Reply to Hauser, 'Social Stratification in Industrial Society: Further Evidence for a Structural Alternative.'" American Sociological Review 45 (August 1980b):712-18.

Beck, E.M.; Horan, P.M.; and Tolbert, C.M. "Stratification in a Dual Economy: A Sectoral Model of Earnings Determination." American Sociological Review 43 (October 1978):704-20.

Becker, G.S. Human Capital: A Theoretical and Empirical Analysis, with Special Reference to Education, 2nd Ed. New York: National Bureau of Economic Research, 1975.

Becker, G.S. The Economics of Discrimination. Chicago: University of Chicago Press, 1957.

Beller, A.H. "Occupational Segregation by Sex: Determinants and Changes." Journal of Human Resources 17, no. 3 (Summer, 1982): pp. 371-92.

Ben-Porath, Y. "The Production of Human Capital and the Life-Cycle of Earnings." Journal of Political Economy 75 (August 1967):352-65.

Bergmann, B.R. "Occupational Segregation, Wages, and Profits When Employers Discriminate by Race or Sex." Eastern Economic Journal 1 (April-July 1974):103-10.

Blau, F.D. Equal Pay in the Office. Lexington, MA: D.C. Heath , 1977.

Blau, F.D., and Jusenius, C.L. "Economists' Approaches to Sex Segregation in the Labor Market: An Appraisal." Signs: Journal of Women in Culture and Society 1, 3, Part 2 (Spring 1976):181-99.

Blinder, A. and Weiss, Y. "Human Capital and Labor Supply: A Synthesis." Journal of Political Economy 84 no. 3, (June 1976): 449-72.

Cain, G. "The Challenge of Segmented Labor Market Theories to Orthodox Theory: A Survey." Journal of Economic Literature 14, no. 4 (December 1976):1215-57.

Corcoran, M. "Work Experience, Labor Force Withdrawals, and Women's Earnings: Empirical Results Using the 1976 Panel Study of Income Dynamics." In Women in the Labor Market, C.B. Lloyd, E. Andrews, and C.L. Gilroy. New York: Columbia University Press, 1979.

Corcoran, M. "The Structure of Female Wages." The American Economic Review (Papers and Proceedings) 68, no. 2 (May 1978):165-70.

Corcoran, M., and Duncan, G.J. "Work History, Labor Force Attachment, and Earnings Differences between the Races and Sexes." Journal of Human Resources 14, no. 1 (Winter 1979):3-20.

Doeringer, P.B., and Piore, M.J. Internal Labor Markets and Manpower Analysis. Lexington, MA: D.C. Heath, 1971.

Duncan, G.J., and Hoffman, S. "On-the-Job Training and Earnings Differences by Race and Sex." Review of Economic Statistics 61, no. 4 (November 1979):594-603.

Duncan, O.D., and Duncan, B. "A Methodological Analysis of Segregation Indexes." American Sociological Review 20 (April 1955):210-17.

Edwards, R. Contested Terrain: The Transformation of the Workplace in America. New York: Basic Books, 1979.

England, P. "The Failure of Human Capital Theory to Explain Occupational Sex Segregation." Journal of Human Resources 17, no. 3(Spring 1982): pp. 358-70.

England, P. "Wage Appreciation and Depreciation: A Test of Neoclassical Economic Explanations of Occupational Sex Segregation." Mimeo, December 1981.

Gronau. R. "Wage Comparisons--A Selectivity Bias." Journal of Political Economy 82, no. 6 (November/December 1974):1119-43.

Gwartney-Gibbs, P. Married Women's Work Experience: Intermittency and Sex-Typed Occupations. Ph.D. dissertation, University of Michigan, 1981.

Hanushek, E.A., and Quigley, J.M. "Life-Cycle Earnings Capacity and the OJT Investment Model." Discussion Paper 7904. Rochester, NY: Public Policy Program, University of Rochester, 1978.

Hauser, R.M. "Comment on Beck et al., ASR, October 1978, 'Stratification in a Dual Economy.'" American Sociological Review 45 (August 1980):702-11.

Hausman, H.H., and Taylor, W.E. "Panel Data and Unobservable Individual Effects." Econometrica 49, no. 6 (November 1981):1377-98.

Heckman, J.J. "Sample Selection Bias as Specification Error." Econometrica 47, no. 1 (January 1979):153-61.

Heckman, J.J. "A Life Cycle Model of Earnings, Learning and Consumption. Journal of Political Economy. 84, no. 4 (August 1976): S11-S44.

Heckman, J.J. "Shadow Prices, Market Wages and Labor Supply." Econometrica 42, no. 4 (July 1974):679-94.

Hill, M.S. "The Wage Effects of Marital Status and Children." Journal of Human Resources 14, no. 4 (Fall 1979):579-94.

Horan, Patrick M. "Is Status Attainment Research Atheoretical?" American Sociological Review 43 (August, 1978): pp. 334-41.

Jones, Ethel B., and Long, James E. "Part-Week Work and Human Capital Investment by Married Women." Journal of Human Resources 14, no. 4 (Fall 1979):463-78.

Jovanovic, B. "Job Matching and the Theory of Turnover." Journal of Political Economy 87, no. 5 (October 1979):972-89.

Jusenius, C.L. "The Influence of Work Experience, Skill Requirement, and Occupational Segregation on Women's Earnings." Journal of Economics and Business 29, no. 2 (Winter 1977):107-15.

Kahn, L.M. "Wage Growth and Endogenous Experience." Industrial Relations 19, no. 1 (Winter 1980):50-63.

Landes, E.M. "Sex Differences in Wages and Employment: A Test of the Specific Capital Hypothesis." Economic Inquiry 15, no. 4 (October 1977):523-38.

Lazear, E. "Age, Experience, and Wage Growth." American Economic Review (September 1976):548-58.

Lloyd, C.B., and Niemi, B.T. The Economics of Sex Differentials. New York: Columbia University Press, 1979.

Medoff, J., and Abraham, K. "Are Those Paid More Really More Productive? The Case of Experience." Journal of Human Resources 16 (Spring 1981).

Mincer, J. Schooling Experience and Earnings. New York: National Bureau of Economic Research, 1974.

Mincer, J., and Ofek, H. "Interrupted Work Careers." Journal of Human Resources 16 (Winter 1982).

Mincer, J., and Polachek, S. "An Exchange: Theory of Human Capital and the Earnings of Women: Women's Earnings

Reexamined." Journal of Human Resources 13, no. 1 (Winter 1978):118-34.

Mincer, J. and Polachek, S. "Family Investments in Human Capital: Earnings of Women." Journal of Political Economy 82, no. 2 (Part 2) (March/April 1974):S76-S108.

Mortenson, D. "Specific Capital and Labor Turnover." Journal of Economics 2 (Autumn, 1978):572-86.

Olsen, R.J. "A Least Squares Correction for Selectivity Bias." Econometrica 48, no. 7 (November 1980):1815-20.

Oppenheimer, V.K. The Female Labor Force in the United States: Demographic and Economic Factors Governing Its Growth and Changing Composition. Westport, CT: Greenwood Press, 1970.

Piore, M.J. "The Dual Labor Market: Theory and Implications." In Problems in Political Economy: An Urban Perspective, D.M. Gordon, pp. 90-94. Lexington, MA: D.C. Heath , 1971.

Polachek, S.W.. "Occupational Self-Selection: A Human Capital Approach to Sex Differences in Occupational Structure." The Review of Economics and Statistics 63, no. 1 (February 1981):60-69.

Polachek, S.W. "Occupational Segregation among Women: Theory, Evidence, and a Prognosis." In Women in the Labor Market, C.B. Lloyd, E.S. Andrews, and C.L. Gilroy, pp. 137-57. New York: Columbia University Press, 1979.

Polachek, S.W. "Occupational Segregation: An Alternative Hypothesis." Journal of Contemporary Business 5, no. 1 (1976):1-12.

Polachek, S.W. "Differences in Expected Post-School Investments as a Determinant of Market Wage Differentials." " International Economic Review 16, no. 2 (June 1975): 451-70.

Prescott, E. and Visscher, M. "Organizational Capital." Journal of Political Economy 88, no. 3 (June 1980):446-61.

Rosen, S. "Learning and Experience in the Labor Market." Journal of Human Resources 7 (Summer 1972):326-42.

Sandell, S.H., and Shapiro, D. "Work Expectations, Human Capital Accumulation, and the Wages of Young Women." Journal of Human Resources 15, no. 3 (Summer 1980):335-53.

Sandell, S.H., and Shapiro, D. "An Exchange: Theory of Human Capital and the Earnings of Women: A Reexamination of the Evidence." Journal of Human Resources 13, no. 1 (Winter 1978):103-17.

Stafford, Frank P. and Duncan, Greg J. "The Use of Time and Technology by Households in the United States." Research in Labor Economics ed. Ronald Ehrenberg, 3, JAI, 1980.

Treiman, D.J., and Hartmann, H.I., ed. Women, Work, and Wages: Equal Pay for Jobs of Equal Value. Washington,DC: National Academy Press, 1981.

Weiss, Y., and Gronau, R. "Expected Interruptions in Labour Force Participation and Sex-Related Differences in Earnings Growth." Review of Economic Studies 58 (October 1981):607-19.

Wolf, W., and Rosenfeld, R. "Sex Structure of Jobs and Job Mobility." Social Forces 56 (1978):823-44.

U.S. Department of Labor, Women's Bureau. 20 Facts on Women Workers, Washington, DC, August, 1979.

Zellner, H. "The Determinants of Occupational Segregation." In Sex, Discrimination, and the Division of Labor, C.B. Lloyd., pp. 125-45. New York: Columbia University Press, 1975.

Appendix A to Chapter 8

PROCEDURE TO DETERMINE "FEMALE"- AND "MALE"-DOMINATED JOBS

The PSID data contain occupation and industry information for all women who were heads and wives for the "income" years 1970-1979. Occupation is coded at the one-digit level for the years 1970-1974 and at the two-digit level for the years 1975-1979. Industry is coded at the two-digit level from 1970 to 1979. In order to maximize the information contained in the data, we determined the "femaleness" of an individual's job using the one-digit occupation/two-digit industry information during 1970-1974, and the two-digit occupation/two-digit industry information during 1975-1979. Below we detail the algorithm used for the two-digit occupation, two-digit industry classifications. The procedure is analogous in the one-digit occupation, two-digit industry case.

We took a single year of data (income from 1975) and computed the fraction of all Panel Study heads and wives in all possible combinations of occupations and industries at the two-digit level who were women. (Table A8.1 lists the two-digit occupation and industry codes.) There were 429 such combinations. After combining homogeneous occupations with fewer than 25 observations, we arrived at a set of estimates of the fraction of adult workers in 74 combinations of occupation and industries who were women. Table A8.2 shows the occupation and industry codes and associated fractions in the form of the OSIRIS IV recode statements used to generate the estimates. These statements, in conjunction with the two-digit occupation and industry definitions contained in Table A8.1, allow the reader to identify the occupation-industry groups and the associated "percent femaleness" of the classification. For example, scrutiny of lines 51 and 58 identify group 1 to be physicians and dentists in any industry, and there were no women in this

group.[38] In some of our analyses, we use the fractions directly,
naming that measure "percent female-dominated." In most of the
analyses, however, we group all jobs into only two categories:
those with more than 50 percent women workers (designated "female
dominated") and those with fewer than 50 percent women workers
(designated "male dominated").

---

[38]In line 51 refer to (10/0-99)=1. The "10" identifies the
occupation (physicians and dentists), the "0-99" identifies the
industry (all industries, in this case). In line 58 refer to
1=0. This says the percentage of females in group 1 equals zero.

Table A8.1

OCCUPATION CODES

Numbers in parentheses represent the 1970 Occupation from Alphabetical Index of Industries and Occupations issued June 1971.

PROFESSIONAL, TECHNICAL AND KINDRED WORKERS (001-195)

10. Physicians (medical & osteopathic), Dentists (062,065)

11. Other Medical and Paramedical: chiropractors, optometrists, pharmacists, veterinarians, nurses, therapists, healers, dieticians (except medical and dental technicians, see 16) (061,063,064,071-076)

12. Accountants and Auditors (001)

13. Teachers, Primary and Secondary Schools (including NA type) (141-145)

14. Teachers, College; Social Scientists; Librarians; Archivists (032-036,091-096,102-140)

15. Architects; Chemists; Engineers; Physical and Biological Scientists (002,006-023,042-054)

16. Technicians: Airplane pilots and navigators, designers, draftsmen, foresters and conservationists, embalmers, photographers, radio operators, surveyors, technicians (medical, dental, testing, n.e.c.) (003-005,025,055,080-085,150-173,183,191)

17. Public Advisors: Clergymen, editors and reporters, farm and home management advisors, personnel and labor relations workers, public relations persons, publicity workers, religious, social and welfare workers (024,026,056,086,090,100-101,184,192)

18. Judges; Lawyers (030-031)

19. Professional, technical and kindred workers not listed above (174,175-182, 185,190,193-195)

MANAGERS, OFFICIALS AND PROPRIETORS (EXCEPT FARM) (201-245)

20. Not self-employed (201-245)

31. Self-employed (unincorporated businesses) (201-245)

CLERICAL AND KINDRED WORKERS

40. Secretaries, stenographers, typists (370-372,376,391)

41. Other Clerical Workers: agents (n.e.c.) library assistants and attendants, bank tellers, cashiers, bill collectors, ticket, station and express agents, etc., receptionists (301-364,374-375,381,392-395)

SALES WORKERS

45. Retail store salesmen and sales clerks, newsboys, hucksters, peddlers, traveling salesmen, advertising agents and salesmen, insurance agents, brokers and salesmen, etc. (206-280)

CRAFTSMEN, FOREMEN, AND KINDRED WORKERS

50. Foremen, n.e.c. (441)

51. Other craftsmen and kindred workers (401-440,442-580)

52. Government protective service workers: firemen, police, marshals, and constables (960-965)

OPERATIVES AND KINDRED WORKERS (601-715)

61. Transport equipment operatives (701-715)

62. Operatives, except transport (601-695)

LABORERS
70. Unskilled laborers--nonfarm (740-785)
71. Farm laborers and foremen (821-824)

SERVICE WORKERS
73. Private household workers (980-984)
75. Other service workers: barbers, beauticians, manicurists, bartenders, boarding and lodging housekeepers, counter and fountain workers, housekeepers and stewards, waiters, cooks, midwives, practical nurses, babysitters, attendants in physicians' and dentists' offices (901-965 except 960-965 when works for local, state, or federal government)

FARMERS AND FARM MANAGERS
80. Farmers (owners and tenants) and managers (except code 71) (801-802)

MISCELLANEOUS GROUPS
55. Members of armed forces
99. Not ascertained

INDUSTRY CODES

Numbers in parentheses represent the 1970 Industries from Alphabetical Index of Industries and Occupation issued June 1971.

11. Agriculture, Forestry, and Fishing (A,017-028)
21. Mining and Extraction (047-057)

MANUFACTURING DURABLES
30. Metal industries (139-169)
31. Machinery, including electrical (177-209)
32. Motor vehicles and other transportation equipment (219-238)
33. Other durables (107-138,239-259)
34. Durables, NA what

MANUFACTURING NONDURABLES
40. Food and kindred products (268-298)
41. Tobacco manufacturing (299)
42. Textile mill products, apparel and other fabricated textile products, shoes (307-327,389)
43. Paper and allied products (328-337)
44. Chemical and allied products, petroleum and coal products, rubber and miscellaneous plastic products (347-387)
45. Other nondurables (388,397)
46. Nondurables, NA what
49. Manufacturing, NA whether durable or nondurable

51. Construction (067-077,B)
55. Transportation (D,407-429)
56. Communication (447-449)
57. Other Public Utilities (467-479)
61. Retail Trade (607-698)
62. Wholesale Trade (507-588)
69. Trade, NA whether wholesale or rental
71. Finance, Insurance, and Real Estate (707-718)
81. Repair Service (757-759)
82. Business Services (727-749)
83. Personal Services (H,769-798)

84. Amusement, Recreation, and Related Services (807-809)
85. Printing, Publishing, and Allied Services (338-389)
86. Medical and Dental and Health Services, whether public or private (828-848)
87. Educational Services, whether public or private (K,857-868)
88. Professional and Related Services other than medical or educational (849,869-897)
91. Armed Services [L(917)]
92. Government, other than medical or educational services; NA whether other [907,L(917),927,M(930)]
99. Not Ascertained

Table A8.2

OCCUPATION AND INDUSTRY RECODES

<u>Line</u>

38: R1120=RECODE R1115,R1116, (1/31)=1 (1/86)=2 (1/87)=3
     (1/88)=4 (1/92)=5 (1/0-99)=6 (2/61)=7 (2/62)=8 (2/71)=9
     (2/87)=10-

39: (2/92)=11 (2/0-86,88)=12 (2/0-99)=13 (3/51)=14 (3/61)=15
     (3/0-99)=16 (4/31)=17 (4/44)=18 (4/55)=19 (4/56)=20-

40: (4/61)=21 (4/62)=22 (4/71)=23 (4/82)=24 (4/85)=25 (4/86)=26
     (4/87)=27 (4/88)=28 (4/92)=29 (4/0-99)=30-

41: (5/30)=31 (5/31)=32 (5/32)=33 (5/33)=34 (5/51)=35 (5/57)=36
     (5/61)=37 (5/81)=38 (5/0-99)=39 (6/30)=40-

42: (6/31)=41 (6/32)=42 (6/33)=43 (6/40)=44 (6/42)=45 (6/43)=46
     (6/44)=47 (6/55)=48 (6/61)=49 (6/62)=50 (6/83)=51-

43: (6/0-85,88)=52 (6/0-99)=53 (7/11)=54 (7/51)=55 (7/55)=56
     (7/61)=57 (7/82)=58 (7/83)=59 (7/86)=60 (7/87)=61
     (7/88)=62-

44: (7/92)=63 (7/0-99)=64 (8/0-99)=65 (9/91)=66 (9/92)=67
     (9/0-99)=68,ELSE=70

45: R1121=BRAC(R1120, 1=.057, 2=.666, 3=.689, 4=.230, 5=.311,
     6=.204, 7=.270, 8=.075, 9=.246, 10=.223, 11=.251, 12=.190,
     13=.190, -

46: 14=.056, 15=.252, 16=.170, 17=.680, 18=.496, 19=.257,
     20=.870, 21=.742, 22=.463, 23=.671, 24=.785, 25=.730,
     26=.982, -

47: 27=.945, 28=.938, 29=.673, 30=.660, 31=.00, 32=.145, 33=.029,
     34=.054, 35=.001, 36=.00, 37=.024, 38=.002, 39=.091,
     40=.147, -

48: 41=.469, 42=.223, 43=.327, 44=.359, 45=.817, 46=.478,
     47=.380, 48=.058, 49=.346, 50=.124, 51=.607, 52=.241,
     53=.452, 54=.110, -

49: 55=.094, 56=.112, 57=.747, 58=.343, 59=.888, 60=.870,
     61=.648, 62=.695, 63=.184, 64=.245, 65=.009, 66=.023,
     67=.008, 68=.252, ELSE=.428)

51: R1120=RECODE R1115,R1116, (10/0-99)=1, (11/0-99)=2
     (12/0-99)=3 (13/0-99)=4 (14/0-99)=5 (15/0-99)=6
     (16/0-85,88)=7 (16/86-87,89-99)=8 (17/0-85,88)=9
     (17/86-87,89-99)=10 (18/0-99)=11-

52: (19/0-99)=12 (20/61)=13 (20/62)=14 (20/71)=15 (20/87)=16
     (20/0-86,88)=17 (20/0-99)=18 (31/51)=19 (31/61)=20
     (31/0-99)=21-

53: (40/0-99)=22 (41/55)=23 (41/56)=24 (41/61)=25 (41/71)=26
     (41/86)=27 (41/87)=28 (41/92)=29 (41/0-99)=30 (45/61)=31
     (45/62)=32 (45/71)=33 (45/0-99)=34-

```
54:  (50/0-99)=35 (51/30)=36 (51/31)=37 (51/32)=38 (51/33)=39
     (51/51)=40 (51/57)=41 (51/61)=42 (51/81)=43 (51/0-99)=44-

55:  (52/0-99)=45 (55/0-99)=46 (61/55)=47 (61/0-99)=48 (62/30)=49
     (62/31)=50 (62/32)=51 (62/33)=52 (62/40)=53 (62/42)=54
     (62/43)=55 (62/44)=56-

56:  (62/61)=57 (62/0-85,88)=58 (62/86-87,89-99)=59 (70/51)=60
     (70/61-62)=61 (70/0-99)=62 (71/0-99)=63 (73/0-99)=64
     (75/61)=65 (75/82)=66-

57:  (75/83)=67 (75/84)=68 (75/86)=69 (75/87)=70 (75/0-85,88)=71
     (75/86-87,89-99)=72 (80/0-99)=73 (99/0-99)=74,ELSE=75

58:  R1121=BRAC(R1120, 1=0, 2=.824, 3=.354, 4=.730, 5=.490,
     6=.023, 7=.186, 8=.576, 9=.301, 10=.577, 11=.062, 12=.335,
     13=.270, 14=.075, -

59:  15=.246, 16=.223, 17=.192, 18=.233, 19=.056, 20=.252,
     21=.170, 22=.992, 23=.146, 24=.887, 25=.894, 26=.848,
     27=.975, -

60:  28=.909, 29=.583, 30=.683, 31=.639, 32=.170, 33=.203,
     34=.283, 35=.091, 36=.0, 37=.195, 38=.037, 39=.056, -

61:  40=.001, 41=.0, 42=.026, 43=.002, 44=.056, 45=.017, 46=0.021,
     47=.068, 48=.104, 49=.154, 50=.486, 51=.246, -

62:  52=.409, 53=.387, 54=.830, 55=.478, 56=.404, 57=.429,
     58=.312, 59=.508, 60=.061, -

63:  61=.256, 62=.026, 63=.277, 64=.995, 65=.773, 66=.351,
     67=.864, 68=.407, 69=.870, 70=.661, 71=.416, 72=.383, -

64:  73=.009, 74=.251, ELSE=.428)
```

Appendix Table B8.1

DYNAMICS OF OCCUPATIONAL SEGREGATION WITH A MORE
RESTRICTIVE DEFINITION OF FEMALE- AND MALE-DOMINATED JOBS

	Women Who Worked at Least 250 Hours in 1975 and 1979		
	White	Black	All
Occupational Change			
Fraction spending <u>all</u> working years in female-dominated jobs	.40 (861)	.48 (527)	.41 (1388)
Fraction spending <u>all</u> working years in male-dominated jobs	.07 (861)	.04 (527)	.07 (1388)
Fraction switching at least once in either direction	.27 (861)	.25 (527)	.27 (1388)
Fraction of those in female-dominated jobs initially who switched to male-dominated jobs	.26 (590)	.20 (386)	.25 (976)
Fraction of those in male-dominated jobs initially who switched to female-dominated jobs	.42 (144)	.59 (73)	.44 (217)

Note: The number of observations is given in parentheses
below each estimate.

A job is designated as female dominated if the percentage
of women workers is greater than or equal to 60. A job is
designated as male dominated if the percentage of women
workers is less than 40.

The table reads: Of the 861 white women, 40 percent spend
all of their working years in female-
dominated jobs.

Appendix C to Chapter 8

SAMPLE SELECTION BIAS CORRECTION

Throughout the chapter we have estimated several variants of a wage change model for women who worked at least two years during 1967-1979, omitting women who never worked or worked in only one year. If the omitted women do not differ systematically from the included women, then the only drawback of using ordinary least squares (OLS) to estimate wage change on the incomplete sample is loss of efficiency. More generally, it may be that the omitted women do differ from the included women in a nonrandom manner. In this case, OLS estimation using the incomplete sample would result in biased parameter estimates and biased standard errors.

Heckman (1979) treats this sample selection bias as a specification error (omitted variable problem) and presents a consistent estimation method that eliminates the specification error in censored samples. The problem, and solution, can be formulated using a two-equation system.

Equation (1) represents the behavioral relationship we are interested in estimating. In terms of our analysis, Y_1 is the change in natural logarithm of the last and first wage rates (Ln W_L - Ln W_F). The vector of independent variables, X_1, contains the time-out variables (h_*, h_L), labor market experience (e_*, e_L), and other variables as specified in the analysis above.

(1) $Y_{1i} = X_{1i}B_1 + u_{1i}$ (behavioral equation)

(2) $Y_{2i} = X_{2i}B_2 + u_{2i}$ (selection equation)

We seek to estimate equation (1) for the entire female population, but data are missing on Y_1 for women who did not work at least two years between 1967 and 1979. The sample selection rule that determines whether a woman has an observation on Y_1 is given by equation (2). Assume data is available on Y_{1i} if $Y_{2i} \geq 0$, otherwise there is no observation on Y_{1i}. In a given year, a woman will work only if her market wage exceeds her reservation wage. Equation (2) would be formulated to capture the relationship between market and reservation wages during the 13-year period such that $Y_{2i} \geq 0$ means the woman works at least two years during 1967-79.

The regression function for the subsample of data is:

(3) $E(Y_{1i}|X_{1i}, Y_{2i} \geq 0) = X_{1i}B_1 + E(u_{1i}|u_{2i} \geq -X_{2i}B_2)$

In the general case, the conditional expectation of u_{1i} is nonzero. OLS estimation of equation (1) omits the final term in equation (3) as an independent variable. The bias produced by sample selection is therefore seen to be a problem of an omitted variable. It can be shown that:

(4) $E(u_{1i}|u_{2i} \geq -X_{2i}B_2) = \sigma_{12}/(\sigma_{22})^{1/2} \lambda_i$

where σ_{12} = covariance (u_{1i}, u_{2i})

σ_{22} = variance (u_{2i})

$\lambda_i = \dfrac{\phi(Z)_i}{1-\Phi(Z_i)}$

$Z_i = -X_{2i}B_2/(\sigma_{22})^{1/2}$

ϕ = density function for standard normal variable

Φ = distribution function for standard normal variable,

So that the conditional regression function can be written as:

(5) $E(Y_{1i}|X_{1i}, Y_{2i} \geq 0) = X_{1i}B_1 + \sigma_{12}/(\sigma_{22}^{1/2}) \lambda_i$.

In practice, one does not know λ_i, but can estimate it as follows. First, estimate the parameters of the probability that $Y_{2i} \geq 0$, (i.e., $B_2/(\sigma_{22})^{1/2}$), using probit analysis for the complete sample of women. Second, from the estimate of $B_2/(\sigma_{22})^{1/2}$, calculate Z_i, and hence, λ_i. Third, enter the estimate of λ_i into equation (5) for the selected subsample of women.

Olsen (1980) has shown that one can use OLS instead of probit analysis when estimating the parameters of the probability that $Y_{2i} \geq 0$ for the complete sample of women. Assuming u_{2i} is uniformly rather than normally distributed, together with the assumption that the conditional expectation of u_{1i}, given u_{2i} is linear in u_{2i}, yields a regression function equal to:

(6) $E(Y_{1i}|X_{1i}, Y_{2i} \geq 0) = X_{1i}B_1 + \rho\sigma_{11}\sqrt{3}(X_{2i}B_2-1)$.

We therefore estimate:

(7) $Y_{1i} = X_{1i}B_1 + \delta(X_{2i}B_2-1) + \varepsilon_i$

where $\delta = \rho\sigma_{11}\sqrt{3}$.

Since B_2 is not typically known, one must use $\hat{B}_2$ from the linear probability model so that the final model estimated is given by:

(8) $Y_{1i} = X_{1i}B_1 + \delta(X_{2i}\hat{B}_2-1) + \eta_i$

where $\eta_i = -\delta X_{2i}(\hat{B}_2-B_2) + \varepsilon_i$.

As Olsen points out, the OLS approach using the $\hat{P}$-1 correction requires the presence of at least one regressor in the linear probability model that does not appear in the behavioral equation. In the context of the wage change model we are estimating, the task of finding variables to exclude from the behavioral equation is a much easier one than for a wage level equation. Independent variables in a typical labor supply equation such as level of education do not appear in the wage change equation unless their coefficients change over time, an unlikely event. Thus our selection equation has as independent variables such measures as education, number of children, the presence of children under age six, whether the woman was married at the start of the 13-year period, and prior labor force experience.

Table C8.1 reports the results of estimating an OLS model based on equation (2). Results conform to expectations and are quite reasonable. The probability that a woman works at least two years during 1967-1979 increases with education, prior work experience, and the number of children in the family, and is negatively related to time out of the labor force, household income, the presence of children under age six, and whether the woman was married.

As detailed in Olsen, the labor supply equation can be used to calculate an expected probability of working ($\hat{P}$), and the quantity ($\hat{P}-1$) can be used in the behavioral equation to adjust for sample selection bias. This procedure was followed in obtaining the estimates given in the columns adjusted for selection bias in Tables 8.4, 8.5, 8.6, and 8.9.

APPENDIX TABLE C8.1

OLS ESTIMATES OF THE PARAMETERS DETERMINING THE
PROBABILITY A WOMAN WORKED AT LEAST TWO YEARS, 1967-1979
(White women aged 23 to 47 in 1967)

	Coefficient and Standard Error
Education (1967)	.017** (.0047)
Pre-1967 experience (full time)	.011** (.0022)
Pre-1967 experience (part time)	.006 (.0041)
Pre-1967 time out of labor force	-.011** (.0022)
Nonlabor income (1967)[a]	-.000007** (.000002)
Number of children in family (1967)	.028** (.0080)
Whether children under six years old in household (1967)	-.091** (.0297)
Whether married (1967)	-.030 (.0405)
Constant	.642
Adjusted R^2	.125
N	1150

Significance levels: *.05 **.01
[a]Consists of total family income minus woman's labor earnings (in dollars).

Note: Standard errors are given in parentheses.

Source: Panel Study of Income Dynamics

Chapter 9

FEMALE HOUSEHOLD HEADSHIP AND THE POVERTY OF CHILDREN[1]

Martha S. Hill

> In the final analysis, a woman heading her
> own household (and in particular a woman
> becoming head of her own household) in all
> too many instances is living in dire economic
> circumstances. (Mott, 1979: xii)

INTRODUCTION

During the past decade, U.S. families have undergone
pervasive changes. Despite an atmosphere continuing to foster
the notion of a "typical" U.S. family consisting of a bread-
winning husband, a home-keeping wife, and two children, in March
1981 only one-fifth (22 percent) of the families with children
satisfied both the number-of-parents and labor-force-
participation criteria of this definition. During the seventies
there were large increases in the number of mothers heading
households and in the number participating in the labor force.
Concern about these changes centers on the implications for
children. As Bane (1976: 3) states: "People are distressed by
these trends not because they signal a decline in the quality and
richness of adult lives but because they seem to threaten the
next generation."

A common belief seems to be that being raised in a family
without a father present or with the mother spending substantial
time away from home is damaging to children not only while they
are growing up but after they reach adulthood as well. The
findings concerning impaired school performance, reduced scores
on intellectual indices, and increased anti-social behavior,

---

[1] This chapter is extracted from a longer paper entitled
"Trends in the Economic Situation of U.S. Families and Children:
1970-1980" prepared for the National Academy of Sciences'
Committee on Child Development Research and Public Policy. It
was presented at the Conference on Families and the Economy,
January 28-29, 1982, and published in the volume of proceedings,
The High Cost of Living: Economic and Demographic Perspectives on
American Families, Richard R. Nelson, (Washington, DC: National
Academy of Sciences, forthcoming June 1983).

while extensive, are not consistent.[2] Indeed, some hypotheses and research suggest that the mother working exerts positive as well as negative effects on child development. In addition, many of the ills associated with single parenthood may in fact be due to the lower economic status of one-parent families: lower economic status for these families is a very consistent finding.

The level of material resources available to children is clearly important to their development. By affecting the degree to which their basic physical needs--food, clothing, shelter--are satisfied, it influences their immediate and possibly longer-term health. Deprivation resulting from low family income during childhood may be detrimental to a child's personality and emotional development and also may influence his or her educational attainment and skill development.

Repeatedly, analysis of the PSID data has shown that changes in family composition are critically important in explaining changes in economic well-being, particularly for women and children (Morgan, 1974; Lane and Morgan, 1975; Duncan and Morgan, 1980). Changes in income are not well explained by differences in the attitudes or skills of family members or by events such as unemployment or migration. Instead, "By far the most important cause of change (in economic well-being) is change in family composition--births, deaths, children leaving home, and especially divorce and marriage" (Duncan and Morgan, 1981a: 21). Marriages and remarriages of parents are the most beneficial of family composition changes, whereas marital disruptions are often detrimental for women and children (Mott, 1979; Morgan, 1974).[3]

Because the living arrangements of the family so strongly influence the economic well-being of children, this chapter

---

[2]See Chapter 6 of Ross and Sawhill (1975) and Chapter 1 of Bane (1976) for discussions of the evidence concerning effects of single parenthood on child development. Chapter 1 of Bane (1976) and Hoffman (1980) addresses the effects of the mother working.

[3]Cross-sectional patterns are consistent with this. For example, toward the end of the Seventies the average level of annual income for two-parent families was about $20,000 and for mother-only households about $8,000. Per capita income differences were also quite large (Bianchi and Farley, 1979). In addition, the proportion of families who were poor was six times greater among mother-only households (Bane and Weiss, 1980), despite the longer work hours and higher personal income of mothers heading their own households relative to those living with their husbands (Bradbury, et al., 1979).

concentrates on what changes have occurred in family life during the past decade and what they have meant for children. It examines the living arrangements that children of the seventies experienced and how this related to their access to income, concentrating on the distinction between a mother-only household and a two-parent household. Race differences in this relationship and the implications of these differences for the economic well-being of children are explored. Increased labor force participation on the part of the mother is examined as one means of improving the economic position of children in low-income families; other means are also examined.

We will begin with a discussion establishing the context for our longitudinal tracking of the economic status of children as they grew up in the 1970s. The initial discussion concentrates first on past findings concerning the effects of family composition changes on economic status. This is followed by a brief look at the major demographic trends of the seventies and the resultant changes in the family situations of children. The empirical analyses reported in the subsequent section of the chapter employ the PSID data to track the changing family situations of children and the accompanying changes in economic status. Following an explanation of the analytical approach, a longitudinal view of children's living arrangements is presented. This is followed by a look at the long-run economic well-being of children in the seventies. The links between living arrangements and economic well-being are a central focus of each of these analyses. The importance of racial differences in living arrangements is investigated as a source of the large racial difference in the economic well-being of children. Finding that the greater propensity of black children to spend time in a mother-only household fails to account for their lower level of long-run per capita income spurs a broader look at factors associated with the long-run level of family income/needs for children, black and nonblack. Results of the empirical investigations are then summarized, with some policy implications discussed in the concluding section of the chapter.

BACKGROUND

Analysis of changes in the well-being of children from 1971 to 1978 (Duncan and Morgan, 1981b) shows that real per capita income grew by 4.7 percent per year for those in stable two-parent households; however, it fell by 4 percent per year for children with parents who became divorced or separated. Other work (Duncan and Morgan, 1976) indicates that from 1968 to 1974 nearly one-quarter of the children losing a father through separation or divorce fell into poverty as a result; marriage of an unmarried household head, on the other hand, helped children climb out of poverty.

There were large race differences in the economic experiences of children, and they seem to be closely linked to female household headship. Hill (1981) finds that blacks are much more susceptible than whites to long-term poverty: over a ten-year period, 20 percent of the individuals temporarily poor were black, whereas 60 percent of those persistently poor were black. Almost half of the individuals who were poor for the whole decade were in female-headed households with children present. Coe (1981) finds that children in general, and black children in particular, were much more likely than adults to be in households receiving welfare at some time during the 1970s. Children--and again, black children especially--also were more likely than adults to be long-term welfare recipients. This was especially true for welfare in the form of food stamps and especially true for young children. Coe finds that presence of young children is a primary factor causing the racial differences in long-term welfare receipt; black household heads are more likely to have young children at home. From his work he concludes that "the presence of young children in households headed by unmarried persons, particularly females and blacks, has a considerable impact on both the incidence and length of time of welfare receipt" (1981: 160).

Subsequent to a marital disruption there is a sharp drop in family income--a drop of 43 percent for divorced women, 51 percent for separated women, and 30 percent for widows (Bane and Weiss, 1980).[4] The decline varies with race. While the absolute decline is greater for white women than black women, the reduction is more likely to place newly formed black female

---

[4]Cross-sectional analysis also has suggested that a married woman could expect about a 40 percent reduction in income as a result of becoming a single head of family (Bradbury et al., 1979).

households in poverty because the income level before the divorce was lower for black women. Small increases in income occur during the two years after the initial decrease, but without remarriage, mothers never again approach the income level they had attained before the marriage dissolved. Here, another race differential comes into play: black mothers are less likely to remarry than white mothers are.

Controlling for living arrangement and race, incomes are consistently higher for children with working mothers (Grossman, 1981). Many children now have a substantial share of support coming from their mother's earnings. This occurs most often when the child is either in a mother-only household or in a two-parent household with the father unemployed or out of the labor force. But is increased labor force participation by the mother an effective way of keeping children out of poverty?

Evidence indicates that the ability of mothers to provide support for children equal to what it was before a marital disruption is limited. The primary source of income for previously married mothers is their own earnings, especially if the mother is divorced (Bane and Weiss, 1980). The percentage of mothers working increases from 66 to 90 percent following a divorce, with entry into the work force greater among white women than among black women.[5] Increases in the percentage working are much smaller for mothers becoming separated or widowed, but as many as half of them do have income from their own work subsequent to their marital disruption.

The long-term separated, though, tend to rely more heavily on public assistance, especially food stamps and Aid to Families with Dependent Children (AFDC), than do other groups of previously married mothers. While increased work effort by the mother would improve the economic situation of these families, the improvement would not be very large. Sawhill (1976) estimates that only one-quarter of such women could increase their income by as much as $1,000 per year by going to work full

---

[5] NLS longitudinal evidence (Mott) shows larger percentages of white women either becoming employed (in the case of mature women) or remaining employed (in the case of young women) right after the transition from a wife to a household head. Finding that such differences were present only among the less educated, though, Mott attributes much of this race differential to the higher proportion of black women with less than a high school education.

time. However, if they were able to earn the higher wages of men with similar qualifications, over one-half would be able to improve significantly their economic well-being by working more. Morgan (1974) also concludes that, in addition to two parents having greater earning capacity than one, men's wage level being higher than women's is important to changes in income accompanying a change in marital status. Thus, a factor in the decline of the economic resources available to children upon a marital disruption is that labor market conditions are more favorable to men than to women.

DETAIL ABOUT THE MAJOR TRENDS AFFECTING CHILDREN

A declining incidence of marriage combined with an increasing incidence of divorce and separation as well as out-of-wedlock births has meant that more children are in families without the father present. Coupled with the increased propensity for independent living arrangements, this has meant that more children are living in households headed by their unmarried mothers.[6] This trend, though a continuation of changes begun earlier, accelerated during the past decade.[7] In 1960 it was relatively rare for children to be living in a one-parent family, but since then it has become increasingly more common. The percentage of children in one-parent families has increased from 9 percent in 1960, to 14 percent in 1970, and to 20 percent in 1980. Throughout this time, about 90 percent of the one-parent families were headed by a female. In the 1970s the proportion of children in two-parent households, while still in the majority, declined steadily. The proportion decreased from 85 percent in 1970 to 76 percent in 1980. Thus, while the two-parent family remains the typical situation for the majority of children, the one-parent, female-headed family has become frequent enough to warrant special attention.

---

[6]See Ross and Sawhill (1975), Bradbury et al. (1979), and Cutright (1974) for discussions of the relative importance of the various demographic factors to the increase in female-headed households with children.

[7]Between 1960 and 1970 the number of one-parent, predominantly female-headed families increased by 49 percent, compared to only an 8 percent increase in two-parent families. During the next eight years not only did one-parent families increase at an even faster rate, increasing by 76 percent, but at the same time two-parent families actually declined by 3 percent.

Most of the recent changes in the composition of children's families have resulted from divorce or separation. However, out-of-wedlock births have also contributed. These differing sources of the increase in mother-only households can have different implications for the well-being of the children living in the households. Recent findings, for example, indicate that out-of-wedlock birth, particularly among teenagers, creates a family form likely to need public assistance (Moore and Hofferth, 1978). Out-of-wedlock births are associated with low levels of educational attainment for the mother as well as larger completed family size, and these are important factors leading to the disproportionately large number of teenage mothers receiving welfare income. Out-of-wedlock birth is more frequent among black women than white. However, early childbirth, with its large proportion of out-of-wedlock births, seems to have a less detrimental effect for blacks over the long run (Hofferth and Moore, 1979). Among black women, early childbirth fosters greater work experience, leading to somewhat higher subsequent income. Early childbirth imparts no such long-run benefits for white women.

Over the last decade, there also have been continuous increases in women's labor force participation rates, with the sharpest rise among married women with children, particularly those with young children.[8] This has led to continuous increases both in the proportion and in the number of children with working mothers. Their number has grown by more than 5 million, despite a decrease of 7.5 million in the total number of children. It has also meant the narrowing, but not the complete elimination, of long-established differentials regarding marital status of working mothers. By 1980, the percentage of children in two-parent households with mothers in the labor force had risen to 52, compared to 62 for the children in mother-only households. There were also marital status differences in labor force commitment among mother-only households (Bradbury et al., 1979). Never married mothers averaged considerably fewer work weeks (20 weeks as opposed to 28 weeks) than did separated/

---

[8]Whereas in 1960 about 28 percent of married women with children were labor force participants, in 1970 the percentage had risen to about 40, and in 1978 the percentage was up to about 53.

divorced/widowed mothers. In fact, the never married mothers averaged about the same number of work weeks as currently married mothers (21 weeks), who were, as a whole, less likely to be labor force participants than were mothers in mother-only households. The ultimate outcome of these changes has been that children with working mothers are now in the majority; as of 1980, 52.8 percent of children had mothers who were labor force participants.

While the changes noted for children in terms of the work status of the mother and two-parent/one-parent living arrangements were pervasive, they were not immutable. Mothers moved both in and out of the labor force, and many married, became divorced, and then remarried.

Female-headed families were strikingly transient, with most ever married mothers remarrying eventually (Wattenberg and Reinhardt, 1979; Ross and Sawhill, 1975; Bane and Weiss, 1980). This has meant that an increasingly familiar pattern for children has been to experience the dissolution of their parents' marriage while they are young, spend several years in a mother-only/ female-headed household, and then spend the rest of their childhood in the family formed by their mother's remarriage. The average length of the time between marriages for the mother is 4.5 years. As Bane and Weiss state "This may be a relatively brief interval for an adult, but it is a significant one in a child's life" (1980: 11).

The changes in labor force participation of women also were pervasive but not usually permanent. Analyses of women's work histories, both retrospective (e.g., Corcoran, 1978) and longitudinal (e.g., Masnick and Bane, 1980; D. Hill, 1977) show considerable movement in and out of work. Among women of childbearing ages stably married from 1968 to 1977, about four out of five worked at least one year during the ten-year period, but less than one-third worked all ten years. Women who were persistently heads of households showed a much greater tendency toward permanent labor force attachment.

EMPIRICAL ANALYSES

Well-Being Measures

The typical level of family money income relative to family needs,[9] a measure of adjusted per capita income, is a fairly good indicator of children's economic well-being. Economic well-being, though, can be affected not only by the typical level of resources available but also by the degree of deviation from this typical level. A family income stream with a great deal of year-to-year variation complicates the choice of the optimal allocation path for a given level of lifetime income. Uncertainty and institutional barriers combine to preclude currently low-income families, even those with high expected lifetime income, from borrowing from future income. Thus, children in families with substantial income instability are in a weaker economic position than children in otherwise similar families with more stable incomes. This means that long-term measures of income are better than measures of one-year income for analyzing children's well-being. Thus, longitudinal data are more appropriate than cross-sectional data.

Analyses of the mean level of childhood per capita income (family income relative to needs), the trend in annual per capita income,[10] and a measure of the degree of instability in annual per capita income[11] are all required for a full description of the typical stream of income available during childhood years. Investigation of additional measures such as long-run exposure to

---

[9] This measure is the ratio of total family cash income divided by estimated total family money needs. The needs estimate is based on the Orshansky "thrifty" needs standard. The number, age, and sex of family members are factors used to determine an estimate of total family weekly money food needs on the basis of the Orshansky standard. Two adjustments for "economies of scale" are made for large families, and the weekly food needs are then translated to a total annual money needs value.

[10] Trend in family income/needs is calculated by adjusting annual family income/needs by the CPI, then regressing annual income/needs, measured in logarithms, on time.

[11] Instability in family income/needs is a measure based on the standard error of the trend regression. It equals the square root of the sum of squared deviations around the trend. It is a measure of the extent to which an individual's per capita income deviates from his or her own trend in per capita income. It could be thought of as an index of unpredictable fluctuations.

poverty,[12] welfare receipt,[13] and welfare dependency[14] can help round out the picture of the typical childhood experience. All of these measures will be examined in the longitudinal analysis.

Unit of Analysis

While family income and family needs form the basis of the economic well-being measures, the child is used as the unit of analysis. As Watts and Skidmore (1979: 75) state:

> The household is, however, ephemeral in the sense that its composition and functional organization change from one period to another. This is not such a handicap for cross-sectional analysis, but it is very troublesome for longitudinal studies.

> The individual who, with other individuals, goes to make up the families and the households is the unit with the necessary identity and continuity through time.

Duncan and Morgan (1981b, 1980) pose a similar argument favoring the individual as the unit of analysis in longitudinal studies.

Data

Several samples from the Panel Study of Income Dynamics are used, all weighted to be representative of the corresponding U.S. population of children. Some cross-sectional figures are presented for the years 1970 and 1979. The longitudinal analyses follow three cohorts of children across time. The primary cohort used for this analysis consists of all sample individuals aged 1 to 6 at the start of the ten-year analysis period, 1970-1979. These children were the only ones to remain within the age range

---

[12]The poverty measure corresponds to the official definition of poverty, with the poverty line set at a ratio of family income/needs equal to 1. A child is counted as in poverty in a given year if his/her family income that year is less than family needs.

[13]Welfare status is based on reports of income from the following sources: AFDC, SSI, General Assistance payments, Old Age Assistance, Aid to the Disabled, or food stamps. A child is counted as a welfare recipient in a given year if he/she is living with a parent who is either the household head or wife and who received income from any of these sources during the previous year.

[14]Welfare dependency is determined by the portion that welfare income is of total annual income of the household head and wife. If the portion is one-half or more, all children in the household are counted as welfare dependents.

1 to 16 throughout those ten years. The other two longitudinal samples follow children for eight years only. One consists of children aged 1 in either 1969, 1970, or 1971. Members of this cohort are followed through their first eight years of life. The other eight-year sample consists of children aged 9 in either 1969, 1970, or 1971. Members of this cohort are followed through ages 9 to 16. These samples of approximate single-year birth cohorts (actually each is the combination of three successive single-year birth cohorts)[15] are used primarily to observe the long-run living arrangements that children born in the 1970s were likely to experience.

The PSID data do not permit a clear analysis concerning out-of-wedlock birth nor unambiguous identification of never-married mothers. Consequently, the research with these data focuses only on the distinction between two-parent and mother-only households, with no separation of the latter according to marital status.

A Longitudinal View of Children's Living Arrangements

Until recently very little was known about the pervasiveness and frequency of family composition changes. Little is known still about the family composition changes children undergo, and many estimates are speculative. A need specifically identified at the 1978 Census Bureau Conference on Issues in Federal Statistical Needs Relating to Women was: "Data on the rapidity of household change and how individuals move over time among various types of households, and the average length of the interval which adults and children spend in different types of households" (Reagan, 1979: 133).

With 20 percent as the highest annual percentage of children in a mother-only household, tentative estimates of the fraction living in a mother-only household at some time during childhood range from one-quarter (Bane, 1976) to one-third (Glick, 1980). Indications are that the length of time spent in these households is much greater for black children than for white children (Bumpass and Rindfuss, 1979) because of the lower remarriage rates of black women (Thornton, 1978). As much as 60 percent of

---

[15]Three successive single-year birth cohorts were combined to represent children born in the middle year of the three-year range. This was done in order to produce a large enough sample size to allow disaggregation by the desired characteristics.

black children are estimated to experience the disruption of
their parents' marriage, and one-third of all black children are
estimated to remain in mother-only households from the time of
the disruption to the end of their childhood years (Bumpass and
Rindfuss, 1979).

Examination of the long-run living arrangements of the
eight-year and ten-year PSID samples (Tables 9.1-9.4) should
substantially improve these estimates. They show that:

*** During the first eight years of their lives, as many as one-
quarter of the children born near the start of the 1970s
decade spent some time in a household with at most one
parent present. Over one-fifth spent some time in a mother-
only household, and 3 percent spent all eight years in
mother-only households (Table 9.1).

*** Among children aged 9 at the start of the decade, almost 30
percent spent some time in the eight years prior to reaching
age 16 in a household with at most one parent present.
About one-quarter spent some time in a mother-only
household, and almost 10 percent spent all eight years in
mother-only households (Table 9.2).

*** Among all individuals aged 1 to 6 at the start of the 1970s
decade, almost one-third spent some time during that decade
in a household with only one parent present. One-quarter
spent some time in a mother-only household, and 5 percent
spent all ten years in mother-only households (Table 9.3).

*** The children born in 1970 who spent some time in a mother-
only household averaged almost four of their first eight
years in such a household. The children aged 9 in 1970 who
spent time in a mother-only household averaged an additional
year, making it over half of their eight years prior to age
16, in mother-only households (Table 9.4).

If the 1980s are similar to the 1970s in terms of changes in
family living situations, the previous estimate of one-quarter of
the children born in the seventies spending some time in a
mother-only household is clearly too low. An estimate of one-
third may, in fact, not be high enough. By age 8, over 20
percent of the children born in 1970 had spent time in mother-
only households. For the cohort eight years older, the
percentage in mother-only households at some time during those
same eight chronological years (but for them, ages 9 to 16) was
even larger--about 25 percent. Thus it seems that the likelihood
of spending time in a mother-only household is somewhat greater
in the second half of childhood than in the first half.
Consequently, one-fifth is certainly a lower bound for the
fraction of the 1970 birth cohort which was ever in mother-only

Table 9.1

PERCENTAGE OF CHILDREN IN VARIOUS FAMILY SITUATIONS
OVER THE LONG RUN
(Eight-year longitudinal sample initially aged one)

Family Situation	Number of Years				
	0	1-2	3-4	5-7	8
Nonblack Children (N=570)					
Father and mother present	3.3	1.7	3.6	12.0	79.3
Mother present, father not present	82.8	8.5	4.4	3.0	1.4
Black Children (N=421)					
Father and mother present	32.1	8.7	8.5	11.3	39.3
Mother present, father not present	51.8	8.6	10.5	14.3	14.7
All (N=991)					
Father and mother present	7.2	2.7	4.3	11.8	74.0
Mother present, father not present	78.7	8.5	5.2	4.5	3.1

Table 9.2

PERCENTAGE OF CHILDREN IN VARIOUS FAMILY SITUATIONS
OVER THE LONG RUN
(Eight-year longitudinal sample initially aged nine)

Family Situation	Number of Years				
	0	1-2	3-4	5-7	8
Nonblack Children (N=497)					
Father and mother present	7.2	4.2	2.4	7.8	78.3
Mother present, father not present	81.0	4.1	4.1	4.9	5.9
Black Children (N=529)					
Father and mother present	38.6	5.9	9.7	7.3	38.5
Mother present, father not present	49.8	5.8	5.2	10.3	28.9
All (N=1,026)					
Father and mother present	12.3	4.5	3.6	7.8	71.9
Mother present, father not present	76.0	4.4	4.3	5.8	9.6

Table 9.3

PERCENTAGE OF CHILDREN IN VARIOUS FAMILY SITUATIONS
OVER THE LONG RUN
(Ten-year longitudinal sample)

Family Situation	Number of Years					
	0	1-2	3-5	6-7	8-9	10
Nonblack Children (N=1,285)						
Father and mother present	3.8	2.0	5.5	5.3	5.9	77.4
Mother present, father not present	79.9	5.7	7.1	2.5	1.7	3.1
Black Children (N=1,086)						
Father and mother present	32.5	7.7	12.0	4.4	9.9	33.6
Mother present, father not present	43.4	9.7	9.9	7.6	11.0	18.4
All (N=2,371)						
Father and mother, present	7.7	2.8	6.4	5.2	6.5	71.5
Mother present, father not present	75.0	6.3	7.6	3.1	2.9	5.2

Table 9.4

AVERAGE NUMBER OF YEARS IN VARIOUS FAMILY SITUATIONS
OVER THE LONG RUN FOR THOSE SPENDING AT LEAST
ONE YEAR IN THAT FAMILY SITUATION
(Eight-year and ten-year longitudinal samples)

| | Average Number of Years | |
Sample Spending at Least One Year in Situation	Father and Mother Present	Mother Present, Father Not Present
Eight-Year Longitudinal Sample Initially Aged 1 Nonblack (N=570)	7.5	3.2
Black (N=421)	6.2	5.3
All (N=991)	7.4	3.8
Initially Aged 9 Nonblack (N=497)	7.4	5.1
Black (N=529)	6.4	6.4
All (N=1,026)	7.3	5.5
Ten-Year Longitudinal Sample Nonblack (N=1,285)	9.2	4.9
Black (N=1,086)	7.5	6.8
All (N=2,371)	9.1	5.5

households. While these figures cannot establish a clear upper bound, they suggest that the upper limit could go as high as one-half for this cohort.

We can add information about mother's work status to get a more complete picture of children's living situations (see Tables 9.5 and 9.6). Doing so, we find that:

*** Between ages 1 and 8, about 15 percent of the 1970 birth cohort were never in a traditional living situation, with both parents present and the mother not working.

*** Only about one-quarter (26.8 percent) of the 1970 birth cohort spent all of their first eight years in two-parent, mother-not-working households.

*** Over two-thirds of the 1970 birth cohort who lived in a mother-only household spent some time with the mother working while heading the household. This compares with about 60 percent of the children in a two-parent household having a working mother.

Figures were similar for the cohort aged 1 to 6 in 1970, with differences mainly reflecting a somewhat greater frequency of market activity among mothers of the older children. Thus, we see that never having a working mother is a rare situation for children of the Seventies. It was somewhat less common for the children in mother-only households never to have had a working mother than it was for the children always living with both parents. Overall, children spending their entire childhood in a two-parent, mother-not-working household constitute a small minority of children.

Race and Family Situation

During the seventies, differences between black and white children widened in terms of the likelihood of being in a two-parent versus a mother-only family. Each year since 1970, a larger proportion of white than black children has been living with two parents. Despite an increase in mother-only, female-headed households among white families with children, this differential grew because of an even larger shift in the same direction among blacks. By the end of the decade this shift among blacks resulted in the majority of black children living in a household without two parents present. In fact, by 1980 equal

Table 9.5

PERCENTAGE IN VARIOUS HEADSHIP/MOTHER'S
WORK HOURS SITUATIONS
(Eight-year longitudinal sample initially aged one)

Headship and Mother's Work Hours	Number of Years					Average Number of Years for Those with Years >0
	0	1-2	3-4	5-7	8	
Nonblack						
Father head and mother's work hours <500	10.5	11.9	12.1	27.3	28.2	5.7
Mother head and mother's work hours >500	87.7	7.3	3.0	1.9	0.0	2.6
Black						
Father head and mother's work hours <500	42.5	16.8	8.3	14.6	17.8	4.8
Mother head and mother's work hours >500	68.7	14.7	9.0	6.8	0.6	3.2
All						
Father head and mother's work hours <500	14.7	12.5	11.7	34.3	26.8	5.6
Mother head and mother's work hours >500	85.2	8.3	3.8	2.6	0.1	2.8

Table 9.6

NUMBER OF YEARS IN VARIOUS HEADSHIP/MOTHER'S
WORK HOURS SITUATIONS
(Ten-year longitudinal sample)

Headship and mother's work hours	Number of Years						Average Number of Years for Those with Years >0
	0	1-2	3-5	6-7	8-9	10	
Nonblack							
Father head and mother's work hours <500	14.6	10.2	16.4	14.8	17.8	26.1	6.9
Mother head and mother's work hours >500	83.7	7.1	4.7	2.5	1.4	0.6	3.9
Black							
Father head and mother's work hours <500	48.3	14.4	14.4	6.7	8.1	8.2	5.2
Mother head and mother's work hours >500	60.1	10.6	11.1	9.7	4.8	3.6	5.1
All							
Father head and mother's work hours <500	19.1	10.7	16.2	13.8	16.5	23.7	6.8
Mother head and mother's work hours >500	80.5	7.5	5.6	3.5	1.9	1.0	4.2

proportions of black children were in two-parent and in mother-only households.[16]

Among the mother-only households there are also important race differences having to do with the marital status of the mother. During the 1970s there was a shift in the marital status mix of mother-only households that affected black and white children differently. At the end of the decade, as at the beginning, the majority of both black and white children in mother-only families was living with a divorced or separated mother. However, there was an increase in the proportion of white children living with a divorced or separated mother, while for black children the proportion actually declined. This differential shift was due to the greater increase among blacks in the proportion with a never-married mother as head of the household. The increase in black households of this type was so large that by the end of the decade over a quarter of black children in mother-only households were living in households headed by a never married mother.[17] This meant that one-tenth of all black children, compared to less than 1 percent of all white children, were in never-married, mother-only families.

Historically, black mothers have been more likely to be labor force participants than white mothers. While this continues to hold, the difference by race is now smaller due to a narrowing of the race difference in participation among married mothers plus no reversal in the race difference among unmarried mothers.

---

[16]By 1979 the percentage of black children living with two parents had dropped to 43 percent, whereas the percentage in mother-only households had risen to 42 percent. Changes for white children were in the same direction but much smaller in magnitude, with 84 percent in two-parent households in 1979, as opposed to 13 percent in one-parent households. Standardizing for changes in the age distribution of children, Bianchi and Farley's (1979) figures provide further evidence of the large race differentials in living arrangements of children widening in recent years.

[17]Of the white children in mother-only households, 76 percent were living with a divorced or separated mother in 1970, and 81 percent were in 1979. The comparable change for blacks was a decrease from 71 to 61 percent. At the same time, the proportion of white children living with never-married mothers increased from 3 to 6 percent of all white children in mother-only households. The comparable change for blacks was an increase from 15 to 28 percent.

Among both married and unmarried mothers, participation rates for blacks and whites increased over the decade. Among married mothers, though, the increase was considerably greater for whites than blacks after the mid-1970s.[8] This led to reductions in the degree to which black married mothers were the more likely participants. The rate of increase in participation for unmarried mothers was, on the other hand, quite similar for blacks and whites.[9] Of the unmarried mothers, though, whites have for some time been the more likely participants. The end result is that, by 1980, the percentage of white children with a mother in the labor force was up to 52 percent, compared to the 57 percent of black children in the same situation.

Racial differences regarding time spent in mother-only households are much more striking than racial differences concerning mother's work status. We find the following:

*** Only 40 percent of the black children born in 1970 spent all of their first eight years of life in two-parent households. This compares with about 80 percent of the nonblack children.

*** Almost 30 percent of the black children born in 1970 spent over half of their first eight years of life in mother-only households. This compares to about 5 percent of the nonblack children.

*** Almost 30 percent of the black children were in mother-only households the entire eight years between ages 9 and 16. The comparable figure for nonblack children was 6 percent.

Adding the work status of the mother as another dimension, we find the following race differences:

*** About 20 percent of the black children (as opposed to 30 percent of the nonblack children) who were born in 1970 spent all of their first eight years of life in two-parent, mother-not-working households.

*** About 7 percent of the black children (as opposed to 2 percent of the nonblack children) who were born in 1970 spent over half of their first eight years of life in mother-only, mother-working households.

---

[8]For white children in two-parent households, the portion with mothers working outside the home increased from 36 percent in 1970 to 51 percent in 1980; correspondingly, for black children the increase was from 52 percent up to 62 percent.

[9]Among the children living with their mother only, 57 percent of the whites, as opposed to 47 percent of the blacks, had working mothers in 1970. As of 1980 these percentages both had increased, to 67 percent for whites and 57 percent for blacks.

*** Almost 4 percent of the black children were in mother-only, mother-working households the entire eight years between ages 9 and 16. The comparable figure for nonblack children was about 1 percent.

These latter differences in living arrangements reflect the influence of two factors--race differences in propensities for living in mother-only households and race differences in the likelihood of the mother working, given the type of household. While black children are more likely to live in mother-only households, and mothers in mother-only households are more likely to be working than those in two-parent households, black children are only somewhat more likely to live in mother-only, mother-working households. These findings are quite consistent with the racial differentials that were cited in the earlier section concerning demographic trends. Thus, the family composition situations of children differ very dramatically by race, and this contributes to the differences in mother's work status for black and nonblack children. However, racial differences in mothers' work status within the different categories of family composition are relatively small.

A CROSS-SECTIONAL VIEW OF CHILDREN'S ECONOMIC WELL-BEING

During the 1970s there were persistent, dramatic differences in the levels of economic well-being between black and nonblack children (see Table 9.7). In both 1970 and 1979, the average level of per capita income of nonblack children was almost twice that of black children. Inequality in the distribution of income/needs around its modal value (GINI coefficient) remained somewhat greater for black than nonblack children; and inequality at the ends of the distribution (top 10%/bottom 10%)[20] remained much greater for blacks. Both in 1970 and 1979, almost no black children occupied the top decile of the income/needs distribution for children, and about one-third were poor. While the percentage of black children who were poor did fall somewhat over the decade, black children continued to be much more likely than white children to be in poverty. On the other hand, the greater likelihood of black children being in a household receiving welfare income declined somewhat, as did the greater likelihood

---

[20] This figure was calculated on the basis of the percentages of the racial subgroup that fell in the top or bottom 10 percent of the distribution of income/needs across all children.

of black children being in a household dependent on welfare income.

A LONGITUDINAL VIEW OF CHILDREN'S ECONOMIC WELL-BEING

The economic environment of the 1970s was favorable, though somewhat less than propitious, for individuals who were children throughout the decade (see Tables 9.8 and 9.9). These children averaged a level of ten-year family income three times as large as their ten-year family needs. However, growth in their annual level of income/needs was small, increasing about 1 percent per year. In addition, many children had negative trends in per capita income. Children also experienced a considerable degree of instability, and the amount of instability differed much more across children than did the level of ten-year per capita income. Between one-quarter and one-third of the children aged one to six in 1970 were poor at some time during the 1970s. Six percent of all children, or one-fifth of the poor ones, were poor at least half of the ten years of the decade. Welfare was received by a large fraction of children--one-third--but only one-tenth were dependent on welfare (welfare comprising over half of family income) at some time. In addition, long-term welfare dependency (six to ten years) was much less common among children than was long-term welfare receipt; only 5 percent of the children were long-term welfare dependents, whereas twice that number were long-term welfare recipients. Interestingly enough,

*** Poverty was a much more frequent occurrence for children than was welfare dependency.

So we see that, despite a high average level of economic well-being for children during the 1970s, poverty was widespread among children, though most of the poverty was of a temporary nature. Welfare receipt was common for children also, but long-term welfare dependency, like long-term poverty, was rare.

The economic experiences of black and nonblack children differed dramatically during the 1970s. Black children averaged much lower levels of long-run per capita income, with a less positive trend and greater instability over time:

*** Average long-run family income/needs was half as large for black children as for nonblack children.

*** Among nonblacks, there were two and one-third times as many children in the highest income/needs decile as there were in

Table 9.7

VARIOUS MEASURES OF FAMILY SITUATION AND ECONOMIC
WELL-BEING FOR ALL CHILDREN IN 1970 AND IN 1979
(Cross-section samples)

	1970			1979		
	Nonblack	Black	All	Nonblack	Black	All
Income/Needs:						
Two-parent families	3.20	2.02	3.08	3.86	2.51	3.66
Mother only	1.89	1.12	1.59	1.99	1.20	1.72
Other families	2.52	1.11	1.82	3.36	1.59	2.58
All families	3.07	1.63	2.85	3.60	1.86	3.35
GINI Coefficient	.307	.389	.330	.306	.371	.330
Top 10%/Bottom 10%	2.04	0.05	1.0	1.98	0.04	1.0
Percent Poor	6.4	36.8	10.9	5.3	31.9	9.1
Percent Receiving Welfare	6.7	36.8	11.2	12.1	44.1	16.7
Percent Dependent on Welfare	3.1	20.1	5.6	4.3	24.7	7.2
Family Situation:						
Percent two parents	89.5	56.9	84.7	84.7	47.9	79.5
Percent mother only	8.2	30.4	11.5	12.6	39.7	16.5
Percent other	2.3	12.8	3.9	2.7	12.4	4.1
Average Number of Children in Family:						
Two-parent families	3.3	4.3	3.4	2.5	3.0	2.5
Mother only	2.9	4.2	3.4	2.2	2.7	2.4
Other families	3.0	3.9	3.5	1.6	2.9	2.2
All families	3.3	4.2	3.4	2.4	2.9	2.5
Percent with Mother's Work Hours:						
Less than 500	65.9	58.2	64.8	53.7	45.8	52.6
500-1,499	16.2	19.0	16.6	20.2	20.3	20.2
1,5000 or more	17.9	22.8	18.6	26.1	33.9	27.2
Average Age of Child	8.5	8.7	8.5	8.4	8.4	8.4
N	3,357	3,310	6,667	3,056	2,497	5,553

Table 9.8

VARIOUS INCOME/NEEDS MEASURES
(Ten-year longitudinal sample)

	Nonblack	Black	All
Average Income/Needs			
Mean	3.32	1.65	3.10
GINI coefficient	.283	.298	.305
Top 10%/bottom 10%	2.30	0.00	1.0
Instability of Income/Needs			
Mean	0.67	0.85	0.69
GINI coefficient	.497	.261	.467
If in top 10%	8.8	17.3	10.0
Trend in Income/Needs			
Mean	0.014	-0.001	0.012
Percent with trend <0	38.8	52.2	40.6
Average Number of Children in Household	2.9	3.9	3.1

Table 9.9

LONG-RUN POVERTY AND WELFARE STATUS BY RACE
(Ten-year longitudinal sample)

	Nonblack	Black	All
Percent in Poverty			
Number of years poor			
0	79.1	30.3	72.5
1-5	18.8	40.1	21.5
6-10	2.3	29.7	5.8
Average Number of Years Poor			
All	0.6	3.5	0.9
Those in Poverty	2.6	5.0	3.4
Percent Receiving Welfare			
Number of Years Receiving Welfare			
0	73.6	25.6	67.1
1-5	20.6	31.4	22.1
6-10	5.8	43.0	10.9
Average Number of Years Receiving Welfare			
All	0.9	4.6	1.4
Those Receiving Welfare	3.6	6.2	4.4
Percent Dependent on Welfare			
Number of Years Dependent on Welfare			
0	92.1	54.0	87.0
1-5	5.6	25.1	8.3
6-10	2.2	20.8	4.8
Average Number of Years Dependent on Welfare			
All	0.3	2.4	0.6
Those Dependent on Welfare	4.1	5.2	4.6

the lowest decile. There were virtually no black children in the highest income/needs decile.

*** Instability in family income/needs was one and one-third times as large for black children as it was for nonblack children.

*** Twice as large a percentage of black children as of nonblack children fell in the top decile of instability in family income/needs.

*** Among nonblack children, the trend in income/needs was positive, but this was not so among black children.

In addition, there were large race differences in poverty and welfare experiences.

*** Even with cash welfare benefits added to family income, the majority (70 percent) of black children was poor at some time during the decade. This compares to 20 percent of nonblack children.

*** Black children were much more likely to be in persistent poverty than were nonblack children (30 percent compared to 2 percent). For both groups of children, though, poverty was more likely to be a temporary than a permanent state.

*** The majority (75 percent) of black children spent some time with a welfare-recipient parent. This compares to 25 percent of nonblack children.

*** Almost half of the black children (46 percent) spent some time with a parent who depended on welfare as the major source of income; one-tenth (8 percent) of nonblack children did so.

Despite these large race differences regarding poverty and welfare use, black and nonblack children were quite similar in one important regard:

*** The majority of children who were long-term welfare recipients, whether black or nonblack, were not long-term welfare dependents.

This indicates that welfare is but one source of income, and not even the largest one, for most children who are long-term recipients.

Long-Run Relationship between Economic Well-Being and Children's Living Situation

The PSID data show a strong negative long-run relationship between economic well-being and the amount of time spent in a mother-only household (Tables 9.10-9.13). Average per capita income declines sharply and percent poor increases dramatically as children spend more of their childhood in a mother-only household. The degree of across-time variability in income is greater for children spending some but not most of the ten years in a mother-only household, as measures of both instability and trend indicate.

Welfare is an important income source--but not the only one--even for children usually in mother-only households. Of these children, over two-thirds received welfare at some time, almost half were long-term recipients, but only one-third were long-term welfare dependents (depending on welfare as the major source of income over half the decade). Apparently income sources other than welfare (and the literature suggests the major one is mother's earnings) are essential to the economic well-being of children even in welfare-recipient, mother-only households.

Long-Run Relationships between Race Differences in Economic Well-Being and Living Arrangements

We have seen that black children tend to fare much worse economically than nonblack children and that they have a much higher propensity for living in mother-only households--which fare worse economically than two-parent ones. This raises a question about the importance of racial differences in children's living arrangements: to what extent are racial differences in the economic situation of children the result of racial differences in family living arrangements? One way to try to answer this question is to decompose the mean value of an economic variable into two components: one based on the distribution of the individuals across household types (mother-only and two-parent), and the other based on the mean values of the economic variable for the individuals within each household type (the mean value of the economic variable for children in mother-only households and the mean value for children in two-parent households). This decomposition of an economic measure is done separately for black and nonblack children; then the mean values for black children by household type are applied to the distribution for nonblack children across the household types. Mean values for black children that are derived in this way are then compared to the actual mean values for nonblack children. Any reduction in the racial difference that is achieved this way is attributable to racial differences in living arrangements,

Table 9.10

LONG-RUN MEASURES OF INCOME/NEEDS BY USUAL FAMILY SITUATION
(Ten-year longitudinal sample)

| Subgroup | Usual Family Situation 1970-1979 | | | | All |
	Always Both Parents	Occasionally Mother Only	Mostly Mother Only	Other	
	Mean of 10-Year Average Income/Needs				
Nonblack	3.50	2.97	2.23	2.93	3.32
Black	2.08	1.77	1.29	1.25	1.65
All	3.41	2.74	1.81	2.29	3.10
	Percent in Top Decile of Ten-Year Average Income/Needs Relative to Percent in Bottom Decile				
Nonblack	3.1	1.8	0.0	0.6	2.3
Black	0.0	0.0	0.0	0.0	0.0
All	2.1	0.9	0.0	0.1	1.0
	Mean of Ten-Year Instability of Income/Needs				
Nonblack	0.61	0.94	0.75	0.63	0.67
Black	0.68	0.98	0.89	0.99	0.85
All	0.62	0.94	0.82	0.77	0.69
	Percent in Top 10 Percent of Ten-Year Instability of Income/Needs				
Nonblack	6.3	22.7	12.5	2.7	8.8
Black	8.0	20.0	22.4	24.1	17.3
All	6.4	22.2	16.9	10.9	9.9
	Mean of Ten-Year Trend in Income/Needs				
Nonblack	0.021	-0.021	-0.007	0.023	0.014
Black	0.024	-0.023	-0.016	0.013	-0.001
All	0.021	-0.022	-0.011	0.019	0.012
	Percent with Ten-Year Trend in Income/Needs <0				
Nonblack	33.2	65.6	53.7	29.5	38.8
Black	35.6	66.1	63.4	39.5	52.2
All	33.5	65.7	57.9	33.3	40.6

Table 9.11

LONG-RUN POVERTY AND WELFARE STATUS BY USUAL FAMILY SITUATION FOR ALL CHILDREN
(Ten-year longitudinal sample)

| | Usual Family Situation | | | | |
	Always Both Parents	Occasionally Mother Only	Usually Mother Only	Other	All
Percent In Poverty					
Number of Years Poor					
0	81.9	53.5	41.0	58.1	72.5
1-5	15.5	39.6	38.1	19.5	21.5
6-10	2.5	6.9	20.9	22.4	5.8
Average Number of Years Poor					
All	0.5	1.3	2.8	2.2	0.9
Those in Poverty	2.9	2.8	4.7	5.2	3.4
Percent Receiving Welfare					
Number of Years Receiving Welfare					
0	77.9	46.5	30.7	44.9	67.1
1-5	18.4	35.0	23.4	41.3	22.1
6-10	3.7	18.5	45.9	13.7	10.9
Average Number of Years Receiving Welfare					
All	0.7	2.4	4.8	2.3	1.4
Those Receiving Welfare	3.1	4.5	7.0	4.2	4.4

Table 9.11 (continued)

	Usual Family Situation				
	Always Both Parents	Occasionally Mother Only	Usually Mother Only	Other	All
Percent Dependent on Welfare					
Number of Years Dependent on Welfare					
0	96.4	71.7	48.3	81.3	87.0
1-5	3.0	24.0	21.5	13.7	8.3
6-10	0.6[a]	4.3[a]	30.1	5.0[a]	4.8
Average Number of Years Dependent on Welfare					
All	0.1	0.9	3.3	0.7	0.6
Those Dependent on Welfare	3.3	3.0	6.3	3.7	4.6

[a]Fewer than 20 observations.

Table 9.12

LONG-RUN POVERTY AND WELFARE STATUS BY USUAL FAMILY SITUATION FOR NONBLACK CHILDREN
(Ten-year longitudinal subsample of nonblack children)

| | Usual Family Situation | | | | |
	Always Both Parents	Occasionally Mother Only	Usually Mother Only	Other	All
Percent In Poverty					
Number of Years Poor					
0	83.6	61.2	62.2	82.5	79.1
1-5	15.1[a]	33.0	31.5[a]	16.2[a]	18.8
6-10	1.3[a]	5.8	6.3[a]	1.2[a]	2.3
Average Number of Years Poor					
All	0.4	0.9	1.5	0.4	0.6
Those in Poverty	2.5	2.4	3.9	2.1*	2.6
Percent Receiving Welfare					
Number of Years Receiving Welfare					
0	80.1	53.6	44.9	57.8	73.6
1-5	17.3	34.9	23.6	39.3[a]	20.6
6-10	2.5	11.4	31.4	2.9[a]	5.8
Average Number of Years Receiving Welfare					
All	0.6	1.8	3.6	0.9	0.9
Those Receiving Welfare	2.9	3.8	6.5	2.1[a]	3.6

Table 9.12 (continued)

	Usual Family Situation				
	Always Both Parents	Occasionally Mother Only	Usually Mother Only	Other	All
Percent Dependent on Welfare					
Number of Years Dependent on Welfare					
0	97.3	79.0	59.0	97.1[a]	92.1
1-5	2.0[a]	20.4	20.4	1.7[a]	5.6
6-10	0.7[a]	0.6[a]	20.6	1.2[a]	2.2
Average Number of Years Dependent on Welfare					
All	0.1	0.5	2.3	0.2	0.3
Those Dependent on Welfare	3.9	2.4	5.7	5.5	4.1

[a] Fewer than 20 observations.

Table 9.13

LONG-RUN POVERTY AND WELFARE STATUS BY USUAL FAMILY SITUATION FOR BLACK CHILDREN
(Ten-year longitudinal sample of black children)

	Usual Family Situation				
	Always Both Parents	Occasionally Mother Only	Usually Mother Only	Other	All
Number of Years Poor	Percent In Poverty				
0	57.0	21.0	14.1	18.4	30.3
1-5	21.4	67.5	46.3	24.8	40.1
6-10	21.5	11.4	39.6	56.9	29.7
	Average Number of Years Poor				
All	2.3	2.9	4.5	5.1	3.5
Those in Poverty	5.3	3.6	5.2	6.2	5.0
	Percent Receiving Welfare				
Number of Years Receiving Welfare					
0	45.6	16.5	12.6	24.1	25.6
1-5	34.5	34.6	23.2	44.7	31.4
6-10	19.8	48.7	64.2	31.3	43.0
	Average Number of Years Receiving Welfare				
All	2.4	4.9	6.5	4.5	4.6
Those Receiving Welfare	4.5	5.9	7.4	6.0	6.2

Table 9.13 (continued)

	Usual Family Situation				
	Always Both Parents	Occasionally Mother Only	Usually Mother Only	Other	All
	Percent Dependent on Welfare				
Number of Years Dependent on Welfare					
0	82.5	40.8	34.8	55.6	54.0
1-5	17.1	39.2[a]	22.9	33.1	25.1
6-10	0.5[a]	20.0[a]	42.3	11.2[a]	20.8
	Average Number of Years Dependent on Welfare				
All Those Dependent on Welfare	0.3	2.3	4.5	1.5	2.4
	1.9	3.9	6.9	3.5	5.2

[a]Fewer than 20 observations.

because that is the only change that has been allowed; racial differences in the economic variable by household type have been held constant.

Table 9.14 presents results of this procedure for several economic values. Comparing the percent of the race difference due to race differences in living arrangements, we find substantial variation across the economic measures. Race differences in living arrangements account for very little of the overall race difference in economic measures based on the level of family income/needs--long-term income/needs and poverty status. Thus, it seems that black children's greater long-run propensity for living in mother-only families plays a relatively minor role in generating their overall lower level of economic well-being.

Turning to other dimensions of family income/needs, we find much stronger effects of the differing propensities that black and nonblack children have for living in mother-only households. Race differences in long-run likelihood of living in a mother-only household account for a great deal of the race differences in both trend and instability of income/needs. Thus, it seems that race differences in living arrangements generate differences regarding variation in the flow rather than the general level of economic resources. This suggests that reduction in black children's greater long-run propensity for living in mother-only families, with no other change, would be of limited help in reducing the racial gap in economic well-being. Bringing the living arrangements of black children more in line with those of nonblack children would help stabilize the flow of income to black children and raise the trend in their income, but it would not substantially increase the level of income. Other changes apparently are needed to bring the level of income of black children up to that of nonblack children. The findings so far suggest that it is factors associated with race differences in the level of economic resources within each kind of household that would need to be changed. This suggests that what is needed to raise the level of income of black children up to that of nonblack children are changes in the wage levels and skills of black household heads, both male and female.

Table 9.14

RACE DIFFERENCES IN VARIOUS INCOME/NEEDS MEASURES
WITH AND WITHOUT ADJUSTMENTS FOR RACE DIFFERENCES
IN CHILDREN'S LIVING ARRANGEMENTS[a]
(Ten-year longitudinal sample)

	Total Race Difference in Means[b]	Percent of Total Race Difference Due to Differences in Living Arrangements
Average Income/Needs		
Mean	1.67	19
Top 10%/bottom 10%	2.3	0
Instability of Income/Needs		
Mean	-0.18	61
If in top 10%	-8.5	74
Trend in Income/Needs		
Mean	0.015	100
Percent with trend <0	-13.4	79
Number of Years Poor		
Mean	-2.9	31
Percent 0	48.8	37
Percent 6 to 10	-27.4	27
Number of Years Received Welfare		
Mean	-3.7	41
Percent 0	48.0	28
Percent 6 to 10	-37.2	43
Number of Years Dependent on Welfare		
Mean	-2.1	71
Percent 0	38.1	50

[a]Here "living arrangement" refers to being in a mother-only
versus two-parent family.

[b]This equals the mean value for nonblack children minus the
mean value for black children.

Factors Associated with Long-Run Level of Family Income/Needs

To investigate these factors, Multiple Classification
Analysis (MCA) was used, with ten-year average family income/
needs as the dependent variable. Separate analyses were
performed for the major race/living arrangement categories of

children. Effects of factors that could be measured in a similar fashion regardless of changes in family composition were investigated. Results of these analyses are presented in Table 9.15.

We find the following factors are important correlates of a child's average level of family income/needs over time: parent's education (average education of the household head),[21] father's average annual work hours for the years when he is present in the child's household,[22] mother's work hours, number of siblings, and years spent in a mother-only household. A child's level of economic well-being increased with parent's education, father's work hours, and mother's work hours. It decreased with number of siblings and years spent in mother-only households. These general patterns were consistent across the differing race and living arrangement subgroups, and their collective explanatory power was quite large for all subgroups.[23]

The PSID data (Corcoran and Duncan, 1979) have helped document large gender and race differentials in wages that persist even with extensive controls for work experience, training, and labor force attachment: women's wages are lower than men's, and blacks' wages are lower than nonblacks'. There are several indications that these differentials are important to the findings of Table 9.15. For children within each household type, father's work hours exerted a stronger effect on a child's level of long-term per capita income than did mother's work hours. The gender differential in wages provides a plausible explanation for additional hours of work of the father having a

---

[21] Education level of the household head is measured by summing years of education of each year's household head, then dividing by ten. The individual who was the household head could, of course, vary.

[22] If no father was present in a given year, father's work hours are zero in that year.

[23] The pattern of R^2s indicates that there must be more important factors missing for nonblack children always in two-parent families than for the other subgroups. Such factors could include the wage rates of fathers and mothers, which are not specified because they were unavailable for all children and inappropriate for some (e.g., children with never-married mothers). Another omitted predictor is the average wealth level of the child's household. This factor could affect the flow of asset income over time as well as the ability to compensate for periods with low labor market earnings. Data limitations, however, precluded analysis of this factor.

Table 9.15

MULTIVARIATE ANALYSIS (MULTIPLE CLASSIFICATION ANALYSIS) WITH TEN-YEAR AVERAGE
INCOME/NEEDS AS THE DEPENDENT VARIABLE, FOR SUBGROUPS BY RACE AND LONG-RUN FAMILY SITUATION
(Ten-year longitudinal sample)

| | Always Two Parents | | | | Mother Only at Some Time | | | |
| | Nonblack | | Black | | Nonblack | | Black | |
	Percentage of Cases	Coef.	Percentage of Cases	Coef.	Percentage of Cases	Coef.	Percentage of Cases	Coef.
Average Formal Education of Head								
No high school	12.0	-1.082	37.9	-0.397	14.5	-0.640	20.1	-0.263
Some high school	20.1	-0.746	22.2	-0.214	38.5	-0.258	51.4	-0.138
High school	30.9	-0.309	32.8	0.395	28.8	-0.166	21.3	-0.332
Some college	18.9	0.518	6.8	1.006	14.2	1.179	7.2	0.749
College or more	18.1	1.536	0.4	a	4.0	a	0.0	a
Beta²		0.208		0.147		0.186		0.120
Average Work Hours of Father								
0	0.2	a	0.6	a	16.4	-0.762	48.7	-0.358
1-499	0.4	a	0.8	a	12.4	-0.317	16.0	0.045
500-1,499	2.7	-0.490	15.1	-1.079	37.3	0.050	21.8	0.496
1,500-1,999	21.3	-0.258	27.4	-0.253	21.6	0.453	10.4	0.512
2,000-2,499	44.6	-0.154	46.0	-0.440	9.2	0.183	0.2	a
2,500 or more	30.7	0.472	10.1	0.435	3.1	a	2.9	a
Beta²		0.030		0.246		0.083		0.199
Average Work Hours of Mother								
0	16.8	-0.097	18.3	-0.306	1.9	a	10.2	0.048
1-499	47.1	-0.142	26.5	-0.048	39.3	-0.179	31.5	-0.221
500-1,499	26.6	0.022	34.1	-0.058	36.8	0.038	43.0	0.011
1,500-1,999	7.7	0.779	19.1	0.388	16.5	0.256	14.0	0.422
2,000 or more	1.8	a	2.0	a	5.4	a	1.3	a
Beta²		0.020		0.045		0.026		0.056
Average Unemployment Hours of Father								
0	56.5	0.148	32.2	-0.095	49.5	0.422	67.3	0.045
1-30 days	31.5	-0.125	55.0	0.021	43.4	-0.409	17.3	-0.040
1 month-60 days	8.5	-0.272	7.2	0.325	5.7	-0.248	11.1	-0.157
2 months-183 days	3.1	-0.606	5.6	-0.077	1.4	a	4.4	a
6 months or more	0.4	a	0.0	a	0.0	a	0.0	a
Beta²		0.010		0.009		0.083		0.007
Number of Years Father Disabled								
0	77.0	0.062	61.2	-0.035	78.1	0.041	78.6	0.058
1-2	11.7	-0.176	9.6	0.167	11.3	-0.159	9.8	0.028
3-5	6.2	-0.259	19.5	0.016	7.7	a	5.4	-0.361
6 or more	5.1	-0.239	9.7	0.024	2.9	a	6.3	a
Beta²		0.004		0.003		0.003		0.032

Table 9.15 (continued)

	Always Two Parents				Mother Only at Some Time			
	Nonblack		Black		Nonblack		Black	
	Percentage of Cases	Coef.	Percentage of Cases	Coef.	Percentage of Cases	Coef.	Percentage of Cases	Coef.
Average Age of Head								
Less than 25	0.6	a	0.0	a	1.9	a	5.0	a
25-34	38.7	-0.030	34.4	-0.101	51.6	0.053	42.7	0.070
35-44	40.5	0.017	36.9	-0.136	35.0	-0.036	37.7	-0.030
45 or more	20.2	0.014	28.8	0.027	11.4	-0.088	14.7	0.094
Beta'		0.000				0.002		-0.179
								0.012
Initial Age of Child								
1 day-2 years	32.4	-0.061	28.4	0.155	25.7	0.052	28.7	0.002
3-5 years	38.8	-0.004	36.8	-0.160	41.5	-0.078	42.2	0.069
6 years	28.8	0.075	34.9	0.043	32.8	0.057	29.1	-0.103
Beta'		0.001		0.013		0.002		0.007
Average Number of Siblings in Family								
Zero	4.3	1.193	2.5	a	9.7	0.670	0.9	a
One	15.2	0.110	7.0	0.418	11.1	0.366	11.7	0.345
Two	10.2	-0.223	6.6	0.019	8.2	-0.501	11.5	0.058
Three or more	70.4	-0.129	83.9	-0.070	71.0	-0.091	76.0	-0.067
Beta'		0.022		0.036		0.038		0.027
Number of Years in Mother-Only Household								
0	100.0		100.0		0.0	0.221	0.0	0.247
1-2					28.3	0.147	17.1	-0.022
3-7					47.6	-0.550	30.9	-0.068
8-10					24.1	0.043	51.9	0.018
Beta'						0.101		0.134
Eta'								
Mean		3.498		2.083		2.698		1.455
R' (adjusted)		0.350		0.557		0.540		0.703
N		932		561		317		411

a Fewer than 20 observations.

stronger effect on a child's economic status than those of the mother.

Wage differentials may also be responsible for the racial difference in importance of the length of a father's absence from the child's household: the effect of years in a mother-only household was considerably stronger among nonblack children than among black children. Lower wages of black men may help account for this since lower wages would mean a smaller loss of income when the father is no longer present in the child's household.

Other factors that show important racial differences in the role of the father in a child's average level of per capita income are father's unemployment hours and years of disability. Both are measures of the extent to which the father was in adverse economic circumstances, and both are important only for children with a father absent at some time. This suggests that income losses from a marital separation are lower, and long-term income is likewise lower, for a child whose father had extensive unemployment or disability before separation. Where the racial difference comes in is in the relative importance of these two types of adversity: unemployment of the father is what matters for nonblack children, whereas disability of the father is what matters for black children. Thus, conditions inhibiting further income contributions from fathers to children from broken homes differ by race. As a method of raising the contribution from father's earnings, unemployment-induced earnings losses would seem more amenable to reduction than would earnings losses due to severe disability. However, concentration on the former, to the neglect of the latter, would place black children from broken homes in an even more disadvantageous position relative to nonblack children.

There is also one important race differential that appears regardless of household type--a difference in the relative

importance of father's education[24] and father's work hours.
While both are quite important in determining the long-term per
capita income of children, regardless of race, father's education
is much more important for nonblack children, whereas father's
work hours is more important for black children. Racial
differences in the distribution of children across the categories
of the variables may account for this differential. Father's
education may be less important for black children because so few
have fathers with a college education; father's work hours may be
more important for them because many have fathers who average
part-time rather than full-time work. This suggests that
redistribution of black children in the direction of having
fathers with higher levels of education--or at least higher
levels of wages that correlate with higher levels of education--
would help reduce the racial gap in the economic well-being of
children. In addition, increases in the work hours of black
fathers, both those in stable marriages and those in unstable
marriages, would also be a big help in reducing this gap.
However, the figures in Table 9.15 caution about the extent to
which large gains in black fathers' work hours could be achieved:
many black children have disabled fathers, and the disability may
be severe enough to preclude large increases in work hours.

It should be recognized that there are also important
constraints to increasing mother's work hours, at least as a
means of achieving large economic gains for children, especially
black children. We have already seen that father's work hours
have a much stronger effect than mother's work hours. That there
is an important effect of mother's work hours, especially among
black children, suggests that increases in mother's work hours

---

[24]Parent's education was relatively more important for
children never in a mother-only household--those always in two-
parent families. For children in two-parent households this
measure reflects father's education only, whereas for children
ever in mother-only households it combines father's and mother's
education in proportion to the fraction of time each parent was
head of the child's household. To the extent that mother's and
father's education differ, the education predictor used in the
analysis will contain a larger measurement error component for
children ever in mother-only households than for children always
in two-parent households. This could be the source of the
difference in predictive power according to the living
arrangement of the child. Since some children never had their
father present in the household, though, father's education could
not be clearly measured for all children.

should be considered as a possible means of improving the economic well-being of children, especially black children. However, a closer look at circumstances brings to light several faults of such an approach. Black mothers averaged at least as long, if not longer, work hours as nonblack mothers. In addition, black mothers heading their own households faced stronger constraints: they were younger than other groups of mothers and they had more children than the nonblack mothers heading their own families. These types of constraints tend to preclude large increases in labor market work, especially when no father is present to share the responsibilities of providing both income and child care. Further, even though black children in two-parent households have mothers who work the longest hours of all, these children averaged long-term per capita income even lower than that of nonblack children in mother-only households.

SUMMARY

During the 1970s the trend in children's per capita income was only slightly upward, and a large proportion of children experienced severe economic difficulties at some time in the decade. Over one-quarter of the children were poor at least one of the ten years. However, poverty was usually a short-term rather than a long-term occurrence for children.

Increased divorce and separation plus growth in out-of-wedlock births resulted in an increasing number of children spending part of their childhood in one-parent families, and one-parent families were more likely than others to have low incomes. Increased labor force participation by mothers helped reduce the economic problems of children, but longer work hours of the mother were often not able to prevent large drops in the economic position of children.

Children in one-parent families, most of them with their mother, averaged ten-year per capita income much lower than that of children in two-parent families the entire ten years. Large reductions in children's per capita income often followed the divorce or separation of parents, and family income after a marital disruption did not usually approach its former level unless the mother subsequently remarried. Most ever-married mothers did eventually remarry, although black mothers were less likely to do so than others.

While level of per capita income is the most crucial determinant of economic well-being, stability in the flow of income over time is also important. And children in mother-only households experienced lower economic well-being on both counts, with greater instability in the flow of income over time adding to problems of a lower level of long-term income.

Some of these families relied on welfare income for help. Contrary to popular beliefs, episodes of welfare use were rather brief in most cases, and welfare income was often mixed with income from other sources, most notably work. Longer term dependence on welfare was the exception rather than the rule.

The large difference in economic well-being of black and nonblack children that existed prior to 1970 persisted into the 1970s decade. Black children were in a much worse economic position at the beginning, at the end, and throughout the decade. This is a consistent finding across all measures of economic well-being--long-term level, trend, and instability in per capita income, as well as poverty status. Average long-term per capita income for black children was half that of other children, and trend in per capita income was positive for nonblack children but zero for black children. Greater instability of income further compounded the poorer economic condition of black children. And, in terms of poverty status:

***   The majority--70 percent--of black children spent part of the decade in poverty, compared to 20 percent of nonblack children.

Most of the greater instability of income for black children was due to the mother-only household being a more common living arrangement for them than for other children.

***   One-half of the black children born in 1970 spent at least one of their first eight years of life in a mother-only household. This compares to one-fifth of nonblack children.

While this greater tendency for being in a mother-only household was largely responsible for black children experiencing more instability in the flow of income over time, it was not the major factor behind their lower level of long-term income. The long-term income of black children in two-parent families throughout the decade was even lower than the long-term income of nonblack children who spent most of the decade in mother-only families. Thus, increasing the proportion of black children growing up in two-parent families would not by itself eliminate very much of the racial gap in the economic well-being of children; changes in the economic circumstances of the parents are needed most to bring the economic status of black children up to the higher status of nonblack children.

The 1970s were a time of large increases in the labor force participation of mothers, both those with and those without husbands. During the decade, mother's labor market activity was an important component of the economic status of many children, both black and white. Mother's work hours were especially important in determining the level of income available to children when no father was present in the household. Among nonblack children, the 1970s were a time when those in mother-only households had mothers working longer hours than those in two-parent households. Still, the economic status of the children in mother-only households lagged a great deal behind that of children in two-parent households. In addition, in all ten years of the decade, children with mothers who worked the most were black children in two-parent families; yet these children averaged lower per capita income than nonblack children who were in mother-only households more often than two-parent ones. These findings are quite consistent with multivariate analysis showing that father's work hours were of greater importance to children's economic status than were mother's work hours. What seems to be a major factor here is that the wages of women were and continue to be only 60 percent of those of men.

Wage differentials may also be responsible for several of the other findings of the multivariate analysis of children's long-term level of per capita income. The lower wages of black men relative to nonblack men seem to account for the differential effects of education and number of years the father was absent from the child's household. The findings suggest that increases in the wages of black fathers would help reduce the large racial gap in the economic well-being of children. Increases in their work hours would also help, but might be prevented by poor health.

CONCLUSIONS

These findings indicate that there are several trends to consider in formulating policies to improve the economic position of children in the 1980s. During the 1970s, the circumstances of

unmarried mothers were of critical importance to the well-being
of children, and indications are that they will be during the
1980s as well. The work hours of these mothers, as well as those
of married mothers, increased substantially as the 1970s decade
progressed. Most children now have mothers who are balancing
childrearing and market work responsibilities, many with no
father present to assist in fulfilling these responsibilities.
The increase in mothers' work hours was accompanied by a sizeable
drop in the birth rate, which reduced the size of families with
children and increased the age of parents when they began having
children. At the same time these changes were taking place,
large racial and gender differences in wage levels continued to
hold.

Several implications of these trends stand out. For one, we
must look to changes other than mothers entering the labor force
or couples having fewer children as primary means of achieving
better economic circumstances for children. Most of the economic
gains to be made by such changes have already been realized: the
changes of the 1970s were large enough to preclude further
changes of the same magnitude in the near future. In addition,
we cannot expect to see increases in the earnings of fathers as
large as those during the 1970s because delays in childbirth have
resulted in fathers being older at the start of the 1980s decade,
and thus less susceptible to large increases in earnings.[25]

Other sources of economic improvements for children in low-
income families would include such things as increases in the
wages of mothers and black fathers, increases in economic support
by fathers of children from broken homes, earnings supplements to
low-income parents for work they do themselves taking care of
their children, as well as transfer payments to low-income
families with children. Future as well as past policy changes in
each of these areas should be evaluated with the effect on the
economic well-being of children in mind. Take recent changes in
the AFDC program as an example. Effective as of September 1981,
the AFDC earned income disregard drops to zero after four months
of work by the mother while participating in the AFDC program.
This means that each dollar of earned income causes the loss of a
dollar of benefits. This locks the family more tightly into a

---

[25] I am indebted to Frank Levy for these valuable insights.

low level of income while reducing the incentive for greater reliance on market work as a major income source. Is this what we want for children in need of income assistance? It is this type of question that should be asked when policies influencing the economic circumstances of adults with children are being evaluated.

References

Allison, Paul D. "Measures of Inequality." American Sociological Review 43 (December 1978):865-80.

Bane, Mary Jo. Here to Stay: American Families in the Twentieth Century. New York: Basic Books, 1976.

Bane, Mary Jo, and Weiss, Robert S. "Alone Together: The World of Single-Parent Families." American Demographics 2, no. 5 (May 1980):11-15,48.

Bianchi, Suzanne M., and Farley, Reynolds. "Racial Differences in Family Living Arrangements and Economic Well-Being: An Analysis of Recent Trends." Journal of Marriage and the Family 41, no. 3 (August 1979):537-51.

Bradbury, Katharine et al. "Public Assistance, Female Headship, and Economic Well-Being." Journal of Marriage and the Family 41, no. 3 (August 1979):519-35.

Bumpass, Larry L., and Rindfuss, Ronald R. "Children's Experience of Marital Disruption." American Journal of Sociology 85 (1979):49-62.

Burr, Wesley R. et al., ed. Contemporary Theories about the Family, Vol. 1. New York: The Free Press, 1979.

Coe, Richard D. "A Preliminary Empirical Examination of the Dynamics of Welfare Use." In Five Thousand American Families--Patterns of Economic Progress, Vol. IX, ed. Martha S. Hill, Daniel H. Hill, and James N. Morgan, pp. 121-68. Ann Arbor: Institute for Social Research, 1981.

Coe, Richard D. "Dependency and Poverty in the Short and Long Run." In Five Thousand American Families--Patterns of Economic Progress, Vol. VI, ed. Greg J. Duncan and James N. Morgan, pp. 273-96. Ann Arbor: Institute for Social Research, 1978a.

Coe, Richard D. "The Poverty Line: Its Functions and Limitations." Public Welfare (Winter 1978b):32-36.

Coe, Richard D. "Sensitivity of the Incidence of Poverty to Different Measures of Income." In Five Thousand American Families--Patterns of Economic Progress, Vol. IV, Greg J. Duncan and James N. Morgan, pp. 357-409. Ann Arbor: Institute for Social Research, 1976.

Corcoran, Mary. "Work Experience, Work Interruption, and Wages." In Five Thousand American Families--Patterns of Economic Progress, Vol. VI, ed. Greg J. Duncan and James N. Morgan, pp. 47-104. Ann Arbor; Institute for Social Research, 1978.

Corcoran, Mary, and Duncan, Greg J. "Work History, Labor Force Attachment, and Earnings Differences between the Races and Sexes." Journal of Human Resources 14, No. 2 (Winter 1979):3-20.

Cutright, Phillip. "Components of Change in the Number of Female Family Heads Aged 15-44: United States 1940-1970." Journal of Marriage and the Family 36 (1974):714-21.

Danziger, Sheldon et al. "The Measurement and Trend of Inequality: Comment." The American Economic Review 67, no. 3 (1977):505-12.

Duncan, Greg J. "An Overview of Family Economic Mobility." Economic Outlook USA 8, no. 2 (Spring 1981):42-43.

Duncan, Greg J., and Morgan, James N. "An Overview of Family Economic Mobility." Mimeo. Ann Arbor: Institute for Social Research, 1981a.

Duncan, Greg J. and Morgan, James N. "Introduction and Overview." In Five Thousand American Families--Patterns of Economic Progress, Vol. IV, ed. Greg J. Duncan and James N. Morgan, pp. 1-22. Ann Arbor: Institute for Social Research, 1976.

Duncan, Greg J., and Morgan, James N. "Persistence and Change in Economic Status and the Role of Changing Family Composition." In Five Thousand American Families--Patterns of Economic Progress, Vol. IX, ed. Martha S. Hill, Daniel H. Hill, and James N. Morgan, pp. 1-44. Ann Arbor: Institute for Social Research, 1981b.

Duncan, Greg J., and Morgan, James N. "The Incidence and Some Consequences of Major Life Events." In Five Thousand American Families--Patterns of Economic Progress, Vol. VIII, ed. Greg J. Duncan and James N. Morgan. pp. 183-240. Ann Arbor: Institute for Social Research, 1980.

Duncan, Greg J., and Morgan, James N. "Young Children and 'Other' Family Members." In Five Thousand American Families--Patterns of Economic Progress, Vol. IV, ed. Greg J. Duncan and James N. Morgan, pp. 155-82. Ann Arbor: Institute for Social Research, 1976.

Garfinkel, Irwin, and Haveman, Robert. "Capacity, Choice, and Inequality." Southern Economic Journal 45, no. 2 (October 1978):421-31.

Glick, Paul C. "Demographic Shifts: Changes in Family Structure." In Work, Family, and Community: Summary Proceedings of an Ad Hoc Meeting, ed. Cheryl D. Hayes, pp. 39-46. Washington, DC: National Academy of Sciences, 1980.

Grossman, Allyson Sherman. "Working Mothers and Their Children." Monthly Labor Review (May 1981):49-54.

Haveman, Robert H. "Tinbergen's Income Distribution: Analysis and Policies--A Review Article." Journal of Human Resources 12, no. 1 (Winter 1977):103-14.

Hayes, Cheryl D., ed. Work, Family, and Community: Summary
    Proceedings of an Ad Hoc Meeting. Washington, DC: National
    Academy of Sciences, 1980.

Hill, C. Russell, and Stafford, Frank P. "Parental Care of
    Children: Time Diary Estimates of Quantity Predictability
    and Variety." Working Paper Series. Ann Arbor: Institute
    for Social Research, 1978.

Hill, C. Russell, and Stafford, Frank P. "Time Inputs to
    Children." In Five Thousand American Families--Patterns of
    Economic Progress, Vol. II, ed. James N. Morgan, pp. 319-44.
    Ann Arbor: Institute for Social Research, 1974.

Hill, Daniel H. "Labor Force Participation of Married Women: A
    Dynamic Analysis." Ph.D. Dissertation, University of
    Michigan, 1977.

Hill, Martha S. "Trends in the Economic Situation of
    U.S. Families and Children: 1970-1980." In The High Costs of
    Living: Economic and Demographic Conditions of American
    Families, ed. Richard R. Nelson. Washington, DC: National
    Academy of Sciences, forthcoming 1983.

Hill, Martha S. "Some Dynamic Aspects of Poverty." In Five
    Thousand American Families--Patterns of Economic Progress,
    Vol. IX, ed. Martha S. Hill, Daniel H. Hill, and James
    N. Morgan, pp. 93-120. Ann Arbor: Institute for Social
    Research, 1981.

Hofferth, Sandra L., and Moore, Kristin A. "Early Childbearing
    and Later Economic Well-Being." American Sociological Review
    44, no. 5 (October 1979):784-815.

Hoffman, Lois, W. "Effects of Maternal Employment on
    Children." In Work, Family, and Community: Summary
    Proceedings of an Ad Hoc Meeting, ed. Cheryll D. Hayes,
    pp. 47-53. Washington, DC: National Academy of Sciences,
    1980.

Johnson, William R. "The Measurement and Trend of Inequality:
    Comment." The American Economic Review 67, no. 3 (June
    1977):502-504.

Kakwani, Nanak C. Income Inequality and Poverty. New York: Oxford
    University Press, 1980.

Kurien, C. John. "The Measurement and Trend of Inequality:
    Comment." The American Economic Review 67, no. 3 (June
    1977):517-19.

Lane, Jonathan P., and Morgan, James N. "Patterns of Change in
    Economic Status and Family Structure." In Five Thousand
    American Families--Patterns of Economic Progress, Vol. III,
    ed. Greg J. Duncan and James N. Morgan, pp. 3-60. Ann Arbor:
    Institute for Social Research, 1975.

Lazear, Edward P., and Michael, Robert T. "Family Size and the
    Distribution of Real Per Capita Income." The American
    Economic Review 70, no. 1 (March 1980):91-107.

Masnick, George, and Bane, Mary Jo. The Nation's Families: 1960-1990. Joint Center Outlook Reports. Cambridge, Mass.: The Joint Center for Urban Studies of MIT and Harvard University, 1980.

Minarik, Joseph J. "The Measurement and Trend of Inequality: Comment." The American Economic Review 67, no. 3 (June 1977):513-16.

Mirer, Thad. "Aspects of the Variability of Family Income." In Five Thousand American Families--Patterns of Economic Progress, Vol. II, ed. James N. Morgan, pp. 201-11. Ann Arbor: Institute for Social Research, 1974.

Moore, Kristin A., and Hofferth, Sandra L. "The Consequences of Age at First Childbirth: Female Headed Families and Welfare Recipiency." Working Paper No. 1146-05. Washington, DC: The Urban Institute, August 1978.

Moore, Kristin A.; Waite, Linda J.; Hofferth, Sandra L.; and Caldwell, Steven B. "The Consequences of Age at First Childbirth: Marriage, Separation, and Divorce." Working Paper No. 1146-03. Washington, DC: The Urban Institute, July 1978.

Morgan, James N. "Family Composition." In Five Thousand American Families--Patterns of Economic Progress, Vol. I, ed. James N. Morgan, pp. 99-122. Ann Arbor: Institute for Social Research, 1974.

Morley, Samuel A. "The Effect of Changes in the Population on Several Measures of Income Distribution." The American Economic Review 71, no. 3 (June 1981):285-94.

Mott, Frank. The Socioeconomic Status of Households Headed by Women. U.S. Department of Labor R&D Monograph 72. Washington, DC: U.S. Government Printing Office, 1979.

Nelson, Eric R. "The Measurement and Trend of Inequality: Comment." The American Economic Review 67, no. 3 (June 1977): 520.

Paglin, Morton. "The Measurement and Trend of Inequality: Reply." The American Economic Review 67, no. 3 (June 1977):520.

Reagan, Barbara B. "In Retrospect: Summary and Issues." In Issues in Federal Statistical Needs Relating to Women. US Census Bureau, Current Population Reports, Special Studies, Series P-23, no. 83, December 1979.

Ross, Heather L., and Sawhill, Isabel V. Time of Transition: The Growth of Families Headed by Women. Washington, D.C.: The Urban Institute, 1975.

Sawhill, Isabel V. et al. Income Transfers and Family Structure. An Urban Institute Paper. Washington, D.C.: The Urban Institute, 1975.

Sawhill, Isabel. "Discrimination and Poverty Among Women Who Head Families." Signs 1, no. 3, part 2 (Spring 1976): 201-11.

Smith, James P., and Ward, Michael P. "Asset Accumulation and Family Size." Demography, 17, no. 3 (1980):243-260.

Spanier, Graham B., and Glick, Paul C. "The Life Cycle of American Families: An Expanded Analysis." Journal of Family History (Spring 1980):97-111.

Strober, Myra H., and Weinberg, Charles B. "Strategies Used by Working and Non-Working Wives to Reduce Time Pressures." Journal of Consumer Research, 6 (March 1980).

Taussig, Michael K. "Trends in Inequality of Well-Offness in the United States Since World War II." Institute for Research on Poverty Special Report Series. Madison, Wis.: Institute for Research on Poverty, 1976.

Thornton, Arland. "Marital Dissolution, Remarriage, and Childbearing." Demography 15, no. 3 (August 1978):361-80.

U.S. Bureau of the Census, Current Population Reports, Series P-60, No. 127. Money Income and Poverty Status of Families and Persons in the United States: 1980 (Advance Report). Washington, D.C.: U.S. Government Printing Office, 1981a.

U.S. Bureau of the Census, Current Population Reports, Series P-20, No. 365. Marital Status and Living Arrangements: March 1980. Washington, D.C.: U.S. Government Printing Office, October 1981b.

U.S. Bureau of the Census, Current Population Reports, Series P-20, No. 366. Household and Family Characteristics: March 1980. Washington, D.C.: U.S. Government Printing Office, September 1981c.

U.S. Bureau of the Census, Current Population Reports, Series P-23, No. 107. Families Maintained by Female Householders 1970-79. Washington, D.C.: U.S. Government Printing Office, October 1980a.

U.S. Bureau of the Census, Current Population Reports, Series P-60, No. 125. Money Income and Poverty Status of Families and Persons in the United States: 1979 (Advance Report). Washington, D.C.: U.S. Government Printing Office, 1980b.

U.S. Bureau of the Census. Statistical Abstract of the United States: 1980. 101st ed. Washington, D.C.: U.S. Government Printing Office, 1980c.

Wattenberg, Esther, and Reinhardt, Hazel. "Female-Headed Families: Trends and Implications." Social Work (November 1979):460-67.

Watts, Harold W. and Skidmore, Felicity. "Household Structure: Necessary Changes in Categorization and Data Collection:

Postscript". In Issues in Federal Statistical Needs
Relating to Women. US Census Bureau, Current Population
Reports, Special Studies, Series P-23, no. 83, December
1979.

Chapter 10

SUMMARY OF OTHER RESEARCH

Abowd, John M., and Farber, Henry S. Job Queues and the Union Status of Workers.

Avery, Robert B.; Hansen, Lars Peter; and Hotz, V. Joseph. Multiperiod Probit Models and Orthogonality Condition Estimation.

Avioli, Paul Smith. The Employment Decision of Married Mothers of Infants.

Black, Matthew. An Empirical Test of the Theory of on-the-Job Search.

Cohn, Elchanan, and Capen, Margaret. The Distribution of Unemployment Insurance Benefits by Income and Earnings Classes.

Cohn, Elchanan, and Capen, Margaret. Labor Supply Effects of Unemployment Insurance Benefits.

Cohn, Elchanan, and Capen, Margaret. Adequacy of Unemployment Insurance Benefits.

Cohn, Elchanan, Kiker, B.F., and Tucker, Irvin B., III. Tenure, Earnings and Productivity: A Test of the Implicit Contract Hypothesis.

Cramer, James C. Fertility and Female Employment in Two Generations.

Faurot, David J., and Sellon, Gordon H. Jr. Analyzing Labor Supply without Considering Income from Assets.

Feinberg, Robert M. Labour Force Participation and the Job Search Theory: Tests of Some Neglected Implications.

Feinberg, Robert M. Earnings-Risk as a Compensating Differential.

Feinberg, Robert M. Employment Instability, Earnings and Market Structure.

Feinberg, Robert M. On the Empirical Importance of the Job Search Theory.

Feinberg, Robert M. Risk Aversion, Risk, and the Duration of Unemployment.

377

Goodman, John L. Jr. Linking Local Mobility Rates to Migration Rates: Repeat Movers and Place Effects.

Harris, Richard J., and Hedderson, John J. Effects of Wife's Income on Family Income Inequality.

Hausman, Jerry A. Labor Supply.

Hausman, Jerry A., and Taylor, William E. Panel Data and Unobservable Individual Effects.

Haveman, Robert H., and Wolfe, Barbara L. Have Disability Transfers Caused the Decline in Older Male Labor Force Participation? A Work-Status Rational Choice Model.

Hutchens, Robert M. Entry and Exit Transitions in a Government Transfer Program: The Case of Aid to Families with Dependent Children.

Jud, G. Donald, and Walker, James L. Racial Differences in the Returns to Schooling and Experience among Prime-Age Males: 1967-1975.

Kiker, B.F. Parental Time Devoted to Children in Two Wage-Earner and One Wage Earner Families.

Kiker, B.F. An Empirical Investigation of the Household Division of Labor.

Kim, Joochul. Characteristics of Migrants within the Framework of Current Migration Direction in the United States: Some Evidence from Micro-Data Analysis.

Kim, Joochul. A Comparative Analysis of Factors Affecting the Current Population Shift among Elderly Migrants.

Kinsey, Jean. The Effect of Wife's Labor Force Participation and Other Sources of Household Income on the Marginal Propensity to Consume Food Away from Home.

Klevmarken, N. Anders. On the Stability of Age-Earnings Profiles.

Knaub, Norman L. The Impact of Food Stamps and Cash Welfare on Food Expenditures, 1971-1975.

Lane, Sylvia, and Kinsey, Jean. Housing Tenure Status and Housing Satisfaction.

Larson, Donald A. Labor Supply Adjustment over the Business Cycle.

Leuthold, Jane H. Taxation and the Consumption of Household Time.

Leuthold, Jane H. Taxation and the Value of Nonmarket Time.

Lillard, Lee A. Wage Expectations in Labor Supply and the Time-Series and Cross-Section Effects of State Unemployment.

McLanahan, Sara. Family Structure and Stress: A Longitudinal Comparison of Male- and Female-Headed Families.

McLanahan, Sara, and Sorensen, Aage. The Incidence and Effect of Life Events over the Life Course.

McLanahan, Sara, and Sorensen, Aage. Life Events and Psychological Distress: A Longitudinal Comparison of Male- and Female-Headed Families.

Mincer, Jacob. Union Effects: Wages, Turnover, and Job Training.

Moen, Phyllis. Developing Family Indicators.

Moen, Phyllis, and Moorehouse, Martha. Overtime over the Life Cycle.

Newman, Sandra; Struyk, Raymond; and Manson, Donald. Poverty, Housing Deprivation, and Housing Assistance.

Nitz, Lawrence H. Intergenerational Mobility and Activity in the Informal Economy.

Null, David George. A Path Model for Black and White Educational Achievement.

Rein, Mildred. Dilemmas of Welfare Policy: Why Work Strategies Haven't Worked.

Rosen, Harvey S. Taxation and on-the-Job Training Decisions.

Shack-Marquez, Janice, and Berg, Ivar. Inside Information and the Employer-Employee Matching Process.

Shorrocks, Anthony F. Income Stability in the United States.

Shorrocks, Anthony F. The Impact of Income Components on the Distribution of Family Incomes.

Smith, Michael J. The Social Consequences of Single Parenthood: A Longitudinal Perspective.

Smith, Michael J. The Economic and Social Consequences of Single-Parenthood: A Longitudinal Perspective.

Smith, Michael J. Economic Conditions in Single-Parent Families: A Longitudinal Perspective.

Sobel, Richard. White Collar Structure and Class: Educated Labor Reevaluated.

Wertheimer, Richard. A Dynamic Model of the Expectations and Fertility of Childless Women.

Williams, Donald R. Racial Differences in the Propensity to Return to School.

Williams, Donald R. Schooling, Market Segmentation, and the Degree of Relative Earnings Mobility.

Yoon, Bong Joon. A Model of Unemployment Duration with Variable Search Intensity.

JOB QUEUES AND THE UNION STATUS OF WORKERS
John M. Abowd, University of Chicago
Henry S. Farber, Massachusetts Institute of Technology
(Forthcoming in Industrial and Labor Relations Review.)

A model of the determination of the union status of workers that allows for the possibility of queuing for union jobs is developed. The empirical results derived from the Panel Study of Income Dynamics are supportive of the queuing hypothesis. The no-queue model can be rejected using a likelihood ratio test. This suggests that a simple probit or logit model for union status is misspecified because it is not based on any consistent behavioral theory.

MULTIPERIOD PROBIT MODELS AND ORTHOGONALITY CONDITION ESTIMATION
Robert B. Avery, Carnegie-Mellon University
Lars Peter Hansen, Carnegie-Mellon University
V. Joseph Hotz, Carnegie-Mellon University
and the University of Chicago
Carnegie-Mellon University Graduate School of
Industrial Administration, Working Paper #62-80-81

This paper considers probit models applicable to panel data for which the underlying disturbances are not independent across time. To estimate such models the authors propose a class of Orthogonality Condition (OC) estimators for the coefficients of such models. Such estimators are consistent and asymptotically normal with covariance matrices that can be consistently estimated. While they are not as asymptotically efficient as a Maximum Likelihood estimator, unlike Maximum Likelihood they are computationally tractable regardless of the covariance structure of the disturbances. In fact, OC estimators do not require that the error covariance structure be specified a priori. To illustrate the tractability of our proposed estimators, they estimate a women's labor force participation model using up to nine years of data on a sample of 500 women from the Panel Study of Income Dynamics. The results compare Maximum Likelihood estimators with the OC estimators as well as the efficiency of alternative OC estimators.

THE EMPLOYMENT DECISION OF MARRIED MOTHERS OF INFANTS
Paula Smith Avioli (Ph.D. dissertation, Rutgers University, 1982)

This study investigates why some married mothers of infants elect to be employed, while other married women remain out of the labor force during the first three years of their child's life. The labor force participation rate of married mothers of infants is now at an unprecedented high and it is expected to continue to rise in the future. This investigation seeks to determine why these women are choosing to be employed in hopes to better understand the problems and benefits associated with maternal employment.

The theoretical approach taken here is that of the life-course perspective, focusing on the interdependence and coordination of the multiple careers of family members and how transitions in the parental and worklife career lines affect both the woman and her family. Data for this research comes from the Panel Study of Income Dynamics. Discriminant function analysis was performed to contrast four groups of women; white employed wives, black employed wives, white full-time housewives, and black full-time housewives.

The patterns of the four groups generated by the discriminant function analysis indicate that each group of women is unique in terms of the constraints and facilitators associated with the group's employment status. Prior work experience and perceived job-family conflict were found to be the most important factors discriminating employed wives from full-time housewives. The study also revealed a number of racial differences in both the importance and the effect of certain determinants of married women's labor force participation. Several factors traditionally found to be related to maternal employment do not appear to be significant predictors of labor force participation for the population of married mothers of infants.

AN EMPIRICAL TEST OF THE THEORY OF ON-THE-JOB SEARCH
Matthew Black
Mathematica Policy Research, Inc.
(Published in The Journal of Human Resources 16, no. 1.)

There are a number of search models in the literature. Yet, surprisingly, the search activity of the employed segment of the labor force has been largely neglected. The purpose of this paper is to examine the factors that prompt employed workers to engage in search activity and to use a logit model to test several hypotheses concerning the probability of on-the-job search (OJS); the data base is a national sample of black and white male workers from the Michigan Panel Study of Income Dynamics. The analysis serves to complement previous studies of quit activity and of unemployed search behavior by providing a test of how appropriate search models are for predicting the likelihood of OJS. The empirical results suggest that OJS is significantly influenced by potential wage gains to be found in the marketplace. A worker's search ability, the costs of switching firms, and several nonwage attributes of the job also play an influential role in motivating OJS.

THE DISTRIBUTION OF UNEMPLOYMENT INSURANCE
BENEFITS BY INCOME AND EARNINGS CLASSES
Elchanan Cohn, University of South Carolina
Margaret Capen, Eastern Carolina University
(Published in Working Papers in Economics DOR-82-13
(Division of Research, College of Business
Administration, USC, Columbia, SC 29208.)

LABOR SUPPLY EFFECTS OF UNEMPLOYMENT INSURANCE BENEFITS
Elchanan Cohn, University of South Carolina
Margaret Capen, Eastern Carolina University
(Published in Working Papers in Economics, DOR-
B-82-09 (Division of Research, College of Business
Administration, USC, Columbia, SC 29208.)

ADEQUACY OF UNEMPLOYMENT INSURANCE BENEFITS
Elchanan Cohn, University of South Carolina
Margaret Capen, Eastern Carolina University
(Work in progress.)

    This study uses 1976 PSID data to analyze the adequacy of UI benefits in terms of nondeferrable and recurrent expenditures. In addition to examining the average adequacy for UI recipients, the study also examines the distribution of recipients by the percentage of net wages covered by UI benefits.

TENURE, EARNINGS AND PRODUCTIVITY: A TEST
OF THE IMPLICIT CONTRACT HYPOTHESIS
Elchanan Cohn, University of South Carolina
B.F. Kiker, University of South Carolina
Irvin B. Tucker III, University of North Carolina-Charlotte
(Work in progress.)

    This study uses 1977 PSID data on self-employed workers to derive a VMP schedule for employees by using a simulation procedure. A comparison of predicted VMP and earnings over a worker's tenure in a firm is used to test Lazear's implicit contract theorem.

FERTILITY AND FEMALE EMPLOYMENT IN TWO GENERATIONS
James C. Cramer, University of California at Davis
(Paper presented at the annual meeting of the Population Association of America, Washington, DC, March 28, 1981.)

This study is based on a sample of the children or stepchildren who left home between 1968 and 1975; they are referred to as "splitoffs." Interviews from the splitoff's original household provide data on parental characteristics. The original household is the first generation, while the new household is the second generation. Mother and father are used as gender-specific terms in the first generation (regardless of blood relationship to the splitoff, in most cases), while husband, wife, male splitoff, and female splitoff all are necessary as gender-specific references in the second generation. In both generations, heads of households usually were respondents, and wives and mothers also were interviewed in 1976. Both male and female splitoffs are included in the sample, so the majority of splitoffs are heads of the new households but some are wives. The 1976 interviews of heads and spouses differed somewhat, so certain data are not available for all female splitoffs or all mothers. Results are generally consistent with the notion of a behavioral tradeoff or choice between marriage/fertility and education/female employment.

ANALYZING LABOR SUPPLY WITHOUT CONSIDERING INCOME FROM ASSETS
David J. Faurot, University of Kansas, Lawrence
Gordon H. Selon Jr.
(Published in Review of Economics and Statistics 63 (August 1981): 458-62.)

Develops a family labor supply model which incorporates asset accumulation into the decision problem and which yields labor supply functions which do not depend on asset income. The form of the model allows us to estimate substitution and income effects in circumstances where there is insufficient variation in exogenous nonwage income which excludes asset income. Empirical results using data from the Michigan Panel Study of Income Dynamics are consistent with the model only for samples of younger families with children. For these families the estimates substitution effects are quite small, suggesting a relatively low sensitivity of the husband and wife to income compensated changes in the wage rate.

LABOUR FORCE PARTICIPATION AND THE JOB
SEARCH THEORY: TESTS OF SOME NEGLECTED
IMPLICATIONS
Robert M. Feinberg, Pennsylvania State University
(Published in Journal of Economic Studies 5 (May 1978): 50-63.)

Two equations on participation are estimated by the use of data from the Panel Study of Income Dynamics. Male heads of households not retired on grounds of disability and residing in large (over 250,000 population) Standard Metropolitan Statistical Areas (SMSAs) comprise the sample used in the study. Three years of the survey data are used, 1969, 1970, and 1971 (each pertaining to labor force activity in the previous year) and sample sizes are 1,526, 1,674, and 1,736, respectively. As the job search theory does not yield the faintest hint of a specification to use in estimating equations, the following procedure has been employed: the 1970 data has been ransacked to find the "best" specification (lowest standard error) for each equation; the admittedly awkward looking specifications obtained in this manner have then been reestimated using the 1969 and 1971 data (separately), and the estimated effects for the three years have been compared for consistency.

EARNINGS-RISK AS A COMPENSATING DIFFERENTIAL
Robert M. Feinberg, Pennsylvania State University
(Published in Southern Economic Journal 48 (July 1981): 156-63.)

This paper examines whether or not the labor market compensates workers for increased earnings-risk, measured by intertemporal variation in earnings. To the extent such a compensating differential exists, a further aim of the study has been to see if the quality of this risk-compensation varies across demographic and occupational groups. Using six years of Panel Study data on 1,419 household heads, regression analysis explained earnings as a function of worker characteristics and earnings instability. The results support the view that a significant part of average hourly earnings reflects compensation for earnings-risk. In addition, the magnitude of the risk premium is significantly lower for women, laborers, and industry-changers--who could be classified as part of the secondary labor force--than for others. This finding is consistent with some statements of segmented labor market theory; it suggests that further empirical work may usefully examine implications of that theory by focusing on how other compensating differentials vary across classes of jobs and workers.

EMPLOYMENT INSTABILITY, EARNINGS AND MARKET STRUCTURE
Robert M. Feinberg, Pennsylvania State University
(Published in Applied Economics 13 (1981): 257-65.)

Recent theorists have suggested that workers accept "implicit contracts" providing for a trade-off between wages (and other benefits) and stability in employment. This paper examines empirically the question, What is the effect of employment instability and earnings instability on a worker's average level of earnings? These issues are examined using six years of data (1971-1976) on individual workers from the Panel Study. Of the four instability measures, only one is significantly different from zero, although the coefficients of two others show the positive sign expected for a "risk premium." The failure of these measures of employment risk to influence hourly earnings may reflect some voluntary aspects of job changing and variability in hours which would not require a risk premium to compensate; in addition, PROB may reflect macroeconomic conditions cutting across industries and not imply wage differentials.

ON THE EMPIRICAL IMPORTANCE OF THE JOB SEARCH THEORY
Robert M. Feinberg, Pennsylvania State University
(Published in Southern Economic Journal
45 (October 1978): 508-21.)

The model developed by McCall is representative of the job search literature and is used to derive most of the hypotheses to be tested here.

Data from the Panel Study of Income Dynamics are used to test the hypotheses, and thus indirectly to test the underlying job search model on which they are based. A large number of implications of the theory are tested, this paper being more concerned with the general predictive power of the theory than with the acceptance or rejection of any one particular implication.

RISK AVERSION, RISK, AND THE DURATION OF UNEMPLOYMENT
Robert M. Feinberg, Pennsylvania State University
(Published in The Review of Economics and
Statistics 59 (August 1977): 264-71.)

This article presents estimates of a reduced-form equation derived from the job search theory and tests the following two hypotheses: (1) as the standard deviation of the distribution of potential wage offers increases, an individual's expected duration of unemployment will increase, ceteris paribus; (2) an individual who is more risk averse than another will have a shorter expected duration of unemployment, ceteris paribus. The empirical results presented tend to support both of these hypotheses.

LINKING LOCAL MOBILITY RATES TO MIGRATION
RATES: REPEAT MOVERS AND PLACE EFFECTS
John L. Goodman, Jr., The Urban Institute
(Forthcoming in Migration, Mobility, and the
Search for Housing, edited by W.A.V. Clark. Croom Helm, 1982.)

Metropolitan areas with high rates of in-migration also tend to have high rates of local residential mobility. This paper specifies a model in which in-migration causes local residential mobility. It estimates the model with data from a longitudinal survey of households.

Chronic movers are found to account for part of the correlation between in-migration rates and local mobility rates. In-migrants to a metropolitan area often soon move a second time, within the area. Some of these subsequent local moves are attributable to the temporary housing many in-migrants initially obtain.

Place effects also contribute to the correlation between in-migration rates and local mobility rates. That is, even after controlling for their own mobility history, families and individuals are more likely to move locally if they live in high-growth counties.

EFFECTS OF WIFE'S INCOME ON FAMILY INCOME INEQUALITY
Richard J. Harris, University of Texas at San Antonio
John J. Hedderson, University of Texas at El Paso

(This article was summarized in Volume IX and was published in
Sociological Methods & Research 10 (November 1981): 211-32.)

LABOR SUPPLY
Jerry A. Hausman, Massachusetts Institute of Tehnology and
National Bureau of Economic Research, Cambridge, MA.
(Published in How Taxes Affect Economic Behavior, edited by
H. Aaron and J. Pechman. Brookings, 1981.)

This paper presents estimates of changes in labor supply and
deadweight loss for three groups: husbands, wives, and female
heads of household. The estimates come from an econometric model
of labor supply that takes account of federal and state income
taxes as well as the payroll tax.

In brief these results show that the current tax system does
significantly reduce labor supply. Husbands work about 8 percent
less than they would in the absence of taxes. The reduction in
work by wives and female household heads is even greater because
they generally face higher tax rates than husbands do. The
results confirm the repeated finding of other studies that the
tax-induced change in the net wage does not greatly affect the
hours worked by husbands, but unlike previous studies, an
important income effect is found. As a result, deadweight loss
is a substantial proportion of tax revenues raised. (See also
Jerry Hausman, "Income and Payroll Tax Policy and Labor Supply,"
in The Supply-Side Effects of Economic Policy, edited by
Laurence Meyer, Federal Reserve Bank of St. Louis, 1981.)

PANEL DATA AND UNOBSERVABLE INDIVIDUAL EFFECTS
Jerry A. Hausman, Massachusetts Institute of Technology
William E. Taylor, Bell Laboratories

(This article was summarized in Volume IX and was
published in Econometrica 49, no. 6.)

HAVE DISABILITY TRANSFERS CAUSED THE DECLINE
IN OLDER MALE LABOR FORCE PARTICIPATION?
A WORK-STATUS RATIONAL CHOICE MODEL
Robert H. Haveman, University of Wisconsin-Madison
Barbara L. Wolfe, University of Wisconsin-Madison
(Discussion paper #674-81, Institute for Research
on Poverty, University of Wisconsin.)

The phenomenon of decreasing labor force participation of
older male workers and increasing disability transfer rolls is

explored in a reduced form probabilistic choice model. Workers are viewed as choosing among work statuses on the basis of the economic returns available in each status. The results of the model indicate that the generosity and leniency of disability transfer benefits is a statistically significant determinant of this discrete choice, but that the magnitude of this incentive is small. This result, which conflicts with those of prior studies, was tested with several variants of the probabilistic choice model and was found to be robust.

ENTRY AND EXIT TRANSITIONS IN A GOVERNMENT
TRANSFER PROGRAM: THE CASE OF AID TO
FAMILIES WITH DEPENDENT CHILDREN
Robert M. Hutchens, University of Wisconsin
(Published in The Journal of Human
Resources 16 (1981): 217-37.)

This study analyzes determinants of entry and exit transitions in the Aid to Families with Dependent Children (AFDC) program using data from the Panel Study of Income Dynamics. The principal findings are that state-controlled policy parameters such as the AFDC "guarantee" (the payment received when earnings are zero) and the "entry income limit" (the income level at which families become eligible for AFDC payments) have a significant but asymmetric impact on these transitions. In addition, evidence on the relationship between wages and such transitions tends to support efforts at reducing welfare dependency through programs which raise wages.

RACIAL DIFFERENCES IN THE RETURNS TO SCHOOLING
AND EXPERIENCE AMONG PRIME-AGE MALES: 1967-1975
G. Donald Jud, University of North Carolina-Greensboro
James L. Walker, University of Nevada-Reno
(Published in Journal of Human Resources
17 (Fall 1982): 622-33.)

Results obtained by estimating a model pooled by race and time indicate that there has been a major decline in the extent of racial discrimination. Given that the sample period examined was characterized by a substantial increase in unemployment, this study provides strong evidence in support of the hypothesis that labor market discrimination declined in the 1970s. While black educational quality improvements are probably responsible for some of the gains registered by blacks, affirmative action programs also have had an important effect. The study indicates that black economic gains have resulted primarily from increased returns to blacks working in southern and urban labor markets where anti-discrimination programs have been most evident.

Black labor market disadvantage stemming from unequal returns to schooling seems to have largely disappeared. During the 1967-1975 period, no evidence of any deterioration in black returns to schooling is found, as might have been expected in a time of slowing economic activity.

Prime-age black males do appear to gain significantly less from both general and specific labor market experience than do whites, and black returns to firm-specific experience appear to have fallen since 1967.

PARENTAL TIME DEVOTED TO CHILDREN IN TWO
WAGE-EARNER AND ONE WAGE EARNER FAMILIES
B.F. Kiker, University of South Carolina
Janet C. Hunt, University of Georgia
(Unpublished paper.)

The principal question addressed in this paper is whether children from one wage-earner households receive more parental time than those from two wage-earner households. If so, and if time spent with preschool children influences cognitive achievement, it can be argued that equal educational programs across different school districts does not necessarily result in equal educational opportunity. Although indirect, our evidence suggests that working and nonworking mothers spend virtually the same amount of time with preschool children. One wage-earner household spends slightly more time with an additional child between the ages of 6 and 12 while devoting less time to teenage sons. The increase in parental time that nonworking mothers devote to a teenage daughter is twice the number of hours the working mother devotes to her daughter.

AN EMPIRICAL INVESTIGATION OF THE
HOUSEHOLD DIVISION OF LABOR
B.F. Kiker, University of South Carolina
Janet C. Hunt, University of Georgia
(Work in progress.)

Using Becker's well-known time allocation model and applying a seemingly unrelated regression technique to PSID data, this study analyzes the effect of wage rates, nonearned income, and college-degree attainment in determining the division of family labor among market work, household production, and leisure time.

CHARACTERISTICS OF MIGRANTS WITH THE FRAMEWORK OF
CURRENT MIGRATION DIRECTION IN THE UNITED STATES:
SOME EVIDENCE FROM MICRO-DATA ANALYSIS
Joochul Kim, Arizona State University
(Published in Policy Sciences 12 (1980): 355-70.)

A COMPARATIVE ANALYSIS OF FACTORS AFFECTING
THE CURRENT POPULATION SHIFT AMONG ELDERLY MIGRANTS
Joochul Kim, Arizona State University
(Forthcoming in Research on Aging.)

THE EFFECT OF WIFE'S LABOR FORCE PARTICIPATION
AND OTHER SOURCES OF HOUSEHOLD INCOME ON THE
MARGINAL PROPENSITY TO CONSUME FOOD
AWAY FROM HOME
Jean Kinsey, University of Minnesota

Using data from 1977 and 1978 PSID, the marginal propensity
to consume food away from home out of different sources of
household income was estimated using Tobit analysis. The
estimating model was patterned after that used by Hymans and
Shapiro in Volume II of Five Thousand American Families.
Differences in the marginal propensity to consume between whites
and nonwhites and from income earned by wives who work full time
and part time were examined through the use of dummy variables
and sample stratification. Total household income was divided
into income earned by the husband, part-time and full-time
working wives, children, transfer income, and income from assets.
All variables were adjusted for the number of standard persons
per household.

Results showed that all sources of income except that earned
by wives who worked full time increased the marginal propensity
to consume food away from home over the marginal propensity to
consume out of husband's income. Contrary to the predictions of
household economic theory, income earned by wives who worked full
time decreased the marginal propensity to consume food away from
home. Whites were found to spend more on food away from home and
to have a higher marginal propensity to consume out of all
sources of income than nonwhites. One implication of this
research is that expenditures on food consumed away from home may
not increase with increased household incomes when the higher
incomes are a result of two full-time earners.

ON THE STABILITY OF AGE-EARNINGS PROFILES
N. Anders Klevmarken, University of Gothenburg
(Published in Scandanavian Journal of
Economics 84 no. 4 (1982): 531-54.

Age-earnings profiles are compared across three countries:
Japan, Sweden, and the United States. In doing this dynamic
changes in period, age, and cohort characteristics are discussed
as well as permanent differences across countries. Observed
differences in profiles are partly explained by intertemporal
country differences in the labor market situation and partly by
institutional differences.

THE IMPACT OF FOOD STAMPS AND CASH WELFARE
ON FOOD EXPENDITURES, 1971-1975
Norman L. Knaub
(Published in Policy Analysis 7, no. 2, (Spring 1981).)

This paper compares the food expenditure behavior of food
stamp recipients with the behavior of food stamp nonrecipients
and analyzes the impact of bonus food stamps on food stamp
recipients. The results indicate that, during the period
studied, the food stamp program successfully restrained
recipients and stimulated greater food purchases than did cash
welfare. As the restrictions of the food stamp program have been
reduced since 1971, however, larger portions of bonus food stamps
have been diverted to nonfood purchases.

HOUSING TENURE STATUS AND HOUSING SATISFACTION
Sylvia Lane, University of California at Davis
Jean Kinsey, University of Minnesota at St. Paul
(Published in The Journal of Consumer
Affairs 14 (Winter 1980): 341-65.)

Increased knowledge concerning the determinants of perceived
consumer satisfaction with housing would permit a more sensitive
response to demand in private markets and in the design of
government programs to improve the supply of housing. In this
study the probability of reporting satisfaction with housing was
examined for those who live in single-family homes, duplexes,
apartments, and mobile homes and for renters and owners.
Findings include: (1) housing characteristics were more
important determinants of housing satisfaction than the
demographic characteristics of housing occupants, (2) mobile-home
dwellers were the least likely to be satisfied with their homes,

and (3) apartment and duplex dwellers had similar preferences for housing characteristics.

LABOR SUPPLY ADJUSTMENT OVER THE BUSINESS CYCLE
Donald A. Larson, College of the Holy Cross
(Published in Industrial and Labor Relations
Review 34 (July 1981): 591-95.)

This study extends one by Kalachek, Raines, and Larson (in the April 1979 Review) of the speed with which labor supply adjusts to changes in demand. The present study uses data from the Panel Study of Income Dynamics that permit a more precise appraisal of whether the speed of supply response varies over the business cycle. Analysis of data for the period 1972-1976, during which a severe recession occurred, shows, as predicted, that as unemployment increases workers are less able to adjust their hours of work in response to changes in their health, wages, and other factors that determine desired work levels. The author also finds, however, that the more rapid response of supply in the recovery phase makes peak-to-peak adjustment relatively complete.

TAXATION AND THE CONSUMPTION OF HOUSEHOLD TIME
Jane H. Leuthold, University of Illinois at Champaign
(Published in Journal of Consumer
Research 7 (March 1981): 388-94.)

The impact of taxation on the allocation of time within households to market work, home production, and child care is empirically examined using a subsample of two-earner families drawn from the 1976 wave of the PSID. Taxes are found to have little effect on the two-earner family's allocation of time, compared with other factors, such as the number and ages of children in the family.

TAXATION AND THE VALUE OF NONMARKET TIME
Jane H. Leuthold, University of Illinois at Champaign
(Published in Social Science Research 10 (1981): 267-81.)

In this study, the value of nonmarket time is estimated for American families using an opportunity cost approach whereby the market wage is taken as a measure of the value of time and used to impute nonmarket income to each household. In cases where the market wage is not observed, a two-stage estimation technique is used to obtain consistent estimates of the wage. Data are drawn from the 1976 wave of the PSID. It is shown that the nonmarket income of families increases with family income and family size, but decreases with age and the number of job holders in the family. The study estimates that for the American family in 1975 home production income was approximately $8400 or 52 percent of family disposable income. By these estimates, home production income represents an important source of untaxed income.

WAGE EXPECTATIONS IN LABOR SUPPLY AND THE TIME-SERIES AND CROSS-SECTION EFFECTS OF STATE UNEMPLOYMENT
Lee A. Lillard, Rand Corporation
(Rand Report #R-2844-DOL.)

This paper is concerned with the estimation of a labor supply model incorporating worker expectation about future life-cycle wage development and autoregressive wage variation and the assessment cross-section versus local time-series effects of local labor market conditions as reflected in the state unemployment rate.

It begins with a model of wage determination and labor supply. The model emphasizes differences among workers and the analysis of a cross-section of individual time-series. The equations of wage determination are based on microeconomic models of human capital investment and incorporate individual worker differences in life-cycle wage paths and autoregressive wage movement over time in deviation from the life-cycle path. Workers are assumed to use knowledge of their life-cycle wage path and the degree of autocorrelation in transitory wages in the determination of current labor supply. The labor supply function is based on intertemporal goods-leisure substitution based on current expectations about future wages. Parameters of the wage and labor supply model are estimated using 11 years of data from the Panel Study of Income Dynamics.

The remainder of the paper is concerned with a characterization of local labor market cycles and with the effects, potential and actual, on workers' wages and hours of work. Local labor markets are characterized by the state unemployment rate.

These local labor market components imply a variety of potential effects on workers' wages and on hours of work. Out of all the possibilities, only two emerge empirically. States with relatively high unemployment rates in low unemployment years, and correspondingly greater cyclic variability on average, pay significantly higher wages. This is a purely cross-sectional result. Conversely, the effects of state unemployment rates on hours of work are purely local time-series in nature. Hours of work vary inversely with the current unemployment rate in the state, even controlling for the direct unemployment experience of the worker through his weeks unemployed. In fact, hours of work are similarly reduced in periods of high unemployment, even for workers who report no unemployment during the eight-year period 1970-1977 used for the analysis. Therefore, the effects of high unemployment are more broadly based than the experience of unemployment by some workers. The basic results remain valid, but magnitudes differ substantially across subgroups of workers.

Taken together, these results imply that workers in local areas are subject to employment variation over local business cycles both through reduced hours of work and through direct unemployment, but that workers in areas with higher long-term unemployment rates are partially compensated by higher wages.

FAMILY STRUCTURE AND STRESS: A LONGITUDINAL
COMPARISON OF MALE- AND FEMALE-HEADED FAMILIES
Sara McLanahan, University of Wisconsin-Madison
(Institute for Research on Poverty Discussion Paper #651-81.)

This paper examines the relationships among life events, psychological well-being, and poverty. The analyses focus on male and female household heads and address the following questions: (1) Do life events have a negative effect on economic status? (2) Does poverty increase the risk of exposure to life events? and (3) Are psychological responses to life events moderated by poverty status?

THE INCIDENCE AND EFFECT OF LIFE EVENTS OVER THE LIFE COURSE
Sara McLanahan, University of Wisconsin-Madison
Aage Sorensen, University of Wisconsin-Madison

In this analysis the authors compare the effects of events on male and female household heads by age groups and by parental status. The focus of the study is to determine if events cluster at particular stages of the life course, if event effects are related to life course stage, and finally, if parental status is an important moderator of event effects.

LIFE EVENTS AND PSYCHOLOGICAL DISTRESS: A LONGITUDINAL
COMPARISON OF MALE- AND FEMALE-HEADED FAMILIES
Sara McLanahan, University of Wisconsin-Madison
Aage Sorensen, University of Wisconsin-Madison

This paper is a study of the effects of life events on
one- and two-parent families. Its primary purpose is to address
some of the conceptual and methodological debates in the life
events/psychological distress literature; namely, (1) Do events
cause changes in levels of distress? (2) Are certain kinds of
events more stressful than others (e.g., change per se versus
"undesirable" change)? and (3) Are event effects related to sex
of head?

UNION EFFECTS: WAGES, TURNOVER, AND JOB TRAINING
Jacob Mincer, Columbia University

This study explores the existence of a net union premium and
of the extent of rationing by quality of the resulting excess
supply. The net union premium was estimated by relating changes
in wages to changes in union status of the same worker in
longitudinal panels (NLS and PSID), and by two cross-section wage
level regressions, a "prospective" and "retrospective" which
permit more direct observation of selectivity in hiring. Over a
half of the cross-section differential of over 20 percent for the
"same" (standardized) worker is a net union rent and much of the
rest reflects a quality adjustment in hiring, as measured by
wages. This conclusion was less reliable for older workers.

Subsequent analysis explores the effects of successful union
wage pressure on: quit rates, fringe benefits, wage profiles,
and training.

The reduction in quit of union joiners depends on the size
of the net wage premium. Quit rate differentials are also
positively related to the gross, cross-section wage differentials
within groups of workers, classified by location, and occupation,
less so by industry.

In Section 4, it is hypothesized that the imposition of
larger fixed labor costs (such as fringes) helps to deter
employers from preferring reductions in hours to reductions in
men, and it helps to stabilize employment in the fact of
fluctuating demand, by a more frequent use of overtime and of
temporary layoffs in the union sector. This hypothesis links the

size of fringe benefits to the union wage gain. An analysis of firms in 70 industries confirms this link.

Union pressure is exerted on the whole tenure profile of wages. The explicit linking of wage levels to seniority reduces incentives for worker investment in general (transferable) training. The total volume of training is indeed reported to be smaller in union jobs, and this is consistent with the flatter profile.

DEVELOPING FAMILY INDICATORS
Phyllis Moen
Cornell University
(Published in Journal of Family Issues
1, no. 1 (March 1980): 5-30.)

This article considers issues involved in the development of measures to be used as yardsticks of family well-being. The utility of such indicators and characteristics of families which will affect their construction are discussed. Suggestions for the development of family measures of well-being include the use of multiple measures, a causal way of thinking, and conceptualization that will link indicators to particular theoretical constructs. Data from the Panel Study of Income Dynamics are used in a case example in the construction of measures of the financial situation of families.

OVERTIME OVER THE LIFE CYCLE
Phyllis Moen, Cornell University
Martha Moorehouse, Cornell University
(In Research in the Interweave of Social Roles, Vol. 3, edited by H. Z. Lopata and J. Pleck. Greenwich, CT: JAI Press, forthcoming.)

This analysis has revealed that the combination of factors influencing the likelihood of family men working overtime are the direct effects of: (1) the opportunity factor reflected in the county unemployment rate; (2) motivational factors of husbands commitment to work and education; and the interaction effects of (3) life-cycle stage with husband's wage rate; (4) life-cycle stage with husband's occupation; and (5) life-cycle stage with wife's employment. More specifically, several tests of the life-cycle squeeze hypothesis were made: According to the hypothesis, men experiencing a ratio of high demands to low income would feel "squeezed" and therefore be more likely to work overtime. Thus, the following factors were expected to contribute to a squeeze:

(1) a family life-cycle stage of one or three (youngest child under six or an adolescent); (2) a low wage rate; (3) a wife out of the labor force; and (4) husband's occupation. Only partial support was found for the hypothesis. Men in stage one, as expected, were more likely to work overtime than men in the other three stages of the life cycle. Men in stage four were more likely, relative to the other stages, to work overtime than expected. Perhaps the squeeze felt by parents of young adults (18-22) with their high educational costs has also been neglected. The effect of life cycle stage was to some extent mediated by wife's employment status, husband's wage rate, and husband's type of job as discussed in the previous sections.

The analysis reported here is the first stage of the investigation and consists of a cross-sectional description of the distribution of overtime among family men in 1975. The second stage will involve longitudinal investigation of movement in and out of the overtime category from 1972 to 1975.

POVERTY, HOUSING DEPRIVATION, AND HOUSING ASSISTANCE
Sandra Newman, Johns Hopkins University
Raymond Struyk, The Urban Institute
Donald Manson, The Urban Institute
(Forthcoming in The Review of Economics and Statistics.)

This paper examines three aspects of the relationship between the permanence of poverty and the housing situation of poor households. The first is whether or not permanent poverty is a good predictor of housing deprivation. That is, do persistently poor families significantly more often than the transiently poor live in dwellings with physical deficiencies, spend an inordinate share of their incomes on housing, or inhabit units that are too small to accommodate comfortably all of their members? A second aspect concerns the permanency of housing deprivation and the relation of permanent deprivation to permanent poverty. Are the permanently poor any more likely than other poor to live persistently in a housing-deprived status, or do they, for example, shift among dwellings with and without key defects, get their landlords to make repairs, or move from higher to lower rent units to relieve the housing expenditure burdens? Clearly the case for concentrating assistance on the permanently poor is stronger the more persistent and severe their housing problems are. The third aspect is whether or not households who are likely to be permanently poor can be identified from among the applicants applying for housing assistance.

The results of the analyses reported in the paper show that households who in 1978 were judged to be permanently poor lived in physically deficient dwellings at substantially higher rates than transiently poor households. Among renters, the rates were 40 percent for the permanently poor and 22 percent for the transiently poor. Blacks and those living in rural areas exhibit even higher rates. Among homeowners, the rates were 34 and 15 percent, respectively.

Permanently poor homeowners were much less likely to be spending an excessive share of their incomes on housing than the transiently poor--26 versus 42 percent. On the other hand, all poor renters were highly likely to be spending more than 30 percent of their incomes on housing.

Permanence of poverty was also associated with occupying a dwelling that has been persistently deficient, relative to the units occupied by the transiently poor. For renters the rates were 30 percent of the permanently poor and 19 percent for the transiently poor; for owner-occupants 30 and 20 percent, respectively. Blacks and those in rural areas again show higher than average rates. Also, the combined incidence of households living in permanently deficient units and currently spending an excessive share of their incomes on housing was found to be low. Hence, those living in permanently deficient units and those with excessive housing expenditures constitute rather separate target populations.

Finally, the permanently poor exhibited rates of persistent housing expense burdens and crowding about twice those of the transiently poor. Of the permanently poor, 43 percent persistently spent an excessive share of their income on housing, and 19 percent lived in crowded conditions.

INTERGENERATIONAL MOBILITY AND ACTIVITY
IN THE INFORMAL ECONOMY
Lawrence H. Nitz, University of Hawaii
(Unpublished paper, 1982.)

This study examines the degree to which participation in the informal economy, namely in doing automobile repairs, making home improvements, and taking on "extra" jobs, serves as a compensatory device to make up for a lack of occupational mobility in the regular labor market. The mobility patterns for respondents from the Panel Study of Income Dynamics are tabulated for "participants" and "nonparticipants" in these three activities, and competing hypotheses based on human capital theory and on notions of redressing unfavorable social comparisons are tested. Under the hypothesis that non-market producers are subject to more status inheritance than nonproducers, the strongest and most persistent effects occur for the home improvement and extra job activities. When examining directional mobility, automotive repair activities appear consistent with compensation for lack of mobility, while home improvements and extra employment support human capital hypotheses.

A PATH MODEL FOR BLACK AND WHITE EDUCATIONAL ACHIEVEMENT
David George Null, California State
Polytechnic University, Pomona, Calif.
(Ph.D. dissertation, City University of New York, 1981.)

This research is an attempt to develop further intergenerational research in educational achievement by refining the "Wisconsin Model of Socioeconomic Achievement." This data, which contained families originally sampled and "spinoff" families that were created by the establishment of a new family by a member of a sample family, was reprogrammed so that the parental characteristics were linked with those of their offspring. The subsample was of all spinoff male heads under 26 who had a parental family sampled in 1972. The subsample is small and potentially unrepresentative; caution should be applied in generalization from the findings of this research.

Path analysis was used as the analytic device because it permits the calculation of both indirect and direct effects in time-ordered data and because it replicates the technique used by other researchers in the "Wisconsin model."

About 40 percent of the variance in offspring educational achievement was explained. The variables which had influence (in declining order of total effect) were: parental education, parental education desires, offspring nAch, parental I.Q., race, parental occupation, number of siblings, and parental nAch. Offspring I.Q. had a spurious relationship with offspring educational achievement.

This research indicates that parental characteristics seem to have strong influences on offspring educational achievement. Unlike earlier research on similar path models, however, the model developed in this dissertation is not characterized by a few clear, strong paths of influence. Instead, this model shows many influences, direct and indirect, but the pattern they follow seems relatively clear.

DILEMMAS OF WELFARE POLICY: WHY WORK
STRATEGIES HAVEN'T WORKED
Mildred Rein
(Published by Prager Publishers, New York, 1982.

TAXATION AND ON-THE-JOB TRAINING DECISIONS
Harvey S. Rosen, Princeton University
(Review of Economics and Statistics (September 1982): 442-49.)

The purpose of this paper is to estimate the effect of income taxation on the decision to engage in one kind of human capital investment, on-the-job training (OJT). The OJT decisions of a group of white American males during 1976 is studied. Questions from the 1976 wave of the PSID are used to classify the men as OJT takers or non-OJT takers, and internal rates of return to OJT are estimated. This internal rate of return, along with a tax variable, is used to explain the OJT decision in a probit equation. The results suggest that the income tax tends to increase the probability that an individual engages in OJT.

INSIDE INFORMATION AND THE EMPLOYER-EMPLOYEE
MATCHING PROCESS
Janice Shack-Marquez, University of Pennsylvania
Ivar Berg, University of Pennsylvania
(Fels Discussion Paper #159, University
of Pennsylvania, August 1982.)

The central purpose of this paper is to address directly the empirical importance to the employer-employee matching process of friendly intermediaries in possession of information about jobs, employers, and prospective job candidates. Using data on workers from the Panel Study of Income Dynamics, the authors analyze the importance of inside information to the matching process.

They found that inside information about a firm leads to better matches between employers and employees and that the returns diminish as one moves into higher-skill occupations.

Also, helpful benefactors and influential benefactors lead to better job matches. Those with more years of education and higher scores on a test of ability are less likely to have used inside information to acquire their job.

INCOME STABILITY IN THE UNITED STATES
Anthony F. Shorrocks
(Published in The Statics and Dynamics of Income, edited by
N. Anders Klevmarken and Johan A. Lybeck. Clevedon, England:
Tieto Ltd., 1981.)

This chapter is concerned with two particular issues: first, the degree to which measured income equality is affected by the choice of accounting period; and second, the problem of characterizing income movements over time in a way that highlights the major influences. One of the main objectives is to show that the computation of the rigidity value R and the construction of stability profiles provide a useful way of summarizing data on income dynamics. The Gini coefficient will tend to indicate much higher stability than other inequality measures. Short-run transitory income fluctuations dominate income movements at young ages.

THE IMPACT OF INCOME COMPONENTS ON THE
DISTRIBUTION OF FAMILY INCOMES
Anthony F. Shorrocks, London School of Economics and
Queen's University, Ontario
(Discussion Paper #417, Queen's
University, Kingston, Ontario, Canada.)

A number of recent studies have attempted to quantify the extent to which inequality in the distribution of total incomes is due to inequality within various income components, such as earnings, investment income, and transfer income. Decompositions of inequality measures related to the variance have been proposed. The Gini coefficient has also been disaggregated into terms involving "pseudo Gini" values. This paper examines the fundamental issues involved in assigning inequality contributions to components of income and discusses the problems that arise from having alternative potential decomposition rules.

A variety of different decompositions are applied to Panel Study data on the distribution of family incomes. It is demonstrated that a wide range of inequality contributions can be obtained, even when attention is restricted to "naturally" derived decomposition rules. Some of the results are plainly absurd and serve to warn against the indiscriminate use of decomposition formulae without first thoroughly investigating their properties.

THE SOCIAL CONSEQUENCES OF SINGLE PARENTHOOD:
A LONGITUDINAL PERSPECTIVE
Michael J. Smith, Hunter College
(Published in Family Relations 29 (1980): 75-81.)

Secondary analysis of interviews with a national sample of families over six years revealed many shifts in the household composition of one parent families over time, a slightly lower level of community participation, and a feeling of powerlessness among single-parent, family heads. These findings cast some doubt on the usefulness of natural support systems for single parents. The findings seem reflective of the societal burdens placed upon lone parents.

THE ECONOMIC AND SOCIAL CONSEQUENCES OF
SINGLE-PARENTHOOD: A LONGITUDINAL
PERSPECTIVE
Michael J. Smith, Hunter College
(Ph.D. Dissertation, Columbia University.)

ECONOMIC CONDITIONS IN SINGLE-PARENT FAMILIES:
A LONGITUDINAL PERSPECTIVE
Michael J. Smith, Hunter College
(Published in Social Work Research and
Abstracts 16 (Summer 1980): 20-24.)

Three different samples of families were selected for analysis: (1) the 1968 cross-sectional sample of one- and two-parent families (472 and 1,573 families, respectively), (2) the panel sample of families that maintained the same status as either a one- or two-parent family from 1968 to 1974 (339 and 1,195 families, respectively), and (3) the transition panel sample of two-parent families with children that became headed by a single parent during the period 1968-1974 (245 families). The transition panel sample included only widowed, divorced, and separated parents.

A one-parent status was found to have a pervasive effect on a family's income. Single-parent families occupied a common economic position resulting, in part, from having only one wage earner. In contrast to their common economic plight, society's response to them was inconsistent and disjointed. Unmarried parents in this study turned to AFDC as a primary source of aid.

Separated parents also used AFDC but not immediately after they had become single parents. In comparison, widowed parents had Social Security as their public transfer system, and Social Security benefits were available to them at the very point of transition to single parenthood.

WHITE COLLAR STRUCTURE AND CLASS:
EDUCATED LABOR REEVALUATED
Richard Sobel, Princeton University
(Ph.D. dissertation, Princeton University.)

The thesis uses PSID data for 1975-1977 in two major sections. First, in a cross-sectional analysis of class in the 1970s, it uses the PSID (1977) data to divide white collar labor into various structurally defined classes, e.g., independents, employers, supervisors, and employees. As the distribution of household heads approximates the distribution of class when family members take class positions from the head of family, in 1977 white collar families were divided into 5 percent independents, 12.5 percent employers, 47.5 percent supervisors, and 35 percent employees. Also, because the PSID asks questions on number of employees overseen and supervisor's powers, supervisors were divided into managers (with more than 3 employees and say in pay or promotion) and other supervisors. Roughly half of white collar supervisors were managers.

A section on the relationship between white collar class and education examines on an initial basis Karabel's suggestion that the stratified system of education parallels the hierarchy in white collar jobs. Specifically technicians are supposed to come from community college, and professionals are supposed to come from upper college or professional schools. While about 90 percent of professionals come from upper college or above, larger proportions of technicians have come from upper college and high school (about one-third for each) than community college (about one-fourth).

Similarly, the study initially tests Bowles and Gintis' hypothesis that there is a correspondence between the social relations of the classroom in which persons are schooled and the social relations on the jobs they enter. It uses number of years of education as a proxy for increasingly less restricted social relations of the classroom, and considers working class (e.g. supervisors and employees) jobs as having more restrictive social relations that nonworking class jobs (e.g. employers and managers). It is found that, in fact, for a younger sample in the PSID (1976) people with more education have gone into more restrictive (i.e., working class) jobs. This challenges the correspondence thesis but gives support to some new working class theories which posit increasing contradictions between education levels and job restrictions in the white collar sectors.

A DYNAMIC MODEL OF THE EXPECTATIONS AND
FERTILITY OF CHILDLESS WOMEN
Richard Wertheimer, The Urban Institute

The 1972 and 1976 waves of the Panel Study of Income Dynamics will be among the data the author intends to analyze as part of a study on the economic correlates and determinants of delayed childbearing. The study focuses on the interaction between fertility expectations and actual fertility behavior within a dynamic framework. That is, an original set of fertility goals and the time path to achieve these goals may be altered over time to reflect unanticipated events. Both fertility expectations and fertility behavior will be adjusted in the light of new information. In particular, the process of adjustment is keenly affected by the age of the women. The study will look strictly at married, childless couples. Other key variables include duration of marriage; husband's age, education, and income; wife's education, wage, and earnings; race; residence; and period economic factors. This study is being funded by NICHD under contract N01-HD-12827. The principal investigator is Roberta Barnes.

RACIAL DIFFERENCES IN THE PROPENSITY TO
RETURN TO SCHOOL
Donald R. Williams, Northwestern University
(Published in Proceedings of the Illinois Economic
Association Meetings, Winter, 1982.)

SCHOOLING, MARKET SEGMENTATION, AND THE
DEGREE OF RELATIVE EARNINGS MOBILITY
Donald R. Williams, Northwestern University
(Work in progress.)

A MODEL OF UNEMPLOYMENT DURATION WITH VARIABLE SEARCH INTENSITY
Bong Joon Yoon, Southern Illinois University
(Published in Review of Economic Statistics 63 (November 1981).)

This study presents a model of unemployment duration with
variable search intensity. In this model, the duration of
unemployment is decomposed into (1) the search time for an offer,
and (2) the unemployment duration due to rejection of offers. It
has been shown that increasing search cost of an offer does not
necessarily imply shorter unemployment duration. If the
elasticity of mean search time for an offer with respect to
search intensity is greater than -1 and less than 0, the increase
in search cost as a result of an increase in the unit cost of
search intensity could, in fact, increase unemployment duration.
This is because the first component of unemployment duration
rises faster than the second falls.

Data from the Panel Study of Income Dynamics have been used
to estimate this model of unemployment duration. From the
empirical results, two important findings emerge. First, the
major portion of unemployment duration for a typical job searcher
is ascribed to his search time for an offer. Only a minor
portion stems from his rejection of received offers. This
contrasts sharply with the implication of the standard search
model which focuses on rejection of offers as a major deterrent
to shortening unemployment duration. Second, the elasticity of
the mean search time for an offer with respect to search
intensity is indeed bounded by -1 and 0. This validates the
theoretical contention that an increase in search cost does not
necessarily shorten unemployment duration. That is, if the
search cost increases as a result of increasing unit cost of
search intensity, then the duration of unemployment actually
increases, on the contrary to the opposite conclusion drawn from
the standard model. This finding does not negate the

406

conventional argument that reducing unemployment compensation lowers unemployment duration. However, it supports an important alternative means of reducing unemployment duration, i.e., lowering the unit cost of search intensity. Examples include improvement in the State Employment Service and provision of tax benefits for the private employment agencies, which will reduce the unit cost of search intensity among unemployed workers, and hence lower the overall rate of unemployment in the economy.

1980 PANEL STUDY OF INCOME DYNAMICS QUESTIONNAIRE

1980 STUDY OF FAMILY ECONOMICS

Project 04

457701

For Office Use Only

OMB NUMBER 85R - 0224

SURVEY RESEARCH CENTER
INSTITUTE FOR SOCIAL RESEARCH
THE UNIVERSITY OF MICHIGAN
ANN ARBOR, MICHIGAN 48106

68 ID	69 ID	70 ID
71 ID	72 ID	73 ID
74 ID	75 ID	76 ID
77 ID	78 ID	79 ID

1. Interviewer's Label

(Do Not Write In Above Space)

2. Home Area _____

3. Your Interview No. _____

4. Date of Interview _____

5. Length of Interview _____ (minutes)

BEFORE YOU BEGIN

Be sure you have prelisted at K36 all eligible Extra Earners in this family unit, using the computer family listing in the 1980 Reinterview Cover Sheet.

6. Date of Edit _____

7. Length of Edit _____ (minutes)

SECTION A: TRANSPORTATION

A1. EXACT TIME NOW: _____

A2. Is there public transportation within walking distance of your house?

| 1. YES | 5. NO | 8. DON'T KNOW |

TURN TO P. 2, A4

A3. Is it good enough so that a person could use it to get to work?

| 1. YES | 3. PRO-CON | 5. NO | 8. DON'T KNOW |

2

A4. Is your house inside the city limits?

1. YES →

5. NO →

   A5. About how far are you from the center of that city?

   1. LESS THAN 5 MILES
   2. 5 - 14.9 MILES
   3. 15 - 29.9 MILES
   4. 30 - 49.9 MILES
   5. 50 OR MORE MILES

8. NA; DON'T KNOW → GO TO A7

A6. About how far are you from the center of the nearest city?

1. LESS THAN 5 MILES
2. 5 - 14.9 MILES
3. 15 - 29.9 MILES
4. 30 - 49.9 MILES
5. 50 OR MORE MILES

A7. Do you (or anyone else in the family here) own a car or truck?

1. YES →

5. NO → TURN TO P. 3, SECTION B

A8. How many cars and trucks do you (and your family living here) own? _____

A9. During the last year, about how many miles did you (and your family) drive in your (car[s]/and truck[s])? _____

3

SECTION B: HOUSING

B1. How many rooms do you have for your family (not counting bathrooms)? _____

B2. Do you live in a one-family house, a two-family house, an apartment, a mobile home, or what?

1. ONE-FAMILY
2. TWO-FAMILY
3. APARTMENT
4. MOBILE HOME
7. OTHER (SPECIFY): _____

B3. How is your (home/apartment) heated--with gas, electricity, oil, or what?

1. GAS
2. ELECTRICITY
3. OIL
8. DON'T KNOW
OTHER (SPECIFY): _____

B4. There are government programs that give money to people to help them pay for heating their homes. Did you receive any such help with bills from this last winter (1979-80)?

1. YES →

5. NO → GO TO B5

B4a. About how much did that amount to?
$_____ (AMOUNT)

B5. Do you own the (home/apartment), pay rent, or what?

1. OWNS OR IS BUYING
5. PAYS RENT → TURN TO P. 4, B14
8. NEITHER OWNS NOR RENTS → TURN TO P. 4, B19

B6. About how much did heat, electricity and water cost you last year?
$_____ UTILITIES IN 1979

B7. Could you tell me what the present value of your (house/apartment/farm) is--I mean about what would it bring if you sold it today?
$_____ HOUSE VALUE

B8. Do you have a mortgage on this property?

1. YES →

5. NO → GO TO B13

                1st MORTGAGE   2nd MORTGAGE

B9. About how much is the remaining principal on this mortgage? $_____ $_____

B10. How much are your monthly mortgage payments? $_____ $_____

B11. About how many more years will you have to pay on it? _____

B12. Do you also have a second mortgage? 1. YES → ASK B9-B11 FOR SECOND MORTGAGE   5. NO → GO TO B13

B13. About how much are your total yearly property taxes including city, county and school taxes?
$_____ PROPERTY TAX PER YEAR

TURN TO P. 5, B23

4

IF R PAYS RENT

B14. About how much rent do you pay a month?

$_____ RENT PER MONTH

B15. Is this (house/apartment) rented fully furnished?

1. YES   5. NO

B16. Do you pay for heat, electricity, or water yourself?

1. YES   5. NO → TURN TO P. 5, B23

B17. About how much did they cost you altogether last year?

$_____ UTILITIES IN 1979

B18. Is heating included in your monthly rent?

1. YES   5. NO

TURN TO P. 5, B23

IF R NEITHER OWNS NOR RENTS

B19. How is that? _____

B20. How much would it rent for if it were rented?

$_____ PER _____
  AMOUNT   MONTH, YEAR

B21. Do you pay for heat, electricity or water yourself?

YES   NO → TURN TO P. 5, B23

B22. About how much did they cost you altogether last year?

$_____ UTILITIES IN 1979

5

B23. Have you (HEAD) moved any time since the spring of 1979?

1. YES   5. NO → GO TO B26

B24. What month was that? (MOST RECENT MOVE)

_____ MONTH

B25. Why did you (HEAD) move? _____

B26. Do you think you might move in the next couple of years?

1. YES, MIGHT OR MAYBE   5. NO   8. DON'T KNOW

TURN TO P. 6, SECTION C

B27. Would you say you definitely will move, probably will move, or are you more uncertain?

1. DEFINITELY   2. PROBABLY   3. MORE UNCERTAIN

B28. Why might you move? _____

6

SECTION C: EMPLOYMENT OF HEAD

C1. We would like to know about what you do--are you (HEAD) working now, looking for work, retired, a student, (a housewife), or what?

```
┌──────────────┐   ┌──────────────┐   ┌──────────────────┐   ┌──────────────┐
│ WORKING      │   │ ONLY         │   │ 3. LOOKING FOR   │   │ 4. RETIRED   │
│ 1. NOW       │   │ TEMPORARILY  │   │    WORK,         │   └──────────────┘
└──────────────┘   │ 2. LAID OFF  │   │    UNEMPLOYED    │   ┌──────────────┐
                   └──────────────┘   └──────────────────┘   │ 5. PERMANENTLY│
                                         TURN TO P. 14,       │    DISABLED   │  CHECK ALL
                                         SECTION D            └──────────────┘  THAT APPLY
                                                              ┌──────────────┐  TURN TO P. 18,
                                                              │ 6. HOUSEWIFE │  SECTION E
                                                              └──────────────┘
                                                              ┌──────────────┐
                                                              │ 7. STUDENT   │
                                                              └──────────────┘
                                                              ┌──────────────────────┐
                                                              │ 8. OTHER (SPECIFY): __│
                                                              └──────────────────────┘
                                                              GO TO C2 IF HEAD HAS JOB, OTHERWISE
                                                              TURN TO P. 18, SECTION E
```

C2. Do you work for someone else, yourself, or what?

```
┌──────────────┐   ┌──────────────────────────┐   ┌──────────────┐
│ 1. SOMEONE   │   │ 2. BOTH SOMEONE ELSE AND  │   │ 3. SELF ONLY │
│    ELSE      │   │    SELF                   │   └──────────────┘
└──────────────┘   └──────────────────────────┘     TURN TO P. 7, C6
```

C3. (In your work for someone else,) do you work for the federal, state, or local government?

```
┌──────────┐          ┌──────────┐
│ 1. YES   │          │ 5. NO    │ ──► TURN TO P. 7, C6
└──────────┘          └──────────┘
```

C4. Is your current job covered by a union contract?

```
┌──────────┐          ┌──────────┐
│ 1. YES   │          │ 5. NO    │ ──► TURN TO P. 7, C6
└──────────┘          └──────────┘
```

C5. Do you belong to that labor union?

```
┌──────────┐          ┌──────────┐
│ 1. YES   │          │ 5. NO    │
└──────────┘          └──────────┘
```

7

OCC ☐☐   IND ☐☐

C6. What is your main occupation? What sort of work do you do?

_____

C7. Tell me a little more about what you do.

C8. What kind of business or industry is that in?

C9. How long have you had your present position?

MOS ☐☐

_____ OR _____
MONTHS   YEARS

C10. INTERVIEWER CHECKPOINT

☐ A. HEAD HAS HAD PRESENT POSITION LESS THAN ONE YEAR

☐ B. HEAD HAS HAD PRESENT POSITION ONE YEAR OR MORE ──► TURN TO P. 8, C16

C11. What month did you start this job?

C12. What happened to the job you had before--did the company go out of business, were you laid off, promoted, were you not working, or what?

```
                                          ┌──────────────────────┐
                                          │ 5. NO PREVIOUS JOB   │
                                          └──────────────────────┘
                                             TURN TO P. 8, C16
```

C13. On the whole, would you say your present job is better or worse than the one you had before?

```
┌──────────────┐   ┌──────────────┐   ┌──────────────┐
│ 1. BETTER    │   │ 5. WORSE     │   │ 3. SAME      │ ──► TURN TO
└──────────────┘   └──────────────┘   └──────────────┘     P. 8, C16
```

C14. Why is it (better/worse)?

C15. Does your present job pay more than the one you had before?

```
┌──────────────┐          ┌──────────────────────┐
│ 1. YES, MORE │          │ 5. NO, SAME OR LESS   │
└──────────────┘          └──────────────────────┘
```

9

C24. Did you miss any work in 1979 because you were unemployed or temporarily laid off?

1. YES   5. NO → GO TO C26

C25. How much work did you miss?

_____ DAYS   _____ WEEKS   _____ MONTHS

C26. Then, how many weeks did you actually work on your main job in 1979?

_____ WEEKS IN 1979

C27. And, on the average, how many hours a week did you work on your main job in 1979?

_____ HOURS PER WEEK IN 1979

C28. Did you work any overtime which isn't included in that?

1. YES   5. NO → TURN TO P. 10, C30

C29. How many hours did that overtime amount to in 1979?

_____ HOURS IN 1979

8

C16. Did you miss any work in 1979 because someone else in the family was sick?

1. YES   5. NO → GO TO C18

C17. How much work did you miss?

_____ DAYS   _____ WEEKS   _____ MONTHS

C18. Did you miss any work in 1979 because you were sick?

1. YES   5. NO → GO TO C20

C19. How much work did you miss?

_____ DAYS   _____ WEEKS   _____ MONTHS

C20. Did you take any vacation or time off during 1979?

1. YES   5. NO → GO TO C22

C21. How much vacation or time off did you take?

_____ DAYS   _____ WEEKS   _____ MONTHS

C22. Did you miss any work in 1979 because you were on strike?

1. YES   5. NO → TURN TO P. 9, C24

C23. How much work did you miss?

_____ DAYS   _____ WEEKS   _____ MONTHS

10

C30. Are you salaried, paid by the hour, or what?

| 1. SALARIED | 3. PAID BY HOUR | 7. OTHER |

SALARIED:

C31. How much is your salary?

$ _____ PER _____

MONTH, YEAR

C32. If you were to work more hours than usual during some week, would you get paid for those extra hours of work?

| 1. YES | 5. NO → TURN TO P. 11, C38 |

C33. About how much would you make per hour for those extra hours?

$ _____ PER HOUR

| TIME AND A HALF |
| DOUBLE TIME |

REG ☐☐☐
OT ☐☐☐

PAID BY HOUR:

C34. What is your hourly wage rate for your regular work time?

$ _____ PER HOUR

C35. What is your hourly wage rate for over-time?

$ _____ PER HOUR

| TIME AND A HALF |
| DOUBLE TIME |

REG ☐☐☐
OT ☐☐☐

OTHER:

C36. How is that?

_____

C37. If you worked an extra hour, how much would you earn for that hour?

$ _____

☐☐☐

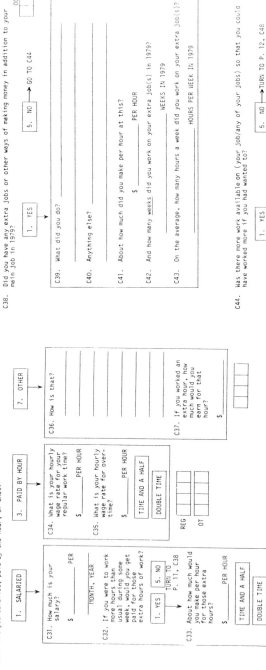

11

OCC ☐☐

C38. Did you have any extra jobs or other ways of making money in addition to your main job in 1979?

| 1. YES | 5. NO → GO TO C44 |

C39. What did you do?

_____

C40. Anything else?

_____

C41. About how much did you make per hour at this?

$ _____ PER HOUR

C42. And how many weeks did you work on your extra job(s) in 1979?

_____ WEEKS IN 1979

C43. On the average, how many hours a week did you work on your extra job(s)?

_____ HOURS PER WEEK IN 1979

C44. Was there more work available on (your job/any of your jobs) so that you could have worked more if you had wanted to?

| 1. YES | 5. NO → TURN TO P. 12, C48 |

C45. How much would you have earned per hour?

$ _____ PER HOUR

C46. Could you have worked less if you had wanted to?

| 1. YES | 5. NO |

TURN TO P. 12, C51

C47. Would you have preferred to work less even if you earned less money?

| 1. YES | 5. NO |

TURN TO P. 12, C51

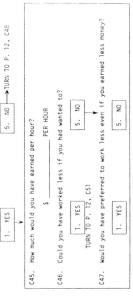

413

12

C48. Would you have liked to work more if you could have found more work?

1. YES
GO TO C51

5. NO

C49. Could you have worked less if you had wanted to?

1. YES
GO TO C51

5. NO

C50. Would you have preferred to work less even if you earned less money?

1. YES

5. NO

C51. About how much time does it take you to get to work each day, door to door?

_____ HOURS   _____ MINUTES   ONE WAY   00. NONE → TURN TO P. 13, C54

C52. About how many miles is to it where you work?

_____ ONE WAY

C53. Do you use public transportation to get to work, (drive with your wife), have a car pool, drive by yourself, walk, or what?

1. PUBLIC TRANS-PORTATION   2. DRIVE WITH WIFE   3. CAR POOL   4. DRIVE BY SELF   5. WALK

7. OTHER (SPECIFY): _____

13

C54. Have you been thinking about getting a new job, or will you keep the job you have now?

1. THINKING ABOUT GETTING A NEW JOB

5. KEEP JOB HAVE NOW → GO TO C56

C55. Have you been doing anything in particular about it?

1. YES

5. NO

C56. Would you be willing to move to another community if you could earn more money there?

1. YES   2. MAYBE   3. DEPENDS

TURN TO P. 20, SECTION F

5. NO

C57. Why is that?

_____

_____

TURN TO P. 20, SECTION F

D7. Would you be willing to move to another community if you could get a good job there?

| 1. YES, MAYBE, OR DEPENDS | 5. NO |

D8. How much would a job have to pay for you to be willing to move?

$ _____ PER _____

D9. Why is that?

_____

_____

_____ WKS [box]

D10. How long have you been looking for work?

_____ [box]

D11. Have you ever had a job?

| 1. YES | 5. NO → TURN TO P. 20, SECTION F |

D12. What sort of work did you do on your last job? What was your occupation?

_____ OCC IND [box]

D13. What kind of business or industry was that in?

_____

_____

D14. What happened to that job--did the company go out of business, were you laid off, or what?

_____

_____

D15. When did you last work?

_____

SECTION D: HEAD LOOKING FOR WORK, UNEMPLOYED IN C1

D1. What kind of job are you looking for?

_____ OCC [box]

D2. How much would you expect to earn?

$ _____ PER _____ [box]

D3. Will you have to get any training to qualify?

| 1. YES | 5. NO | 8. DON'T KNOW |

D4. Have you been doing anything in the last four weeks to find a job?

| 1. YES | 5. NO → GO TO D6 |

D5. How many places have you been to in the last four weeks to find out about a job?

| 0. NONE | 1. ONE | 2. TWO | 3. THREE | 4. FOUR | 5. FIVE OR MORE | 8. DON'T KNOW | [box]

D6. What is the lowest wage or salary you would accept on any job?

$ _____ PER _____

415

16

D16. INTERVIEWER CHECKPOINT

[ ] A. HEAD WORKED IN 1979 OR 1980

[ ] B. HEAD DID NOT WORK IN 1979 OR 1980 ──→ TURN TO P. 20, SECTION F

D17. Did you take any vacation or time off during 1979?

1. YES

5. NO ──→ GO TO D19

D18. How much vacation or time off did you take?

____ DAYS   ____ WEEKS   ____ MONTHS

D19. Did you miss any work in 1979 because someone else in the family was sick?

1. YES

5. NO ──→ GO TO D21

D20. How much work did you miss?

____ DAYS   ____ WEEKS   ____ MONTHS

D21. Did you miss any work in 1979 because you were sick?

1. YES

5. NO ──→ GO TO D23

D22. How much work did you miss?

____ DAYS   ____ WEEKS   ____ MONTHS

D23. Did you miss any work in 1979 because you were on strike?

1. YES

5. NO ──→ TURN TO P. 17, D25

D24. How much work did you miss?

____ DAYS   ____ WEEKS   ____ MONTHS

17

D25. Did you miss any work in 1979 because you were unemployed or temporarily laid off?

1. YES

5. NO ──→ GO TO D27

D26. How much work did you miss?

____ DAYS   ____ WEEKS   ____ MONTHS

D27. Then, how many weeks did you actually work on your job in 1979?

____ WEEKS IN 1979

D28. And, on average, how many hours a week did you work when you worked?

____ HOURS PER WEEK IN 1979

D29. On your last job, how much time did it take you to get to work each day, door to door?

____ HOURS   ____ MINUTES   ONE WAY   00. NONE ──→ TURN TO P. 20, SECTION F

D30. About how many miles was it to where you worked?

____ ONE WAY

D31. Did you use public transportation to get to work, (drive with your wife,) have a car pool, drive by yourself, walk, or what?

| 1. PUBLIC TRANS-PORTATION | 2. DRIVE WITH WIFE | 3. CAR POOL | 4. DRIVE BY SELF | 5. WALK |

7. OTHER (SPECIFY): ____

TURN TO P. 20, SECTION F

SECTION E: HEAD IS RETIRED, HOUSEWIFE, STUDENT, PERMANENTLY DISABLED IN C1

E1. INTERVIEWER CHECKPOINT

[ ] 1. HEAD IS RETIRED

[ ] 5. HEAD IS PERMANENTLY DISABLED, HOUSEWIFE, STUDENT OR OTHER →GO TO E3

E2. In what year did you retire?

E3. During 1979, did you do any work for money?

[1. YES]

[5. NO] TURN TO P. 19, E10

E4. What kind of work did you do? What was your occupation?

OCC [ ] IND [ ]

E5. What kind of business or industry was that in?

E6. How many weeks did you work last year? _____ WEEKS IN 1979

E7. About how many hours a week did you work? _____ HOURS PER WEEK IN 1979

E8. Are you still working?

[1. YES] TURN TO P. 19, E10

[5. NO]

E9. What happened to that job--did the company go out of business, were you laid off, or what?

E10. Are you thinking of getting (a/another) job in the future?

[1. YES]

[5. NO] → TURN TO P. 20, SECTION F

E11. When might that be? (How soon?)

E12. What kind of job do you have in mind?

E13. Would you have to get any training to qualify?

[1. YES] [5. NO] [8. DON'T KNOW]

E14. Have you been doing anything in the last four weeks to find a job?

[1. YES]

[5. NO] → TURN TO P. 20, SECTION F

E15. How many places have you been to in the last four weeks to find out about a job?

[0. NONE] [1. ONE] [2. TWO] [3. THREE] [4. FOUR] [5. FIVE OR MORE] [8. DON'T KNOW]

SECTION F: EMPLOYMENT OF WIFE/FRIEND

F1. INTERVIEWER CHECKPOINT

1. HEAD IS MALE WHO HAS WIFE IN FU (REMEMBER: FEMALE FRIEND LIVING IN FU ONE YEAR OR MORE IS CONSIDERED WIFE)

2. HEAD IS MALE WHO DOES NOT HAVE WIFE IN FU ──TURN TO P. 30, SECTION J

3. HEAD IS FEMALE ──TURN TO P. 30, SECTION J

F2. We would like to know about what your (wife/friend) does--is she working now, looking for work, retired, a student, a housewife, or what?

1. WORKING NOW

2. ONLY TEMPORARILY LAID OFF

3. LOOKING FOR WORK, UNEMPLOYED
TURN TO P. 25, SECTION G

4. RETIRED

5. PERMANENTLY DISABLED

6. HOUSEWIFE

7. STUDENT

8. OTHER (SPECIFY):

CHECK ALL THAT APPLY TURN TO P. 28, SECTION H

GO TO F3 IF HAS JOB, OTHERWISE TURN TO P. 28, SECTION H

F3. Does your (wife/friend) work for someone else, herself, or what?

1. SOMEONE ELSE   2. BOTH SOMEONE ELSE AND SELF   3. SELF ONLY
TURN TO P. 21, F7

F4. (In her work for someone else) does she work for the federal, state, or local government?

1. YES   5. NO

F5. Is her current job covered by a union contract?

1. YES   5. NO ──TURN TO P. 21, F7

F6. Does she belong to that labor union?

1. YES   5. NO

21

F7. What is your (wife's/friend's) main occupation? What sort of work does she do?

OCC [ ]   IND [ ]

F8. Tell me a little more about what she does.

F9. What kind of business or industry is that in?

F10. How long has your (wife/friend) had her present position?

MONTHS   OR   YEARS

F11. INTERVIEWER CHECKPOINT

A. WIFE HAS HAD PRESENT POSITION LESS THAN ONE YEAR

B. WIFE HAS HAD PRESENT POSITION ONE YEAR OR MORE ──TURN TO P. 22, F14

F12. What month did she start this job?

MOS [ ]

F13. What happened to the job she had before--did the company go out of business, was she laid off, promoted, not working, or what?

5. NO PREVIOUS JOB

F24. Then, how many <u>weeks</u> did your (wife/friend) actually work on her main job in 1979?

_____ WEEKS IN 1979

F25. And, on the average, how many <u>hours</u> a week did your (wife/friend) work on her main job in 1979?

_____ HOURS PER WEEK IN 1979

F26. Did your (wife/friend) work any overtime which isn't included in that?

　　1. YES

　　5. NO ──→ GO TO F28

F27. How many hours did that overtime amount to in 1979?

_____ HOURS IN 1979

F28. Is your (wife/friend) salaried, paid by the hour, or what?

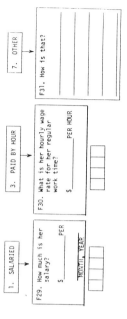

　　1. SALARIED　　　　3. PAID BY HOUR　　　　7. OTHER

F29. How much is her salary?

$ _____ PER

_____ MONTH　YEAR

F30. What is her hourly wage rate for her regular work time?

$ _____ PER HOUR

F31. How is that?

_____
_____
_____

F14. Did your (wife/friend) miss any work in 1979 because you or someone else in the family was sick?

　　1. YES

　　5. NO ──→ GO TO F16

F15. How much work did she miss?

_____ DAYS　　_____ WEEKS　　_____ MONTHS

F16. Did your (wife/friend) miss any work in 1979 because <u>she</u> was sick?

　　1. YES

　　5. NO ──→ GO TO F18

F17. How much work did she miss?

_____ DAYS　　_____ WEEKS　　_____ MONTHS

F18. Did your (wife/friend) take any vacation or time off during 1979?

　　1. YES

　　5. NO ──→ GO TO F20

F19. How much vacation or time off did she take?

_____ DAYS　　_____ WEEKS　　_____ MONTHS

F20. Did your (wife/friend) miss any work in 1979 because she was on strike?

　　1. YES

　　5. NO ──→ GO TO F22

F21. How much work did she miss?

_____ DAYS　　_____ WEEKS　　_____ MONTHS

F22. Did your (wife/friend) miss any work in 1979 because she was unemployed or temporarily laid off?

　　1. YES

　　5. NO ──→ TURN TO P. 23, F24

F23. How much work did she miss?

_____ DAYS　　_____ WEEKS　　_____ MONTHS

24

F32. Did your (wife/friend) have any extra jobs or other ways of making money in addition to her main job in 1979?

OCC [ ]

1. YES ↓   5. NO →GO TO F36

F33. What did she do?
_____

F34. And how many weeks did your (wife/friend) work on her extra job(s) in 1979?
_____ WEEKS IN 1979

F35. On the average, how many hours a week did she work on her extra job(s)?
_____ HOURS PER WEEK IN 1979

F36. About how much time does it take your (wife/friend) to get to work each day, door to door?
_____ HOURS _____ MINUTES   ONE WAY
00. NONE →TURN TO P. 30, SECTION J

F37. About how many miles is it to where your (wife/friend) works?
_____ ONE WAY

F38. Does she use public transportation to get to work, drive with you, have a car pool, drive by herself, walk, or what?

1. PUBLIC TRANS-PORTATION   2. DRIVE WITH HEAD   3. CAR POOL   4. DRIVE BY SELF   5. WALK

7. OTHER (SPECIFY): _____

TURN TO P. 30, SECTION J

25

OCC [ ]

SECTION G: WIFE/FRIEND LOOKING FOR WORK, UNEMPLOYED IN F2

G1. What kind of job is your (wife/friend) looking for?

G2. Has she been doing anything in the last four weeks to find a job?

1. YES   5. NO →GO TO G4

G3. How many places has your (wife/friend) been to in the last four weeks to find out about a job?

0. NONE   1. ONE   2. TWO   3. THREE   4. FOUR   5. FIVE OR MORE   8. DON'T KNOW

G4. How long has she been looking for work?
_____ WKS

G5. Has your (wife/friend) ever had a job?

1. YES   5. NO →TURN TO P. 30, SECTION J

G6. What sort of work did your (wife/friend) do on her last job? (What was her occupation?)
_____   OCC [ ]   IND [ ]

G7. What kind of business or industry was that in?
_____

G8. What happened to that job--did the company go out of business, was she laid off, or what?
_____

G9. When did your (wife/friend) last work?
_____

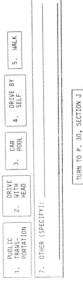

420

G19. Did your (wife/friend) miss any work in 1979 because she was unemployed or temporarily laid off?

1. YES

5. NO → GO TO G21

G20. How much work did she miss?

_____ DAYS   _____ WEEKS   _____ MONTHS

G21. Then, how many weeks did she actually work on her job in 1979?

_____ WEEKS IN 1979

G22. And, on average, how many hours a week did she work when she worked?

_____ HOURS PER WEEK IN 1979

G23. On her last job, how much time did it take her to get to work each day, door to door?

_____ HOURS   _____ MINUTES   ONE WAY   00. NONE → TURN TO P. 30, SECTION J

G24. About how many miles was it to where she worked?

_____ ONE WAY

G25. Did your (wife/friend) use public transportation to get to work, drive with you, have a car pool, drive by herself, or what?

1. PUBLIC TRANS-PORTATION   2. DRIVE WITH HEAD   3. CAR POOL   4. DRIVE BY SELF   5. WALK

7. OTHER (SPECIFY): _____

TURN TO P. 30, SECTION J

G10. INTERVIEWER CHECKPOINT

A. WIFE WORKED IN 1979 OR 1980

B. WIFE DID NOT WORK IN 1979 OR 1980 → TURN TO P. 30, SECTION J

G11. Did your (wife/friend) take any vacation or time off during 1979?

1. YES

5. NO → GO TO G13

G12. How much vacation or time off did she take?

_____ DAYS   _____ WEEKS   _____ MONTHS

G13. Did your (wife/friend) miss any work in 1979 because you or someone else in the family was sick?

1. YES

5. NO → GO TO G15

G14. How much work did she miss?

_____ DAYS   _____ WEEKS   _____ MONTHS

G15. Did your (wife/friend) miss any work in 1979 because she was sick?

1. YES

5. NO → GO TO G17

G16. How much work did she miss?

_____ DAYS   _____ WEEKS   _____ MONTHS

G17. Did your (wife/friend) miss any work in 1979 because she was on strike?

1. YES

5. NO → TURN TO P. 27, G19

G18. How much work did she miss?

_____ DAYS   _____ WEEKS   _____ MONTHS

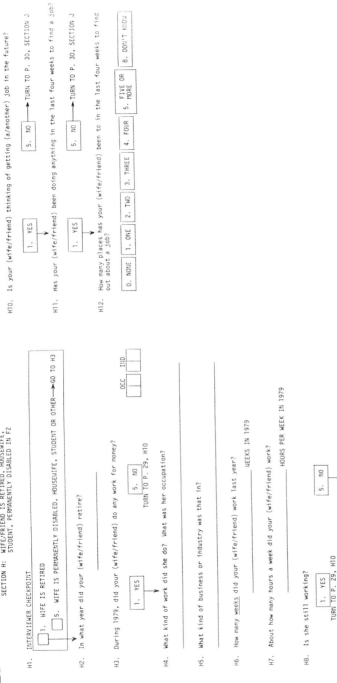

SECTION H: WIFE/FRIEND IS RETIRED, HOUSEWIFE, STUDENT, PERMANENTLY DISABLED IN F2

H1. INTERVIEWER CHECKPOINT

☐ 1. WIFE IS RETIRED

☐ 5. WIFE IS PERMANENTLY DISABLED, HOUSEWIFE, STUDENT OR OTHER ──→GO TO H3

H2. In what year did your (wife/friend) retire?
_____

H3. During 1979, did your (wife/friend) do any work for money?

1. YES   5. NO
                 TURN TO P. 29, H10

H4. What kind of work did she do? What was her occupation?   OCC |___|___| H10
_____

H5. What kind of business or industry was that in?
_____

H6. How many weeks did your (wife/friend) work last year?
_____ WEEKS IN 1979

H7. About how many hours a week did your (wife/friend) work?
_____ HOURS PER WEEK IN 1979

H8. Is she still working?

1. YES   5. NO
TURN TO P. 29, H10

H9. What happened to that job--did the company go out of business, was she laid off, or what?
_____
_____

H10. Is your (wife/friend) thinking of getting (a/another) job in the future?

1. YES   5. NO ──→ TURN TO P. 30, SECTION J

H11. Has your (wife/friend) been doing anything in the last four weeks to find a job?

1. YES   5. NO ──→ TURN TO P. 30, SECTION J

H12. How many places has your (wife/friend) been to in the last four weeks to find out about a job?

0. NONE   1. ONE   2. TWO   3. THREE   4. FOUR   5. FIVE OR MORE   8. DON'T KNOW

SECTION J: HOUSEWORK AND FOOD

J1. Are you (HEAD) married, widowed, divorced, separated, or single?

| 1. MARRIED | 2. SINGLE | 3. WIDOWED | 4. DIVORCED | 5. SEPARATED |
| GO TO J4 | | GO TO J4 | | |

J2. Were you ever married?

1. YES   5. NO → GO TO J4

J3. What happened to your last marriage--were you widowed, divorced, separated, or what?

3. WIDOWED   4. DIVORCED   5. SEPARATED   7. OTHER (SPECIFY): _____

J4. INTERVIEWER CHECKPOINT

1. HEAD IS MALE WHO HAS WIFE IN FU (REMEMBER: FEMALE FRIEND LIVING IN FU ONE YEAR OR MORE IS CONSIDERED WIFE)

2. HEAD IS MALE WHO DOES NOT HAVE WIFE IN FU → GO TO J6

3. HEAD IS FEMALE → GO TO J6

J5. About how much time does your (wife/friend) spend on housework in an average week-- I mean time spent cooking, cleaning and doing other work around the house?

_____ HOURS PER WEEK

J6. About how much time do you (HEAD) spend on housework in an average week? (I mean time spent cooking, cleaning, and doing other work around the house?)

_____ HOURS PER WEEK

J7. INTERVIEWER CHECKPOINT

A. ANY OTHER PEOPLE LIVE WITH HEAD (AND WIFE) IN FU, INCLUDING CHILDREN → TURN TO P. 32, J12

B. HEAD (AND WIFE) LIVE ALONE IN FU → TURN TO P. 32, J12

J8. Does anyone else here in the household help with the housework?

1. YES   5. NO → TURN TO P. 32, J12

J9. Who is that? (LIST RELATIONSHIP TO HEAD AND ASK J10 FOR EACH.)

J10. About how much time does (he/she) spend on housework in an average week?

J9 RELATIONSHIP TO HEAD	AGE		SEQ #
_____	____	_____	☐
_____	____	_____	☐
_____	____	_____	☐
_____	____	_____	☐

J11. Anyone else? (LIST IN J9 AND ASK J10 FOR EACH PERSON.)

32

J12. Did you (or anyone else now living in your family) receive government food stamps last month?

☐ YES

☐ NO → TURN TO P. 33, J20

J13. For how many members of your family were stamps issued? _____

J14. How many dollars' worth of food stamps did you get?
$ _____ PER _____
   AMOUNT   MONTH

J15. In addition to what you bought with food stamps, did you (or anyone else in your family) spend any money on food that you use at home?

☐ YES → J16. How much? $ _____ PER _____
               AMOUNT   WEEK, MONTH

☐ NO → GO TO J17

J17. Do you have any food delivered to the door which isn't included in that?

☐ YES → J18. How much do you spend on that food? $ _____ PER _____
               AMOUNT   WEEK, MONTH

☐ NO → GO TO J19

J19. About how much do you (or anyone else in your family) spend eating out, not counting meals at work or at school?
$ _____ PER _____
   AMOUNT   WEEK, MONTH

TURN TO P. 33, J24

33

J20. How much do you (or anyone else in your family) spend on food that you use at home in an average week?
$ _____ PER _____
   AMOUNT   WEEK, MONTH

J21. Do you have any food delivered to the door which isn't included in that?

☐ YES → J22. How much do you spend on that food? $ _____ PER _____
               AMOUNT   WEEK, MONTH

☐ NO → GO TO J23

J23. About how much do you (and everyone else in your family) spend eating out, not counting meals at work or at school?
$ _____ PER _____
   AMOUNT   WEEK, MONTH

J24. Did you (or anyone else in your family) use government food stamps at any time in 1979?

☐ YES

☐ NO → TURN TO P. 34, J27

J25. How many dollars' worth of stamps did you get in 1979?
$ _____ PER _____
   AMOUNT   MONTH

J26. For how many months did you use food stamps in 1979? _____ MONTHS

TURN TO P. 35, SECTION K

34

J27. Did you think you were eligible for food stamps at any time in 1979?

1. YES | 3. MAYBE | 5. NO | 8. DON'T KNOW

GO TO J31

J28. Did you try to get the stamps last year (in 1979)?

1. YES | 5. NO → GO TO J30

J29. Why couldn't you get them? (Any other reasons why?)

_____

_____

TURN TO P. 35, SECTION K

J30. Can you tell me why you didn't try? (Any other reasons why?)

_____

_____

TURN TO P. 35, SECTION K

J31. Can you tell me why you thought you weren't eligible? (Any other reasons why?)

_____

_____

_____

_____

35

SECTION K: INCOME

To get an accurate financial picture of people all over the country, we need to know the income of all the families that we interview.

K1. INTERVIEWER CHECKPOINT

[ ] 1. HEAD IS FARMER, OR RANCHER

[ ] 5. HEAD IS NOT A FARMER OR RANCHER ──→ GO TO K5

K2. What were your total receipts from farming in 1979, including soil bank payments and commodity credit loans? $ _____ A

K3. What were your total operating expenses, not counting living expenses? $ _____ B

K4. That left you a net income from farming of? (A - B =) $ _____ A-B

K5. Did you (or anyone else in the family here) own a business at any time in 1979, or have a financial interest in any business enterprise?

1. YES | 5. NO ──→ GO TO K8

K6. Was it a corporation or an unincorporated business, or did you have an interest in both kinds?

1. CORPORATION | 2. UNINCORPORATED | 3. BOTH | 8. DON'T KNOW

GO TO K8

K7. How much was your (family's) share of the total income from the business in 1979--that is, the amount you took out plus any profit left in?

$ _____ IN 1979

K8. How much did you (HEAD) receive from wages and salaries in 1979, that is, before anything was deducted for taxes or other things?

$ _____ IN 1979

K9. In addition to this, did you have any income from bonuses, overtime or commissions?

YES | NO ──→ TURN TO P. 36, K11

K10. How much was that?

$ _____ IN 1979

36

K11. I'm going to be reading you a list of other sources of income you might have. Did you (HEAD) receive any other income in 1979 from professional practice or trade? (FOR EACH "YES" TO K11, ASK K12 AND K13.)

	K11		K12 How much was it?	K13 During how much of 1979 did you get this income?
a. PROFESSIONAL PRACTICE OR TRADE?	NO	YES	$ ___ PER ___	FOR ___
b. from farming or market gardening?	NO	YES	$ ___ PER ___	FOR ___
c. roomers or boarders?	NO	YES	$ ___ PER ___	FOR ___
d. dividends, interest, rent, trust funds, or royalties?	NO	YES	$ ___ PER ___	FOR ___
e. ADC, AFDC	NO	YES	$ ___ PER ___	FOR ___
f. Supplemental Security Income (the gold/tan/yellow checks)?	NO	YES	$ ___ PER ___	FOR ___

TURN TO P. 37, K20

K14. INTERVIEWER CHECKPOINT
[ ] 1. HEAD AGE 65 OR OLDER
5. HEAD UNDER 65 ——> TURN TO P. 37, K20

K15. We are interested in the government's Supplemental Security Income Program. Did you think you were eligible for Supplemental Security Income in 1979?
1. YES   3. MAYBE   5. NO   8. DON'T KNOW
(NO) TURN TO P. 37, K19

K16. Did you try to get SSI last year (1979)?
1. YES   5. NO ——> TURN TO P. 37, K18

K17. Can you tell me why you couldn't get SSI? (Any other reasons why?)

TURN TO P. 37, K20

37

K18. Can you tell me why you didn't try? (Any other reasons why?)
GO TO K20

K19. Can you tell me why you thought you weren't eligible? (Any other reasons why?)

K20. Did you (HEAD) receive any income in 1979 from other welfare? (FOR EACH "YES" TO K20, ASK K21 AND K22.)

	K20		K21 How much was it?	K22 During how much of 1979 did you get this income?
a. OTHER WELFARE?	NO	YES	$ ___ PER ___	FOR ___
b. Social Security?	NO	YES	$ ___ PER ___	FOR ___
c. Other retirement pay, pensions or annuities?	NO	YES	$ ___ PER ___	FOR ___
d. Unemployment compensation?	NO	YES	$ ___ PER ___	FOR ___
e. Workers compensation?	NO	YES	$ ___ PER ___	FOR ___
f. Alimony?	NO	YES	$ ___ PER ___	FOR ___
g. Child support?	NO	YES	$ ___ PER ___	FOR ___
h. Help from relatives?	NO	YES	$ ___ PER ___	FOR ___
j. Anything else? (SPECIFY):	NO	YES	$ ___ PER ___	FOR ___

K23. Did anyone (else) not living here now help (you/your family) out financially-- I mean give you money, or help with your expenses during 1979?
YES   NO ——> TURN TO P. 38, K25

K24. How much did that amount to last year? $ ___ IN 1979

Page 38

K25. INTERVIEWER CHECKPOINT

- [ ] A. HEAD IS MALE AND HAS WIFE IN FU
- [ ] B. HEAD IS MALE, DOES NOT HAVE WIFE IN FU —→TURN TO P. 39, K36
- [ ] C. HEAD IS FEMALE —→TURN TO P. 39, K36

K26. Did your (wife/friend) have any income during 1979?

YES / NO —→TURN TO P. 39, K36

K27. Was any of it earnings from her work?

YES / NO —→GO TO K29

K28. How much did she earn from work in 1979 before deductions?

$_____ IN 1979

K29. Did she receive any unemployment compensation in 1979?

YES / NO —→GO TO K31

K30. How much was that? $_____ IN 1979

K31. Did she receive any Social Security in 1979?

YES / NO —→GO TO K33

K32. How much was that? $_____ IN 1979

K33. Did she have any other income in 1979 such as interest, dividends, or rent?

YES / NO —→TURN TO P. 39, K36

K34. What was it from? _____ SOURCE

K35. How much did that amount to in 1979? $_____ IN 1979

(DO NOT WRITE IN THIS SPACE)

HEAD TYPE INCOME:	
TAXABLE	TRANSFER
L A	

(DO NOT WRITE IN THIS SPACE)

WIFE TYPE INCOME:	
TAXABLE	TRANSFER
L A	

Page 39

K36. PRELIST

- ALL PERSONS 16 OR OLDER AT THE TIME OF THE 1980 INTERVIEW. (THESE PERSONS ARE LISTED ON THE FAMILY LISTING LABEL, PAGE 3 OF THE COVER SHEET.)
- DO NOT PRELIST "HEAD" OR "WIFE."

UPDATE

- LIST ANYONE 16 OR OLDER WHO HAS MOVED IN SINCE THE 1979 INTERVIEW. (THESE PERSONS LISTED IN ITEM 12, PAGE 3 OF THE COVER SHEET.)
- LIST ANYONE SHOWN AS "HEAD" OR "WIFE" ON FAMILY LISTING LABEL WHO HAS MOVED OUT SINCE THE 1979 INTERVIEW.

EXCEPTION

- DO NOT ASK AN EXTRA EARNER SECTION FOR ANYONE WHO MOVED OUT BEFORE JANUARY 1, 1979.

EXTRA EARNERS' GRID

EXTRA EARNER NUMBER	RELATIONSHIP TO HEAD	SEX	AGE

K37. INTERVIEWER CHECKPOINT

- [ ] 1. ANY ELIGIBLE PERSON(S) LISTED ABOVE —→ASK AN EXTRA EARNER SECTION (K38-K52) FOR EACH
- [ ] 5. NO ELIGIBLE PERSON(S) LISTED ABOVE —→TURN TO P. 46, K54

40 FIRST EXTRA EARNER: RELATIONSHIP TO HEAD: _____ AGE: [ ]

K38. INTERVIEWER: THIS PERSON IS DECEASED: 1. YES [GO TO K40]   5. NO

K39. We would like to know about what (INDIVIDUAL) does--is (he/she) working now, looking for work, retired, a student, keeping house, or what? (CHECK ALL THAT APPLY.)

| 1. WORKING NOW | 2. ONLY TEMPORARILY LAID OFF | 3. LOOKING FOR WORK, UNEMPLOYED | 4. RETIRED | 5. PERMANENTLY DISABLED |

| 6. KEEPING HOUSE | 7. STUDENT | 8. OTHER (SPECIFY): | 9. DON'T KNOW |

K40. During 1979 did (he/she) have a full-time or part-time job (not counting work around the house)?

FULL-TIME JOB | PART-TIME JOB | DID NOT HAVE A JOB [GO TO K45]

K41. What kind of work did (he/she) usually do?

K42. About how much money did (he/she) earn from work last year?
$_____ IN 1979

K43. About how many weeks did (he/she) work last year?
_____ WEEKS IN 1979   DON'T KNOW

K44. During the weeks that (he/she) worked about how many hours did (he/she) usually work per week?
_____ HOURS PER WEEK   DON'T KNOW

K45. Did (he/she) have any (other) income last year?
YES   NO [TURN TO P. 41, K48]

K46. What was that from?

K47. How much was that last year? $_____ IN 1979

41

K48. During 1979 was there any time when (he/she) was laid off or looking for work and could not find a job?
YES   NO [GO TO K50]   DON'T KNOW

K49. About how many weeks was that? _____ WEEKS IN 1979

K50. During 1979 was (he/she) enrolled in school as a full-time or part-time student?

1. FULL-TIME STUDENT | 3. PART-TIME STUDENT | 5. NOT ENROLLED IN SCHOOL [GO TO K52] | 8. DON'T KNOW

K51. How many weeks did (he/she) attend school in 1979? _____ WEEKS IN 1979

K52. What is the highest grade or year of school that (he/she) has completed? _____ GRADE/YEAR

K53. INTERVIEWER CHECKPOINT:

A. MORE THAN 1 EXTRA EARNER LISTED IN K36 → GO TO P. 42, SECOND EXTRA EARNER SECTION

B. ONLY 1 EXTRA EARNER LISTED IN K36 → TURN TO P. 46, K54

TAXABLE   TRANSFER [ ]   TX [ ][ ][ ]   WRKHRS [ ][ ]
L   A   UNEMP [ ]   TR [ ][ ][ ]

42 SECOND EXTRA EARNER: RELATIONSHIP TO HEAD: _____ AGE: [ ]

K38. INTERVIEWER: THIS PERSON IS DECEASED: 1. YES   5. NO
                                                          └─GO TO K40

K39. We would like to know about what (INDIVIDUAL) does--is (he/she) working now,
looking for work, retired, a student, keeping house, or what? (CHECK ALL THAT
APPLY.)

| 1. WORKING NOW | 2. ONLY TEMPORARILY LAID OFF | 3. LOOKING FOR WORK, UNEMPLOYED | 4. RETIRED | 5. PERMANENTLY DISABLED |

| 6. KEEPING HOUSE | 7. STUDENT | 8. OTHER (SPECIFY): | | 9. DON'T KNOW |

K40. During 1979 did (he/she) have a full-time or part-time job (not counting work
around the house)?

| FULL-TIME JOB | | PART-TIME JOB | | DID NOT HAVE A JOB |
                                                  └─ GO TO K45

K41. What kind of work did (he/she) usually do?

K42. About how much money did (he/she) earn from work last year?
$ _____ IN 1979

K43. About how many weeks did (he/she) work last year?
_____ WEEKS IN 1979 | DON'T KNOW |

K44. During the weeks that (he/she) worked about how many hours did (he/she) usually
work per week?
_____ HOURS PER WEEK | DON'T KNOW |

K45. Did (he/she) have any (other) income last year?

| YES | | NO | ──► TURN TO P. 43, K48

K46. What was that from?

K47. How much was that last year? $ _____ IN 1979

43

K48. During 1979 was there any time when (he/she) was laid off or looking for work
and could not find a job?

| YES | | NO | | DON'T KNOW |
                  └─ GO TO K50

K49. About how many weeks was that?
_____ WEEKS IN 1979

K50. During 1979 was (he/she) enrolled in school as a full-time or part-time student?

| 1. FULL-TIME STUDENT | 3. PART-TIME STUDENT | 5. NOT ENROLLED IN SCHOOL |
                                                         └─ GO TO K52

K51. How many weeks did (he/she) attend school in 1979?
_____ WEEKS IN 1979 | 8. DON'T KNOW |

K52. What is the highest grade or year of school that (he/she) has completed?
_____ GRADE/YEAR

K53. INTERVIEWER CHECKPOINT

[ ] A. MORE THAN 2 EXTRA EARNERS LISTED IN K36 ──► GO TO P. 44, THIRD
       EXTRA EARNER SECTION

[ ] B. ONLY 2 EXTRA EARNERS LISTED IN K36 ──► TURN TO P. 46, K54

| TAXABLE | TRANSFER |
| L | A | |

TX [ ][ ][ ][ ]   TRANSFER [ ][ ]   WRKHRS [ ][ ]

UNEMP [ ][ ]   TR [ ][ ][ ][ ]

44. THIRD EXTRA EARNER: RELATIONSHIP TO HEAD: _____ AGE: _____ [ ]

K38. INTERVIEWER: THIS PERSON IS DECEASED: 1. YES → GO TO K40   5. NO

K39. We would like to know about what (INDIVIDUAL) does--is (he/she) working now, looking for work, retired, a student, keeping house, or what? (CHECK ALL THAT APPLY.)

1. WORKING NOW   2. ONLY TEMPORARILY LAID OFF   3. LOOKING FOR WORK, UNEMPLOYED   4. RETIRED   5. PERMANENTLY DISABLED

6. KEEPING HOUSE   7. STUDENT   8. OTHER (SPECIFY):   9. DON'T KNOW

K40. During 1979 did (he/she) have a full-time or part-time job (not counting work around the house)?

FULL-TIME JOB   PART-TIME JOB   DID NOT HAVE A JOB → GO TO K45

K41. What kind of work did (he/she) usually do?

K42. About how much money did (he/she) earn from work last year?
$ _____ IN 1979

K43. About how many weeks did (he/she) work last year?
_____ WEEKS IN 1979   DON'T KNOW

K44. During the weeks that (he/she) worked about how many hours did (he/she) usually work per week?
_____ HOURS PER WEEK   DON'T KNOW

K45. Did (he/she) have any (other) income last year?
YES   NO → TURN TO P. 45, K48

K46. What was that from?

K47. How much was that last year? $ _____ IN 1979

K48. During 1979 was there any time when (he/she) was laid off or looking for work and could not find a job?

YES   NO → GO TO K50

K49. About how many weeks was that?
_____ WEEKS IN 1979

K50. During 1979 was (he/she) enrolled in school as a full-time or part-time student?

1. FULL-TIME STUDENT   3. PART-TIME STUDENT   5. NOT ENROLLED IN SCHOOL → GO TO K52

K51. How many weeks did (he/she) attend school in 1979?
_____ WEEKS IN 1979   8. DON'T KNOW

K52. What is the highest grade or year of school that (he/she) has completed?
_____ GRADE/YEAR

K53. INTERVIEWER CHECKPOINT

[ ] A. MORE THAN 3 EXTRA EARNERS LISTED IN K36 → USE EXTRA EARNER SUPPLEMENTAL SECTION (BLUE)

[ ] B. ONLY 3 EXTRA EARNERS LISTED IN K36 → TURN TO P. 46, K54

TAXABLE   TRANSFER   TX [ ][ ][ ][ ]   WRKHRS [ ][ ]
L   A [ ]   UNEMP [ ][ ]   TR [ ][ ]

K60. Are you covered by some medical or hospital insurance like Medicare, Blue Cross or Blue Shield?

1. YES   5. NO

K61. Can you get free hospital or medical care as a veteran, or through Medicaid, or any other way?

1. YES   5. NO

K62. During the past year, has anyone in the family received medical care which has been or will be paid for by Medicare or Medicaid (Medi-Cal, Medical Assistance, Welfare, Medical Services)?

1. YES   5. NO → GO TO K64

K63. Which program was it?

1. MEDICARE   2. MEDICAID, MEDI-CAL, MEDICAL ASSISTANCE, WELFARE, MEDICAL SERVICES

7. OTHER (SPECIFY): _____   8. DON'T KNOW

K64. Did you get any other money in 1979--like a big settlement from an insurance company, or an inheritance?

1. YES   5. NO → TURN TO P. 48, K66

K65. How much did that amount to?

$ _____ IN 1979

K54. Did anyone else living here in 1979 have any income in 1979? (INCLUDING CHILDREN UNDER 16.)

YES   NO → TURN TO P. 47, K60

K55. Who was that? (LIST EACH PERSON AND ASK K56-K58)

RELATIONSHIP TO HEAD AGE   RELATIONSHIP TO HEAD AGE   RELATIONSHIP TO HEAD AGE

K56. About how much was that?

$ _____ IN 1979 $ _____ IN 1979

K57. What was that from?

K58. (IF WORK MENTIONED AT K57) About how many hours of work was that?

_____ HOURS IN 1979   _____ HOURS IN 1979

K59. Did anyone else living here in 1979 have any income in 1979?

YES   NO → TURN TO P. 47, K60

ASK K55-K58 ABOVE

TAXABLE   TRANSFER   TAXABLE   TRANSFER   TAXABLE   TRANSFER
L   A   L   A   L   A

TX   TX   TX

WRKHRS   WRKHRS   WRKHRS

TR   TR   TR

48

K66. Last year did you help support anyone who doesn't live here with you now?

1. YES → / 5. NO → GO TO K71

K67. How many? ___

K68. How much money did that amount to in the last year? $ ___ IN 1979

K69. Were any of these people dependent on you for more than half of their total support?

1. YES / 5. NO → GO TO K71

K70. How many? ___

K71. People sometimes have emergencies and need help from others--either time or money. Let's start by talking about time. In the last five years have you (or anyone living with you) spent a lot of time helping either a relative or friend in an emergency?

1. YES / 5. NO → GO TO K74

K72. Was the person you helped a relative of (yours/anybody who lives here)?

1. YES / 5. NO

K73. What kind of help was that? ___

K74. Suppose there were a serious emergency in your household. Is there a friend or relative living nearby whom you could call on to spend a lot of time helping out?

1. YES / 3. DEPENDS / 5. NO → TURN TO P. 49, K77 / 8. DON'T KNOW
TURN TO P. 49, K80

K75. Would that be a relative?

1. YES / 5. NO

K76. What is that person's relationship to you? ___

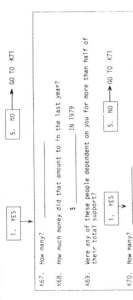

49

K77. How much would that person mind spending time helping you out--a lot, a little bit, or not at all?

1. A LOT / 3. A LITTLE BIT / 5. NOT AT ALL / 8. DON'T KNOW

K78. Would you feel you had to repay that person in some way?

5. NO / 8. DON'T KNOW

K79. If that person were not available, is there someone else you could call on?

5. NO / 8. DON'T KNOW

K80. Do you have a relative or friend who doesn't live near you who could come to help you in an emergency?

1. YES → / 5. NO → GO TO K83

K81. Is that person a relative?

1. YES → / 5. NO → GO TO K83

K82. What is that person's relationship to you? ___

K83. In the last five years has either a friend or a relative spent a lot of time helping you in an emergency?

1. YES → / 5. NO → TURN TO P. 50, K85

K84. What kind of help did you receive? (Did you receive any other kind(s) of help?) ___

50

K85. We've talked about time, now let's talk about money. Do you have any savings such as a checking or savings account, or government bonds?

1. YES   5. NO → GO TO K88

K86. Would they amount to as much as two months' income or more?

1. YES   5. NO → GO TO K88

K87. Would they amount to as much as a year's income or more?

1. YES (GO TO K89)   5. NO

K88. Was there a time in the last five years when you had as much as two months' income saved up?

1. YES   5. NO

K89. Suppose in an emergency you needed several hundred dollars more than you had available or could borrow from an institution. Would you ask either a friend or a relative for it?

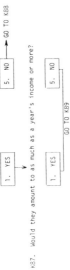

1. YES   3. DEPENDS   5. NO → TURN TO P. 51, K92   8. DON'T KNOW → TURN TO P. 51, K95

K90. Is the person you would ask a relative?

1. YES   5. NO → TURN TO P. 51, K92

K91. What is that person's relationship to you?

51

K92. How much would that person mind helping you out with money--a lot, a little bit, or not at all?

1. A LOT   3. A LITTLE BIT   5. NOT AT ALL   8. DON'T KNOW

K93. Would this money be a loan or a gift?

1. LOAN   5. GIFT → GO TO K95

K94. Would you expect to pay interest on it?

1. YES   5. NO

K95. In the last five years have you received any amount such as several hundred dollars from either a friend or relative?

1. YES   5. NO → TURN TO P. 52, K98

K96. Was it a loan or a gift?

1. LOAN   5. GIFT → TURN TO P. 52, K98

K97. Did you pay interest on it?

1. YES   5. NO

52

K98. In the last five years have you helped out either a friend or a relative in an emergency by giving or loaning them several hundred dollars or more?

1. YES →

5. NO → GO TO K103

K99. Was the person you helped a relative?

1. YES →

5. NO → GO TO K101

K100. What is that person's relationship to you?

K101. Was that a loan or a gift?

1. LOAN

5. GIFT → GO TO K103

K102. Did (he/she) pay interest on it?

1. YES

5. NO

K103. Prices and costs have been rising generally--are there some particular increases that have hit you especially hard?

1. YES →

5. NO → TURN TO P. 53, K107

K104. What are they?

K105. Have you been able to do anything about it?

1. YES

5. NO → TURN TO P. 53, K107

K106. What have you done?

53

K107. Has inflation caused you to change your ideas about retirement?

1. YES

5. NO → GO TO K109

K108. How have they changed?

K109. Do you belong to a labor union?

1. YES

5. NO

K110. INTERVIEWER CHECKPOINT

1. THERE IS A WIFE IN FU

5. NO WIFE IN FU → GO TO K112

K111. Does your wife belong to a labor union?

1. YES

5. NO

K112. Do you (HEAD) have any physical or nervous condition that limits the type of work or the amount of work you can do?

1. YES

5. NO → TURN TO P. 54, SECTION L

K113. Does it limit your work a lot, somewhat, or just a little?

1. A LOT

3. SOMEWHAT

5. JUST A LITTLE

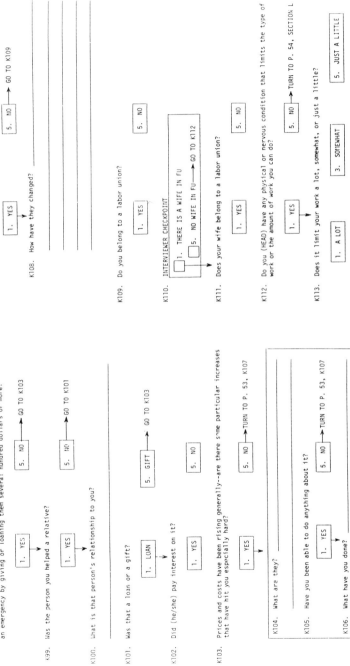

SECTION M: NEW HEAD

M1. INTERVIEWER CHECKPOINT

1. HEAD IS A NEW HEAD THIS YEAR

   5. HEAD IS THE SAME HEAD AS IN 1979 →

   TURN TO P. 4 OF COVERSHEET.
   (REINTERVIEW)→ITEM 13
   (SPLITOFF)→ITEM 14

   M1a. EXACT TIME NOW: _____

M2. Now I have some questions about your (HEAD'S) family and past experiences. Where did your father and mother grow up? (FROM BIRTH TO 18 YEARS OF AGE.)

ST. CO- FA

Father: _____
         (STATE IF U.S., COUNTRY IF FOREIGN)   (COUNTY OR TOWN)

ST. CO- MA

Mother: _____
         (STATE IF U.S., COUNTRY IF FOREIGN)   (COUNTY OR TOWN)

M3. What was your father's usual occupation when you were growing up?

OCC. ☐☐

M4. Thinking of your (HEAD'S) first full-time regular job, what did you do?

OCC. ☐☐

M5. Have you had a number of different kinds of jobs, or have you mostly worked in the same occupation you started in, or what?

   0. NEVER WORKED
      TURN TO P. 56, M6

_____

_____

_____

SECTION L: NEW WIFE

L1. INTERVIEWER CHECKPOINT

1. HEAD HAS NEW WIFE THIS YEAR (REMEMBER: FEMALE FRIEND LIVING IN FU ONE YEAR OR MORE IS CONSIDERED WIFE)

   5. HEAD IS FEMALE ──────────→ TURN TO P. 55, SECTION M
   5. HEAD IS MALE WITH NO WIFE ─→ TURN TO P. 55, SECTION M
   5. HEAD IS MALE WITH SAME WIFE AS IN 1979 → TURN TO P. 55, SECTION M

L2. How many grades of school did your (wife/friend) finish?

GRADES OF SCHOOL

| 00 | 01 | 02 | 03 | 04 | 05 | 06 | 07 | 08 | 09 | 10 | 11 | 12 |

COLLEGE

| 13 | 14 | 15 | 16 | 17+ |

L3. Did she have any other schooling?

   1. YES   5. NO →GO TO L8

L4. What other schooling did she have?

_____

L5. What college was that?

_____

L6. Does she have a college degree?

   1. YES   5. NO
              GO TO L8

L7. Does she have any advanced degrees?

   1. YES   5. NO

L8. How much education did your (wife's/friend's) father have? _____

L9. How much education did your (wife's/friend's) mother have? _____

L10. How many years altogether has your (wife/friend) worked for money since she was 18?

   _____ YEARS   00. NONE →TURN TO P. 55, SECTION M

L11. How many of these years did she work full-time for most or all of the year?

   _____ YEARS   ALL →TURN TO P. 55, SECTION M

L12. During the years that she was not working full-time how much of the time did she work? (PROBE FOR TIME PERIOD)

_____

☐
☐
☐

56.

M6. Do you (HEAD) have any children who don't live with you?

YES   NO → GO TO M9

M7. How many? _____ NUMBER

M8. When were they born? ___ YEAR BORN ___ YEAR BORN ___ YEAR BORN

    1st   2nd   3rd

M9. Did you (HEAD) have any children who are not now living?

YES   NO → GO TO M11

M10. When were they born? ___ YEAR BORN ___ YEAR BORN ___ YEAR BORN

    #

M11. How many brothers and sisters did you (HEAD) have?

_____ NUMBER

0. NONE → GO TO M13

BY 25

M12. Were any of your brothers or sisters older than you?

1. YES   5. NO

M13. Did you (HEAD) grow up on a farm, in a small town, in a large city, or what?

1. FARM   2. SMALL TOWN   3. LARGE CITY   OTHER (SPECIFY): _____

M14. In what state and county was that? (EXAMPLE: ILLINOIS, COOK COUNTY)

ST____ CO-H____   STATE_____ COUNTY

(IF DON'T KNOW TO M14)
M15. What was the name of the nearest town? _____ TOWN

M16. What other states or countries have you lived in, including time spent abroad while in the armed forces?

M17. Have you (HEAD) ever moved out of a community where you were living in order to take a job somewhere else?

1. YES   GO TO M19   5. NO

M18. Have you ever turned down a job because you did not want to move?

1. YES   5. NO

M19. Were your parents poor when you were growing up, pretty well off, or what?

_____

M20. How much education did your (HEAD'S) father have? _____

(IF LESS THAN 6 GRADES)
M21. Could he read and write?

M22. How much education did your (HEAD'S) mother have? _____

(IF LESS THAN 6 GRADES)
M23. Could she read and write?

M24. Are you (HEAD) a veteran?

1. YES   5. NO

M25. How many years have you worked since you were 18?

_____ YEARS   00. NONE → TURN TO P. 58, M28

M26. How many of these years did you work full-time for most of the year?

_____ YEARS   ALL → TURN TO P. 58, M28

M27. During the years that you were not working full-time, how much of the time did you work?

_____

58

M28. How many grades of school did you (HEAD) finish?

GRADES OF SCHOOL
| 00 | 01 | 02 | 03 | 04 | 05 | 06 | 07 | 08 | 09 | 10 | 11 | 12 |

COLLEGE
| 13 | 14 | 15 | 16 | 17+ |

M29. Did you get any other training?

1. YES → 5. NO GO TO M31

M30. What was it? _____

M31. Do you have any trouble reading?

M32. Did you have any other schooling?

1. YES → 5. NO GO TO M37

M33. What other schooling did you have? _____

M34. What college was that?

M35. Do you have a college degree?

1. YES   5. NO GO TO M37

M36. Do you have any advanced degrees?

1. YES   5. NO

M37. Now we would like to ask for your religious preference. This involves a right that is protected by the United States Constitution. You are under no obligation to answer these questions, and, if for any reason, you decide you do not wish to answer them, we will accept and respect your decision. The information requested is important to us, and we hope you will decide to answer them.

May we record your religious preference?

1. YES   5. NO → TURN TO P. 4 OF COVERSHEET, (REINTERVIEW)→ITEM 13 (SPLITOFF)→ITEM 14

M38. Is your religious preference Protestant, Catholic, or Jewish, or what?

7. PROTESTANT   8. CATHOLIC   9. JEWISH   OTHER (SPECIFY): _____

TURN TO P. 4 OF COVERSHEET, (REINTERVIEW)→ITEM 13 (SPLITOFF)→ITEM 14

M39. What denomination is that? _____

TURN TO P. 4 OF COVERSHEET, (REINTERVIEW)→ITEM 13 (SPLITOFF)→ITEM 14

M40. EXACT TIME NOW: _____

59

SECTION N: BY OBSERVATION ONLY

N1. Who was respondent (relation to Head)? _____

N2. Number of calls? _____

THUMBNAIL SKETCH: MUST BE FILLED OUT. EXPLAIN FAMILY INTER-RELATIONSHIPS SUCH AS WHO IS DEPENDENT UPON WHOM--AND PLEASE DO NOT EVER USE NAMES IN QUESTIONNAIRE (THIS IS A CARDINAL RULE FOR INTERVIEWERS.)